SPECIAL FORCES

IN THE WAR ON TERROR

OSPREY
PUBLISHING

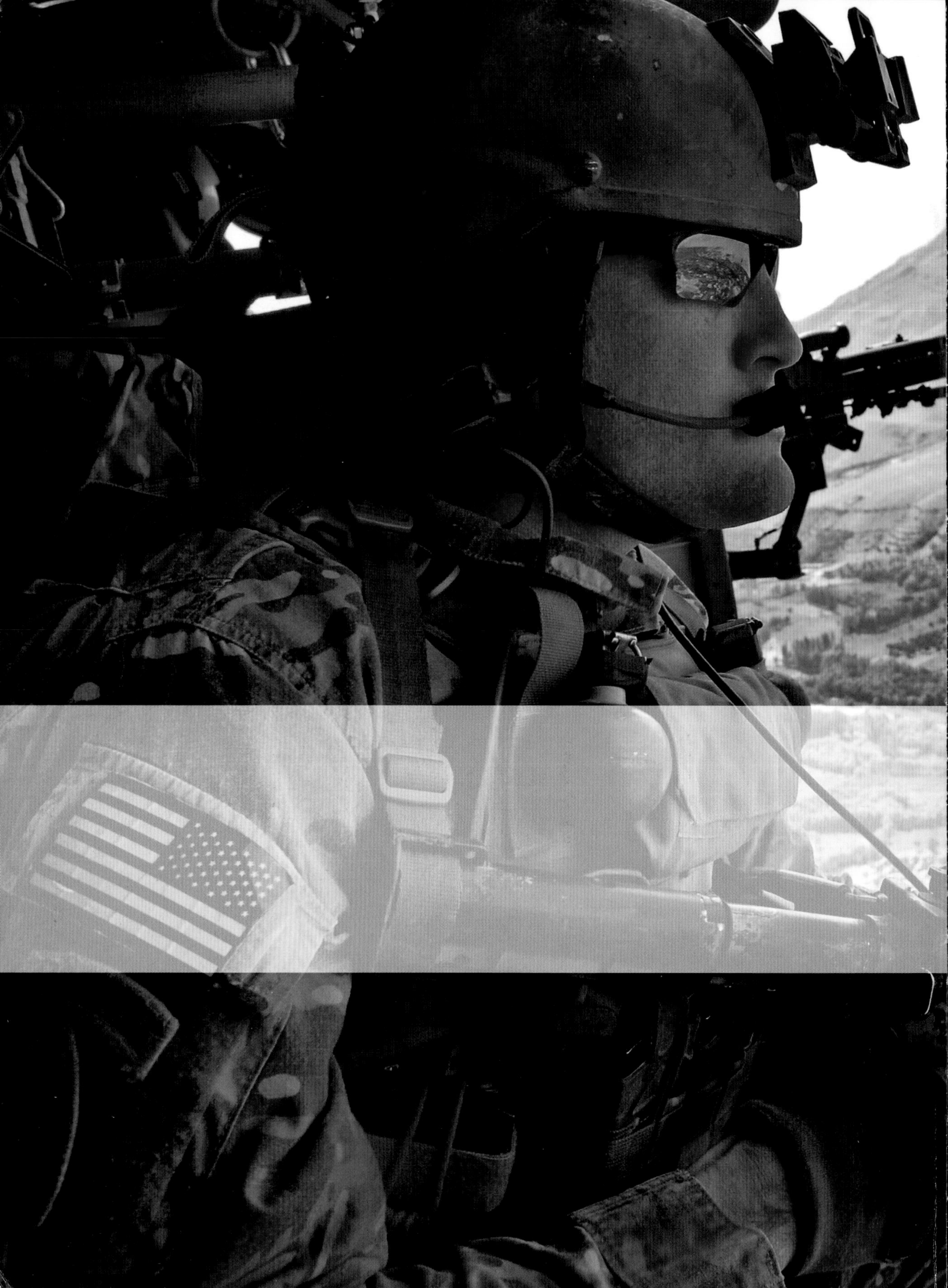

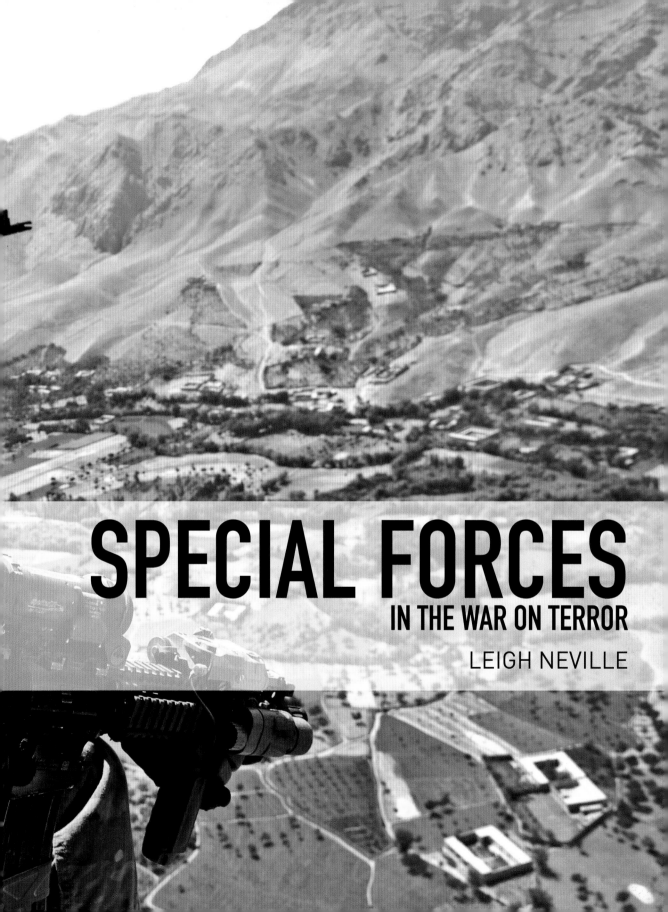

SPECIAL FORCES
IN THE WAR ON TERROR

LEIGH NEVILLE

First published in Great Britain in 2015 by Osprey Publishing,
PO Box 883, Oxford, OX1 9PL, UK
PO Box 3985, New York, NY 10185-3985, USA

E-mail: info@ospreypublishing.com

Osprey Publishing is part of Bloomsbury Publishing PLC

A CIP catalog record for this book is available from the British Library

Leigh Neville has asserted his right under the Copyright, Designs and
Patents Act, 1988, to be identified as the Author of this Work.

Print ISBN: 978 1 4728 0790 8

Index by Alison Worthington
Typeset in Adobe Garamond Pro and DIN Schrift
3D BEVs by Alan Gilliland
Originated by PDQ Media, Bungay, UK
Printed in China through Worldprint Ltd.

15 16 17 18 19 10 9 8 7 6 5 4 3 2 1

Osprey Publishing is supporting the Woodland Trust, the UK's leading
woodland conservation charity, by funding the dedication of trees.

www.ospreypublishing.com

DEDICATION
This work is dedicated to all who have served in special operations
units. All gave some, some gave all.

EDITOR'S NOTE
Some of the material in this book has been previously published as
Elite 163: *Special Operations Forces in Afghanistan*, ELI 170: *Special
Operations Forces in Iraq*, and RAID 39: *Takur Ghar – The SEALs and
Rangers on Roberts Ridge, Afghanistan 2002*, all by the same author.

TITLE PAGE
A US Army Green Beret surveys Uruzgan Province below him from a
UH-60 Blackhawk. He carries an M4A1 with Spectre DR sight. Note
the two M67 fragmentation grenades worn on his plate carrier. (Petty
Officer Third Class James Ginther; US Navy)

CONTENTS

1 **INTRODUCTION** 6
The World Before 9/11

2 **ENDURING FREEDOM** 16
Afghanistan 2001-2002

3 **IRAQI FREEDOM** 84
Iraq 2003

4 **COUNTERING INSURGENCY** 136
Afghanistan 2002-2009, Iraq 2003-2011, and the
Philippines 2002 onward

5 **INDUSTRIAL COUNTERTERRORISM** 186
Hunting al-Qaeda in Iraq 2003-2012

6 **KILL OR CAPTURE** 228
Afghanistan 2006-2014

7 **NEW THEATERS** 278
Somalia, Libya, Yemen, Mali, and Syria

8 **THE LONG WAR** 308

Glossary 318

Select Bibliography 326

Index 330

CHAPTER 1
INTRODUCTION
THE WORLD BEFORE 9/11

September 11, 2001 ushered in a new form of terrorism – a mass casualty suicide bombing on a scale never before imagined, and a new form of terrorist – young, fanatical and inspired by radical clerics to strike against their Great Satan, the United States. Schooled in terrorist training camps in Afghanistan, the Philippines, Chechnya and Pakistan, this new generation of terrorist did not follow in the footsteps of their forefathers who seized airliners for the release of political prisoners held in Israeli or Egyptian jails. Instead, these terrorists seized airliners to use as weapons in a terrifying new asymmetric war.

The Bush White House responded with the War on Terror – a largely meaningless, and often derided, term to group all operations by the US and Coalition militaries against al-Qaeda (AQ) and AQ related groups. A war on al-Qaeda would have been a more accurate and honest term. The United States' closest allies, the United Kingdom, Canada, and Australia, as well as a wider 'coalition of the willing' including much of Western Europe, joined this new war. Russia, despite its own history of conflict with Islamic terrorist separatists in Chechnya and Uzbekistan, largely stayed on the sidelines, granting basing and overflight rights in exchange for the West ignoring human rights abuses in Chechnya.

A forward scout from a patrol of Australia's 2 Commando somewhere in Afghanistan, 2011. He wears a Crye MultiCam uniform and an A-TACS Arid/Urban pattern assault pack displaying how well both patterns work in the mountainous environment. (Australian SOCOMD)

Many elements and tactics used in the War on Terror, or more formally the Global War on Terror, will be debated and questioned for decades to come. Was it right to detain prisoners in military prisons? Should they not have been dealt with as common criminals? Where did harsh interrogation end and torture begin? Is torture ever justified? Along with these philosophical quandaries, the War on Terror also brought tremendous advances in counterterrorist and law enforcement technologies and techniques that have undoubtedly saved many lives. One area which has seen both rapid growth and tremendous evolution has been that of military Special Operations Forces (SOF).

Special Operations Forces became, from the outset, the figurative and literal tip of the spear. Along with their CIA brethren, they were the first on the ground in Afghanistan barely weeks after the Twin Towers fell. They were the first to

A vintage shot of US Navy SEALs from the 1990s. Note the use of the Woodland pattern Battle Dress Uniforms (BDUs) that still find favour with SEALs, Marine Special Operations Command (MARSOC) and Army Special Forces today in parts of Afghanistan. Also interesting are the relatively "vanilla" weapons. The lead SEAL's M4 mounts an M203 grenade launcher, but features none of the lasers, lights and optics so common today. (PH1 Mussi; US SOCOM)

deploy to the Philippines to assist the Filipino military in their hunt for Abu Sayyaf and Jemaah Islamiyah. Again alongside the CIA, they were deployed to northern Iraq up to a year before the invasion began. In dozens of countries around the world, SOF training teams worked with local and national Special Forces to develop their counter-terrorist and counter-insurgency capabilities. And in the shadows, the 'black', or covert, SOF of the Joint Special Operations Command (JSOC) conducted kill or capture missions targeting the senior terrorist leadership, financiers, and logisticians.

JSOC had been formed in December 1980 after the abortive Operation *Eagle Claw* to Iran. It began life with narrow responsibilities for hostage rescue and later, nuclear proliferation. Along with endless training to rescue hijacked airliners, JSOC became the command responsible for capturing rogue nuclear weapons (it has long been rumored that JSOC units have been trained to seize Pakistani nuclear facilities in the event of a jihadist takeover). They were, however, considered the "Ferrari in the garage that never gets driven" as their operational deployments were few and far between. Their capabilities were largely unknown outside SOF and they were an expensive resource, often considered as "cowboys" by their conventional counterparts.

Special Operations Command (SOCOM) was established a number of years later in 1987 to act as the overall command for each service's SOF and the parent

A very rare shot of a Delta Force hide site in the western Iraqi desert during Operation *Desert Storm*, 1991. The vehicle is the little-seen six-wheel Pinzgauer Special Operations Vehicle modified for Delta's particular requirements. (Photographer unknown)

AH-6 Little Birds from the 160th Special Operations Aviation Regiment operating from the deck of a US Navy aircraft carrier in the Persian Gulf during Operation *Prime Chance*, late 1980s. Note the MH-60 Blackhawks in the background. The pioneering work accomplished by 160th SOAR and the US Navy SEALs would pave the way for later post-9/11 operations conducted from the so-called "floating bases." (US SOCOM)

Delta Force's A Squadron again during Operation *Desert Storm* in western Iraq, 1991. The operators carry an interesting mix of Colt carbines, which are equipped with early Aimpoint sights and Colt scopes, some with suppressors and M203 grenade launchers. Their uniforms are still the 'chocolate chip' desert pattern and there is a conspicuous lack of body armor. (Photographer unknown)

command of JSOC. It aimed to ensure events such as the invasion of Grenada never happened again. In the 1980s, SOF had suffered from being deployed on operations ill-suited to their unique skills. The majority of the operations conducted by Delta Force and SEAL Team 6 during the Grenada intervention in 1983 were both unnecessary and poorly conceived or could have been conducted by the Rangers or even conventional Marine or Army units. There was a feeling within the Pentagon that the SOF units needed to be blooded, and so missions were created for them, often by conventional commands unused to working with SOF.

SOCOM (Special Operations Command) gave SOF their own command and for the first time they had a voice in how and when their units were deployed. One of its first successes was the SEAL and the 160th Special Operations Aviation Regiment campaign in the Persian Gulf during the latter part of the decade, protecting civilian shipping from Iranian attacks. The mission would also offer proof of a number of concepts that would feature in the later War on Terror – deploying both SEALs and Army SOF helicopters from Navy ships as floating forward staging areas and conducting opposed VBSS (Visit Board Search and Seizure) missions.

SOF spent the 1990s employed in a number of global hotspots and in several different ways. The Balkans became one of their longest-running campaigns, beginning with British SAS (Special Air Service) teams guiding in NATO airstrikes, and leading to the hunt for war criminals by SEAL Team 6. Delta Force and the Rangers had fought in the now legendary Day of the Rangers in Mogadishu, honing their credentials as man hunters. The British conducted their own very successful hostage rescue in Sierra Leone in 2000, rescuing a number of their own from a drug-addled militia. The Green Berets had worked alongside the Colombian military targeting the narco-terrorists of FARC. The Australian SOF had their first combat deployment in many years with the East Timor intervention and then the Gulf War of 1991.

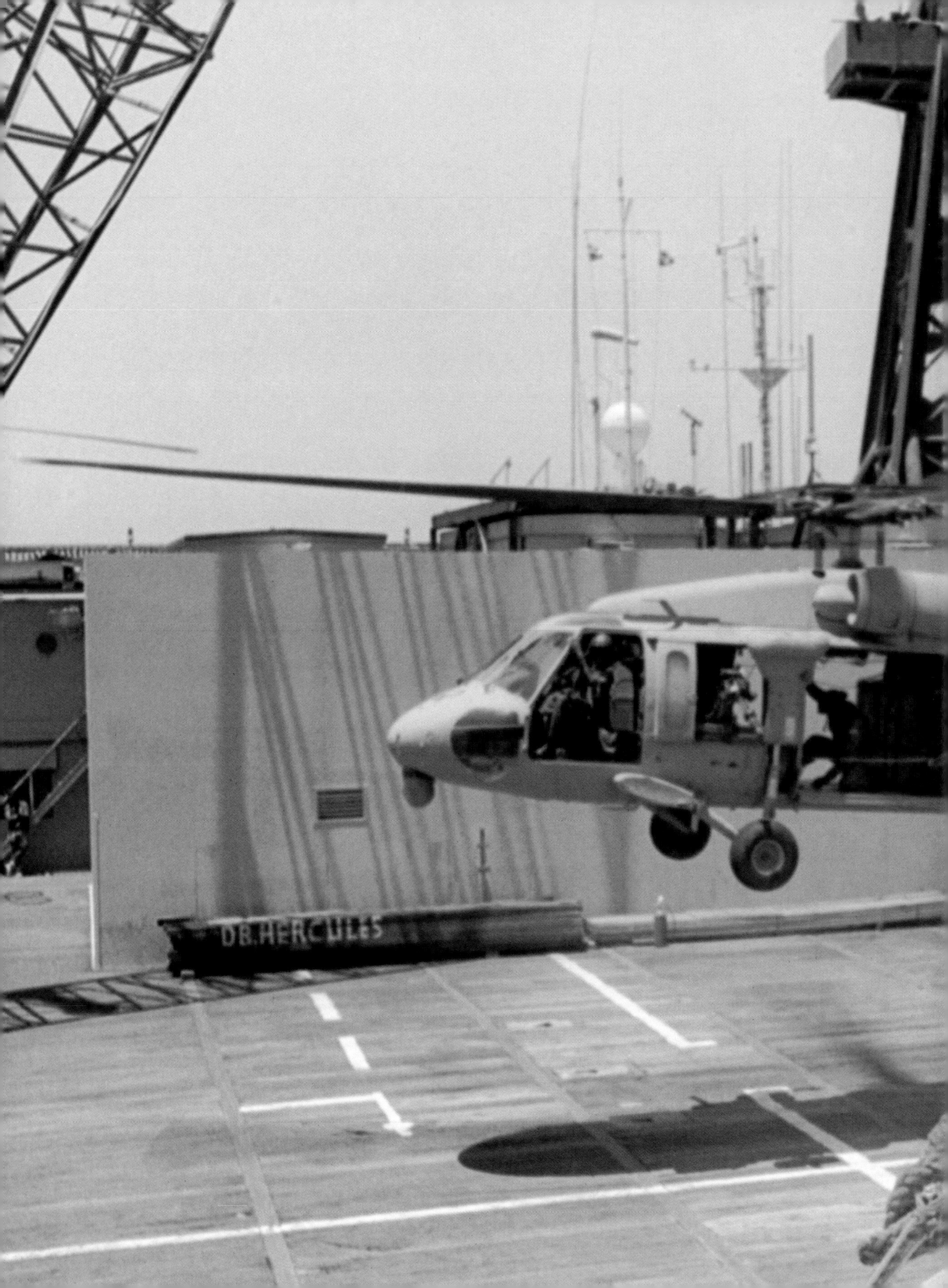
DB.HERCULES

A 160th Special Operations Aviation Regiment MH-60 helicopter deployed in support of the SEALs during Operation *Prime Chance*. Normally, Nightstalker aircraft are painted in an almost black olive-drab, but for operations in the Gulf they were painted in a light grey tone (although their accompanying Little Birds stayed in their olive-drab finishes). (US SOCOM)

US Army Special Forces Operational Detachment Alpha 525 moments before launching on its famous special reconnaissance mission, which saw it compromised in the Iraqi desert by Iraqi children who stumbled across its hide site. The team was rapidly surrounded by Iraqi Army units, and only through accurate shooting and Danger Close airstrikes did it manage to break contact, allowing a pair of Nightstalker MH-60s to extract it. The team carry an interesting mix of M16A2 rifles, M203 under barrel grenade launchers and suppressed MP5SD3 sub-machine guns with early laser sights. (Photographer unknown)

Operation *Desert Storm* saw the Green Berets conducting a range of missions – from mobile Scud hunting in the western desert and long-range reconnaissance to embedded training teams with other Coalition nations. Famously, the SAS also hunted Scuds, later joined by their comrades from Delta Force. The SEALs were the first into the recaptured Kuwait City in their Desert Patrol Vehicle dune buggies and Marine Force Reconnaissance (Force Recon) was instrumental in the famous Battle of Khafji. *Desert Storm* was also the first truly joint special operations theater with British Special Forces and the Polish GROM (the Grupa Reagowania Operacyjno Mobilneho or Operational Reserve Group) working alongside their US counterparts.

US Navy SEALs conducting range work from a Navy ship during Operation *Prime Chance*, late 1980s. The sniper rifles appear to be an early McMillan .50 and a Marine M40A1 in 7.62mm. Over twenty-five years later, similar skills were used to rescue Captain Richard Phillips from Somali pirates. (US SOCOM)

The experience and lessons learned from these earlier actions directly informed how SOF was deployed in the wake of 9/11. SOCOM and JSOC had legitimized their presence on the battlefield and their deployments in the 1990s had established their capabilities on a wide variety of missions. The British SOF had required no such painful legitimacy as they had long been viewed as the surgical tool of choice for British foreign policy. Even so, they also received their own

The famous image of Rangers in their distinctive patrol hats, post their successful airfield seizure at Point Salines, Grenada as part of Operation *Urgent Fury*, 1983. Most of the planned special operations in support of the Grenada intervention were aborted or went badly wrong, leading directly to the formation of the United States Special Operations Command (SOCOM). The Rangers conducted their first opposed airfield seizure, a role they had long practiced and something they would become particularly adept at during the initial incursions into Afghanistan and Iraq. (US DOD)

Directorate of Special Forces in the same year SOCOM was raised, bringing Army, RAF, Navy and Royal Marine SOF under the one, unified command.

Following 9/11, the Green Berets were the obvious choice to send to Afghanistan to mentor, train and advise the Afghans of the Northern Alliance. Along with target designation skills and equipment perfected in the Balkans, the Green Berets had long trained for exactly this mission; in fact the famous Robin Sage exercise at the culmination of their grueling US Army Special Forces Qualification Course was based around a similar scenario, of Army Special Forces infiltrating a hostile nation state (called Pineland), making contact with and training and mentoring a local guerrilla army.

The SEALs had been lobbying hard for access to land-based operations beyond their maritime and littoral, close to shore, origins. Afghanistan gave them that opportunity and despite some costly setbacks and naysayers within Army SOF, they began to silence their critics. If the SOF were the tip of the spear for this war, JSOC was the dagger that killed quietly in the shadows. Delta and SEAL Team 6 evolved into the premier kill or capture force. United States SOF, and those of its key allies, had finally come of age. The War on Terror was not a war of conventional armies, massed tank battles or strategic bombing; it was a special operations war.

CHAPTER 2
ENDURING FREEDOM
AFGHANISTAN 2001–2002

THE LAND OF WAR

Afghanistan is a land that has rarely known peace. From the Great Game of the nineteenth century that saw both the First and Second Anglo-Afghan Wars end in bloody disaster for the British through to the current Taliban insurgency, Afghanistan has been fought over by rival governments, factions and warlords for hundreds of years. It has also resisted every foreign invader and occupier since Alexander the Great in 330 BC – Afghans do not look kindly upon foreign intervention in their affairs.

The event which arguably sowed the seeds for the terrorist attacks of September 11, 2001, and the eventual Global War on Terror, was the Soviet invasion of Afghanistan in 1979. Installing a puppet government in the capital Kabul, the Soviets boasted they would crush the anti-communist mujahideen ("holy warrior") resistance in a few short months. Ten years later, they finally withdrew their forces with casualty estimates ranging from 35,000 to 50,000 troops killed and a thoroughly demoralized and psychologically crippled Red Army.

Fighting alongside the anti-Soviet mujahideen were what became known as Afghan Arabs, an eventual 30,000-strong volunteer force from across the Islamic world, fuelled by a religious imperative to jihad in the defense of fellow Muslims (in a situation not markedly different to today's foreign volunteers fighting in Syria or Iraq). These foreign fighters would travel to Pakistan, where, with the covert assistance of the Pakistani Inter-Services Intelligence (ISI), they would cross the border into Afghanistan and via a series of safe houses, eventually arrive at the frontline.

Ironically, these Arab volunteers were neither particularly liked nor trusted by the Afghan mujahideen, but were tolerated as they often brought hard currency and much-needed medical supplies with them. The mujahideen would often deploy these foreigners in the most dangerous positions on the battlefield, which thanks to their fanaticism, the Arabs would accept without comment. Not surprisingly, many were killed when they discovered religious zeal did not make one invincible to Soviet bullets and bombs.

THE BASE

Among these Afghan Arabs was a man whose name would rise to notorious prominence in the years to follow – Usama bin Laden. The son of a wealthy Saudi Arabian construction magnate, bin Laden established an Islamic charity in Afghanistan to support the Afghan Arabs. This charity, centered on a guest house for foreign fighters in Peshawar, was known as al-Qaeda or The Base. Bin Laden became a well-known figure in the anti-Soviet resistance, not the least because of his deep pockets and willingness to share his father's fortune.

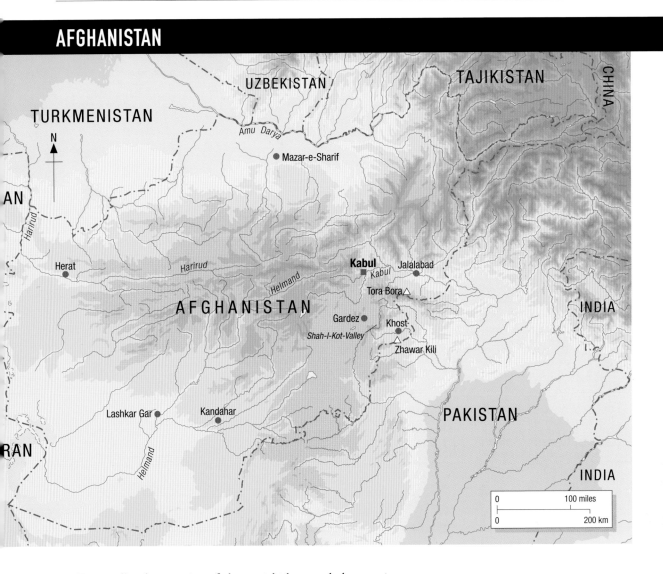

Eventually, the tenacity of the mujahideen and the massive covert support from the US, China, the UK, and Pakistan forced the Soviets to withdraw from Afghanistan, their forces bleeding and battered. In the vacuum left by the departing Soviets, the mujahideen factions fought against the ailing communist central government before its inevitable collapse in 1992. The Afghan Arabs, now blooded by war and supported by donations from wealthy Gulf State sponsors, went on to fight in numerous Islamic insurgencies from Chechnya to the Philippines to Kashmir.

In Afghanistan hope for a new central government was short lived as the seven major rival mujahideen factions descended into a bitter civil war for control of the country. It was during this civil war that the Taliban first appeared. From humble

Black and White

Black and white SOF are terms used to describe units that conduct primarily covert (black) and overt (white) operations. Despite what may be presented in video games, there are no specific 'Black Ops' units, however there are black SOF units such as Delta Force or the Intelligence Support Activity whose personnel are identity protected and who conduct unacknowledged missions. Euphemisms such as 'Other Coalition Forces' are used to avoid describing exactly what these units are when referencing their operations.

Another confusing concept is the idea of a tier system somehow ranking United States SOF. This tier system, depending on who you talk to, is either based on deployment readiness, overall competency or the level of funding a particular unit receives. The idea has gained currency in the media thanks again to video games where the phrase 'Tier One operator' is often used as shorthand for a member of Delta, the SAS or DEVGRU. The existence of the tier system within organizations such as JSOC cannot be confirmed but its use informally by members of units such as the Rangers and DEVGRU indicates that it may have some basis in reality.

The use of the term 'operator' also deserves some discussion. It has now moved into common usage to describe a member of a special operations force. The term was once the exclusive preserve of Delta Force, however. Its founder, Colonel Charlie Beckwith, wanted a term to differentiate the members of his newly founded unit from those of others. As the CIA already used the title 'operative' and the FBI had 'agent,' Beckwith settled on 'operator' and its six-month Operator Training Course was thus named.

beginnings as a small group of Pashtun (the predominant ethnic group within Afghanistan) religious students known as Talibs in southern Afghanistan, under the leadership of the one-eyed cleric, Mullah Muhammad Omar, they became a popular movement, railing against the brutal excesses of the warlords. The Taliban also opposed the country's opium trade and dealt with banditry and corruption with an iron fist. Ironically, their devout views on opium production would be tempered by financial realities during the post-9/11 insurgency. Supported by, and some would say created by, Pakistani intelligence (the ISI), the Taliban movement grew quickly from its traditional power base in Kandahar.

ISI saw in the Taliban a strategic buffer to contain the chaos of its neighbour. Some accounts suggest ISI even embedded intelligence officers within the Taliban, a practice that had become commonplace in the mujahideen in the 1980s (and allegedly during the most recent insurgency, Pakistani officers were discovered in Afghanistan supporting Taliban cells; including one who was inadvertently killed by UK Special Forces). Certainly ISI actively recruited and trained thousands of Pakistani volunteers to join the Afghan Taliban.

Into this morass, bin Laden returned. He had lost his Saudi citizenship after the Gulf War and had retreated to Sudan for a time before he was forced out under increasing US pressure. Now he extended the hand of friendship to Mullah Omar. Returning to Afghanistan in 1996, he brought with him a cadre of al-

A mounted US Army Special Forces Operational Detachment Alpha (ODA) riding alongside their Northern Alliance allies in Afghanistan, October 2001. Few of the Special Forces men were accomplished riders, and combined with the relatively short stature of Afghan horses and traditional wooden saddles, it made it a memorable experience. (US SOCOM)

Qaeda fighters and soon attracted many of the Afghan Arab veterans he had supported during the Soviet–Afghan War.

As a gift to Mullah Omar, bin Laden donated vehicles, built roads, and recruited the largest jihadist army of modern times – al-Qaeda's Brigade 055 (or the 55th Arab Brigade) – which bin Laden deployed alongside the Taliban against the Shura Nazar, or Northern Alliance, of anti-Taliban forces. Brigade 055 soon gained an unenviable reputation for the barbaric murder of civilians – including decapitation of prisoners; another grim portent for future jihadist outrages.

The civil war ground on with the Northern Alliance holding out in roughly a third of the country. Two days before the terrorist attacks which killed 2,973 people in New York, Virginia, and Pennsylvania, Ahmad Shah Masoud, leader of the Northern Alliance, was assassinated in a suicide bombing by two al-Qaeda terrorists posing as journalists in his mountain headquarters in the Panjshir Valley. Al-Qaeda had cannily eliminated the West's closest ally in Afghanistan.

After the attacks of 9/11, the world rallied to the United States and offers of military support were pledged by many nations, from Canada to France to their closest ally, the United Kingdom. Indeed, on September 12 and for the first time in its history NATO invoked Article 5 of its charter providing for mutual protection of member states against attack, paving the way for NATO participation in Afghanistan and the eventual deployment of the International Security Assistance Force (ISAF).

A US Army Green Beret uses an AN/PEQ-1 Special Operations Forces Laser Marker (SOFLAM) to 'paint' targets for US airstrikes supporting the Northern Alliance, late 2001. His mix of Western and Afghan clothing was common at the time in an effort to make the ODAs blend in (or at least not stand out so much as Western soldiers). Note that as well as his map and compass he wears a Suunto-type wrist compass on his right wrist – a common Special Forces accruement. (US SOCOM)

Mullah Omar and the Taliban were given the opportunity to surrender bin Laden and his top lieutenants such as Khalid Sheikh Mohammed. They refused, so Operation *Crescent Wind* was launched. The first American boots on the ground arrived in Afghanistan a scant 15 days after the events of 9/11. Perhaps surprisingly for some, these men were not members of a military SOF unit. They had arrived covertly from the former Soviet airbase of Karshi-Khandabad (generally referred to as the more easily pronounced K2) in Uzbekistan where a formidable US presence was building in preparation for an extended campaign in Afghanistan.

FIRST IN

The eight men who landed in Afghanistan's Panjshir Valley in a Russian-built but CIA-piloted Mi-17 helicopter in the pre-dawn darkness of September 26, 2001 were members of the Central Intelligence Agency. Known by the callsign

CIA Special Activities Division

The CIA had lost much of its human intelligence and paramilitary capacity during the post-Vietnam years when numerous scandals resulted in a severe degradation of both capabilities. Rebuilding only began in the 1990s as new threats emerged after the break-up of the USSR. The events of 9/11 forced a rapid expansion as the CIA took the lead role in covert operations in Afghanistan, the Philippines, and later Iraq.

The Special Activities Division is divided into several different units known as branches. Chief among these is SAD-Ground Branch. Ground Branch is the home of the CIA's shooters and surveillance operators. They conducted extraordinary renditions of terrorist suspects and guarded the overseas black sites into which those same suspects disappeared. They were the

first into Afghanistan and the first into northern Iraq, a year ahead of Army SOF in the latter case.

Most are recruited from SOF units with many former Delta, Special Forces and SEALs among them. They have their own training facility but are sent to specialist schools to learn or refresh skills in the black arts of high-speed driving, lock-picking, surveillance, and HALO parachuting. When they deploy they often dress and arm themselves like locals. The two SAD officers at the infamous Taliban prison uprising at Mazar-e-Sharif on 25 November 2001 both wore traditional Afghan Shalwar Kameez and Chinese chest rigs, and carried AK-47s.

Along with Ground Branch, SAD has its own pilots and aircraft (including unmarked civilian Little Birds) in Air Branch. Air Branch aircraft specially modified for signals intercept missions, such as the Dash-8, have often been spotted in the skies above Afghanistan. SAD-Maritime Branch provides waterborne insertion and extraction expertise to Ground Branch and recruits heavily from the Navy's Special Boat Teams.

A CIA-owned and -operated former Soviet Mi-17 transport helicopter pictured in Afghanistan in late 2001. The figures around the aircraft are CIA SAD personnel. This MI-8 was used to ferry the Jawbreaker teams around the country and was used for aerial reconnaissance over the Shahikot Valley prior to Operation *Anaconda*. (CIA)

Jawbreaker, the team were volunteers drawn from the Agency's paramilitary Special Activities Division (SAD) and Counterterrorist Centre (CTC). Later, to the men of the Special Forces who would soon be working alongside them, they would be known simply and euphemistically as the OGA or Other Government Agency.

Comprised of former special operators, communications and linguistics experts, the Jawbreaker team brought with it satellite communications enabling its intelligence reports to be instantly available to headquarters staff at both the CIA's

The Spartan accommodation of the first CIA Jawbreaker team into Afghanistan. Note the commercial civilian hiking packs and gear and Soviet-made AKM assault rifles. The Jawbreaker teams dressed in civilian clothing and carried sterile AKMs and 9mm Browning Hi-Power pistols, devoid of serial numbers and any link with the CIA. (CIA)

Langley HQ and Central Command (CENTCOM) – responsible for Operation *Crescent Wind* and what would soon be called Operation *Enduring Freedom*. Jawbreaker also carried with it $3 million of US currency in non-sequential, $100 bills, which would be used to shore up Afghan support (an old Afghan proverb claims that while you may never buy an Afghan, you can certainly rent one).

The Jawbreaker element also facilitated the planned insertion of the first US Army Special Forces teams with Northern Alliance commanders; assessed potential air targets for *Crescent Wind*; provided an in-extremis Combat Search and Rescue (CSAR) capability should the worst happen and a Coalition aircraft was downed in Afghanistan; and could provide bomb damage assessments (BDAs) for the air campaign.

ENDURING FREEDOM

Operation *Enduring Freedom-Afghanistan* (OEF-A) officially began on the evening of October 6, 2001 with Operation *Crescent Wind*, the Coalition air campaign, targeting the Taliban's aging command and control and air defense sites. Most of the Taliban's outdated Soviet-built SA-2 and SA-3 surface to air missile (SAM) platforms, as well as its attendant radar and command units, were destroyed on the first night along with the Taliban's small fleet of MiG-21 and Sukhoi Su-22 fighter aircraft.

With the threat of high-altitude SAMs negated and total air dominance established, aerial targeting soon focused on Taliban infrastructure, leadership nodes and troop concentrations along with any known al-Qaeda training camps. These were struck by a myriad of United States Air Force (USAF), United States

Navy (USN) and Royal Air Force (RAF) aircraft types, including the venerable B-52H and B-1B long range bombers and AC-130 Spectre fixed-wing gunships operating from both K2 and a classified forward base in Pakistan. Operation *Enduring Freedom-Afghanistan*, and the Global War on Terror, had begun.

Under the overall leadership of US Army General Tommy Franks, Coalition Forces Commander (CENTCOM), four major task forces were raised to support OEF: the Combined Joint Special Operations Task Force (CJSOTF), the Combined Joint Task Force-Mountain (CJTF-Mountain), the Joint Interagency Task Force-Counterterrorism (JIATF-CT), and the Coalition Joint Civil-Military Operations Task Force (CJCMOTF).

CJSOTF was a mixture of black and white SOF and comprised of three subordinate task forces, all named after types of blades: Joint Special Operations Task Force-North (JSOTF-North) known as Task Force Dagger; Joint Special Operations Task Force-South (JSOTF-South) better known as Task Force K-Bar; and the secretive Task Force Sword (later renamed Task Force 11).

TASK FORCES
DAGGER

Task Force Dagger, established 10 October 2001, was led by Army Green Beret Colonel John Mulholland and was formed around his 5th Special Forces Group with helicopter support from the Nightstalkers of the 160th Special Operations Aviation Regiment (160th SOAR). Dagger was assigned the north of Afghanistan and tasked with infiltrating Special Forces ODA (Operational Detachment Alpha) teams to advise and support the warlords of the Northern Alliance. These Green Beret ODAs were generally composed of a Special Forces ODA A-Team (the common term for an ODA of 12 Green Berets, see below) supported by an Air Force Special Tactics element, and would work closely with the CIA Jawbreaker teams already on the ground.

A defining image of the early war in Afghanistan – SSgt Bart Decker, an Air Force Combat Controller attached to US Army Special Forces ODA 595, astride an Afghan horse. (US SOCOM)

US Army Special Forces

In the 1960s and 1970s, the most famous SOF in the United States was the Green Berets of the US Army Special Forces. The Special Forces could trace their battle honors back to the wartime Office of Strategic Services' Jedburgh teams – the job of which was to parachute deep behind German lines to conduct guerrilla operations.

Any Special Forces soldier will tell you that a Green Beret is a hat, not a person, but the term stuck, particularly after John Wayne's performance in the classic Vietnam era movie, *The Green Berets*. Their motto of *De Oppresso Libre* (To Liberate the Oppressed) hints at one of the key skills of Army Special Forces – Foreign Internal Defense or FID. FID sees Green Berets training and mentoring friendly forces in counterguerrilla tactics and counterinsurgency. Conversely, Green Berets can also raise, train and advise indigenous guerilla armies – a skill that came in handy in Afghanistan.

To conduct their FID mission, Green Berets need advanced language and cultural skills along with a mixture of civil and military expertise – they could be building a rural health clinic one day and instructing on the finer points of bounding overwatch (a common fire and movement tactic) the next. Organized into 12-man teams known as an Operational Detachment Alpha, or ODA, each operator has a different primary specialty – from demolition to communications, medicine or engineering – and are cross-trained in at least two other subjects.

Although Foreign Internal Defense is their bread-and-butter day job, Army Special Forces are experts in Unconventional Warfare (literally the behind-the-lines commando stuff of legend – ambushes, sabotage, and subversion and training foreign forces in such tactics); Long-Range Reconnaissance (true to their Vietnam roots, but known today as Special Reconnaissance); and Direct Action – kicking in doors. Like the British and Australian SAS, each ODA also has a team specialty based on an infiltration method – some ODAs are dive teams trained in Military SCUBA while others are Military freefall parachuting specialists.

Each ODA is identified by a four-digit number that defines its Group, Battalion, Company, and Team – thus ODA 5225 would be the 5th Special Forces Group's 2nd Battalion, Bravo Company's 5th ODA (the addition of a fourth digit, representing the battalion is a recent change as a fourth battalion was added to each Group – ODAs in the early days of Afghanistan and Iraq only had three-digit numbers).

ODAs can operate in a covert capacity (as seen by their mixture of military and local attire worn in the opening months of OEF-A) or in uniform. They have become well known for their beards which are grown as a sign of cultural respect. Afghan elders will simply not take a clean-shaven American seriously, although the image of the bearded, Oakley-wearing operator has since entered the mythology of the Special Forces.

Green Berets examine an operable Soviet-made 12.7mm DShK heavy machine gun on an anti-aircraft tripod. (JZW)

K-BAR

The second special operations task force, also established on 10 October 2001, was Task Force K-Bar with a geographic responsibility for the south of the country. K-Bar (named after a Marine fighting knife) was led by Navy SEAL Captain Robert Harward and formed around a Naval Special Warfare Group consisting of SEAL Teams 2, 3 and 8 and the Green Berets of the Army's 1st Battalion of the 3rd Special Forces Group. The task force principally conducted Special Reconnaissance (SR) and Sensitive Site Exploitation (SSE) missions – intelligence gathering at former enemy locations, although some 3rd Special Forces Group ODAs were also given the Foreign Internal Defense and Unconventional Warfare role, advising anti-Taliban militias.

K-Bar was assigned a number of Coalition SOF units while Dagger was originally an all-American affair. These Coalition SOF included the German KSK (Kommando Spezialkräfte), Canada's Joint Task Force 2 (JTF2) and New Zealand's 1st Special Air Service Group (NZSAS). Many of these units slotted in

A Navy SEAL watches munitions captured in a Sensitive Site Exploitation mission being destroyed in the valley below, February 2002. Note the German KSK operators just visible to his lower right. (Photographer's Mate 1st Class Tim Turner; US Navy)

US Navy SEALs

The SEALs (Sea, Air and Land – describing their different insertion methods) are the US Navy's Special Warfare units. Their formation dates back to the World War II Underwater Demolition Teams, which conducted beach reconnaissance and combat diving tasks. The SEALs expanded on that role during the Vietnam War, during which they became skilled in littoral reconnaissance, along rivers such as the Mekong Delta, and Direct Action missions which included ambushing the Viet Cong in their base areas.

Today's SEALs still maintain a focus on littoral and maritime operations and are officially tasked with naval special operations, but have expanded into land warfare roles, much to the skepticism and sometimes hostility of Army SOF. Modern SEALs are trained in traditional reconnaissance and water-based skills, but are also increasingly conducting Unconventional Warfare (UW) and Foreign Internal Defense (FID) missions. Movies such as *Act of Valor* show the range of SEAL operations.

Like the Army Special Forces, each SEAL is trained in an individual specialist area – such as medical, communications, surveillance, or breaching – and cross trained in others, but unlike the Green Berets, SEAL platoons are not based on a team specialty – all SEALs are SCUBA, HALO (High-Altitude Low-Opening military parachuting), mobility and small boat qualified. Each SEAL Team is given specific geographical responsibilities in much the same way as their Army counterparts.

The SEALs are generally structured into 16-man platoons, six of which comprise a numbered SEAL Team. On the West Coast of the United States are SEAL Teams 1, 3, 5 and 7 and on the East Coast are SEAL Teams 2, 4, 8 and 10. The unit popularly known as SEAL Team 6, celebrated in movies such as *Zero Dark Thirty*, is actually known as the Naval Special Warfare Development Group (DEVGRU) and does not appear on SEAL organizational charts.

A US Navy SEAL operating in a desert environment in 2002 with dust goggles and his NVG mount covered by tape. Note also the tape helping secure the AN/PEQ-4 infra-red illuminator on the forward top rail on his M4A1 carbine – accessories can be easily knocked off-line or lost during combat operations and are often secured with extra tape or equipment ties. (Staff Sergeant Aaron D. Allmon II; US Air Force)

Special Forces ODA 574 with Afghan President Hamid Karzai, 5 December 2001, minutes before an errant 2,000lb bomb landed amid friendly lines, killing three Special Forces soldiers and gravely wounding a number of others. (US SOCOM)

well with their US counterparts, although some did not bring their own ground vehicles, which both restricted the types of missions they could be given and forced a reliance on borrowed US vehicles.

SWORD

The third SOF task force, established in early October 2001, was Task Force Sword – a black SOF unit under the direct command of the Joint Special Operation Command (JSOC). This was the so-called hunter-killer force with the primary objective of capturing or killing senior leadership high-value targets (HVTs) within both al-Qaeda and the Taliban. Sword was initially structured around a two-squadron component of operators from Delta and the Naval Special Warfare Development Group (DEVGRU), supported by Ranger force protection teams and Intelligence Support Activity (ISA) signals intercept and surveillance operators.

Each of these components was further identified by color – a technique still in use today and used as a form of shorthand for the JSOC units. Delta was Task Force Green, DEVGRU was Task Force Blue, the Rangers were Task Force Red, ISA (Intelligence Support Activity) was Task Force Orange and the 160th SOAR was Task Force Brown.

A number of Coalition SOF elements were sometimes attached to Sword to support specific operations, but only UK Special Forces, particularly the SBS (Special Boat Service), were integrated directly into the Sword structure. "Early on, Task Force 11 had no real presence outside of US/UK, other Coalition troops were used predominantly in SR (Special Reconnaissance) and some SSEs (Sensitive Site Exploitation)", explained one US special operator. Another added that "there was a lot of 'hey there's a war and everyone wants to come' going on back then – only we

A US Air Force Combat Controller and members of an ODA, late 2001, working alongside Northern Alliance fighters (who can be seen in the background standing near what appears to be a ZU-23 anti-aircraft cannon). A SOFLAM laser designator stands ready for use. (US SOCOM)

[the US] were running the show and needed to be the ones that nailed the big bad guys for the press!" Certainly the vaunted British SAS felt that missions were continually denied to them in favour of US units.

MOUNTAIN

Alongside the SOF task forces operated the largely conventional CJTF-Mountain Task Force. Mountain was also initially comprised of three subordinate commands. Only one was special operations – Task Force 64, a Special Forces Task Group built around a Sabre Squadron from the Australian Special Air Service Regiment (SASR).

The US Marines contributed Task Force 58, comprised of the 15th Marine Expeditionary Unit (MEU), which was later replaced by the now legendary Task Force Rakkasan, formed of elements of the 101st Airborne, the 10th Mountain Division, and the Canadian Light Infantry. The final task force under Mountain was Jacana, a Battle Group of some 1,700 personnel drawn from 45 Commando, Royal Marines, and the largest Coalition presence in Afghanistan at the time (November 2001).

The Australians of Task Force 64 conducted reconnaissance for Task Force Mountain and later for Task Force Sword as well as some direct action taskings. Task Force 58 provided the conventional forces for securing Forward Operating Bases (FOBs) and for conducting larger-scale follow-on operations. Task Force Jacana was established to eliminate al-Qaeda remnants following Operation *Anaconda*. Jacana was involved in locating and destroying a number of insurgent caves and bunkers before returning to the UK in July 2002.

BOWIE

Intelligence gathering, processing, and dissemination were conducted by the Joint Inter Agency Task Force-Counter Terrorism (JIATF-CT), better known as Task Force Bowie. Bowie was an intelligence integration and fusion activity manned by personnel from all OEF-A participating units, both US and Coalition, alongside a number of civilian intelligence and law enforcement agencies.

Led by Brigadier General Gary Harrell, a former Delta officer and a hugely experienced special operator (Harrell commanded Delta's C Squadron during Operation *Gothic Serpent* in Mogadishu), Bowie established the Coalition's interrogation facility at Bagram and provided intelligence to the special operations

Another CIA-owned and operated Mi-8 Hip providing an aero-medical evacuation service for wounded Northern Alliance fighters. Note the ODA members by the tail and the CIA SAD Ground Branch operative helping to carry the wounded man to the cargo HMMWV. (US SOCOM)

task forces. At its largest, Bowie numbered 36 US military personnel and 57 from agencies such as the FBI, NSA and CIA as well as liaison officers from a number of Coalition SOF.

Administratively embedded within Bowie was Advanced Force Operations (AFO). AFO was a 45-man reconnaissance unit made up of Delta recce specialists augmented by selected SEALs from DEVGRU and supported by ISA's technical experts. Rather than being a full-time standing unit, AFO had been raised solely to support Sword and was tasked with intelligence preparation of the battlefield, working closely with the CIA. AFO's operators were split between AFO-South and AFO-North with a headquarters element based at Bagram within Task Force Bowie's hanger but reporting directly to Task Force Sword.

AFO conducted covert reconnaissance – sending small, two- or three-man teams into al-Qaeda's backyard along the border with Pakistan. The AFO operators would deploy into observation posts known as hides, often high in the mountains, to watch and report on insurgent movements and numbers. They also carried out what are known as environmental recons – the mapping of a particular area to understand the geography and feasibility of infiltrating teams through or into that area. Much of this work was done on foot or on specially adapted All Terrain Vehicles with infrared headlights allowing them to be driven while wearing night-vision goggles.

The final task force supporting OEF-A was the Combined Joint Civil-Military Operations Task Force (CJCMOTF). It was eventually headquartered in Kabul but with two geographically divided subordinate commands; Civil-Military Operations Centre-North and Civil-Military Operations Centre-South. These had responsibility for managing civil affairs and humanitarian efforts. These operations later evolved in 2002 into the Provincial Reconstruction Teams (PRT), of which over 30 teams were eventually deployed across Afghanistan.

As the *Crescent Wind* aerial campaign began to wind down, Task Force Dagger was planning to insert their first teams from K2 in Uzbekistan. Aviators from the 2nd Battalion of the 160th SOAR maintained their MH-47E Chinooks and

A pair of MH-47E transport helicopters of the 160th Special Operations Aviation Regiment at Bagram Airbase. Both helicopters are equipped with the nose-mounted refuelling probe to extend their operational range. (US SOCOM)

MH-60L Blackhawks at a constant state of readiness, awaiting a break in the poor weather that would allow the helicopters to safely negotiate the notorious Hindu Kush Mountain.

INFIL

With two weeks of preparatory aerial bombardment (and the Air Force fast running out of targets), the first Army units were infiltrated into Afghanistan on the evening of October 18, 2001 and into the early hours of the 19th. The first team to touch down was the 12-man ODA 555 (the Triple Nickel), which immediately linked up with Jawbreaker at a helicopter landing zone (HLZ) in the Panjshir. The Green Berets were taken to a safe house to meet representatives of warlord Fahim Khan, Masoud's successor as military commander of the Northern Alliance. Early the next day, the men of the Special Forces began operations alongside Khan's militia.

Although the 160th SOAR had been given clearance to fly, the weather that night had been dangerous enough to force back two escorting MH-60L Direct Action Penetrators (DAPs). The MH-47E Chinook they were accompanying, carrying the second Green Beret team – ODA 595 – continued on alone in the

OPERATION *ENDURING FREEDOM*
AFGHANISTAN, TASK FORCE INSERTIONS, OCTOBER TO DECEMBER 2001

Operation Enduring Freedom–Afghanistan,
October to December 2001:
Task Force Insertions
1) Combined Joint Special Operations
   Task Force–North (Task Force Dagger)
2) Combined Joint Special Operations
   Task Force–South (Task Force K-Bar)
3) Task Force 58 (USMC) and Task Force 64 (SASR)

night. As well as potentially deadly ice build-ups on their rotors, and the treacherous 16,000ft peaks of the Hindu Kush, the aviators struck a sandstorm on the way into Afghanistan. Despite these appalling conditions, the Nightstalker crew courageously completed their mission, touching down at 0200hrs local time in the Dari-a-Souf Valley just south of the regional capital, Mazar-e-Sharif. This second team was met at the HLZ by the militia of ethnic Uzbek warlord General Abdur Rashid Dostum, commander of the largest Northern Alliance faction.

Dostum maintained a strong powerbase around Mazar-e-Sharif and was an accomplished political player, having previously struck alliances with the Soviets, the former Kabul puppet government and the Taliban. These kinds of shifting loyalties are not considered unusual in Afghanistan, where the local Taliban commander could be your cousin and the local head of police your uncle. Tribal loyalties are far more important to the Afghan than any nominal government and insurgent divide.

RHINO

At roughly the same time as the first Green Beret teams were being inserted into northern Afghanistan (on the night of 19 October 2001), two other special operations were taking place – both in southern Afghanistan. Some 200 Army Rangers from the 3rd Battalion of the 75th Ranger Regiment conducted a daring night-time combat drop from MC-130P Combat Talon aircraft, parachuting on to a remote desert airstrip southwest of the city of Kandahar. The site had been softened up by airstrikes from B-2 Spirit stealth bombers and AC-130 Spectre fixed-wing gunships that remained orbiting over the drop zone (DZ) in case the Rangers ran into trouble.

Led by a small Pathfinder team to mark the DZ, the Rangers met almost no resistance (a solitary Taliban fighter who attempted to engage the Rangers was quickly shot and killed) and the location, code-named Objective Rhino, was secured. A small Taliban force mounted in pick-up trucks that attempted to investigate was spotted and destroyed by the AC-130s. The only casualties among

Members of a US Army Special Forces ODA meet with General Tommy Franks, October 2001, Afghanistan. Note the Mk12 Special Purpose Rifle nicknamed "Sara Jane" carried by the central operator. (US DOD)

Delta Force

The 1st Special Forces Operational Detachment – Delta, the Combat Applications Group, the Army Compartmented Element, Delta Force – all various names for the US Army's special mission unit. Known simply as the Unit by its members and as Delta or CAG by those who work with it, it was founded in the late 1970s as a response to an ongoing wave of international terrorism that followed the Munich Massacre in 1972 when 11 Israeli athletes were murdered at the Summer Olympics.

Delta's first operation ended in failure in the Iranian desert. A 1980 joint operation to rescue American hostages at the Tehran Embassy went disastrously wrong. After several helicopters developed mechanical problems at a forward airstrip, the operation was aborted. As Delta and the Rangers climbed aboard their aircraft to leave, a Navy RH-53 transport helicopter collided with an Air Force EC-130E cargo aircraft carrying part of the Delta assault element. In the ensuing explosion and fire, eight US servicemen tragically died.

Following the Iran disaster, Delta operated in Grenada, Lebanon, Panama, the first Gulf War, Somalia, the Balkans, and many other failed states. The first Gulf War gave Delta an opportunity to demonstrate that it was not simply a hostage rescue team as it conducted extended length mobility patrols in the western Iraqi Desert hunting for Scud launchers. Somalia and the Balkans cemented Delta's reputation as a man-hunting force. It would need both sets of skills in Afghanistan.

Delta, like most military counterterrorist units, is based around the British SAS model and is considered the Army's primary direct action, hostage rescue and special reconnaissance unit. The unit consists of four

Squadrons (A, B, C, and the recently raised D) each of which is further divided into three Troops – two consisting of assaulters and snipers and one, called Recce Troop, which contains the most experienced operators. Members of Recce Troop are expected to be able to infiltrate virtually any location, in any weather, to conduct covert reconnaissance or surveillance tasks for extended periods of time.

Another rare image of Delta Force during the famous Scud hunt during *Desert Storm*. The two vehicles in the fore and middle ground are DUMVEES (Desert Mobility Vehicles) – one of the earliest incarnations of what later became the GMV (Ground Mobility Vehicle) special operations HMMWV (High Mobility Multipurpose Wheeled Vehicle, also known as a Humvee). Behind the DUMVEES is what appears to be a Pinzgauer Special Operations Vehicle. Interestingly, the machine gun mounted on a bipod on the roof of the centre DUMVEE is an FN MAG58, later known as the M240 in US service. At the time, the M240 hadn't yet been formally adopted by the US military. (Photographer unknown)

the Rangers were two soldiers who had suffered light injuries in the jump itself. The Rangers provided security while a Forward Arming and Refuelling Point (FARP) was established using fuel bladders flown in on the MC-130s.

The parachute drop and some equally grainy night-vision footage of the airstrip seizure was later televised by the Pentagon as proof that US forces could seize any location in Afghanistan, a strong psychological message to the Taliban leadership. The Ranger mission also paved the way for the later use of the airstrip by the Marines of 15th MEU as FOB Rhino who would be among the first conventional forces to set foot in Afghanistan.

No casualties were suffered in the Rhino operation itself, but two Rangers assigned to the Combat Search and Rescue (CSAR) element supporting the mission were sadly killed when their MH-60L helicopter crashed at Objective Honda in Pakistan, a temporary staging site secured by a company of Rangers from 3/75th Ranger Regiment. The crash was the result of what is termed a brown-out (a dust storm caused by rotor downdraft that temporarily blinds the aircrew) rather than from any enemy action. Brown-outs were an occupational hazard when operating in arid, dusty environments and had been suffered by the 160th SOAR back in the first Gulf War, but the tragic deaths were nonetheless sobering for the young Rangers.

At the same time, another much less publicized operation was being conducted outside of Kandahar at a location known as Objective Gecko. The details of the operation remain classified primarily because of the units involved – a squadron of Delta Force from Task Force Sword. Its target was none other than Mullah Omar himself. The mission was launched from the USS *Kitty Hawk*, which was serving as a floating SOF base in the Indian Ocean. Four MH-47Es ferried a total of 91 soldiers to the objective from the *Kitty Hawk* – the assault teams were drawn from Delta while teams from the Rangers secured the perimeter and manned blocking positions. In a similar fashion to Rhino, the target was softened up by preparatory fire from both AC-130s and MH-60L Direct Action Penetrators.

The Gecko target itself was a "dry hole" – there was no sign of the Taliban leader. The assaulters had met zero resistance on the target and immediately switched to exploiting the target location for any intelligence while their helicopters landed at Rhino to refuel at the newly established FARP. As the assault teams prepared to extract and summoned their rides, a sizeable Taliban force approached the compound and engaged the ground forces with small arms fire and RPGs.

The Rangers and Delta operators engaged the insurgents and a heavy firefight developed. An attached Combat Controller directed deadly fires from the orbiting AC-130s and DAPs, allowing the assault force to break contact and withdraw to an emergency HLZ for extraction. One of the MH-47Es lost a wheel assembly after striking a compound wall in the scramble to extract the ground force – the Taliban unsurprisingly claimed this as evidence that it had shot down one of the American helicopters. Some 30 insurgents were killed in the battle at Gecko. No one on the raiding force was killed but a dozen were wounded including several seriously. Delta's plans to leave a stay-behind reconnaissance team in the area were aborted by the Taliban response.

US Army Rangers prepare to head out on a night operation. Note the sniper pair to the left carrying a 7.62mm SR-25/ Mk11 and his partner carrying the big .50 M82A1 with thermal day/night sight. (JZW)

21ST-CENTURY CAVALRY

While Task Force Sword carried out the Kandahar raids, the Green Berets of ODA 595 were striking up a healthy relationship with the Uzbek warlord General Dostum. The ODA had split into two elements – Alpha and Bravo – with Alpha riding on horseback with Dostum to his headquarters to plan the impending attack on Mazar-e-Sharif. Bravo was tasked with clearing the Dari-a-Souf Valley of the Taliban and travelled high into the Alma Tak Mountains to get a good look at its area of operations.

The horseback riding posed particular challenges for the American operators – only one had any real riding experience and the traditional wooden Afghan saddles used by Dostum's riders were far from comfortable. Afghan horses are closer to ponies in stature which also did not help matters. The wooden saddles led to one of the most unusual resupply requests – for civilian manufacture saddles – which were duly airdropped to their location, along with copies of a World War II-era Army field manual on conducting operations with pack animals.

On October 20, 2001, the Alpha element of ODA 595 guided in the first JDAM (Joint Direct Attack Munition) GPS-guided bomb from an orbiting B-52. Dostum was suitably impressed: "You made an aircraft appear and drop bombs. General Dostum is very happy!" he was quoted as saying by the official SOCOM history, *Weapon of Choice*. Dostum was soon taunting his Taliban opponents over their radio frequencies – a curious facet of the war between the Taliban and the Northern Alliance and a crude example of Afghan psychological warfare. "This is General Dostum speaking. I am here and I have brought the Americans with me!" he declared, much to the amusement of the Special Forces.

A US Army Special Forces ODA takes a break during a mounted patrol, eastern Afghanistan, 2002. (JZW)

The United States conducted its own psychological warfare operations with EC-130E Commando Solo aircraft beaming radio transmissions in both Dari and Pashtu to the Afghan civilian population. Radios were dropped with humanitarian packages that were fixed to receive only news and Afghan music from a Coalition radio station. Air Force Special Operations aircraft also dropped huge numbers of Psy Ops leaflets decrying the Taliban and al-Qaeda as criminals who had ruined Afghanistan and promoting the $25 million reward placed on bin Laden's head.

The ODA 595 Bravo team was conducting its own airstrikes in the Dari-a-Souf Valley, cutting off and destroying Taliban reinforcements and frustrating its attempts to relieve its embattled forces to the north. Cumulatively, the near constant airstrikes had begun to have a decisive effect and the Taliban began to withdraw toward Mazar-e-Sharif. Dostum's forces and the men of ODA 595 Alpha followed, pausing only to drop further bombs on Taliban stragglers using their SOFLAM (Special Operations Forces Laser Marker – a device that emits a laser-aiming point that can be followed by a smart bomb such as a JDAM).

DAISY CUTTER

On the Shomali Plains, ODA 555 and the CIA Jawbreaker team attached to Fahim Khan's forces began calling in airstrikes on entrenched Taliban positions at the southeastern end of the former Soviet air base at Bagram. The Green Berets set up an observation post in a disused air traffic control tower and with perfect lines of sight, guided in two 15,000lb BLU-82 Daisy Cutter bombs (the Daisy Cutter

OPERATION *ENDURING FREEDOM*
AFGHANISTAN, INFILTRATION ROUTES AND AREAS OF RESPONSIBILITY, 2001

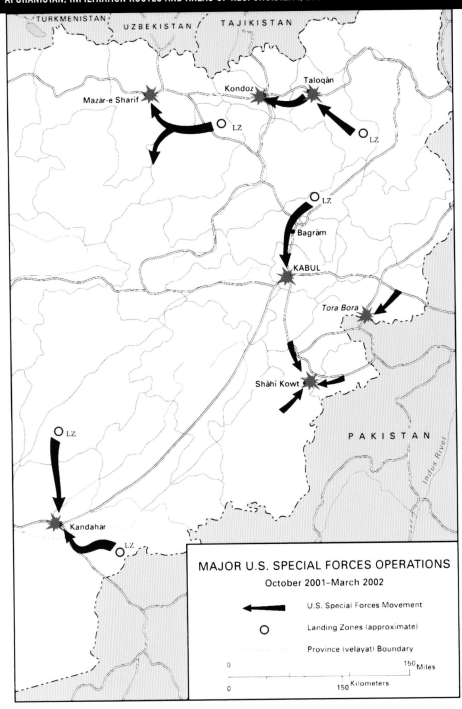

MAJOR U.S. SPECIAL FORCES OPERATIONS

October 2001–March 2002

← U.S. Special Forces Movement

○ Landing Zones (approximate)

Province (velayat) Boundary

0   150 Miles

0   150 Kilometers

is so big it must be pushed out of an MC-130 transport plane) which devastated the Taliban lines, both physically and psychologically.

By November 5, 2001, the advance of Dostum and his horsemen was stalled at the Taliban-held village of Bai Beche in the strategically vital Dari-a-Souf Valley. Two earlier Northern Alliance attacks had been driven back by the entrenched defenders. While ODA 595 organized airstrikes from B-52s, Dostum prepared his men to follow the bombs with a cavalry charge. According to a member of the ODA, one of Dostum's lieutenants misunderstood the call to stand-by for a signal to attack and sent 250-odd Uzbek horsemen charging toward the Taliban lines as the B-52 made its final approach. Quoted in Max Boot's *War Made New*, an operator explains:

"Three or four bombs hit right in the middle of the enemy position. Almost immediately after the bombs exploded, the horses swept across the objective – the enemy was so shell-shocked. I could see the horses blasting out the other side. It was the finest sight I ever saw. The men were thrilled; they were so happy. It wasn't done perfectly, but it will never be forgotten." The potential for fratricide and the resulting political fallout may have severed Dostum's key relationship with the Americans and slowed the pace of the war. Thankfully, fate played its hand and Dostum's cavalry charge succeeded in breaking the back of the defenders, with a little help from a B-52.

Other Green Beret ODAs were inserting at regular intervals across the country as the pace of operations increased (and the flying weather improved). On October 23 ODA 585 was infiltrated near Konduz to work alongside the warlord Burillah Khan. On November 2, the ten-man ODA 553 inserted into Bamian and linked up with General Kareem Kahlili's forces. ODA 534 was also inserted on November 2 into the Dari-a-Balkh Valley after again being delayed by the weather for several nights. Its role was to support General Mohammed Atta, a sometime associate of General Dostum, and head of the powerful Jaamat-e-Islami militia. Alongside the Green Berets was a small element from the CIA's Special Activities Division. As one of the CIA operators on the team explained to the author a number of years later:

The team was finally able to infil [infiltrate] northern Afghanistan by Chinook on the night of 2 November after several days of bad weather. If the helo insertion [had] failed, an airborne [parachute] operation was scheduled for the following evening. In addition to the 12-man ODA and two Air Force CCTs, three Agency (CIA) Officers were attached. The Agency team consisted of a Case Officer/Dari Linguist, a former SEAL Officer, and a former Special Forces medic Med Officer.

The team was met on the HLZ by Atta's forces and an Agency CTC Officer [from Jawbreaker] who had infiltrated two weeks prior and had been working with Dostum. He [the Jawbreaker Officer] now took command of the Agency team, while the rest of his group and another ODA [595] remained with Dostum and his men. The ODA team leader's Russian did come in handy once the RON [Remain-Over-Night] site was reached and the team split, but the primary source of interpretation between the team and Atta and his men was the Agency Case Officer.

The pace of operations continued without pause. Special Forces ODAs 586 and 594 were infiltrated into Afghanistan on November 8 in MH-47s and picked up on the Afghan/Tajik border by CIA-flown Mi-17s crewed by SAD Air Branch contractors. ODA 586 deployed into Konduz with the forces of General Daoud Khan and ODA 594 deployed into the Panjshir to assist the men of the Triple Nickel.

MAZAR-E-SHARIF

ODA 534 had fought through the Dari-e-Souf Valley with Atta's militia and had linked up with Dostum outside Mazar-e-Sharif to develop a plan of attack against the Taliban-held city. At the critical Tangi Pass, the gateway from the Balkh Valley to the city of Mazar-e-Sharif and an obvious defensive location, Taliban forces were dug in aiming to halt the Northern Alliance's rapid advance on the city.

On November 9, members of the two ODAs and the CIA team positioned themselves in mountainside hides and began calling in airstrikes against the defenders of the pass. The Taliban responded with indirect fire from BM-21 Grad rockets, which were quickly suppressed by orbiting air support. The airstrikes took their toll on the Taliban and at a signal from Atta and Dostum, the Northern Alliance forces – some on foot, some on horseback, some in pickups, and some in captured BMP armored personnel carriers – raced toward the gates of the city in a pell-mell attack.

Mazar-e-Sharif fell to the Northern Alliance and with it came the first hint

A Ranger (on the right) and a CIA SAD operative known only as "Dave" at an undisclosed Forward Operating Base. Dave was one of two CIA operatives caught up in the prison uprising at Mazar-e-Sharif; his partner Mike Spann was tragically killed. (JZW)

that the war may not be the bloody year-long affair predicted by the Pentagon and the media. US Army Civil Affairs Teams from the 96th Civil Affairs Battalion and Tactical Psychological Operations Teams from the 4th Psychological Operations Group, both assigned to the Green Berets of Task Force Dagger, were immediately deployed into Mazar-e-Sharif to assist in winning the proverbial hearts and minds of the inhabitants. A medical clinic and humanitarian rations, along with pens, notepads, and footballs for the children went a long way toward meeting that goal.

In the central north of Afghanistan, Special Forces ODA 586 was advising General Daoud Khan outside of the city of Taloqan (the capital of Takhar Province) and coordinating a batch of preparatory airstrikes when the General surprised everyone including the ODA by launching an impromptu massed infantry assault on the Taliban holding the city. Before the first bomb could be dropped, Taloqan fell. Often, the Afghan warlords could read the local conditions and the will of the opposition far more accurately than the ODAs – the Afghans knew their opponents, often personally, and knew how conflicts in Afghanistan were resolved. As long as the Taliban made a show of resistance before it retreated, its honor would escape intact.

LITTLE BIRDS

While the ODAs and their Afghan allies captured city after city, the Rangers carried out their second combat parachute drop into Afghanistan on the night of November 13. A platoon-sized Ranger security element, including Team 3 of the elite Regimental Reconnaissance Detachment, accompanied by eight Air Force Special Tactics operators, dropped into a site southwest of Kandahar codenamed Bastogne to secure a FARP for a follow-on operation by the Nightstalkers of the 160th SOAR.

A pair of MC-130 cargo aircraft soon landed at the improvised strip and deposited four AH-6J Little Bird gunships. The flight of Little Birds lifted off to hit a Taliban target compound near Kandahar code named Objective Wolverine. After successfully destroying the target, the AH-6J "Six Guns" returned to the desert FARP to rearm and refuel before launching another strike against a second site called Objective Raptor. With their missions complete, the Little Birds returned to the FARP, loaded on to the MC-130s, and the combined team flew back to Pakistan.

Several nights later, a similar attack mission codenamed Operation *Relentless Strike* was also successfully flown – this time with the Rangers driving in their modified HMMWVs and Land Rovers to secure a remote desert strip. These were the first missions in Afghanistan conducted by the Little Bird pilots of the 160th SOAR, as the helicopters could not operate at the higher attitudes in the mountains.

Navy SEALs watch a Taliban cave complex go up in smoke. Note the Desert Patrol Vehicle in the foreground. (US SOCOM)

Two US Navy DEVGRU operators providing close protection for Afghan President Hamid Karzai, early 2002, while a contractor force was being hired. DEVGRU saved Karzai's life more than once including in September 2002 when a gunman attempted to shoot him at close range with a pistol. The gunman and at least two bystanders were killed by DEVGRU fire. (US SOCOM)

Three days after the historic fall of Mazar-e-Sharif, Kabul itself, the capital of Afghanistan, fell to General Fahim Khan supported by the men of ODA 555. Surviving Taliban and al-Qaeda members retreated toward Kandahar, the spiritual home and birthplace of the Taliban movement, and the inhospitable mountain ranges of Tora Bora (a location which the mujahideen had used as base areas during the Soviet–Afghan War).

On November 14, ODA 574 inserted into the southern Afghan village of Tarin Kowt in Uruzgan Province in four MH-60Ks, bringing with them the soon-to-be President of Afghanistan, the Pashtun leader Hamid Karzai. As the key cities fell in rapid succession, Task Force Dagger's attention focused on the last northern Taliban stronghold, Konduz. General Daoud and ODA 586 initiated massive Coalition airstrikes to demoralise the Taliban defenders of Konduz. After some 11 days of continual aerial bombardment, Daoud took the traditional Afghan step of opening negotiations with his enemies and successfully negotiated the Taliban's surrender on November 23. Now only Kandahar remained.

KANDAHAR

Two days later, Forward Operating Base Rhino was established outside Kandahar (at the former air base the Rangers had seized a month earlier), adding further pressure on the beleaguered Taliban in and around the city. A SEAL recce team from SEAL Team 8 conducted a reconnaissance before the Marines landed, but were mistakenly engaged by orbiting AH-1W Cobra attack helicopters. Luckily they managed to get a message through to the Marines and suffered no casualties from the friendly fire. Cleared in by the SEALs, the 15th Marine Expeditionary Unit later landed a battalion-sized force at Rhino. Task Force 64 soon followed with an initial SASR complement.

Meanwhile, President Elect Karzai, with ODA 574, had begun moving toward Kandahar, gathering fighters from friendly local Pashtun tribes until his militia force eventually numbered some 800 gunmen. His militia fought for two days with the Taliban dug into ridgelines overlooking the strategic Sayd-Aum-Kalay Bridge before managing to seize the bridgehead, with the help of American airpower, opening up the road to their final objective, Kandahar.

In spite of the ongoing success of the campaign, tragedy struck Special Forces ODA 574 accompanying Karzai. On December 5 a 2,000lb GPS-guided bomb landed among the Special Forces, killing three members of the ODA outright and wounding all of the rest of the team, some with life-changing injuries. Over 20 of Karzai's militia were also killed and Karzai himself was slightly wounded in the blast. A Delta Force unit that had been operating nearby on a classified reconnaissance mission arrived in their Pinzgauers and secured the site while Delta medics worked with the less injured Green Berets on their seriously wounded comrades. Along with a Marine CH-53 casualty evacuation helicopter with a Marine medical team on board, ODB 570 and ODA 524 were immediately dispatched by helicopter to assist with the wounded and to eventually replace the fallen operators of 574.

A former ODA operator explained to the author how he believed the accident occurred: "When the PLGR GPS [Precision

No bag limit! A humorous hunting permit worn on a Green Beret's body armor. (JZW)

Lightweight GPS Receiver] batteries go dead and you put new ones in, it defaults to showing the GPS location of itself (the PLGR unit, not the target coordinates). The TACP [Tactical Air Control Party] with 574 wasn't trained for that and put new batteries in, looked at the unit and called the GPS location in to the bird. The bird asked for confirmation because the data had changed since [the] last call and 574 confirmed that it was correct at which time they dropped the JDAM".

The following day, after being informed that he was indeed to be the next President of Afghanistan, Karzai successfully negotiated the surrender of both the remaining Taliban forces around Sayd-Aum-Kalay and of the entire city of Kandahar itself. ODA 524 and ODB 570 mounted up with Karzai's militia to begin the final push to clear and secure the city. Another Green Beret team was also fighting its way toward Kandahar City. ODA 583 had infiltrated into the Shin-Narai Valley, southeast of Kandahar to support Gul Agha Sherzai, the former governor of Kandahar. By November 24, ODA 583 had established covert observation posts, which allowed it to call in devastating airstrikes on Taliban positions at Kandahar Airport.

On December 7, the Taliban had finally had enough punishment from the American bombs and Sherzai's forces seized Kandahar Airport. Informed by the Special Forces of Karzai's surrender deal with the Taliban in Kandahar City, Sherzai controversially entered the city just before President Karzai. Apparently it was around this time that Mullah Omar, the leader of the Taliban in Afghanistan, escaped the city on a motorcycle with a handful of his closest followers. The campaign had taken just under two months – 49 days to be precise – from the insertion of the first Green Beret teams to the fall of Kandahar. It was accomplished by several hundred highly trained and motivated SOF and CIA officers supported by their allies in the Northern Alliance and the awe-inspiring might of American airpower.

TORA BORA

After the dramatic fall of Kabul and Kandahar, al-Qaeda elements, including bin Laden himself and other key leadership figures, withdrew to the ancient eastern city of Jalalabad, the capital of Nangarhar Province. Jalalabad was only a short distance from the mountains of the Tora Bora region and the network of caves and prepared defenses used by the mujahideen in its war against the Soviets.

Tora Bora, part of the famous White Mountains, lies only 20km from the porous border with Pakistan, offering an ideal if physically demanding smuggler's route into Pakistan and the lawless tribal lands which stretch along the border. The area was very familiar to bin Laden as he had spent time with the mujahideen there in the 1980s and knew the mountainous caverns would provide the perfect stronghold against Coalition bombing. Indeed, it was one the Soviets never fully managed to conquer.

Signals intercepts and interrogations of captured Taliban and al-Qaeda pointed toward the presence of significant numbers of foreign fighters and possible-high value targets moving from Jalalabad to take refuge in Tora Bora. With resistance from the higher echelons of both the White House and the Pentagon to committing conventional forces on the ground in Tora Bora – in a misplaced fear of replicating the Soviet experience – a decision was made to continue to use American SOF supporting locally recruited Afghan Militia Forces (AMF).

Special Forces ODA 572 and a small group of SAD Ground Branch operators were dispatched to Tora Bora to advise eastern anti-Taliban forces under the command of two warlords; Commanders Hazrat Ali and Mohammed Zaman (regrettably, two warlords with a deep-seated distrust, if not open hostility, toward each other). Using CIA hard currency, some 2,500 to 3,000 Afghan Militia Forces were recruited for the operation to isolate and destroy the al-Qaeda elements using Tora Bora as a final strongpoint.

As tactical command of the forthcoming operation would rest with him, the leader of the CIA Jawbreaker team requested a battalion of Rangers – the 3rd Battalion of the 75th Rangers – who were at that time in-country supporting Task Force Sword to be dropped into the mountains to establish blocking positions along potential escape routes out of Tora Bora and into Pakistan. They would serve as the anvil while the Green Berets with their Afghans would be the hammer. With attached Air Force Combat Controllers, the Rangers could direct airstrikes on to enemy concentrations or engage them directly in conventional ambushes. The other seemingly obvious choice would have been the 10th Mountain Division, elements of which were already forward deployed to nearby Bagram. However, despite its name the Division had not trained in mountain warfare for many years. Either way, the request for the Rangers or indeed any significant increase in the size of the US footprint was denied.

A grainy but rare shot of a Delta Force team at Tora Bora. Again the team wear a mix of military and high-end civilian hiking gear. Delta at the time could be identified by the custom forward grips it used on its M4s (which also featured a switch for its light mounts) and its preference for EO Tech holographic weapons sights – commonplace today, but rarer during the early days of the War on Terror. (US SOCOM)

Certainly, the logistics, particularly in terms of helicopter lift capability, would have been difficult to manage, although the Jawbreaker leader and the respected Marine General, James Mattis, both believed that it could have been done. They also believe that using the Rangers to seal the trails may well have succeeded. As a counterpoint, it must also be remembered that up until Tora Bora, the use of Afghan militias directed and mentored by the Green Berets had been a consistent formula for success. The Pakistanis would be informed of the operation and it was hoped their Frontier Scouts, an irregular paramilitary police, would mop up escaping al-Qaeda members as they entered Pakistan.

At the outset of the Afghan-led operation into the mountains, ODA 572, with its attached Combat Controller, called in daily precision fires from the air – plus another 15,000lb Daisy Cutter – while their Afghan militias launched what amounted to a number of poorly executed and poorly coordinated attacks on established al-Qaeda positions with a predictable degree of success. The Green Berets discovered that these new militias lacked both the heart and the skills for the fight. According to ODA members who were there, the militias would gain ground in the morning in the wake of American airstrikes, only to relinquish control of those very gains later the same day. Similarly, the Afghans would retreat to their base areas each night to sleep. The handful of Green Berets and CIA officers, rightly concerned about being overrun by the numerically superior al-Qaeda, were forced to concede ground and fallback with them.

With the Afghan militia offensive all but stalled, despite intensive and prolonged aerial bombing, the decision was finally made to bring more Americans into the fight. The Special Forces and Jawbreaker teams were stretched thin, so

Navy SEALs meeting local residents during a Sensitive Site Exploitation (SSE) mission in the Jaji Mountains of Paktia Province. (Photographer's Mate 1st Class Tim Turner; US Navy)

instead 40 operators from Delta Force's A Squadron were forward deployed to Tora Bora. They would assume tactical command of the operation from the CIA. With the Delta squadron were several patrols from the British SBS.

The Delta operators deployed in small teams embedded within the militias and sent their own Recce operators out to pick up bin Laden's trail. Eventually, now with Green Berets, Delta and CIA operators cajoling the Afghan militia, some halting progress was made. The Delta squadron commander agreed with Jawbreaker's assessment of the situation and also requested blocking forces or the scattering of aerially sown minefields to deny the mountain passes to the enemy. If he couldn't have Rangers, he requested that his operators, who had all completed recent and grueling mountaineering training, be dropped behind the al-Qaeda forces to act as the much-needed anvil. All of his requests were flatly denied by General Franks.

On December 12, two weeks into the operation and in typical Afghan fashion, Militia Commander Zaman opened negotiations with the trapped al-Qaeda and Taliban in Tora Bora. Much to the frustration of the Americans and British, a temporary truce was called until 0800hr the following morning to allow al-Qaeda time to supposedly agree surrender terms by Shura (group meeting). This was a ruse played to allow as many as several hundred al-Qaeda, including members of the notorious Brigade 055, to escape overnight into the mountain paths toward Pakistan.

THE ESCAPE

The following day, a handheld ICOM radio recovered from the body of a dead al-Qaeda fighter allowed members of the Delta squadron and the CIA to finally hear bin Laden's voice, apparently apologizing to his followers for leading them to Tora Bora and giving his blessing for their surrender. This was now thought to have been addressed directly to his men who stayed to fight a rearguard action to allow "the Sheikh" to escape. It has also been long suspected that the locally recruited militias actively assisted in the escape. Credible rumors of cash payments by bin Laden to at least one of the warlords abound. The reluctance of the militias to press the attack may have also been influenced by similar bribes. Gary Berntsen, leader of the CIA Jawbreaker team at Tora Bora, believes that two large al-Qaeda groups escaped.

The smaller group consisted of some 130 fighters who headed east into Pakistan, while the second group, which included bin Laden himself and 200 Saudi and Yemeni jihadists, took the snow-covered route across the mountains to the Pakistani town of Parachinar, which lies just over the border in the tribal lands. The Delta Force Major believes that bin Laden physically crossed the border into Pakistan sometime around December 16.

US Navy SEALs from Task Force K-Bar and attached Explosive Ordnance Disposal (EOD) teams search a Taliban cave complex at Zawar Kili. Note the burn marks at the cave entrance – a sign of an earlier airstrike. (US Navy)

Inside one of the Taliban caves at Zawar Kili as SEALs and EOD teams catalogue the finds and prepare them for later demolition. (US Navy)

With the majority of their quarry gone, the Battle of Tora Bora drew to an anticlimatic close. Official tallies claiming hundreds of al-Qaeda dead at Tora Bora are difficult to confirm, particularly since many of the bodies were buried in cave-ins or simply vaporized by aerial bombs. Only a handful of prisoners were taken. A Delta Recce team with the callsign Jackal had spotted a tall man wearing a camouflage jacket entering a cave with a large number of foreigners with the obvious presumption that it was bin Laden. The Recce team called in multiple airstrikes on the cave mouth, but later DNA analysis of the recovered remains did not match bin Laden's.

Another Special Forces team, ODA 561, was inserted into the White Mountains on December 20 to support ODA 572 in conducting sensitive site exploitations of the caves and to assist with the grim task of recovering DNA samples from enemy bodies. Although primitive bunkers were discovered formed from natural caves, none of the vast cave complexes described in the news media was ever located. Another newspaper-fuelled myth was that a British SAS squadron had been involved in close-quarter battle through one of these very same cave complexes. In fact, the only UK Special Forces in Tora Bora were the dozen or so operators from the SBS.

Eight years later, in a sad addendum to the story of the Battle of Tora Bora, the United States Senate Committee on Foreign Relations held a series of hearings on the matter. The Senate Committee eventually found that reluctance to insert US forces to man blocking positions on the part of both the Pentagon and the White House facilitated bin Laden's escape and probably extended the length of the Afghan War.

In January 2002, another series of caves used by al-Qaeda was discovered in Zawar Kili, just south of Tora Bora. Airstrikes hit the sites before SOF teams were infiltrated into the area. A SEAL platoon from SEAL Team 3, including several of their Desert Patrol Vehicle dune buggies, accompanied by a German KSK element

Order of Battle

Operation ANACONDA

Task Force DAGGER
ODAs, 5th Special Forces Group (Airborne)
Company B, 2nd Battalion, 160th Special Operations Aviation Regiment
Combat Tactical Air Controllers, AFSOC

Afghan Militia Forces (AMF)
Commander Zia (Task Force HAMMER)
Kamil Khan (Task Force ANVIL)
Zakim Khan (Task Force ANVIL)

Task Force RAKASSAN
3rd Brigade, 101st Airborne Division (Air Assault)
1st Battalion, 187th Infantry
2nd Battalion, 187th Infantry
1st Battalion, 87th Infantry, 10th Mountain Division

Task Force COMMANDO
2nd Brigade, 10th Mountain Division
4th Battalion, 31st Infantry
3rd Battalion, Princess Patricia's Canadian Light Infantry

Task Force 64
1 Squadron, Australian SASR

Task Force K-BAR
ODAs, 3rd Special Forces Group (Airborne)

Task Force BOWIE
Advanced Force Operations

Task Force SWORD
Mako 30, 31, and 21, Task Force Blue

and a Norwegian SOF team, spent some nine days conducting an extensive SSE. They cleared an estimated 70 caves and 60 structures in the area, recovering a huge amount of both intelligence materials and munitions, but they did not encounter any al-Qaeda fighters.

ANACONDA

In February 2002, a Special Forces intelligence analyst working for Task Force Bowie began to identify patterns that led him to believe that surviving al-Qaeda forces were massing in the Lower Shahikot Valley, some 60 miles south of Gardez. The Lower Shahikot bordered the Pakistani tribal lands where many al-Qaeda fighters were believed to have escaped to from Tora Bora. Others within Advanced Force Operations (AFO) and the CIA were making the same connections.

The Shahikot, which translates as the Place of the King, stretches 9km in length and is 5km across at its widest point. It is composed of two distinct areas, the Lower and Upper Shahikot which run roughly parallel to each other. In the Lower Shahikot several imposing mountains dominate the landscape; chief among them is Takur Ghar at the southeastern end of the valley. To the northeast is Tsapare Ghar, dominating the northern entrance to the valley.

The famed Afghan authority Lester Grau has established that a mujahideen commander called Malawi Nasrullah Mansoor was in charge of the valley during the Soviet–Afghan War and invited foreign jihadists to base themselves in the Lower Shahikot. Mansoor soon fortified the valley, digging trench systems, building bunkers, and firing positions into the ridgelines, many of which would be put to deadly effect some 20 years later. As the intelligence mounted on the suspected enemy concentration in the Lower Shahikot, AFO began developing plans to conduct both environmental reconnaissance and pattern-of-life surveillance on the valley and its inhabitants.

An environmental reconnaissance is conducted to gain a detailed understanding of a particular area in terms of environmental factors that may influence a military operation. This could include, for example, the relative difficulty in traversing a mountain trail, the amount, type, and depth of snow in a given area, the availability of water sources, or the height of a specific terrain feature. It is defined doctrinally by the US Department of Defense as "operations conducted to collect and report critical hydrographic, geological, and meteorological information."

Pattern-of-life surveillance instead entails maintaining covert surveillance over an area of interest to develop an understanding of that area and its inhabitants. This is generally a longer-term Special Reconnaissance mission as time is required to monitor and understand the atmospherics of the target location. Pattern-of-life surveillance allows operators and analysts to spot when something changes in the area of interest – for example, on a certain day the villagers take food into the hills. Is it to feed insurgents (as it was on Operation *Anaconda*) or are they simply having a community meal?

For the AFO operators, it meant a lot of cold, backbreaking work infiltrating the Shahikot in a particularly harsh Afghan winter. Its commander, Delta Lieutenant Colonel Pete Blaber made the call early in the planning phase that "there will be no direct helicopter infiltrations of AFO teams anywhere near the valley" to ensure they didn't spook their quarry. He felt that heliborne insertions made it impossible to surprise the enemy, giving forewarning of the operation and that the tactic limited opportunities for the teams to develop superior methods of infiltrating a target area.

Instead, AFO chose to conduct vehicle recons of the routes into and around the valley in locally procured Toyota four-wheel-drive vehicles and at night on specially adapted Polaris All Terrain Vehicles (ATVs). These ATVs were modified by unit mechanics with Infrared headlights, GPS receivers, and suppressed exhausts. They also sent two teams of highly experienced Delta operators from their squadron's Reconnaissance and Surveillance Troop into the area surrounding the Shahikot to conduct the environmental recons.

These two small teams, codenamed Juliet and India with five and three operators respectively, climbed high into the mountains and gorges of the Shahikot, often in the most extreme weather conditions to gain an appreciation of the area of operations. Their vital intelligence was fed back to the AFO and would prove invaluable once Operation *Anaconda* was launched. General Franks at CENCOM was reading the AFO daily situation reports and became convinced that an operation was needed to destroy what appeared to be a sizeable enemy presence in the Shahikot. Franks believed the time was right to deploy conventional forces into what could well become a final large scale, and decisive, battle against al-Qaeda in Afghanistan.

THE PLAN

In simple terms, the concept of operations for the coming battle was for the conventional forces of Task Force Rakkasan to air assault into the valley in CH-47D Chinook transport helicopters supported by six AH-64A Apache attack helicopters. The Rakkasans would then occupy a number of blocking positions along the eastern ridgeline of the Shahikot. Apart from organic 60mm mortars and a single 120mm tube, Task Force Rakkasan would be reliant upon the Apaches and Air Force, Marine, and Navy fighter and ground attack aircraft for fire support.

The conventional troops would act as the anvil, manning a total of seven blocking positions along the eastern ridges and destroying enemy forces fleeing from the hammer. This hammer was based around a Special Forces force element of 450 Afghan Militia Fighters led by Commander Zia Lodin, and was to be considered in military planning terms, the main effort. Lodin's AMF, suitably codenamed Task Force Hammer, would enter the valley from the northern entrance in a ground assault convoy after a preplanned aerial bombardment of previously identified enemy positions. They would then assault through the villages of Serkhankheyl and Marzak, where intelligence indicated the enemy were concentrated, and channel fleeing enemy into the sights of the Task Force Rakkasan soldiers manning the blocking positions. Two other locally recruited militias were tasked with establishing an outer cordon to stop any enemy squirters (a US military term for escaping enemy forces) from fleeing into Pakistan.

If bin Laden or another significant high-value target (HVT) was located during the operation, all offensive operations were to be paused and conventional forces tasked to place a cordon around the location of the HVT, ensuring that no enemy could escape or be reinforced. They would then await the arrival of Task Force 11's (the newly renamed Task Force Sword) direct action assault elements that would conduct the capture.

On February 28, 2002, three AFO teams were covertly infiltrated into the valley in preparation for the final air assault. Juliet was a Delta element comprised of five operators including one signals intelligence specialist from ISA. The team entered from the north using Delta's specially modified ATVs and drove through

OPERATION *ANACONDA*

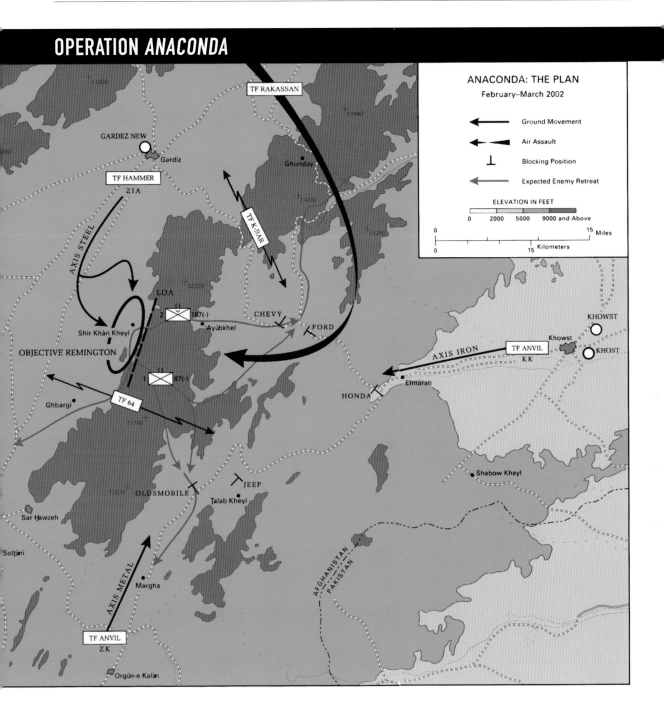

ANACONDA: THE PLAN
February–March 2002

Ground Movement

Air Assault

Blocking Position

Expected Enemy Retreat

ELEVATION IN FEET

0   2000   5000   9000 and Above

0   15 Miles

0   15 Kilometers

TF RAKASSAN

GARDEZ NEW

Gardiz

Ghunday

TF HAMMER

ZIA

TF K-BAR

AXIS STEEL

LOA

2   187(-)

Ayübkhel

CHEVY

FORD

KHOWST

Khowst

KHOST

Shir Khàn Kheyl

TF ANVIL

KK

AXIS IRON

OBJECTIVE REMINGTON

1   87(-)

HONDA

Elmarah

Ghbargi

TF 64

11740

Shabow Kheyl

Sar Hawzeh

11930

OLDSMOBILE

JEEP

Talab Kheyl

Soltàni

AFGHANISTAN
PAKISTAN

AXIS METAL

Margha

TF ANVIL

ZK

Orgûn-e Kalàn

A Chechen insurgent photographed by DEVGRU SEALs on "The Finger," shortly before Operation *Anaconda* was launched. The 12.7mm DShK was well maintained and wrapped in plastic to protect it from the elements. The SEALs were so surprised to find the Chechens so high in the mountains that they checked to ensure they weren't British Special Forces. This Chechen and his colleagues were later killed by the SEALs and an orbiting AC-130 gunship. (US SOCOM)

snow, rain, and high winds using its night-vision devices to reach eventually a covert hide on the eastern side of the valley. The second team was also an Army Delta element with an attached ISA operator and was codenamed India. This three-man team walked into the valley through the same incredibly fierce weather and climbed to establish its hide in the southwest of the valley, in a location known as the Fish Hook.

The final team, Mako 31, was from DEVGRU and comprised three SEALs from their Recce Squadron, an Air Force Combat Controller, and curiously a Navy Explosive Ordnance Disposal (EOD) operator. It is unclear what support an EOD specialist could possibly provide to a covert surveillance team, and his inclusion on the mission has never been explained. EOD operators were often attached to direct action teams to either deal with IEDs or unexploded ordnance discovered on the targets or to provide specialist demolition skills. Mako 31 also infiltrated on foot via the southern edge of the valley to set up an observation post on a terrain feature known as The Finger.

All three teams were tasked with confirming enemy strengths and dispositions including antiaircraft emplacements, ensuring the designated Rakkasan HLZs were clear of obstructions and providing terminal guidance for air support both prior to and during the insertion of the conventional forces. While the teams settled into their hides, other SOF teams were also inserting into the valley. These teams were drawn from Task Force K-Bar and Task Force 64 and were tasked with establishing their own observation posts which "had to be tenable, afford good reconnaissance, and cover the identified escape routes, or 'rat lines' into Pakistan" according to one of the US planners.

It was a truly international affair. Twenty-five teams from US and Coalition SOF, including Navy SEALs from Teams 2, 3, and 8; Green Berets from the 3rd Special Forces Group; and small teams from Canada's JTF2, Australia's SASR, New Zealand's SAS, Germany's KSK, Norway's Jaegerkommando, the Dutch Korps Commando Troepen, and the Danish Army's Jaegerkorpset, inserted into the outer edges of the valley to cut off any escape. These Special Reconnaissance teams remained uncompromised throughout the duration of *Anaconda* – three NZ SAS patrols remained in place without resupply for some ten days – and provided vital intelligence that allowed air support to intercept enemy squirters and inhibited the ability of the enemy to reinforce their positions.

H-HOUR

The SEAL team on The Finger meanwhile discovered that they were not alone. A group of foreign fighters was positioned on the peak where it had planned to establish its observation post. The enemy had an established location manning a 12.7mm DShK heavy machine gun with clear views down the valley. If the DShK was not disabled before the conventional forces arrived in their lumbering Chinooks, it could easily shoot one down. The SEALs planned on ambushing the enemy fighters in the pre-dawn darkness just hours before the Rakkasans flew into the valley.

Luck was not with them, however, and they were spotted by one of the Uzbek insurgents and a brief firefight ensued, killing five of the seven foreign fighters (two of the SEALs had stoppages with their rifles, perhaps due to the freezing conditions, leaving one man to do most of the shooting before the stoppages could be cleared). As another insurgent began taking them under fire with a PKM machine gun, the SEALs broke contact and brought in an orbiting AC-130 fixed-wing gunship which pounded the peak with Danger Close 105mm howitzer rounds, destroying the enemy encampment.

After completing the fire mission against the insurgent position on The Finger, the same AC-130 made a fatal mistake. Spotting a ground convoy of apparent insurgents heading toward the valley and with a malfunctioning navigation system that was incorrectly plotting their location, the AC-130 engaged the ground convoy. A small combined element led by CWO Stanley Harriman had broken off from the main convoy to establish a planned observation post and it was his convoy that came under fire. Harriman received a fatal fragmentation wound, two other Green Berets were wounded and several Afghans were killed before the AC-130 ceased fire after being informed by AFO of the potential fratricide.

Soon after, the main element of Task Force Hammer, already rattled by the AC-130 incident and a frustrating lack of preparatory bombing (the true cause of which has never been established), were engaged by mortar fire from al-Qaeda positions on the slopes. This was the straw that broke the camel's back and the Afghans scattered, refusing to advance any further. Like Tora Bora, it was beginning to look like an over-reliance on the Afghans would prove to be a mistake. Coupled with late breaking CIA intelligence that the al-Qaeda forces were apparently living in the peaks surrounding the valley rather than down in the villages, it did not bode well for the incoming air assault.

With no opportunity to alter operational timings, the Chinooks of Task Force Rakkasan began their air assault into the Shahikot. Incredibly, the enemy appeared to be surprised and did not take the Chinooks under fire. This may perhaps be

Calling in airstrikes during Operation *Anaconda*. To the right of the image can be seen one of the Special Tactics Combat Controllers attached to the Advanced Force Operations recce teams. (US SOCOM)

explained by the distraction of Task Force Hammer's advance or the fact that the various groups of foreign fighters did not communicate effectively between themselves (apparently, there was a sort of caste system between the jihadists). Whatever the reason, the first shots only began to ring out as the infantry took up security positions around the HLZs as the Chinooks lifted off and departed.

It did not take long for the enemy to join the battle and the conventional forces were soon in the fight of their lives. The orbiting Apaches attempted to suppress enemy mortar teams, but ran into a wall of RPG and 12.7mm fire with one Apache losing all of its electronics to an RPG hit. It was estimated that there were between 750 and 1,000 al-Qaeda fighters in and around the valley, a far cry from original estimates. The insurgents used their DShK and ZPU-1 antiaircraft guns and bracketed small arms fire against the attack helicopters supporting Rakkasan.

They also began firing their RPG rockets into the air, intending for the self-destruct mechanism that automatically detonates the warheads at 920m to catch the helicopters in lethal flak bursts of shrapnel. The Afghan mujahideen had long experience of using the RPG as a field-expedient antiaircraft weapon and these skills had been shared with their allies. The insurgents in the Shahikot began to use another of these Soviet–Afghan War tactics, launching barrages of RPGs just ahead of the helicopters as the Apaches navigated through the valley.

Two Apaches were taken out of the fight early on the first day as they were peppered with RPG and machine-gun fire and forced to return to base. One AH-64A was hit by an RPG which destroyed its left-side Hellfire mount sending shrapnel through the airframe. The same Apache was also simultaneously engaged by a DShK, rounds from which penetrated the cockpit narrowly missing the pilots. When the damaged helicopter limped home, the crew counted more than 30 bullet holes in the fuselage in addition to the RPG damage.

Despite heavy opposition, Task Force Rakkasan managed to secure its blocking positions to the north by the middle of that first morning. Task Force Rakkasan and the Green Berets of Hammer fought all day with the AFO teams calling in continuous airstrikes on al-Qaeda positions while the Apaches valiantly protected the Rakkasans on the valley floor. AFO's only frustration was that Rakkasan had priority of fires over AFO and the other SOF reconnaissance teams dotting the valley. This meant that if a Rakkasan ETAC (Enlisted Terminal Attack Controller – now known as a JTAC or Joint Tactical Air Controller) requested an airstrike, his request would take precedence as they were classed as troops in contact.

As darkness finally fell on a long day of combat, the mighty AC-130s returned over the Shahikot and began to pummel enemy firing points. The infantrymen on the valley floor marked targets by goading the enemy into firing at them. The return fire registered on the AC-130's thermal sensors and was rapidly engaged with 105mm howitzer rounds. Eventually the more exposed Rakkasan and 10th Mountain troops were extracted by Chinook that night after suffering numerous wounded during the first day.

At AFO, alarming news was received from the leadership of Task Force 11. Essentially, they were ordering the Delta AFO commander to pass control of the AFO portion of *Anaconda* to the SEALs of Task Force Blue, who were moving teams in from Bagram to Gardez for this very purpose. The message was couched in terms of AFO needing "to be out looking for the next battlefield," but was insistent that the SEALs be given the opportunity to join the fight. The Task Force 11 commander put it bluntly; "Put both of those SEAL teams into the fight tonight. That's an order."

Replacing the immediate chain of command during an operation is never considered a sound move, and to do so with operators ill-prepared for the coming operation (and without the extensive local knowledge of both the environment and the enemy that AFO had built up) was risky indeed. To do so for what seemed like political reasons, to "blood" the SEALs, was to risk men's lives.

SEAL Team 6

Once known as SEAL Team 6 but now known as the Naval Special Warfare Development Group (they have since changed their name once more but the new name is classified), the unit is considered by many as the maritime equivalent of the Army's Delta Force.

DEVGRU are structured in a similar manner to the Army unit with each squadron numbering some 50 to 60 operators based on Assault and Recce Troops and the two units are now considered interchangeable by JSOC. The unit is composed of four assault squadrons – Blue, Gold, Red, and the most recently added Silver – along with a surveillance and reconnaissance squadron – Black (known simply as Recce Squadron within DEVGRU).

SEAL Team 6 was originally conceived as a SEAL maritime component of Delta Force, but a simple alteration of paperwork by its first commander, the charismatic Richard Marcinko, led to the unit being established as its own command, rather than as part of Delta. The name SEAL Team 6 came from a deliberate deception attempt by Marcinko to keep the Soviets guessing as to the true number of SEAL Teams the US Navy possessed.

Team 6 has conducted operations in support of every major US military operation since their inception including Grenada, Panama, the Gulf, Somalia, and the Balkans. It has been heavily committed to Afghanistan since 9/11. DEVGRU now sits under direct JSOC command and conducts full-spectrum special operations, for instance, DEVGRU protected Afghan President Hamid Karzai soon after he was installed in office until an Afghan security team could be trained to take over the role, although hostage rescue and direct action missions, such as the bin Laden raid in Abbottabad, remain their primary role.

TAKUR GHAR

The SEALs' initial plans were straightforward – the first team, Mako 21, would link up with AFO team Juliet at the northern end of the valley, resupply it, and then establish a hide site on the eastern ridge above Task Force Rakkasan's blocking positions. The second team, Mako 30, would insert on to a HLZ over 1km northeast of Takur Ghar before climbing to the peak to establish their hide. Takur Ghar, the highest mountain in the area, gave commanding views of the Shahikot and was an obvious site for an observation post. The two teams would insert that night by two MH-47Es: Razor 03 and Razor 04.

After delays from an inbound B-52 strike and a faulty helicopter, the teams were eventually launched in the early hours of March 4 but they were running out of precious darkness. After a request to delay until the following night was denied, the Mako 30 team leader was forced to make the unenviable decision to insert directly on to the peak of Takur Ghar.

An AC-130H Spectre swept the peak with its sensors and declared the landing zone "cold" or uninhabited by enemy. The Mako 30 team leader felt uneasy at the speed with which the sweep was conducted and wondered whether the Spectre had the right mountain. In any case, he soon dismissed his doubts and trusted to the AC-130's technology as Razor 03 began its final approach on to the peak of

Takur Ghar. As they flared to land, the Nightstalker pilots saw a curious sight – an apparently abandoned DShK 12.7mm heavy machine gun position and goat carcasses hanging from trees. He informed the SEALs over the intercom.

As the SEAL team leader prepared to order his team off the helicopter, an RPG came screaming past the cockpit. Moments later, machine gun fire erupted from the tree line and rounds began to punch through the thin, unarmored sides of the Chinook. A second RPG flew toward them and this time hit home, striking just behind the cockpit and starting a fire in the cabin. Yet another RPG struck seconds after the first hit, exploding into the Chinook's right-side radar pod. This hit also blew out all electrical power to the aircraft, leaving many of the navigation

A pair of US Army Rangers in eastern Afghanistan, late 2001. Note the Ranger to the left is man-packing a 60mm mortar. (JZW)

systems out of action and the electrically powered miniguns useless (this incident led to 160th SOAR developing a battery-powered backup system for the miniguns, which remains in use today).

Another RPG impacted outside the aircraft, sending razor-sharp fragments through the Chinook. Yet another RPG struck a moment later, hitting the right-side turbine. They were also taking heavy automatic weapons fire from at least three distinct firing points. Thankfully the helicopter had set down in a slight depression, shielding it from the DShK the pilots had seen. The pilot made the call to save his passengers, and the aircraft, by getting out of the ambush as quickly as possible. He yanked the controls to bring the Chinook back into the air.

As he did so, swerving the helicopter violently to present a more difficult target to the enemy, the SEAL closest to the ramp, PO1 Neil Christopher 'Fifi' Roberts, fell and slid towards the edge. One of the SOAR crew chiefs, wearing a restraining tether, managed to grab hold of the SEAL's pack, but lost his grip as the helicopter again swerved to avoid ground fire. The SEAL disappeared over the edge of the ramp and was lost to the night. Leaking hydraulic fluid, the crippled helicopter made an emergency landing several kilometres away on the valley floor.

Roberts, a ten-year veteran of the SEALs, had toppled from the open ramp of the MH-47E. He had fallen some 10ft into the knee-deep snow covering the peak of Takur Ghar. He carried only his SAW (Squad Automatic Weapon – a light machine gun), his SIG Sauer 9mm pistol, and several grenades. Realizing his

TAKUR GHAR: The Rangers' battle on the peak
MARCH 4, 2002

MUJAHIDEEN TENT

US MILITARY PERSONNEL
LOCATIONS, c.06:21 1 - 12

1 Staff Sergeant Gabe Brown USAF

2 Technical Sergeant John A. Chapman USAF (KIA)

3 Staff Sergeant Ray DePouli

4 Private First Class David Gilliam

5 Specialist Anthony Miceli

6 Petty Officer First Class Neil Roberts USN (KIA)

7 Captain Nate Self

8 Chief Warrant Officer Class 5 Don Tabron

9 Specialist Aaron Totten-Lancaster

10 Staff Sergeant Kevin Vance USAF

11 Sergeant Joshua Walker

12 Sergeant Brian Wilson

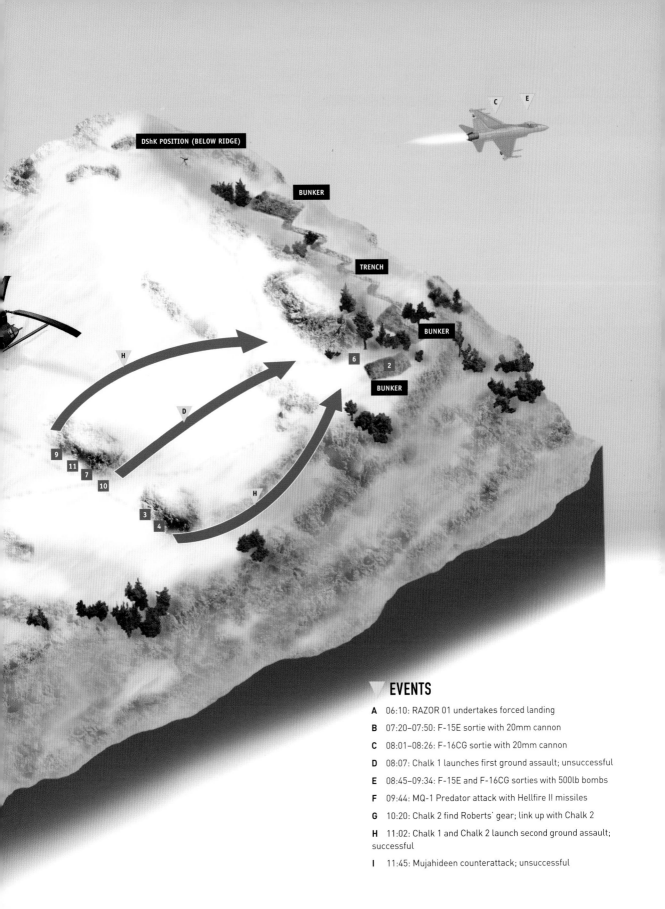

DShK POSITION (BELOW RIDGE)

BUNKER

TRENCH

BUNKER

BUNKER

C
E

H

D

9
11
7
10

3
4

H

6

2

EVENTS

A 06:10: RAZOR 01 undertakes forced landing

B 07:20–07:50: F-15E sortie with 20mm cannon

C 08:01–08:26: F-16CG sortie with 20mm cannon

D 08:07: Chalk 1 launches first ground assault; unsuccessful

E 08:45–09:34: F-15E and F-16CG sorties with 500lb bombs

F 09:44: MQ-1 Predator attack with Hellfire II missiles

G 10:20: Chalk 2 find Roberts' gear; link up with Chalk 2

H 11:02: Chalk 1 and Chalk 2 launch second ground assault; successful

I 11:45: Mujahideen counterattack; unsuccessful

The Ranger Regiment

The United States Army 75th Ranger Regiment can trace its lineage to Rogers' Rangers, a guerrilla unit formed during the French–Indian War of 1757. The Rangers were drawn from frontiersmen who could operate in small groups, raiding and ambushing before disappearing into the woods. Ranger units were raised in both the American War of Independence and the American Civil War.

Modern Rangers date from World War II when the 1st Ranger Battalion was formed in 1942. The Rangers fought in North Africa and the Middle East with the unit expanding into a regiment a year later, serving with distinction in Italy before participating in the D-Day landings in 1944. Famously they captured German gun positions near Pointe du Hoc after scaling a sheer cliff under enemy fire.

Post-war, Ranger companies were raised to serve in both Korea and Vietnam as specialist reconnaissance teams, and a Ranger battalion was formed in 1974. The Rangers soon added airfield seizures to their core skills in long-range reconnaissance and raiding. Members of the battalion saw action supporting Delta Force during the Operation *Eagle Claw* rescue in Tehran and an airfield capture during Operation *Urgent Fury* in Grenada.

The 75th Ranger Regiment was raised in 1986 serving in Operation *Just Cause* in Panama – again seizing airfields – and Operation *Desert Storm* in Kuwait where it conducted a daring helicopter-borne raid against Iraqi communication facilities and supported JSOC units during the famous 'Scud Hunt.' Since 9/11, the Rangers have been in constant combat in Iraq and Afghanistan.

In 2014 the Ranger Regiment consists of three Ranger battalions and a Regimental Special Troops Battalion (RSTB). The RSTB includes a military intelligence company, a communications company, a selection and training company, and the fabled Regimental Reconnaissance Company (RRC). The RRC, formerly known as the Regimental Reconnaissance Detachment (RRD), is thought to comprise of nine six-man teams and provides Special Reconnaissance expertise to JSOC units.

Rangers man a cut-off position while another SOF team conducts a search of a target compound, hunting for a high-value target in Helmand Province, 2013. The SAW gunner is equipped with the Mk46 light machine gun. Note the rest of the Ranger squad almost hidden in the depression. (Specialist Justin Young; US Army)

The only known, and poor quality, image of the downed Razor 01 MH-47E on the peak of Takur Ghar Mountain taken during the firefight. (US SOCOM)

predicament, Roberts quickly activated the infrared strobe that all Task Force 11 members carried to mark their positions at night.

For Mako 30 team, retrieving the missing operator was its primary objective. The team was picked up by another MH-47E, and about 30 minutes after Roberts had fallen off the ramp his team mates went back to rescue him. The al-Qaeda defenders of Takur Ghar could not believe their luck when yet another US helicopter landed on the mountain peak. They quickly manned their positions and the heavy 12.7mm DShK opened fire on the Chinook as it flared to land. Remarkably, it landed on the peak relatively unscathed and the SEALs charged down the ramp.

At first, the enemy didn't spot the SEALs in the early morning darkness and concentrated their fire on the MH-47E. Finally the helicopter lifted off, miraculously escaping the lethal barrage. Mako 30 had split up into two-man buddy pairs to conduct bounding movement and they were making good ground until the enemy finally spotted them. One team ran across a concealed al-Qaeda bunker, killing three fighters before the SEALs were suppressed by other fighters with a PKM machine gun. The firefight lasted some 20 minutes before the team leader made another difficult decision and ordered his team to break contact.

With their Air Force Combat Controller tragically killed and several SEALs wounded, the Mako 30 team leader had little choice. Retreating off the peak, another SEAL was struck by a 12.7mm round in the ankle almost blowing his foot off. Finally hunkering down in some cover, the team made an urgent request for the standby Ranger Quick Reaction Force (QRF).

Thirty-five Rangers from 1st Battalion of the 75th Rangers led by Captain Nate Self had been assigned the QRF (Quick Reaction Force) duty for all Task Force 11 operations. Only half of the platoon was available that day as the remainder was conducting live-fire training at Tarnak Farms, a former home to none other than bin Laden himself. The Ranger QRF launched immediately in two MH-47Es with the callsigns Razor 01 and Razor 02.

Razor 01 was directed to land on the peak, unaware of the significant enemy presence and that the SEALs had already withdrawn. During the flight, the Ranger commander received information that his team was to land and extract a "SEAL sniper team" that was in contact with the enemy. At that point, the information the QRF was receiving indicated, falsely as it turned out, that Roberts had already linked up with the Mako 30 element.

As Razor 01 began its final approach, it was engaged by intense RPG, DShK and small arms fire and was forced to crash land when an RPG struck and destroyed one of its engines. Three Rangers and one of the aircrew were killed immediately. The other Rangers broke from the stricken aircraft and began firing back. The Ranger commander fell back on his training, saying: "Return fire and seek cover. Locate the enemy. Suppress the enemy. Attack."

He decided to suppress the enemy firing points immediately and launch a counterattack against the peak. He issued his quick battle orders and all of the Rangers stood up and began firing at both known and suspected enemy positions while they bounded forward in subteams; one team firing to suppress while the other moved and vice versa much as the SEALs had earlier. They advanced about 20m before the weight of enemy fire drove them to seek cover.

Razor 02 saw its sister aircraft's fate and landed its team of Rangers at the off-set HLZ, from which the team began an arduous climb to the peak to link up with colleagues. The Rangers on the peak called in several Danger Close gun runs from orbiting F-15E and F-16C strike aircraft to suppress the enemy before again attempting another ground assault. The Rangers had covered about half the 50m distance to the enemy positions when they were engaged by PKM fire. The Ranger commander then realized that what they had assumed was simply fallen logs and foliage up ahead was a fortified bunker. He ordered his Rangers to withdraw in bounds, firing to suppress as they moved. They did not have enough men to start clearing bunkers and other prepared positions – particularly without Light Antitank rockets or similar "bunker busters."

The attached Combat Controller continued to vector in airstrikes to keep al-Qaeda forces at bay until the rest of the Rangers could negotiate the climb and reinforce them. The Combat Controller dropped a number of bombs on the peak, well within normal safety limits, to attempt to dislodge the entrenched defenders. He also called in the first recorded use of the MQ-1 Predator UAV (Unmanned Aerial Vehicle, or drone) as close air support. The Predator launched two Hellfire missiles – one missed but the second struck the bunker dead-on, collapsing it.

A grainy and unfortunately low-resolution shot of airstrikes hitting the peak of Takur Ghar in support of the trapped Rangers, March 2002. (US SOCOM)

After an exhausting climb, the second Ranger troop arrived and the combined force launched a final assault, charging up the slope as quickly as the snow would allow under the covering fire of two M240 machine gun teams. The fire teams reached the first bunker and cleared through, killing an enemy fighter before discovering a second bunker and trench line. They posted grenades into the bunker, which detonated a number of stored RPG warheads, destroying the bunker in the blast. A final al-Qaeda fighter hiding further up the slope was killed before the peak was finally secured.

Unfortunately, it was not over for the reunited Rangers. They were soon engaged by al-Qaeda reinforcements who attempted to retake Takur Ghar. An SASR observation post on a mountain some 4km distant directed airstrikes on these reinforcements as they attempted to flank the Rangers. Eventually that night, after some 16 hours of pitched combat, the Rangers and SEALs were extracted.

Sadly, the efforts to locate and rescue Roberts were in vain. The SEAL appears to have died soon after falling from the helicopter; despite putting up a ferocious resistance with his SAW, he was overcome by the sheer weight of numbers after his weapon was disabled by an enemy round and he was shot through the thigh. He was soon captured and executed by the al-Qaeda fighters with a single gunshot wound to the head.

As for Operation *Anaconda*, a new plan was hatched to relieve the embattled conventional forces still in the valley. The 2nd Battalion of the Rakkasans air assaulted into the eastern end of the valley on March 4, immediately attacking the heights under Apache cover. Meanwhile, the 3rd Battalion were dropped into the northern end of the valley with the objective of linking up with the stranded forces at the blocking positions. Supported by the combined might of 16 Apaches, five Marine Cobras and several Air Force A-10A ground attack aircraft, the Rakkasans methodically cleared an estimated 130 caves, 22 bunkers and 40 buildings to finally secure the valley.

The exhausted Rakkasans were replaced by fresh elements from the 10th Mountain on March 12, who continued to clear the southern end of the Shahikot. AFO teams launched further Recce teams into the nearby Naka Valley, hunting

for al-Qaeda forces who had escaped but came up empty handed. Operation *Anaconda* officially ended on March 19, 2002. Al-Qaeda had been driven from the Shahikot Valley or they were killed where they stood – estimates of enemy dead range from between 200 and 500. Coalition forces lost eight men killed in action – seven of those on Takur Ghar.

One of the Ranger SAW gunners, Ranger SPC Anthony Miceli on Takur Ghar during the battle. Note he wears Gortex camouflage gear and carries an M249 Para mounting an M68 Aimpoint sight. (US SOCOM)

ANACONDA POSTSCRIPT

On March 17, 2002, Task Force 11 received time-sensitive intelligence that a possible high-value target was traveling within a convoy of al-Qaeda fighters who were attempting to escape by vehicle from the Shahikot into neighboring Pakistan. A Predator UAV had the convoy under surveillance showing that the convoy consisted of three SUVs of the type al-Qaeda HVTs preferred, including a Toyota pickup truck carrying a large security element of hooded gunmen.

The Task Force 11 element assigned the mission included SEAL operators from DEVGRU (commanded by the SEAL who had led the Mako 30 mission on Takur Ghar) to conduct the vehicle stop with a mixed force of Rangers as back-up. The operators and an assigned CSAR team boarded three MH-47Es while the Rangers

22 Special Air Service Regiment

The Special Air Service Regiment or SAS are perhaps the world's most recognized, admired and emulated special operations unit. Their cap badge of a winged Excalibur sword speaks to their regimental motto, "Who Dares Wins," and is almost as well known as the unit itself. Devised by a British officer, David Stirling, the SAS began as a desert raiding force in World War II, operating alongside a sister unit called the Long Range Desert Group.

The SAS, so named to confuse the Germans as to the true intentions of the unit, was best known for its trademark lightning raids on Luftwaffe airfields, shooting up the parked planes from their machine-gun-equipped Willys Jeeps. Ironically, it was originally intended to parachute into their targets. Later in the war the SAS did parachute into occupied territory and conducted sabotage missions alongside the partisans of the resistance. The unit also maintained its reconnaissance role, using its heavily armed Jeeps to scout ahead of advancing Allied forces as Western Europe was liberated.

Postwar, the SAS fought in all of Britain's "small wars;" post-colonial counterinsurgencies from Malaya and Borneo to Aden and Oman. The Regiment also operated extensively in Northern Ireland, often as a plain-clothes direct action force with the covert surveillance operators of 14 Intelligence Company (which later became the Special Reconnaissance Regiment).

Perhaps the SAS's most famous operation was the successful assault on the Iranian Embassy in London in May 1980. The Embassy had been seized by a number of separatist terrorists who held staff, several visitors, and a policeman hostage for six days. The terrorists began murdering hostages when their demands were not met, so the regiment's B Squadron stormed the building under the lens of the world's media. Five of the six terrorists were shot dead in the assault with one hostage murdered as the assaulters broke in – the remaining 24 hostages were rescued. Operation *Nimrod*, as it was codenamed, made the SAS a household name. The Falklands and later the Gulf War cemented that reputation.

The SAS's fighting strength is comprised of four Sabre Squadrons of around 60 men apiece – A, B, D, and G. Within each squadron are four Troops each of around 16 men. Each Troop has a speciality based on an insertion method – Air, Boat, Mountain, or Mobility (vehicles). Each SAS soldier is also trained as a specialist in communications, medicine, demolitions, or languages and cross-trained in another.

climbed aboard a pair of MH-60G Blackhawks. The five helicopters launched from Bagram in the early morning, flying low and fast toward the target area.

The three MH-47Es carrying the SEALs soon caught up with their targets. The helicopters flew up behind the small convoy at a height of less than 50ft. The lead Chinook levelled out and landed on the road directly in front of the column. As the occupants leapt from their vehicles raising their weapons, the doorgunner hosed the vehicles down with his minigun, cutting down a number of al-Qaeda fighters in their tracks. The second Chinook overshot the column and raked it with minigun fire as it passed. The Task Force 11 operators added their firepower, having earlier gained permission to punch out the Plexiglas side windows in the MH-47Es to enable them to fire their M4 carbines and SR-25 marksman's rifles from inside the helicopter.

Two Chinooks landed their passengers in cover nearby and the operators took up positions overlooking the convoy, while the third landed a team nearby to investigate another suspicious vehicle. Both teams of SEAL operators now opened fire down on the enemy fighters in a vicious crossfire. As fighters attempted to move to cover or return fire, they were engaged and killed. In minutes the contact was over and the operators moved down into the wadi to secure the dead and wounded. Of the 18 enemy fighters in the three vehicles, 16 had been killed outright. Two were seriously wounded and were patched up by SEAL medics before being detained.

The fighters appeared to be a mix of Uzbeks, Chechens and Afghan Arabs and were well equipped. One wore a makeshift suicide vest of fragmentation grenades concealed in a harness under his arms while another had disguised himself by wearing a burkha. The operators also recovered a US-made suppressor; a number of US fragmentation grenades of a lot issued to Task Force 11, and a Garmin handheld GPS later traced to one of the crew of Razor 01.

UK SPECIAL FORCES
OPERATION *TRENT*

The first UK Special Forces unit deployed in support of Operation *Enduring Freedom-Afghanistan* was a two-squadron group from 22 SAS in mid-October 2001. A and G Squadrons, both having recently completed desert training in Oman, were given the mission by the Director of Special Forces, bypassing D Squadron which was on standby duty as Hereford's resident Counterterrorist (or Special Projects) team and B Squadron which was on long-term overseas training. Both squadrons were reinforced by personnel from the Territorial Army SAS regiments and brought their own transportation with them in the form of a mix of their Land Rover Desert Patrol Vehicles (known as Pinkies), and modified ATVs which were becoming increasingly popular with Coalition SOF.

The British SAS squadrons deployed initially to the north west of Afghanistan to conduct a series of largely uneventful reconnaissance tasks known as Operation *Determine*. Members of the SAS had assumed that their involvement in OEF-A, particularly with their strong ties to United States SOF, would center on direct action strike operations against high-value targets. The squadrons were both surprised and not a little disappointed to be given rather more mundane special reconnaissance roles resulting in zero enemy contacts. After a fortnight and with the missions drying up, both squadrons returned to their new base in Credenhill on the Welsh Borders – an inauspicious start for the vaunted SAS in the War on Terror.

On November 10, C Squadron of the SBS inserted into the recently captured Bagram Air Base and caused an immediate political quandary with the Northern Alliance leadership which claimed that the British had failed to consult it on the deployment. M Squadron also deployed to Afghanistan (with at least one SEAL

Two British Special Boat Service (SBS) operators, December 2001, prior to operations at Tora Bora. Note the mix of civilian and military clothing, the camouflage painted and ACOG equipped Diemaco C8 carbine preferred by UK Special Forces, and the Minimi Para light machine gun carried by the operator on the right. (Photographer unknown)

on secondment), and were tasked with several missions – some deploying to work with TF Sword, eventually at Tora Bora – and others with General Dostum's forces around Mazar-e-Sharif.

While their Royal Marine counterparts were embroiled in heated discussions with the Northern Alliance leaders at Bagram, A and G Squadrons from the SAS landed under their very noses. After political intercession by Prime Minister Tony Blair, the SAS had been given a direct-action task – the destruction of an allegedly al-Qaeda-linked opium processing plant.

The target was a low priority for the US and probably would have been hit from the air if the British hadn't argued for a larger slice of the pie. As mentioned earlier, American SOF commanders were jealously guarding the juicy targets for their own units, and it was not until later in the war that the target folders would start to open up to Coalition units. Whether the task was a good fit for SAS capabilities is still open to question, with many commentators believing it was more suited to a light infantry or commando unit such as the Parachute Regiment or Rangers. Indeed the UK's Special Forces Support Group (SFSG) would later be formed to conduct such larger-scale operations.

Operation *Trent*, as the operation was named, became the largest British SAS operation in history with both squadrons tasked to assault an opium processing facility located 250 miles southwest of Kandahar. Intelligence indicated that the facility was manned by between 80 and 100 foreign fighters and was defended by trench-lines and several make-shift bunkers. Its strategic significance has never been fully explained.

Incredibly, the SAS were ordered to assault the complex in full daylight – very much against the standard tactics of all SOF. The timelines had been mandated by CENTCOM and were based on the availability of air support assets – only one hour of on-call close air support was to be provided. The timings also meant that the squadrons could not carry out a detailed reconnaissance of the site prior to the assault being launched. Both of these factors should, and evidently did, raise significant red flags at Hereford.

Despite this, the general feeling within UK Special Forces Group was that if the CO of 22 SAS declined the operation, little else in terms of targeting would be passed to the Regiment by the US, so he accepted the mission. Another first in SAS history gained during the opening stages of Operation *Trent* –the first wartime High Altitude Low Opening (HALO) parachute jump. An eight-man patrol from G Squadron's Air Troop were parachuted in at night to test a barren desert site in Registan for its suitability as an improvised airstrip for the landing of the main assault force in its C-130 Hercules transport planes.

The Air Troop advanced team gave the site the thumbs up and later that day a fleet of C-130s, each only touching down long enough to disgorge its SAS cargo, began to land. The men of A and G Squadrons drove directly off the ramps as the planes trundled along the desert strip before the aircraft again took to the sky. The 40 vehicles comprised of 38 Pinkies, two logistics vehicles and eight outriders on Kawasaki dirt bikes soon formed up and set off toward their target.

An early setback struck the ground assault force with a Pinkie breaking down with engine problems not far from the landing strip. The vehicle, armed with a twin General Purpose Machine Gun (GPMG) mount, had to be left behind with its three-man crew to protect it. The crew would be recovered on the way out as the assault force exfiltrated from the target. With the motorcycle outriders covering the front, rear and flanks of the convoy, the assault force drove to a previously agreed forming-up point and split into two elements – the main assault force and the fire support base (FSB).

A Squadron were given the task of assaulting the target facility in their Pinkies while G Squadron took the FSB role to suppress the enemy, allowing A Squadron to close on the target. This fire support task was essential, particularly in view of the lack of artillery fires (as they were out of range of Coalition guns), and the limited nature of the close air support available. The FSB teams were armed with vehicle-mounted GPMGs, .50cal Browning Heavy Machine Guns (HMGs) and Milan antitank missiles along with a brace of 81mm mortars and the fearsome .50cal Barrett M82A1 sniper rifle for long-range precision fire.

An exceedingly rare image of Britain's famed SAS conducting close-quarter battle training. These operators, from the Regiment's B Squadron, are accompanied by a muzzled Combat Assault Dog. In combat, SAS dogs have been seen sporting shark's teeth painted on these muzzles to further terrify the enemy. (Photographer unknown)

The assault began with a preparatory airstrike before A Squadron gunned its engines and raced away from its start line, firing its weapons as it drove down the treacherous terrain, pulling up meters from the outer perimeter to dismount from its vehicles and close on the target on foot. All the while the FSB team dropped mortar rounds on the facility and pounded it with .50cal and GPMG fire. The air support flew sorties until it ran out of munitions (known as "Winchestering" in aircrew terminology), although on its final pass strafing a bunker with its 20mm cannon, one US Navy Hornet narrowly missed several G Squadron vehicles with an ill-timed burst.

The Regimental Sergeant Major in command of the FSB joined in the action; bringing forward teams to reinforce A Squadron when he believed the assault was stalling. They were only several hundred meters from the enemy positions when the RSM himself was hit in the leg by an AK-47 round, the second wounded man of the operation. Several other SAS soldiers were saved by their body armor and helmets (most disliked wearing the helmets and allegedly had to be ordered to do so), although they suffered four casualties in total – thankfully none with life-threatening wounds.

With the bunker destroyed and teams clearing the trench-lines, the main assault force swept into the compound to mop up the remaining enemy. Up against the SAS the enemy stood little chance and the British quickly secured the compound buildings. Once cleared, the site exploitation phase of the operation begun with other teams tasked to search for intelligence materials. After just under four hours on target, both squadrons mounted up and rendezvoused with a Chinook, which evacuated the SAS casualties from the battle.

PRISON UPRISING AT QALA-I-JANGHI

Meanwhile, M Squadron SBS was involved in one of the most infamous incidents of the early part of the war – the prisoner uprising at the ancient fort of Qala-i-Janghi on November 25, 2001. The mud and brick-built fortress, known as "The Fort of War," was a sprawling structure dating from the nineteenth century and had been General Dostum's headquarters until co-opted to hold prisoners from the battle for the city of Mazar-e-Sharif.

Two CIA officers from the Special Activities Division who had been deployed with Dostum's forces were conducting tactical questioning of al-Qaeda and Taliban prisoners at the fort. Unfortunately, the prisoners had been poorly searched by the Northern Alliance militia and many concealed grenades, pistols and knives under their loose Afghan clothing. While questioning detainees, both CIA officers were attacked by prisoners carrying these hidden weapons and one, former Marine Captain Johnny "Mike" Spann, was killed. His partner, known only as "Dave," managed to barely escape with his life.

A small team of British SBS operators providing close protection duties for an Afghan Northern Alliance commander. The operator on the left rear of the pick-up truck carries a Heckler & Koch MP5KA1 sub-machine gun while the one on the right-hand side of the vehicle carries a Diemaco C8 assault rifle mounting an AG36 under barrel grenade launcher. (Photographer unknown)

Dave managed to make contact with CENTCOM who relayed his urgent request for assistance to the inhabitants of the School House, a Task Force Dagger safe house in Mazar-e-Sharif housing members of Delta, some Green Berets, and a small team from M Squadron of the SBS. A quick reaction force was immediately formed of whoever was in the School House at the time: a headquarters element from the 3rd Battalion, 5th Special Forces Group, a pair of US Air Force liaison officers, a handful of CIA SAD operators, and the SBS team.

"The individual in Air Force uniform was not a CCT (Combat Controller) or SF-TACP (Special Forces-Tactical Air Control Party). He was a USAF Lieutenant Colonel who happened to be at the Mazar HQ when the call came in. There were not many shooters available at the time, since the next big fight was anticipated to be at Konduz, so the Lieutenant Colonel and another USAF Major came along with the ad-hoc team to see if they could help out. "The SBS really saved the day on the 25th", explained an American special operator who fought alongside the SBS at the Fort of War.

Arriving in short wheelbase Land Rover 90s painted white and reminiscent of NGO or UN vehicles (apart from the rather obvious L7A2 GPMG mounted on the roof of each vehicle), the eight-man SBS team deployed alongside the Green Beret and CIA operators (who had arrived in a pair of similarly colored minivans) in civilian clothes and with just their carbines and pistols. The teams had been ordered to maintain a low profile, particularly with the number of journalists on the ground in Afghanistan and a uniform appearance may well have antagonized some of the Afghan militias with which they were forced to work.

The resourceful patrol commander, the late Sergeant Paul 'Scruff' McGough (who tragically died in a hang gliding accident in June 2006), immediately realized the need for heavier weapons, and with the assistance of another SBS operator used his trusty Leatherman multi-tool to dismount the GPMGs from the vehicles. He quickly emplaced them on the parapets overlooking the main square of the fort under a growing amount of small arms fire. The prisoners had managed to break into the fort's armory and soon had armed themselves with an array of AK-47s and RPG launchers. Dave, the surviving CIA operative – himself only armed with an AK-47 and a Browning pistol – and Dostum's ragtag militia had been fighting a losing battle against the overwhelming numbers of prisoners until the ad-hoc quick reaction force arrived to reinforce them.

The Americans and British began fighting a pitched battle against the prisoners in an effort both to stem the tide and to rescue Dave. Scruff was famously filmed by a camera crew at the fort, firing the heavy GPMG from the hip to stop a Taliban charge. Dave eventually managed to escape over a wall during the night and link up with his colleagues. The special operators then began to focus their attention on recovering the body of the fallen Mike Spann.

Over the course of four days, the battle at Qala-i-Janghi raged. The Green Berets called in multiple airstrikes as the Taliban prisoners tried to overwhelm the hard-pressed defenders. During one close-air support mission, a JDAM was misdirected (again after a battery change in a PLGR GPS unit) and slammed into the ground close to the Coalition and Northern Alliance positions. The blast seriously wounded five Green Beret soldiers and four SBS operators were also wounded to varying degrees.

"I think we had one 'short' bomb on day one of the uprising. It landed in a field to the north of the fort and caused no casualties. The other JDAMs that day were on target in the prison area. These bombs came in Danger Close, and I appreciated the skill of the pilots and the guy who called in the drop," explained one of the participants to the author.

"Day two is when the JDAM hit the wall of the fort and killed several Afghans and wounded some friendlies. That was the fault of the guy who passed the coordinates to the pilot from the ground. Apparently, he sent his own position instead of the target, which was a few hundred meters away. A similar situation happened to another ODA farther south, and several of them were killed", explained

A mix of British and American SOF, November 2001. The two operators with the green shemaghs covering their faces are from the SBS while the operator to the right in three-color desert camouflage and carrying the suppressed M4A1 is probably from the 5th Special Forces Group. The central figure is more enigmatic as his weapon indicates Delta Force or the Naval Special Warfare Development Group (DEVGRU), but he wears what looks like desert DPM (Disruptive Pattern Material) webbing along with US-pattern trousers. This leads the author to suspect he may be a SEAL known to be on secondment with the SBS at the time and who was later decorated for his actions at the Mazar-e-Sharif prison uprising. (Photographer unknown)

the special operator, referencing the friendly fire incident which happened to ODA 574 protecting Hamid Karzai.

Circling AC-130s kept up the aerial barrage throughout the night. The following day, Tuesday November 27, the siege was finally broken as Northern Alliance T-55 tanks were brought into the central courtyard to fire main gun rounds into several block houses containing die-hard Taliban. Fighting continued sporadically throughout the week as the last remnants of Taliban resistance were mopped up by Dostum's forces. The combined Green Beret and SBS team finally recovered Mike Spann's body only to discover it had been booby trapped with a live hand grenade. The trap was successfully disarmed and Spann's body returned to the United States and his family.

The CIA showed its appreciation of the SBS contribution by attempting to have the operators recognized with US decorations. Due to political and military bureaucracy, the decorations were never awarded, although a chromed Taliban commander's PPSh-41 submachine gun now sits above the stairs on the way to the CO's office in the SBS headquarters in Poole in Dorset; a token of gratitude from the CIA. "All [of the SBS] were extremely professional, aggressive, and cool under fire," added the American operator.

The SBS went on to carry out more work with both Task Force Sword and the CIA – the Battle of Qala-i-Janghi having put them on the map with the Americans. The SAS weren't so lucky. Following Operation *Trent*, A and G Squadrons were again deployed on uneventful reconnaissance tasks in the Dasht-i-Margo desert before a mid-December return to Hereford. Small numbers of SAS remained from both of the Territorial Army (Reserve) SAS regiments to provide close protection for members of the British Secret Intelligence Service (MI6).

COALITION SPECIAL OPERATIONS FORCES
AUSTRALIA

The Australian Special Air Service Regiment (SASR) deployed under the Australian Operation *Slipper* in November 2001 and was known as Task Force 64. Initially under attachment to Task Force 58, elements of 1 Squadron flew in directly from Kuwait to the recently captured FOB Rhino. This early SASR presence comprised a small team of 1 Squadron operators, one of their Long Range Patrol Vehicles (LRPV), and a headquarters section including both the squadron commander and the commanding officer of the SASR.

The rest of 1 Squadron soon followed and it immediately began launching patrols, pushing upwards of 100km out from FOB Rhino, conducting a range of missions including securing a compound in Lashkar Gah in Helmand Province owned by Mullah Omar. As the Marines of Task Force 58 planned the move to Kandahar, 1 Squadron conducted advanced reconnaissance for them.

Australian SOF returned to Afghanistan from 2005 onward. Here, SOTG Commando is operating at an undisclosed location in southern Afghanistan. Note the Blackhawk, possibly carrying a cut-off or sniper group, flying over the village. This image again proves the validity of the MultiCam pattern. (Australian SOCOMD)

February 2002 saw the SASR suffer its first casualty on a vehicle-mounted reconnaissance in the Helmand River Valley. Sergeant Andrew Russell died from a Soviet-era land mine which destroyed the LRPV he was riding in (a month earlier, the SASR had suffered their first serious casualty outside Kandahar, also from a Soviet-era mine). Soon after, in March 2002 1 Squadron was committed to Operation *Anaconda* in which it played an important role inserting small reconnaissance teams high up in the Shahikot and embedding with American units as liaison teams.

Later that month in Operation *Mountain Lion*, SASR teams targeted al-Qaeda elements along the Pakistani border near Khost, including the longest mounted patrol conducted by any unit during the history of the Afghan campaign – a grueling 52 days in duration. The SASR later received a US Meritorious Unit Citation for actions in support of Operation *Slipper*.

1 Squadron was replaced by 3 Squadron in April 2002 and 3 Squadron in turn was relieved by 2 Squadron in August. A pause in deployments to Afghanistan coincided with the build-up training and deployment of an SASR squadron to Iraq in support of Operation *Falconer*. However, the SASR would return to Afghanistan in 2005, shaping the environment for a later 2006 deployment of an Australian Reconstruction Task Force.

CANADA

Joint Task Force Two (JTF2), the Canadian Army's Special Mission Unit, deployed 40 operators in December 2001 under Task Force K-Bar command. JTF2 worked extensively with the 3rd Special Forces Group. One of their first missions in Afghanistan was what Admiral Hayward later described as "the first Coalition direct action mission since the Second World War." The joint operation with a team of Green Berets targeting a Taliban command node almost ended in disaster when JTF2's Chinook was forced to make a hard landing near the target site.

The unit's deployment was controversial in Canada as JTF2 had allegedly deployed prior to the Army formally receiving Canadian Prime Minister Jean Chrétien's approval for the mission. Soon after, three JTF2 operators were photographed herding several shackled detainees from an American aircraft. Segments of the Canadian media made much of Special Forces handing over detainees who may have been bound for the American facility at Guantanamo Bay.

JTF2 later deployed reconnaissance teams during Operation *Anaconda*, assisted in the massive SSE at Zawar Kili, conducted close-

US Navy SEALs and German KSK operators conducting a Sensitive Site Exploitation (SSE) mission, February 2002. This image caused some controversy as the deployment of the German KSK (Kommando Spezialkräfte), to Afghanistan was not publicly acknowledged at the time. (Photographer's Mate 1st Class Tim Turner; US Navy)

protection tasks and participated in numerous direct action missions, allegedly including the siege at Mirwais Hospital where a Special Forces ODA killed a group of al-Qaeda gunmen hiding in a hospital ward. It also carried out numerous operations with the New Zealand SAS. JTF2's first rotation returned to Canada in May 2002 to be replaced by a second, shorter term, deployment until October 2002.

DENMARK

The Danes deployed a 100-man force from the Army Jaegerkorpset (Hunter Corps) and Navy Fromandskorpset (Frogman Corps) to Afghanistan in December 2001. They primarily carried out Special Reconnaissance tasks including designating targets for airstrikes. However, they were also involved in the capture of Taliban Mullah Khairullah Kahirkhawa whose vehicle convoy was ambushed by heliborne Danish SOF and SEALs in February 2002.

FRANCE

It is rumored that French SOF elements were deployed before the fall of the Taliban, although the secrecy surrounding French SOF makes the SAS look like

OPERATION *ENDURING FREEDOM–AFGHANISTAN,*
MAJOR OPERATIONS 2001 AND 2002

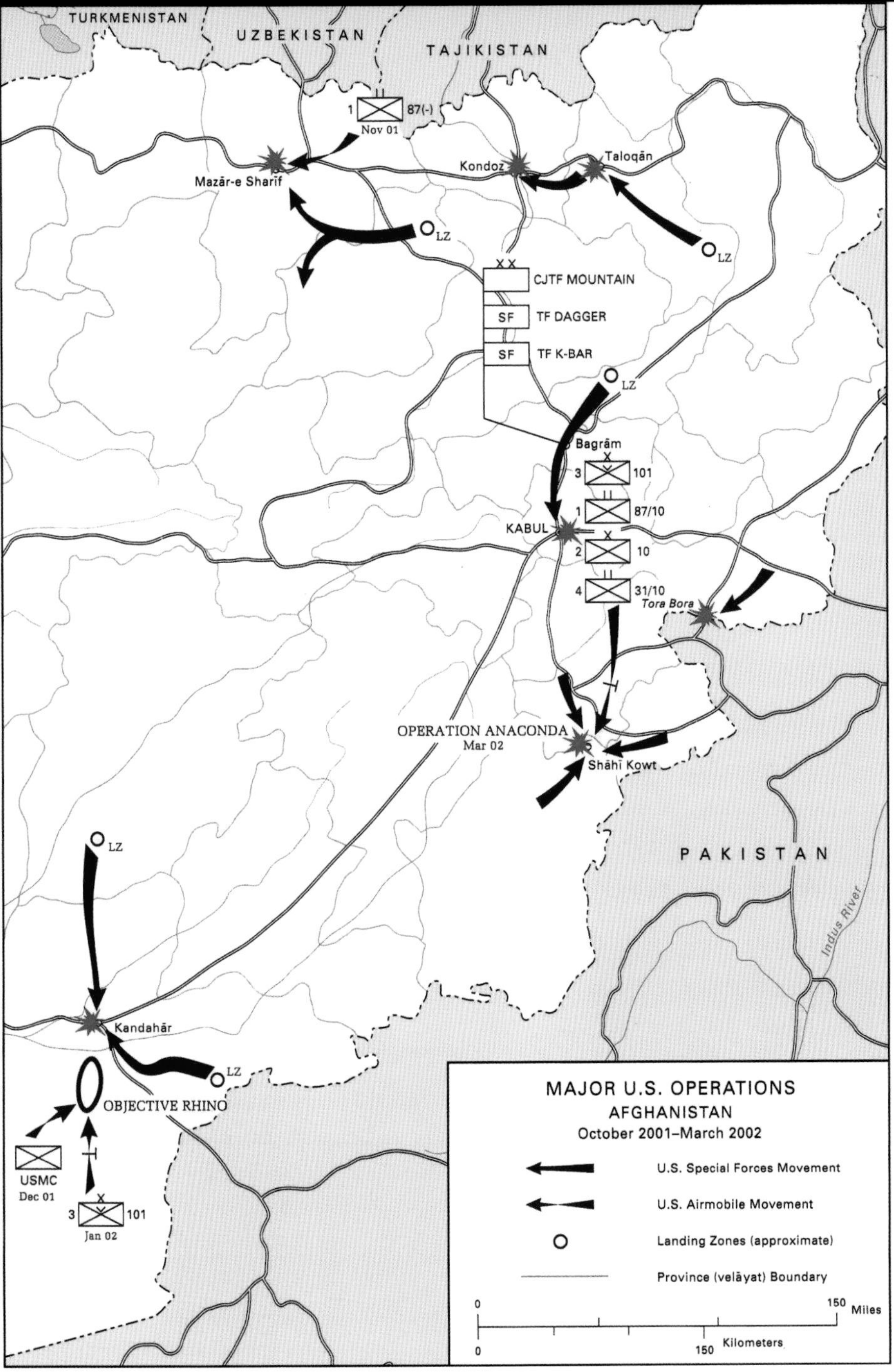

TURKMENISTAN

UZBEKISTAN

TAJIKISTAN

1 ☒ 87(-)
Nov 01

Mazār-e Sharif

Kondoz

Taloqān

○ LZ

○ LZ

XX	CJTF MOUNTAIN
SF	TF DAGGER
SF	TF K-BAR

○ LZ

Bagrām

3 ☒ 101

KABUL

1 ☒ 87/10

2 ☒ 10

4 ☒ 31/10

Tora Bora

OPERATION ANACONDA
Mar 02

Shāhi Kowt

PAKISTAN

Indus River

○ LZ

Kandahār

○ LZ

OBJECTIVE RHINO

☒
USMC
Dec 01

3 ☒ 101
Jan 02

MAJOR U.S. OPERATIONS
AFGHANISTAN
October 2001–March 2002

←	U.S. Special Forces Movement
←	U.S. Airmobile Movement
○	Landing Zones (approximate)
——	Province (velāyat) Boundary

0   150 Miles

0   150 Kilometers

Sergeant Bill "Willie" Apiata, Victoria Cross Recipient

An NZ SAS soldier, Lance Corporal Willie Apiata, was awarded his country's highest military honor, the Victoria Cross for New Zealand (New Zealand's version of the British VC) for saving the life of a comrade during a June 2004 ambush in which one of their patrol vehicles was disabled and two NZ SAS operators were wounded.

A large force of insurgents had attacked their evening laager, opening the engagement with PKM and RPG fire. One of the RPG warheads detonated near Apiata, wounding two of his colleagues, one seriously. Apiata decided he had to get the seriously wounded operator back to safety with the main SAS force.

As the Victoria Cross citation reads:

In total disregard of his own safety, Lance Corporal Apiata stood up and lifted his comrade bodily. He then carried him across the seventy meters of broken, rocky and fire swept ground, fully exposed in the glare of battle to heavy enemy fire and into the face of returning fire from the main Troop position. That neither he nor his colleague were hit is scarcely possible. Having delivered his wounded companion to relative shelter with the remainder of the patrol, Lance Corporal Apiata re-armed himself and rejoined the fight in counter-attack.

an open book. It is known that 50 Army Commandement des Opérations Spéciales (COS) operators deployed in 2001 although which exact units these men came from is unknown. It is known that the COS has carried out operations in cooperation with Task Force K-Bar elements in the south and incurred a number of casualties.

GERMANY

The Kommando Spezialkräfte or KSK are the Army Special Forces of Germany. The KSK initially deployed around 100 operators in mid-December 2001 as part of Task Force K-Bar. Its deployment was marred by a lack of missions, much like the experience of the British SAS under US command. The KSK was also assigned low-priority targets and reconnaissance missions until its deployment on Operation *Anaconda*. The KSK was deployed on several SSEs in early 2002, most often alongside US Navy SEALs.

NEW ZEALAND

The initial deployment to Afghanistan of the New Zealand 1 Special Air Service Group (NZ SAS) under Task Force K-Bar in December 2001 numbered around 40 operators and served for a rotation of six months. Two further deployments continued in May to September 2004 and June to November 2005. NZ SAS later redeployed to the country between 2009 and 2012.

The NZ SAS specialized in long-range reconnaissance, both vehicle mounted and on foot, with teams deployed in the field for upwards of three weeks at a time. In the 2005 deployment, they used 11 newly purchased Pinzgauer 6x6 Special Operations

Vehicles (similar to those used by Delta), while on earlier rotations they were forced to depend on borrowed HMMWVs from the resident Special Forces Group.

In Afghanistan, the NZ SAS teams worked extensively with other Coalition special operations units including the SEALs and the 3rd Special Force Group. In December of 2004, the NZ SAS Group attached to Task Force K-Bar was awarded the US Presidential Unit Citation, along with other Coalition units attached to K-Bar, for conducting "extremely high risk missions, including search and rescue, special reconnaissance, sensitive site exploitation, direct action missions, destruction of multiple cave and tunnel complexes, identification and destruction of several known al-Qaeda training camps (and) explosions of thousands of pounds of enemy ordnance."

Three US Army Green Berets at a safe house in eastern Afghanistan, March 2002. The operator on the right wears a jacket made in the obsolete US Desert Night Camouflage pattern – designed to counter older night vision systems. (JZW)

NORWAY

Norwegian special operations units from the Army, Jaegerkommando (HJK), and Navy, Marinekommando (MJK), collectively known as NORSOF, were first deployed in support of Task Force K-Bar in January 2002. Seventy-eight Army and 28 Navy personnel formed the first deployment. Operating alongside US Navy SEALs, they carried out several SSEs, and their Special Reconnaissance teams also inserted into the Shahikot during Operation *Anaconda*.

POST-*ANACONDA* SPECIAL OPERATIONS

The International Security Assistance Force (ISAF) was established under NATO command to provide security and reconstruction across Afghanistan. ISAF (International Security Assistance Force) command included some Coalition SOF units. Years later, as the insurgency grew, an ISAF special operations command alternately commanded by a British or Australian officer controlled all ISAF SOF.

In the years to come Coalition SOF would return in numbers to Afghanistan, to fight the insurgency and train Afghan forces. Here, US Air Force Para Rescue Jumpers in an HH-60G Pedro aero medically evacuate a wounded Afghan National Army Commando during a partnered Green Beret mission in Nuristan province, Afghanistan, April 2012. (Mass Communication Specialist Second Class Clay Weis; US Navy)

The US Combined Joint Special Operations Task Force (CJSOTF) became a single integrated command under the broader CJTF-180, the Combined Joint Task Force that commanded all US forces assigned to Operation Enduring Freedom-Afghanistan. It was built around an Army Special Forces Group (often manned by National Guard units) and SEAL teams. A small element from the JSOC Task Force (formerly Task Force Sword/11), not under direct CJTF command, embedded within CJSOTF. The JSOC element was manned by a joint SEAL and Ranger element that rotated command. The CJSOTF was not under ISAF command, although sometimes it operated in support of NATO operations.

The majority of Coalition SOF left Afghanistan in 2002. US units were withdrawn in preparation for the upcoming war in Iraq (originally due to be launched late in 2002) leaving a skeleton crew of isolated ODAs, SEALs, and Coalition SOF in an undermanned, under-resourced and undervalued effort at developing a failed state, winning hearts and minds and staving off a burgeoning insurgency.

CHAPTER 3
IRAQI FREEDOM
IRAQ 2003

A PRELUDE TO WAR

Planning for what was eventually to become Operation *Iraqi Freedom* began in December 2001 even as Coalition Forces continued to battle Taliban and al-Qaeda elements in Afghanistan under Operation *Enduring Freedom*. Drawing on a pre-existing battle plan, US Central Command's harried leader, General Tommy Franks, began to develop options for an invasion of Iraq under the orders of then Defense Secretary Donald Rumsfeld. Franks was literally to design one war while still fighting another.

The plan soon evolved into a concept of operations which required far fewer resources than originally conceived and one which called for a concurrent start for the air and ground components rather than the protracted bombing campaign seen in Operation *Desert Storm* ten years earlier. Special operations were an integral part of the plan and their role would only increase in light of the early successes of SOF in Afghanistan.

CENTCOM's Special Operations Command Central (SOCCENT) joined the planning process formally in March 2002 as the conventional forces of Combined Joint Task Force 180 took over command and control of SOF in Afghanistan. Brigadier General Gary "Shooter" Harrell, fresh from leading Task Force Bowie in Bagram, assumed command of SOCCENT in June 2002. Harrell had the pedigree after having previously served with Delta Force along with earlier stints with the 10th and 7th Special Forces Groups.

Harrell and Franks developed a concept of operations that would see Coalition SOF deployed in three major geographies. In the western deserts of Iraq, SOF would hunt down mobile Iraqi Scud B TEL (transporter erector launcher) units while providing Special Reconnaissance and screening tasks in support of conventional forces. In the north, SOF would work with the Kurdish Peshmerga ("Those Who Face Death") guerrillas to draw Iraqi forces away from reinforcing Baghdad while capturing strategic sites to allow conventional follow-on forces to deploy, a task which grew in importance with Turkey's refusal to allow conventional forces to deploy from their soil. In the south, SOF would seize the national oil production facilities before providing reconnaissance support for the advancing conventional forces. A fourth, covert or black SOF unit would carry out the hunt for weapons of mass destruction and high-value leadership targets within the regime of Saddam Hussein.

Once the plan was signed by President George W. Bush, D-Day for Operation *Iraqi Freedom* was set for March 20, 2003. An air campaign known for using the concept of "shock and awe" would herald proceedings while SOF teams quietly infiltrated into Iraq ahead of conventional forces. In reality, the first conventional operation of the war would occur during the early morning of March 19 when

The Australian Special Forces Task Group, known as Task Force 64, patrolling in the western desert of Iraq. Both six-wheel Perentie Long Range Reconnaissance Vehicles (LRRV) and four-wheel Surveillance Reconnaissance Vehicles (SRV) are pictured. Note the incredible amounts of stowage carried, including Javelin guided missiles. (Australian DOD)

intelligence indicated that Saddam Hussein and his sons Uday and Qusay were holding a meeting at a location known as Dora Farms outside Baghdad.

Four 2,000lb laser-guided bombs struck the Dora Farms complex, dropped from a pair of F-117A Night Hawks, followed immediately by a salvo of Tomahawk cruise missiles fired from ships stationed in the Gulf. Disappointingly, the targets of this "decapitation strike" were not present. Operation *Iraqi Freedom* officially began in the early hours of March 20 after the deadline for Saddam and his sons to leave the country had expired.

As the air campaign got underway, conventional forces crossed the Kuwaiti border with the 3rd Infantry Division (3ID) taking the lead for V Corps across the western desert heading north for Najaf, Karbala and finally Baghdad. The 1st Marine Expeditionary Force (1MEF) headed up through the rough centre of southern Iraq toward Nasiriyah and al Kut as the British 1st Armoured Division advanced across the east of the country bound for Basra in the south. The planned northern attack by the 4th Infantry Division (4ID) was stymied by Turkey and thus it fell to SOF in the north to carry out the attack there and become the main effort.

COMBINED JOINT SPECIAL OPERATIONS TASK FORCE-WEST

Resurrecting the Task Force Dagger moniker from its operations in Afghanistan, the Combined Joint Special Operations Task Force-West (CJSOTF-West) was again led by Colonel John Mulholland and based around his 5th Special Forces Group (Airborne). His Operational Detachment Alpha (ODA) teams were tasked with two core missions. The first was to counter the SCUD theater ballistic missile threat by both locating and destroying the SCUD TELs and by denying the Iraqi military the use of potential launch sites. Their second objective was to provide both an intelligence-gathering and screening function in support of the conventional forces to build up an accurate picture of Iraqi force dispositions in the west of Iraq.

The Green Beret ODAs were deployed under the command and control of Operational Detachment Bravo (ODB) teams which operated as roving Advanced Operating Bases (AOBs). These AOBs provided a mobile resupply function using their modified M1078 "War Pig" Light Medium Transport Vehicles. The concept was first developed in the mid-1990s based on the SAS use of Acmat and Unimog "Motherships" during the first Gulf War. It meant that Green Beret patrols could operate for extended periods in enemy territory before linking up with a fighting patrol that would escort in the Motherships for a combat resupply.

The 5th Special Forces Group was assigned responsibility for two distinct sectors of western Iraq – the western and southern Joint Special Operations Areas

The M1078 LMTV War Pig carried fuel, water, ammunition, and all manner of logistical supplies forward to Green Beret mounted patrols. This particular vehicle mounted an M2 and M240 for protection and carries a range of aerials for satellite communications. (CROSSSUD)

(JSOAs, otherwise known as Ops Boxes). One element, termed Forward Operating Base 51 (FOB 51) and commanded by AOB 520 and AOB 530, was composed of the ODAs of the 1st Battalion. These teams staged out of H-5 airfield in Jordan and were responsible for the western JSOA. The 2nd and 3rd Battalions deployed from Ali al-Salim Air Base in Kuwait as FOB 52 and 53 respectively, dedicated to the southern JSOA. Assigned to all teams were Special Tactics airmen from the 23rd Special Tactics Squadron trained to guide in close air support and manage the airspace above the ODA teams, including negating any possible friendly fire.

A company element from the 19th Special Forces Group (National Guard) was attached to Task Force Dagger as were several regular Army and National Guard infantry companies to provide FOB security and to act as a Quick Reaction Force (QRF); a role previously provided by the Rangers in Afghanistan. As the prospect of war grew, the ODAs of A Company, 1st Battalion, 19th Special Forces were tasked with liaison roles supporting conventional forces – ODA 911 and 913 were to support the 1st Marine Expeditionary Force (1MEF); ODA 914 was divided into two sub-teams with one assigned to the 3rd Infantry Division (3ID) alongside ODA 916 and the other to the British 1st Armoured Division; while ODA 915 was attached to the 101st Airborne Division following 3ID across the western desert. A final 19th Special Forces Group ODA, 912, was tasked with providing the Personal Security Detail (PSD) for General Harrell, commander of what was now termed Combined Forces Special Operations Component Command (CFSOCC).

Coalition SOF

In addition to American SOF, Task Force Dagger included the largest component of Coalition SOF of any of the four special operations task forces deployed to Iraq. The British deployed under Operation *Row*. Known as Task Force 7, the UK Special Forces contribution included two squadrons of the SAS and M Squadron of the SBS, along with support personnel and the RAF Special Forces Flight. B and D Squadrons of the SAS would be involved in mobility operations in the western desert while M Squadron was earmarked for a heliborne assault on several Iraqi oil facilities that had their own desert airstrips. These would be captured for later use as SOF staging areas.

The Australian Special Operations Command (SOCOMD) contributed 1 Squadron from the SASR and a company from 4th Battalion (Commando), Royal Australian Regiment (4RAR) to support the SASR patrols. The Australians also resurrected their codename from Afghanistan and were termed Task Force 64. The British and Australian Special Forces were assigned the northern and central JSOAs respectively also deployed from H-5 in Jordan.

The Australians readily agreed to be under US command while the UK Special Forces required

significant convincing before they relinquished operational command. An additional issue arose around IFF (Identification Friend or Foe) measures, with the UK eventually leasing the top secret Blue Force Tracker units from the US. The Australians followed their experiences working with US SOF in Afghanistan and had USAF Combat Controllers embedded with each SASR patrol, bringing with them the indispensable Blue Force Tracker (the BFT shows all friendly and known enemy positions and is constantly updated by GPS signal).

SASR troopers patrolling the perimeter of the captured Al Asad Air Base. Note the destroyed ZPU anti-aircraft gun in the background. (Australian DOD)

The aviators of 3rd Battalion of the 160th Special Operations Aviation Regiment (SOAR) deployed as the Joint Special Operations Air Detachment-West with eight MH-47E Chinooks, four MH-60L Direct Action Penetrators and two MH-60M Black Hawk helicopters. In addition, a flight of Air National Guard A-10A ground attack aircraft and a flight of USAF F-16C strike aircraft to serve as dedicated SOF close air support (CAS) were deployed to Jordan. The UK's Task Force 7 also had its own dedicated CAS at H-5 from two flights of RAF GR7 Harriers and a flight of CH-47 Chinooks from 7 Squadron along with C-130s from the RAF Special Forces Flight of 47 Squadron.

COMBINED JOINT SPECIAL OPERATIONS TASK FORCE-NORTH

Responsibility for special operations in the north was assigned to Combined Special Operations Task Force-North (CJSOTF-North), known as Task Force Viking in tribute to the European origins of its core component, the 10th Special

IRAQ

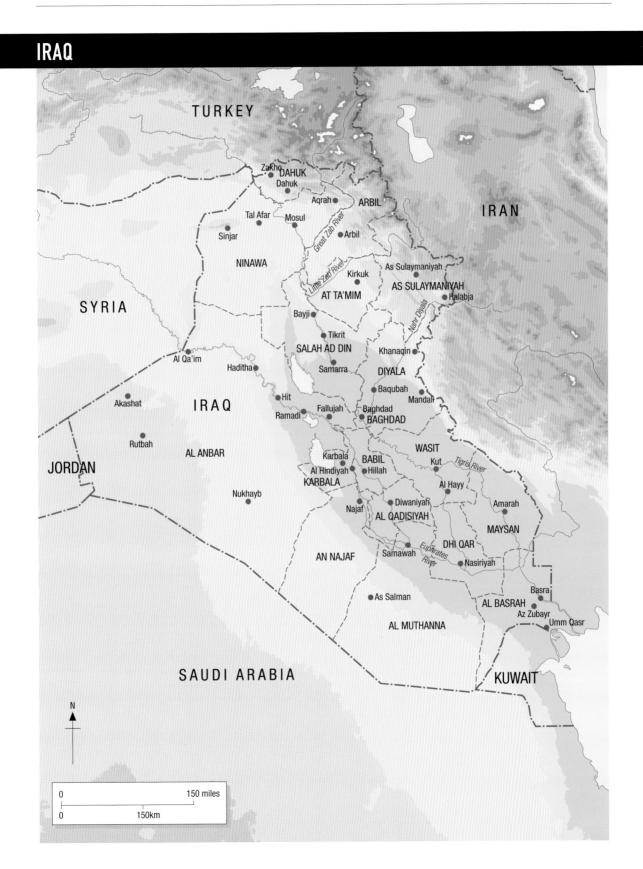

TURKEY

Zakho
DAHUK
Dahuk

Aqrah
ARBIL

IRAN

Tal Afar
Mosul

Sinjar

Arbil

NINAWA

Great Zab River

Little Zab River

As Sulaymaniyah
AS SULAYMANIYAH

Kirkuk
AT TA'MIM

Halabja

SYRIA

Bayji

Nahr Diyala

Tikrit

SALAH AD DIN

Khanaqin

Al Qa'im

Haditha

Samarra

DIYALA

Baqubah

Hit

Mandali

Akashat

IRAQ

Fallujah
Ramadi

Baghdad
BAGHDAD

Rutbah

AL ANBAR

WASIT

Karbala
BABIL
Al Hindiyah
Hillah
KARBALA

Kut

Tigris River

JORDAN

Al Hayy

Nukhayb

Najaf
AL QADISIYAH

Diwaniyah

Amarah

MAYSAN

DHI QAR

AN NAJAF

Samawah

Euphrates
River

Nasiriyah

Basra

As Salman

AL BASRAH

Az Zubayr

SAUDI ARABIA

AL MUTHANNA

Umm Qasr

KUWAIT

N

0 ———— 150 miles
0 ———— 150km

Forces Group (Airborne). With its extensive experience between 1991 and 1996 in Kurdistan during Operation *Provide Comfort*, a United Nations-led operation to save the Kurds living in northern Iraq from persecution by Saddam Hussein, 10th Special Forces was the obvious choice.

Working alongside the 10th Special Forces would be the men of 3rd Battalion, 3rd Special Force who had recently returned from Afghanistan. The 20th Special Forces Group (National Guard) and the 2nd Battalion of the 7th Special Forces Group had assumed the role of CJSOTF-Afghanistan in September 2002, freeing up 3rd Special Forces to contribute to Viking. The 123rd Special Tactics Squadron, an Air National Guard AFSOC (Air Force Special Operations Command) unit were slated to support the Viking ODAs on the ground. Additionally, conventional infantry units were attached to Viking in the form of the 173rd Airborne Brigade and several companies from 2nd Battalion, 14th Infantry Regiment of the 10th Mountain Division.

Originally, the war plan called for Task Force Viking to support the 4th Infantry Division's march south toward Baghdad from Turkey. With Turkey denying staging rights to US forces and the 4ID mission consequently scrubbed, Viking was assigned the task of keeping Iraqi forces in the north from reinforcing Baghdad. The men of Viking began to look for other infiltration routes, bypassing Turkish airspace. As the official history, *All Roads Lead to Baghdad*, succinctly explains that after Turkey denied permission "CJSOTF-North transitioned from being a supporting element to being a supported command. Without a strong infantry presence in the north, it fell to the 10th Special Forces Group to organize the Kurdish Peshmerga and keep thirteen Iraqi infantry and armoured divisions north of Baghdad busy" – a tall order for the lightly equipped Special Forces.

In 2002, several teams of mixed 10th Special Forces and Central Intelligence Agency Special Activities Division operatives had been infiltrated into Kurdistan in advance of hostilities. They were based in the Harir Valley outside of the Kurdish capital, Irbil, and tasked to develop ground truth intelligence while organizing and training the Peshmerga. They were also there to monitor the presence of an al-Qaeda-related group – Ansar al-Islam – and plan for future offensive operations against them. These teams now paved the way for the eventual insertion of the Viking ODAs in much the same way as the CIA Jawbreaker teams in Afghanistan had in October 2001.

The men of the 10th Special Forces Group were not equipped with the Ground Mobility Vehicles (GMVs) of the 5th Special Forces Group (which had actually left many of their vehicles in Afghanistan with 3rd Special Forces and consequently had to embark on a hasty and extensive program of refitting standard HMMWVs to GMV specifications before their deployment to Jordan), and so civilian vehicles had to be procured. Some 230 Non-Standard Tactical Vehicles (NTVs) – the

A rare image of Delta Force operating as part of Task Force Wolverine, western Iraqi desert. The vehicle is a heavily modified Pinzgauer Special Operations Vehicle. (Photographer unknown)

majority white Land Rover Defenders along with some 30 Toyota Tacoma pick-up trucks – were purchased and modified to their requirements. These vehicles had to be driven covertly from warehouses in Turkey under continual petty interference from the Turkish authorities until finally crossing the border into Kurdish territory. They may have had transport, but when the first ground operations of the war began in the pre-dawn hours of March 19, 2003, Task Force Viking was still trying to find a way into northern Iraq.

TASK FORCE 20

Assigned to the western desert along with Task Force Dagger was another special operations task force known as Task Force 20. It was based on the concept of Task Force 11/Task Force Sword in Afghanistan and was structured around similar black SOF units drawn primarily from the Joint Special Operations Command (JSOC). Task Force 20 was commanded by Major General Dell Dailey, a former commander of the 160th SOAR and former commander of Task Force 11 in Afghanistan during the Takur Ghar debacle.

For Iraq, Task Force 20 was initially composed of B Squadron from Delta Force led by Dailey's old sparring partner, Lieutenant Colonel Pete Blaber, former commander of the AFO in Afghanistan. Alongside the special operators of Delta were all three battalions of the 75th Ranger Regiment; a battalion-strength element from the 82nd Airborne serving both as a heavier infantry punch and as a QRF; and a truck-mounted M142 High Mobility Artillery Rocket System (HIMARS) battery to provide mobile indirect fire support. Later in the campaign, another Delta squadron and even a company of M1A1 Abrams main battle tanks was attached to Task Force 20.

In a repeat performance of their relationship in Afghanistan, the commander of the Delta squadron wanted to push his operators out into the western desert and conduct lightning strikes against enemy concentrations, tying up enemy

Another unit formed in the aftermath of the Tehran Embassy tragedy was the 160th Special Operations Aviation Regiment – known as the Nightstalkers owing to their preferred method of flying: blacked out in the dead of night wearing night-vision goggles. The Nightstalkers became the first dedicated special operations helicopter unit within the US Army. The Nightstalkers have a close relationship with their customers and guarantee a plus or minus 30 seconds time on target – a guarantee that is rarely broken.

The unit flies a number of helicopters. The biggest is the MH-47E, a Chinook variant that can be refuelled in-flight, is equipped with sophisticated threat detection and Forward Looking Infrared Radar (FLIR) sensors, and can carry a platoon of fully equipped special operators. The Nightstalkers also fly a modified Blackhawk called the MH-60 series, which can also be refuelled in-flight, and is equipped with similar FLIR and detection systems to its bigger brother. Both the MH-60 and MH-47 carry 7.62mm M134 miniguns to protect themselves and their passengers.

A second distinct type of MH-60 flown by the Nightstalkers is the MH-60L DAP or Direct Action Penetrator. The DAP was the brainchild of a 160th SOAR

pilot who sadly lost his life in Mogadishu in 1993. It is designed to escort in the other two helicopter types, conduct preparatory fires on a target location and suppress any hostiles in the immediate area of the HLZ.

To do this, the DAP carries a frightening array of weapons systems, which includes 2.75in unguided rocket pods, a 30mm cannon and 7.62mm miniguns. It can even be configured to fire Hellfire antitank missiles. The DAP is preferred over attack helicopters such as the Apache, as the DAP has larger fuel tanks for longer operational range and can be aerially refuelled. It can even, at a pinch, carry a four-man patrol of operators.

The smallest of the Nightstalkers' fleet is the diminutive Little Bird, developed from the Hughes 500 and its Vietnam-era cousin, the OH-6 Loach. The Little Bird comes in two variants: the 6 Pax, which is the nickname for the unarmed MH-6 transport version, as it can carry up to six passengers on its external pods (although four is far more common); and the attack version, the AH-6, which is referred to as a Six Gun (and leads to the motto "Nightstalkers Don't Quit, Six Guns Don't Miss.") Normally, the AH-6 is equipped with two 7.62mm M134 miniguns and two 2.75in rocket pods.

An excellent close-up view of a 160th Special Operations Aviation Regiment MH-47E carrying a full component of Army Rangers just prior to lift-off from Kandahar Air Field, 2014. (Sergeant Troy B Tippett; US Army)

forces that could otherwise be sent to reinforce against the conventional Marine and Army advances from the south. Such operations would also effectively deceive the Iraqis as to the true intentions of the Coalition Forces and precisely where the main effort would be concentrated.

Dailey wanted the Delta squadron to stay at Ar'ar Air Base in Saudi Arabia and only launch against suspected Weapons of Mass Destruction (WMD) sites or high-value targets (HVT) in much the same way as Task Force 11 operated at Bagram. Eventually, the disagreement was decided by General Franks who went with Blaber's plan and Delta was assigned raiding and deception operations in the western desert.

Instead, a squadron from the Naval Special Warfare Development Group (DEVGRU) also operated under Task Force 20 to conduct heliborne direct action raids – the SEALs would launch after any HVTs that were spotted. CIA SAD operatives worked alongside the Task Force operators, as did members of the Intelligence Support Activity, which had formally been placed under JSOC command. Dedicated special operations aviation was provided by 1st Battalion of the 160th SOAR with its MH-60M Blackhawks, MH-60L Direct Action Penetrators and MH-6M transport and AH-6M Little Birds.

The Task Force was covertly based at Ar'ar in western Saudi Arabia and was tasked with seizing key targets including airfields deep in Iraq and capturing high-value targets along with providing long-range Special Reconnaissance. One of its primary targets in pre-war planning was the seizure of Baghdad International Airport (BIAP), an operation that saw two full-scale dress rehearsals carried out but which was never mounted, as conventional forces eventually seized BIAP after the success of the two armored Thunder Runs on the capital.

NAVAL SPECIAL OPERATIONS TASK GROUP

The Naval Special Operations Task Group, more commonly known simply as the Naval Task Group, was the fourth and final special operations task force assigned to Operation *Iraqi Freedom*. It was built around a core component of US Navy SEAL Teams 8 and 10; the Polish special operators of GROM; the Royal Marines of 40 and 42 Commando under the command of HQ 3 Commando Brigade and attached US Psy Ops and Civil Affairs teams.

The Naval Task Group was principally tasked with the capture of the port of Umm Qasr, Iraq's only deep-water port; the oil pipeline facilities of the al Faw Peninsula, and the two off-shore platforms the pipelines fed. Once these initial target sets were secured, the Task Group would support conventional forces in the south, conducting reconnaissance and raiding activities. Aviation was provided by both Marine Air of the 15th MEU and the Air Force's 20th Special Operations Squadron.

BLACK SWARM

First blood in Operation *Iraqi Freedom* went to the aviators of the US Army's elite 160th SOAR. A flight of two MH-60L DAPs and four Black Swarm flights were assigned the mission – each comprised of a pair of AH-6M Little Birds and a FLIR (Forward-Looking Infrared Radar) equipped MH-6M to identify and paint the targets for the AH-6s. Additionally, each Black Swarm flight was assigned a pair of A-10As to deliver Maverick antitank guided missiles against any hardened targets the AH-6s couldn't handle with their miniguns and 2.75in unguided rockets.

At 2100hr on March 19, 2003, the DAPs and the Black Swarm flights engaged their first targets – Iraqi visual observation posts along the western and southern borders of Iraq. The DAPs engaged their targets with Hellfire missiles and followed up with bursts from their 30mm cannons. The Black Swarm teams relied on their MH-6M flight leads that guided in the strikes or called in the orbiting A-10As. In the space of just seven hours of darkness, more than 70 sites were destroyed, effectively depriving the Iraqi military of any early warning of the coming invasion. It was a remarkable effort and a significant feather in the cap for the Nightstalkers.

As the sites were eliminated, special operations air corridors were opened and the first heliborne SOF teams were launched from H-5 in Jordan including vehicle-mounted patrols from the British and Australian SOF components transported by the MH-47Es of the 160th SOAR. Ground elements from Task Force Dagger, Task Force 20, Task Force 7 and Task Force 64 breached the sand berms along the Iraqi border with Jordan, Saudi Arabia and Kuwait in the early morning hours and drove into Iraq. At least officially that was the case. Unofficially, the British had been in Iraq for several weeks as had the Australians and Task Force 20.

UGLY BABY

For Task Force Viking in the north, the delay in infiltrating all of its ODAs into Iraq was becoming increasingly frustrating. Planners finally developed a punishing route from 10th Special Forces Group's forward staging area in Constanta, Romania to northern Iraq via two undisclosed countries. It was codenamed Ugly Baby – allegedly from a flippant description of the air route by a Green Beret officer.

March 22 saw this epic lift completed with the majority of the 2nd and 3rd Battalion landing near Irbil aboard six MC-130H Combat Talons. The lift was not without its perils as several MC-130s were engaged by Iraqi air defense on the way in. One aircraft was sufficiently damaged by antiaircraft fire to make an

A pair of AH-6J Little Birds from the US Army's 160th Special Operations Aviation Regiment launch for a mission in southern Iraq. (Staff Sergeant Shane Cuomo; US DOD)

emergency landing at, ironically enough, Incirlik Air Base in Turkey. The initial lift had deployed a total of 19 Green Beret ODAs and four ODBs into northern Iraq. The next day Turkey relented and allowed over flights and the three final MC-130s flew in to Bashur, outside the Kurdish capital of Irbil.

Eventually Task Force Viking would number 51 ODAs and ODBs alongside some 60,000 Kurdish Peshmerga militia of the Patriotic Union of Kurdistan (PUK). The Special Forces had to make do with locally procured civilian transport as the first of their new trucks were still several days away. On March 26, the 173rd Airborne Brigade conducted a successful combat jump from C-17 cargo planes into Bashur airfield, which had already been secured by the Green Berets and the Peshmerga. The 173rd were assigned the task of securing the vital Kirkuk oil fields.

The men of Task Force Viking deployed initially to the Green Line, a north–south demarcation of the boundary of Kurdish territory. Their initial objectives were threefold – to prevent the reinforcement of Baghdad by tying up the estimated 13 Iraqi Army divisions operating to the north; to advance on the cities of Kirkuk and Mosul; and to carry out a direct-action operation against the Ansar al-Islam terrorist training camp along the Iranian border. That operation would be known as Operation *Viking Hammer*.

VIKING HAMMER

Viking Hammer was scheduled to launch on March 21, however the ground component was set back by several days owing to the issues around infiltrating the majority of the 3rd Battalion into Iraq. A Tomahawk cruise missile strike was set

OPERATION *IRAQI FREEDOM,*
COMBINED JOINT SPECIAL OPERATIONS TASK FORCE AREAS OF RESPONSIBILITY AND INFILTRATION ROUTES, APRIL 2003

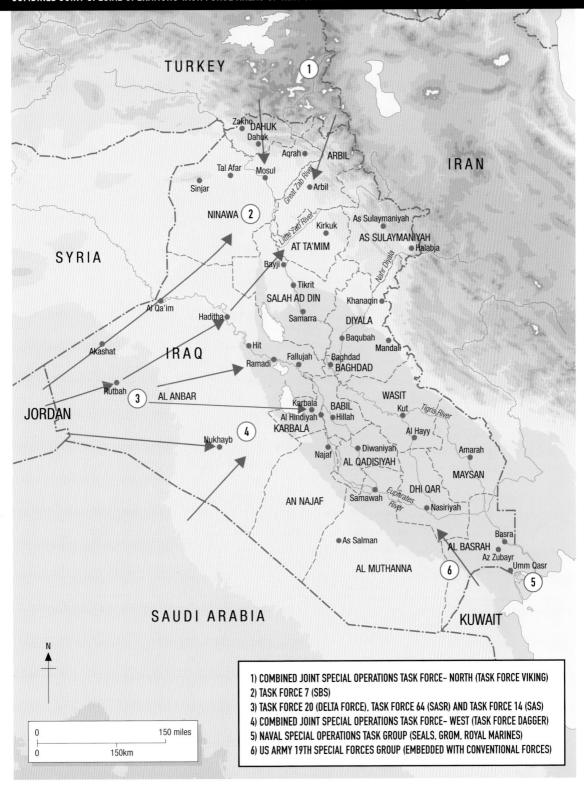

TURKEY

IRAN

Zakho
DAHUK
Dahuk

Aqrah
ARBIL

Tal Afar
Mosul
Arbil

Sinjar

NINAWA ②

Great Zab River

Little Zab River

As Sulaymaniyah
Kirkuk
AS SULAYMANIYAH
Halabja

SYRIA

AT TA'MIM

Bayji

Nahr Diyala

Al Qa'im

Tikrit
SALAH AD DIN

Khanaqin

Haditha

Samarra

DIYALA

Akashat

Hit

Baqubah
Mandali

IRAQ

Fallujah
Baghdad
BAGHDAD

Ramadi

Rutbah ③
AL ANBAR

Karbala
BABIL
WASIT

JORDAN

Al Hindiyah
Hillah
Kut
Tigris River

KARBALA
Al Hayy

Nukhayb ④

Najaf
Diwaniyah
Amarah

AL QADISIYAH
MAYSAN

DHI QAR

AN NAJAF
Samawah
Euphrates River
Nasiriyah

As Salman
Basra

AL BASRAH
Az Zubayr
Umm Qasr ⑤

AL MUTHANNA ⑥

SAUDI ARABIA
KUWAIT

N

0   150 miles
0   150km

1) COMBINED JOINT SPECIAL OPERATIONS TASK FORCE– NORTH (TASK FORCE VIKING)
2) TASK FORCE 7 (SBS)
3) TASK FORCE 20 (DELTA FORCE), TASK FORCE 64 (SASR) AND TASK FORCE 14 (SAS)
4) COMBINED JOINT SPECIAL OPERATIONS TASK FORCE– WEST (TASK FORCE DAGGER)
5) NAVAL SPECIAL OPERATIONS TASK GROUP (SEALS, GROM, ROYAL MARINES)
6) US ARMY 19TH SPECIAL FORCES GROUP (EMBEDDED WITH CONVENTIONAL FORCES)

for midnight as a preparatory barrage, however the strike could not be delayed because of the high tempo of operations elsewhere in the theater. In the early hours a grand total of 64 Tomahawks struck the Ansar al-Islam camp and surrounding sites with Green Berets maintaining surveillance to carry out a Bomb Damage Assessment (BDA) on the target.

Ansar al-Islam was a Sunni terrorist group which counted as one of its formative members Abu Musab al Zarqawi, a Jordanian former thug and drug dealer turned international terrorist who would later rise to prominence as the self-appointed head of al-Qaeda in Iraq (AQI). According to surveillance, around 700 Ansar al-Islam members inhabited the valley along with a small Kurdish splinter faction. They had prepared a number of defensive positions, including antiaircraft machine guns, and maintained a facility that US intelligence suspected at which biological or chemical agents may have been developed or stored for use in future terrorist attacks.

The ground attack element of *Viking Hammer* was finally launched on March 28 with a six-pronged advance up into the valley. Each prong was composed of several ODAs from the 3rd Battalion and upwards of 1,000 Kurdish Peshmerga fighters. The main advance set off toward Sargat, the location of the suspected chemical and biological weapons site. It was soon pinned down by DShK 12.7mm heavy machine gun fire from the surrounding hills. A pair of Navy F/A-18s responded to an urgent CAS request and delivered two 500lb JDAMs against the Ansar al-Islam machine gun nests. The F/A-18s obligingly then strafed the positions with their 20mm cannon before exiting the valley, low on fuel.

The advance began again only to be halted once more by fire from prepared DShK and PKM machine gun nests. Special Forces ODA 081 deployed a 40mm Mk19 automatic grenade launcher from the back of a Toyota Tacoma and suppressed the gun positions, allowing the Peshmerga to assault and wipe out the Ansar defenders. The Peshmerga captured the charmingly named town of Gulp and moved on to its primary target, the village of Sargat.

Sargat was heavily defended by fortified fighting positions mounting DShKs and mortars along with several BM-21 Grad rocket systems firing in support. Unable to call in airstrikes owing to the close proximity of the Peshmerga, a Special Forces sergeant known as Cosmo instead used a dismounted .50cal M2 heavy machine gun to suppress the entrenched terrorists. His actions allowed the Peshmerga to bring forward their own 82mm mortars and Grads which eventually forced the Ansar al-Islam fighters to retreat.

Task Force Viking advanced to secure the Daramar Gorge which was surrounded by caves in the rock walls. The Peshmerga was again engaged by small arms and RPG fire, which it and the ODAs enthusiastically returned with .50 fire and 40mm grenades. However, it soon became obvious that they could

advance no further without air support to dislodge the defenders of the gorge. Covering their withdrawal with the dismounted .50cal, the Combat Controllers attached to the ODAs vectored in Navy F/A-18s. Six 500lb JDAMs shut down any further resistance.

During the night four AC-130 gunships maintained the pressure on the retreating Ansar al-Islam terrorists as they pulled back toward the Iranian border. The next day Task Force Viking seized the high ground and pushed down through the valley, surrounding and killing small pockets of Ansar al-Islam remnants. With *Viking Hammer*'s primary objectives complete, the 3rd Battalion and their Peshmerga returned to the Green Line to assist in the push on Kirkuk and Mosul.

A specialist SSE (Sensitive Site Exploitation) team was brought in to document the finds at Sargat. The team recovered traces of several chemicals including Ricin along with stocks of NBC (Nuclear, Biological, and Chemical) protective suits, atropine injectors (used to counteract the effects of chemical weapon exposure) and Arabic manuals on chemical weapons and IED construction. Sargat would ironically become the only known site in Iraq that was in the process of actually developing WMDs.

Examination of the bodies at the site showed many of the Ansar al-Islam to be foreign fighters from a variety of countries. Estimates of enemy dead numbered over 300. Only 22 Peshmerga fighters had been killed. Despite the ferocity of the fight, the Special Forces suffered no casualties.

Operators ride in the open doors of a MH-60L Blackhawk, piloted by the Nightstalkers of the 160th Special Operations Aviation Regiment – note the flight number made from tape, a tradition that continues today. (US SOCOM)

MOSUL

Task Force Viking regrouped before launching an operation to seize the town of Ayn Sifni, which straddles the main highway into Mosul and thus was of strategic importance; once Ayn Sifni fell, the coast would be clear to advance on Mosul. Following the lead from their brother teams in the west, the 10th and 3rd Special Forces Group ODAs called in airstrikes on the Iraqi garrisons in and around Ayn Sifni, resulting in many of the Iraqi conscripts retreating or deserting their posts. By April 5 there appeared to be only two largely intact Iraqi platoons left in the town. The next day three ODAs; 051, 055, and 056, launched a final assault.

ODA 051 would lead the actual assault with some 300 Peshmerga fighters. ODAs 055 and 056 would act as fire support groups along with Peshmerga heavy weapons teams. As ODA 051 advanced cautiously toward the village it came under intense fire – the two platoons of defenders turned out to be closer to battalion strength and heavily equipped with 82mm mortars, antiaircraft guns and even an artillery piece. They were also far more determined than the average Iraqi conscript and held their positions against the Americans and the Kurds.

After some four hours of F/A-18 airstrikes and constant heavy weapons fire from ODAs 055 and 056, the assault force finally entered Ayn Sifni. Soon after, an Iraqi infantry counterattack, supported by several mortars, attempted to retake the town, but it was beaten back by 051 and the Kurds. On the same day, southeast of Ayn Sifni, another battle was occurring that would go down in Green Beret history – the Battle of the Debecka Crossroads.

THE BATTLE OF THE DEBECKA CROSSROADS

The Debecka crossroads divided both the main roads leading to Kirkuk and Mosul – seizing the road junction would effectively eliminate Iraqi capabilities to reinforce the north of the country. Overlooking this strategic crossroads was the Zurqah Ziraw Dagh Ridge, which was occupied by Iraqi forces protecting these crossroads.

The American operation, codenamed *Northern Safari*, commenced with timed B-52 strikes against the Iraqi defenders on the ridgeline. In the wake of the airstrike, Special Forces ODA 044 with 150 Peshmerga fighters advanced toward Objective Rock, a T junction leading to the crossroads and to the town of Debecka itself. Supporting the ODA were two 3rd Special Forces Group ODAs – 391 and 392 – providing fire support from their GMVs. To their immediate north, two groups of some 500 Peshmerga fighters advanced on the ridgeline. Further north, ODA 043 with 150 Kurds, and with ODAs 394 and 395 acting as fire support, attacked Objective Stone, a commanding hilltop occupied by Iraqi forces.

US Army Special Forces operators launching a Javelin missile at approaching Iraqi tanks and armored personnel carriers at the Debecka Crossroads in April 2003. (US SOCOM)

The central columns of Peshmerga reached their objectives first and ran into only token resistance, successfully seizing their sector of the ridgeline. ODAs 394 and 395 began suppressing the defenders of Objective Stone after a scheduled airstrike failed to soften up the defenses (only four JDAMs were dropped and of these only one hit its target). The two ODAs were engaged by Iraqi DShK heavy machine gun fire and 120mm mortar fire. Due to the poor results of the airstrike, ODA 043's Peshmerga initially refused to move forward.

The Green Berets finally managed to talk in additional close air support, which covered the withdrawal of the fire support ODAs back out of mortar range and finally suppressed the majority of Objective Stone's defenders. ODAs 394 and 395 quickly resupplied, as they had been burning through .50cal and 40mm ammunition, and raced forward once again to join the battle. However, they were not yet in place when ODA 043 convinced the Peshmerga to start advancing again and closed on the objective. Thankfully, the Peshmerga quickly routed the remaining Iraqi defenders and captured the hilltop objective.

To the south, ODAs 044, 391 and 392 ran into a dirt berm the Iraqis had built across the road leading to Objective Rock, scattering mines over the roadway. While the Peshmerga attempted to clear the mines, the ODAs went cross-country to bypass the roadblock. As the teams crested the ridge, they contacted Iraqi infantry in prepared positions and bunkers who soon surrendered under the firepower of the GMVs. One of the prisoners, an Iraqi Colonel, related that an Iraqi Army armored unit that had been supporting them had withdrawn to the south.

The Special Forces teams returned to breach the dirt berm on the road behind them with demolition charges in case a hasty retreat was required and moved up on to a ridge (known later as Press Hill) overlooking the concealed southern approach. The ODAs then advanced down to the Debecka crossroads themselves. At the edge of Debecka, ODA 392 pursued several Iraqi light mortar teams until it was engaged at long range by a ZSU-57-2 (a tracked, twin-barrel 57mm antiaircraft vehicle), while ODA 391 destroyed several trucks and armed technicals heading from Debecka with its Javelin antitank guided missiles and .50cal heavy machine gun fire.

Soon after, the ODAs spotted a number of Iraqi MTLB tracked armored personnel carriers appear out of the haze, advancing cautiously toward the crossroads and using their smoke generators to lay down a smoke screen behind them – the MTLBs were from the armored unit the Iraqi Colonel had mentioned. Engaging the aging Soviet-designed personnel carriers with their .50cal machine guns and Mk19 grenade launchers, the Green Berets attempted to suppress them and halt their advance.

A 3rd Special Forces Group Ground Mobility Vehicle (GMV) near the Debecka Crossroads, northern Iraq. This GMV mounts a .50cal M2 heavy machine gun and a swing mount 7.62mm M240 medium machine gun. This vehicle also carries a Javelin launcher and several AT-4 (M136) anti-tank rockets. (US SOCOM)

The American operators needed to buy themselves time to call in an airstrike and to warm up the Command Launch Units (CLU) of their Javelins (portable antitank guided missiles). At that moment, four Iraqi T-55 main battle tanks – an elderly design but still lethal, particularly against lightly armed infantry – pulled out from behind the MTLBs. Their smoke screen had been cannily used to cover the tanks' approach – someone in the Iraqi armored unit knew what he was doing.

The T-55 tanks began firing their 100mm main guns directly at the Special Forces positions. Abandoning the plan to engage with Javelins as the CLUs were taking too long to warm up, the ODAs quickly mounted their GMV trucks and pulled back to a ridgeline some 900m from the crossroads. They dubbed the site their "Alamo," a SOF term meaning a site to hold a last-ditch defense while awaiting reinforcement. The operators continued to request air support only to be told it would take a further 30 minutes to arrive on-station. The Javelin units were finally ready to fire and the teams began killing MTLBs.

Having brought only a few spare missiles for each launcher, they soon began running low, although the sudden onslaught of missiles had knocked the wind from the Iraqis' sails and temporarily halted their attack, buying the Green Berets much-needed time for the Navy strike aircraft to arrive. The T-55 tanks, again showing unusual tactical skill, meanwhile used a dirt defensive berm to approach the crossroads slowly, effectively shielding them from a "lock on" from the Javelins.

Finally, some 35 minutes after the initial TIC (troops in contact) request was made, two Navy F-14 Tomcats arrived. After talking in the first bombing run on the priority target – the T-55s – the unthinkable happened. The first 2,000lb bomb landed among friendly forces, including the Green Beret Advanced Operational Base (AOB) located back at Objective Rock. The Tomcat pilot had somehow become confused and targeted an old rusting hulk of a similar T-55 at

Objective Rock rather than the four actively engaging the ODAs. The bomb killed some 18 Peshmerga and wounded 45 along with the four AOB operators and a BBC camera crew accompanying the Peshmerga. Veteran BBC journalist, John Simpson, was among those injured. A half team from ODA 391 immediately drove to the scene and began treating the casualties.

The rest of the Special Forces were forced to pull back from the Alamo to Press Hill as Iraqi artillery now began to bracket them. One of the ODA operators managed to use his Javelin to destroy a T-55 that broke cover and attempted to advance toward them. Finally a pair of Navy F/A-18 Hornets arrived overhead and drove off the remaining tanks with several bombs. With the battle over, the results were tallied – 26 Army Green Berets had managed to blunt an attack by a reinforced company of mechanized Iraqi infantry in armored personnel carriers, supported by a platoon of well-trained and led tanks and under artillery support. Ironically, a day after the battle, Task Force 1-63 Armor arrived in Irbil, the Kurdish capital, with its company of M1A1 Abrams main battle tanks and M2A2 Bradley Infantry Fighting Vehicles (IFV) – a force that would have been ideally suited to assist the defenders of the crossroads at Debecka.

THE FALL OF THE NORTH

On April 9 the Peshmerga and the nine ODAs from FOB 103 encircled the city of Kirkuk after fierce fighting to capture ridges overlooking the approaches to the city. The earlier capture of the nearby city of Tuz had largely broken the will of the Iraqi Army and only Fedayeen Saddam ("Saddam's Men of Sacrifice" – a Ba'athist militia loyal to the dictator who wore civilian clothes or all black uniforms including bizarre Darth Vader-style helmets and drove armed technicals) remained in Kirkuk. The first ODA units entered the city the next day to a Normandy-like reception from the civilian inhabitants. A week later, the conventional forces of the 173rd Airborne had taken over responsibility for Kirkuk and the city was firmly in Coalition hands with the surviving Fedayeen fleeing after a number of minor skirmishes.

A day after the first Green Beret teams entered Kirkuk, an advance element from FOB 102 numbering no more than 30 operators, including the 2nd Battalion's commanding officer, drove unopposed through abandoned Iraqi lines and into Mosul itself. The prize had been captured. The advance had followed several days of heavy airstrikes on three Iraqi divisions defending Mosul. April 13 saw the 3rd Battalion of the 3rd Special Forces, a battalion from the 10th Mountain Division and the 26th Marine Expeditionary Unit (who had infiltrated into Irbil some days earlier) ordered into Mosul to relieve the 10th Special Forces Group teams and their loyal Peshmerga allies.

THE BATTLE OF THE DEBECKA CROSSROADS

APRIL 6, 2003

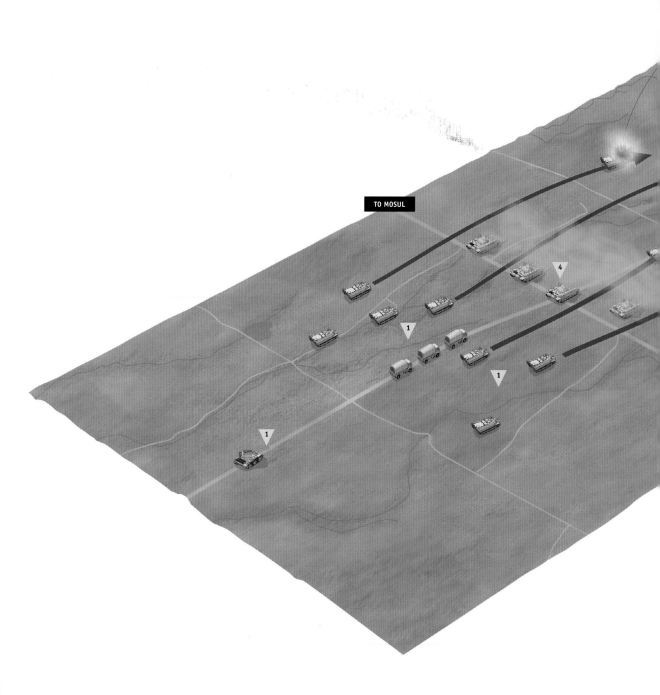

TO MOSUL

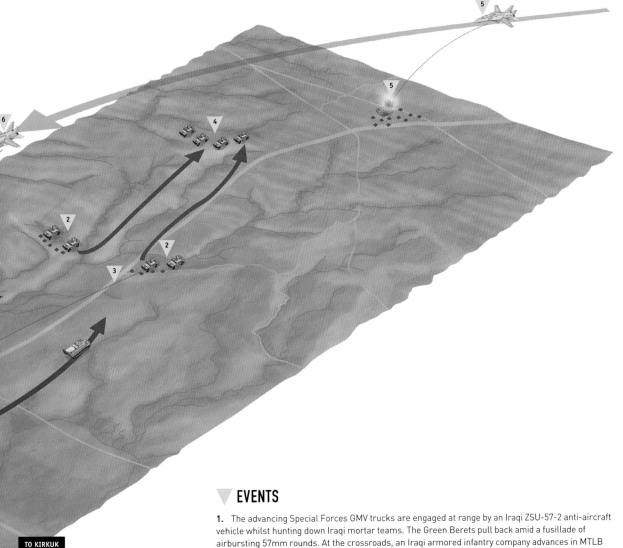

TO KIRKUK

▼ EVENTS

1. The advancing Special Forces GMV trucks are engaged at range by an Iraqi ZSU-57-2 anti-aircraft vehicle whilst hunting down Iraqi mortar teams. The Green Berets pull back amid a fusillade of airbursting 57mm rounds. At the crossroads, an Iraqi armored infantry company advances in MTLB armored personnel carriers. The MTLBs produce smoke to cover the advance of truck-borne Iraqi infantry and, more ominously, a platoon of T-55 main battle tanks

2. The GMVs withdraw to an Iraqi antitank berm and begin engaging the MTLBs with their machine guns and grenade launchers

3. The Green Berets try to engage the MTLBs and emerging T-55s with their Javelin anti-tank guided missiles but the CLU (Command Launch Units) for the Javelins are taking too long to warm up and lock-on. With the T-55s now firing directly at the Special Forces positions with their main guns, the Americans decide to fall back to an Alamo position.

4. From the Alamo ridge, the Green Berets buy enough time to get the CLUs warmed up and start engaging Iraqi vehicles with the top-attack function on the Javelin easily destroying Iraqi armor. As the Javelin gunners hold back the Iraqi attack, the teams' attached Combat Controller desperately calls for emergency close air support

5. Close air support in the form of two Navy F-14 Tomcats finally arrived over the battlefield. Their arrival ended in tragedy as one F-14 mistakenly drops a 2,000lb bomb on the Special Forces position known as Press Hill, killing a large number of Peshmerga fighters and wounding both a number of Green Berets and journalists gathered at the site

6. Eventually the aircraft are vectored onto the correct targets and the F-14s help break the Iraqi attack. The Green Berets pull back from the Alamo to Press Hill to assist with the wounded

3rd Special Forces Group operators and their GMV secure a crossroad in northern Iraq. (SSgt Jeremy T. Lock; US DOD)

SPRINT

Meanwhile in the west, Bravo and Charlie Companies of 1st Battalion, 5th Special Forces crossed the Kuwaiti border at H-Hour with ODA 531 using breaching demolition charges to clear a path through the defensive sand berms. Charlie's seven ODAs in some 35 vehicles took to the southeastern Ops Box of the western desert heading toward the towns of Nukyab, Habbariya, and Mudyasis. ODA 534 split off to head for the area surrounding Nukyab, searching for mobile Scud-B TEL launch sites.

Bravo Company set out for the central western town of Ar Rutba and the Iraqi airbase west of it codenamed H-3 with six ODAs and a support Operational Detachment Bravo traveling in the War Pig Motherships. ODAs 523 and 524 searched a suspected Scud-B storage facility while ODAs 521 and 525 were tasked with clearing several abandoned airfields. With no sign of Scud launchers, ODA

A mass of GMVs and militarized All-Terrain Vehicles (ATVs) from Task Force Dagger prepares to enter western Iraq at the onset of hostilities, April 2003. (US SOCOM)

525 was retasked to deploy a Special Reconnaissance team to conduct pattern of life surveillance on the town of Ar Rutba itself. A two-man reconnaissance team was inserted on to a hill overlooking the town and almost immediately called in a pair of nearby F-16C Fighting Falcons to destroy an Iraqi Army radio direction-finding facility they had identified.

ODA 525 had deployed a second reconnaissance team covering the two highways leading to Ar Rutba itself. This team was soon compromised by roving Bedouins who informed the Iraqi Army's Ar Rutba garrison of the team's presence and location (a similar compromise to that experienced by the men of the SBS further north at about the same time which will be detailed later in this chapter). A pick-up truck leading four armed technicals, each apparently mounting a DShK heavy machine gun and carrying black-helmeted members of the Fedayeen Saddam drove out from the garrison, apparently searching for the covert hide site.

The Green Berets mounted up and pulled out in their GMVs, quickly utilizing the Falcon View mapping software on their Toshiba Toughbook laptops to view the surrounding terrain and plan a hasty ambush of their pursuers. As the Fedayeen Saddam drove into range, they were engaged by .50cal and 40mm grenades from the GMVs who had positioned themselves in partially concealed, hull-down positions. Under the weight of fire, the Fedayeen beat a hasty retreat.

Realizing that the hilltop reconnaissance team could be compromised and easily overrun, the ODA 525 GMVs attempted to link up with the two-man team and extract it back to safety, but before they could, large numbers of Iraqi vehicles began driving out of Ar Rutba at a great rate of knots. Pulling into prepared defensive positions around the southwest of the city and waiting until all were in place, the Iraqi technicals began advancing up the hill towards the reconnaissance team.

Recognizing the danger, the ODA team leader immediately broadcast the emergency brevity code 'Sprint' on the Guard Net emergency channel, which is heard by all nearby Coalition aircraft (again in a remarkable parallel to the

A US Army 5th Special Forces GMV, western Iraq. The .50cal gunner wears the unusual military motorcycle helmet. Note also the Aimpoint sight mounted on the swing-arm M240. (CROSSSUD)

Another detailed image of a US Army 5th Special Forces GMV. Of particular interest are the painted M240 machine gun, orange VS-17 identification friend-or-foe panel and custom camouflage nets. (CROSSSUD)

compromised SBS squadron near Tikrit). The brevity code is only used when friendly ground call signs are in imminent danger of being overrun by the enemy and is not to be used lightly. An AWACS (Airborne Warning and Control System) aircraft flying high overhead immediately responded and an urgent request for close air support was made.

While the ODA awaited the arrival of the strike aircraft, the reconnaissance team began engaging individuals among the Fedayeen forces at the base of the hill with their suppressed Mk12 sniper rifle – anyone who appeared to be issuing commands became a priority target. The team leader, meanwhile, managed to contact his sister team of ODA 521, which had been clearing suspect sites east of Ar Rutba. Informed of the situation, it raced to reinforce ODA 525. Within minutes of the Sprint call, the first F-16C Fighting Falcons were vectored in and "rolled in hot" to engage the enemy vehicles advancing up the hill.

The response to the brevity code emergency call was breathtaking. Speaking directly with the AWACS aircraft, ODA 525's attached ETAC (Enlisted Terminal Attack Controller) stacked flights of strike aircraft as they arrived over the battlespace. He then assigned flights which were called in to their targets by the two-man reconnaissance team – one man talked the pilots on with his line of sight MBITR (Multi-Band Inter-Team Radio) while the other continued firing his Mk12, picking off Fedayeen. At one point there were as many as four flights of strike aircraft stacked up, awaiting tasking – so many that mid-air refueling was needed.

After four hours of constant, punishing airstrikes on the encircling Fedayeen Saddam, the eight GMV trucks of ODAs 525 and 521 managed to extract the exposed reconnaissance team under the cover of nothing less than a B-1B strategic bomber which shadowed the teams' vehicles back to ODB 520's staging area in a dry wadi bed south of Ar Rutba. A conservative bomb-damage assessment added up to over 100 Fedayeen Saddam killed. The other ODA operators had also had their hands full. Another Fedayeen convoy attempting to outflank ODA 525 ran into the guns of the neighboring ODA 524.

In the resulting three-hour contact, four armed technicals were destroyed and the Green Berets repelled a ground assault by an estimated company of enemy infantry. ODA 525's ETAC, although busy with keeping the heat on the Fedayeen advancing up the hill toward the isolated reconnaissance team, managed to also vector in strike aircraft to support ODA 524.

To the west, ODA 523 had moved to reinforce ODA 524, but they ran into trouble in the form of a pair of armed technicals on the highway. Both were engaged and destroyed by the GMVs. The operators ceased fire when a civilian station wagon, packed with Iraqi children, drove straight through the middle of the blazing firefight. ODA 522 had also identified two Fedayeen armed technicals proceeding down the highway toward ODA 523 in response to its earlier firing and set a hasty vehicular ambush. Catching the Iraqi militia completely unawares, both armed technicals were disabled by machine gun and grenade launcher fire, killing 15 black-clad Fedayeen in the process.

H-3

The strategic intent of the Special Forces ODAs had been to shut down the main supply routes and deny access around Ar Rutba and the strategically important H-3 airfield, before slowly tightening the noose around both. H-3 appeared to be defended by a battalion of Iraqi troops and significant numbers of both mobile and static antiaircraft guns. From March 24, the surrounding ODAs, supported by Coalition SOF from Task Force 7 (the British SAS) and Task Force 64 (the Australian SASR), called in a constant 24 hours of precision airstrikes on H-3 utilizing their SOFLAM (Special Operations Forces Laser Aiming Marker) target designators. The aerial bombardment seemed to have done the trick when the next day saw two long columns of Iraqi military vehicles leave H-3 at high speed heading east toward Baghdad during a brief respite in the bombing.

ODA 521 was overwatching that particular section of highway and managed to spring an ambush on the harried Iraqi column. The Green Berets destroyed the lead vehicle in the first convoy, a truck-mounted ZU-23 antiaircraft cannon, with a Javelin missile set to "top attack" mode. With the convoy halted in disarray unsure of where the firing was coming from, ODA 521 made an urgent call for any orbiting strike aircraft to bomb the stalled vehicles. As fortune would have it, a sudden sandstorm swept across the desert forcing a temporary pause in air support. Using the cover of the sandstorm, and some incredible luck, the Iraq convoy scattered into the desert and escaped in all directions. H-3 now looked rather unoccupied, so on the next day Bravo Company and the Coalition SOF patrols moved cautiously into the airfield.

An Australian SASR patrol from Task Force 64, western Iraq. Its Perentie LRPV is heavily armed with both .50cal and 7.62mm machine guns and a number of M72 LAW anti-tank rockets ready to hand. Note the plastic "skate" helmet hanging behind the passenger's head. Combat experience in Iraq and Afghanistan would see these non-ballistic helmets replaced by armored versions capable of stopping an AK-47 round. (Australian DOD)

They found a French Roland mobile surface-to-air missile (SAM) system; around 80 assorted antiaircraft cannon guns including a tracked, four-barreled ZSU-23-4 Shilka; SA-7 Grail handheld SAMs and an enormous amount of ammunition. H-3 was established as an Advanced Operating Base for Bravo Company with supplies delivered by C-130 cargo aircraft (that could land on the desert strip) and MH-47E Chinooks. An ODA 581 vehicle checkpoint managed to capture the Iraqi General formerly in command of H-3 as he was trying to escape dressed in civilian attire in the back seat of a taxi. He was quickly secured and flown out by an unmarked CIA SAD Air Branch Little Bird on March 28 for further interrogation. Additionally, the special operators of ODA 523 discovered what may have been chemical weapons samples in a laboratory on the grounds of H-3.

AR RUTBA

Bravo Company's attention soon turned to Ar Rutba itself. Signals intercepts by the attached SOT-A (Support Operations Team-Alpha) along with the development of an informer network among both the Bedouin and the Ar Rutba inhabitants indicated that around 800 Fedayeen Saddam remained in the city. The Fedayeen still occasionally patrolled outside the city. However, most of these were engaged by the surrounding Green Beret teams and taken prisoner.

The noose tightened as the ODAs guided in precision airstrikes against Fedayeen antiaircraft gun positions around the outskirts of the city. The airstrikes struck concentrations of Fedayeen militiamen with the Javelin again on top attack mode, leading the Iraqis to suspect a much larger force, with artillery, was encircling the city. On April 8, all nine ODAs from Bravo Company secured the main roads into Ar Rutba and commenced a day of near continuous final airstrikes from both fixed-wing strike aircraft and Apache attack helicopters. A delegation of civilians eventually approached the American blocking positions, pleading for the bombardment to stop. The Green Berets struck a deal with the residents and the next day at precisely 0600hr, Bravo Company entered the city.

Not a round was fired as the GMV trucks drove in under the ominous shadows of an orbiting B-52 and a pair of F-16C Fighting Falcons that conducted repeated Show-of-Force missions over the city (a Show of Force entails a strike aircraft flying in low over enemy positions at full speed with afterburners engaged in an attempt to whittle down the opponent's morale). Surprisingly, the majority of the Fedayeen Saddam had not fled, being far more used to beating civilians than facing professional soldiers; and those that remained were attempting to blend in with the population.

The Operational Detachment Bravo team quickly transitioned to Civil Affairs mode and coordinated with the local civilian leadership to have a new mayor of Ar Rutba elected. The Special Forces operators wisely allowed former Ba'athists to

A US Army 5th Special Forces Group mounted patrol camouflaged in a desert hide site. The GMVs underneath the nets are only betrayed by their radio aerials, which would not be visible at a distance. (CROSSSUD)

hold local government positions if they signed documents disavowing their former affiliations (a tactic that could have been used across Iraq to prevent or at least blunt the later insurgency).

The ODAs lent local traders their satellite telephones to allow them to order their goods from across the border in Jordan, so within days the markets were again thriving. Sixty percent of the electricity grid was back on within a few days and the water supply was repaired, providing living conditions that were actually measurably better than under Saddam Hussein. It was a remarkably effective "hearts and minds" program by seasoned practitioners of counterinsurgency and should have been the model for the rest of Iraq.

Bravo Company continued operations in the region, using Ar Rutba as its base. ODAs 521 and 525 stopped several buses carrying foreign fighters from Syria – an ominous sign of things to come. The operators disarmed them, noted their passport details and sent them back toward the Syrian border with a warning that if they returned, they would be killed. In early May, the teams were finally relieved in place by the conventional mechanized forces of the 3rd Armored Cavalry Regiment.

KARBALA

Another important operation undertaken by the 5th Special Forces Group was the infiltration of ODA 551 on a strategic Special Reconnaissance to provide eyes-on surveillance of the Karbala Gap. The mission became legendary in Green Beret history as one of the longest in its history. It was also of vital strategic importance as conventional forces, in this case the 3rd Infantry Division, would have to pass through the Karbala Gap to reach Baghdad. The Gap itself was some 8km wide and lay between Lake Razzaza and Karbala itself, an ideal ambush site. Intelligence suggested that it would also be the logical choice for a chemical or biological weapons strike by Saddam Hussein's forces.

A detail shot of the front of a US Army 5th Special Forces Group Ground Mobility Vehicle in western Iraq. The Green Beret crew wear Gentex Military Motorcycle Helmets in preference to the more common MICH helmet. The vehicle has been fitted with camouflage nets that can be quickly deployed to obscure the vehicle's shape. (CROSSSUD)

A Green Beret team flanked by two M1078 LMTV War Pig logistics vehicles at a captured airbase in the western Iraqi desert. The ZU-23-1 anti-aircraft gun, PKM medium machine gun and Iraqi flag were all captured from the airbase's former owners. (CROSSSUD)

On the night of March 19, ODA 551 infiltrated into the Gap on board three MH-47Es, accompanied by a pair of MH-60L DAPs. The helicopters were forced to fly under a 300ft ceiling owing to the continuing "shock and awe" air campaign. The news channel, CNN, had inadvertently compromised the operation the night before when a retired US General, who really should have known better, pointed out the strategic significance of the Gap to an international audience and the specific need for an SOF reconnaissance team to be inserted there.

Landing off-set by some 100km from their proposed hide site, the team drove its GMVs straight off the back of the MH-47Es and headed into the night. Arriving at their chosen site, a seemingly disused quarry, the operators camouflaged their GMVs and settled in to their observation posts to begin their surveillance. Almost immediately they began calling in airstrikes on Iraqi military traffic on the nearby highway.

To their surprise they found the area itself did not contain the massed Iraqi armor that intelligence had claimed, but instead only a small Iraqi Army garrison and local Fedayeen Saddam. The team wore its MOPP (Mission Oriented Protective Posture) suits initially, fearful of being "slimed" if the chemical weapons intelligence proved correct, but took them off after seeing civilians moving freely about the area. Fedayeen Saddam patrolled regularly and came to within 400m of the team's position but never discovered it.

A FRAGO (Fragmentary Order) mission was received when a Patriot SAM battery mistakenly engaged and shot down a Navy F/A-18 – the ODA was to search for the downed pilot if practicable. On March 26, Apache attack helicopters probing through the Gap in advance of the 3rd Infantry Division (which had been delayed owing to a sandstorm) were battered by the significant Iraqi antiaircraft defenses in Karbala.

One of the Apaches was shot down by antiaircraft fire, but famously claimed by an Iraqi farmer with an old bolt action rifle. The helicopter came down on the far side of Karbala – unfortunately too far away for the ODA to assist. The first reconnaissance elements of the 3rd Infantry Division began arriving several days later and ODA 551 eventually drove out of its hides on March 30 (the antiaircraft threat was now considered too high to extract the team by helicopter).

ODA 551 discovered later from captured Iraqis that the CNN report had been seen, and acted upon – the Fedayeen Saddam had been actively searching for them. A second surprise was the reason Iraqi forces had not entered the quarry – it was discovered that the area was a former firing range used by Iraqi artillery and was littered with unexploded ordnance.

BASRA AND NAJAF

To the south, the 2nd Battalion of the 5th Special Forces Group was tasked with two key roles: Charlie Company would support the Marines and the British Battle Group around the southern city of Basra while Bravo Company would conduct reconnaissance and develop targets around Najaf for the 101st Airborne Division. ODA 554 crossed the border on March 21, driving into Iraq with the Marine Corps advanced elements. The special operators were to support the seizure of the Rumaylah oilfields which would later be secured by UK follow-on forces. A half team drove to the outskirts of Basra to pick up four Iraqi oil industry technicians, who had earlier been recruited by the CIA to assist in safeguarding the oilfields from destruction.

The half team successfully contacted the technicians, who were passed to the Marines, and ODA 554 rejoined the other half of its team after several gunfights with roving bands of Fedayeen Saddam. The team's new mission was to infiltrate undercover with a CIA-recruited Sheikh to assist British forces in identifying targets around Basra. The team encountered a surprising amount of resistance from Fedayeen in the city.

The ODA soon established an informer network with the Sheik's assistance and supported by a handheld mini UAV called the AeroVironment Pointer (AVP). ODA 554 eventually assisted the British in rounding up some 170 Fedayeen Saddam and Ba'athist Party die-hards, and leadership targets in and around Basra City. They were replaced by elements of G Squadron of the British SAS as the ODA had a somewhat strained relationship with UK conventional forces in the area (allegedly the Green Berets felt their input was not being acted upon by the British conventional forces and that the British were not responsive enough when a target was presented to them).

ODA 544 was infiltrated into Wadi al Khirr Airfield by MC-130 and drove the 80km to Najaf. Upon arrival in the city it began setting up temporary VCPs (Vehicle Check Points) to gather local intelligence. As it turned out, it was not the first Special Forces team into Najaf. ODA 572 had accidentally driven into the

A US Army Green Beret GMV, near Najaf, Iraq, March 2003, its crew scanning for hostiles. This angle shows the rear bed of the GMV and the rear swing-mount M240 machine gun to good effect. (US SOCOM)

city after being given an incorrect grid reference, but they had quickly withdrawn under enemy mortar fire. The 3rd Infantry Division had bypassed Najaf on its way to Karbala and ODA 544 linked up with the follow-on forces of General David Petraeus' 101st Airborne Division which entered the city on March 30.

The 101st Airborne secured the city, leaving a brigade to clear up scattered Fedayeen and Ba'ath Party hold-outs. ODA 544 stayed with the brigade and assisted by setting up a locally recruited security force to act as police. It also worked on developing a functioning local civilian government. While operating in Najaf, the Green Berets ran into a character whose name would later become synonymous with violence in southern Iraq – Moqtada al Sadr. In Najaf, al Sadr organized the killing of a moderate cleric who had been supported by the Special Forces.

Meanwhile, ODA 563 worked in support of the Marines around Diwaniyah. Again working with local Sheikhs and their militias (in a flashback to its Afghanistan experiences), and supported by the AV-8Bs and F/A-18s of Marine Air Wing, the Green Berets managed to capture the city of Qwam al Hamza. The following day ODA 563, their local Sheikh, his militiamen, and a small Force Recon team captured the bridge leading to Diwaniyah. The Sheikh's militia entered the city to pinpoint enemy positions, which were then engaged by Marine strike aircraft with 500lb JDAMs to limit collateral damage.

The surgical bombing worked and the Iraqi Army and Fedayeen Saddam withdrew from the city toward Baghdad, chased by Marine aviators all the way. The Green Berets immediately transitioned to reconstruction mode: setting up a local police service, restoring 80 percent of the city's electricity within two weeks, reopening schools and hospitals and even foiling a bank robbery. ODA 563's Civil Affairs efforts in Diwaniyah were the fastest return of civil services within Iraq, and again a template that should have been followed across Iraq.

NASIRIYAH

On the first attempt by ODA 553 to insert into Nasiriyah, the left front tire of its MH-53J transport helicopter struck a sand dune west of the city, flipping the aircraft. A CSAR (Combat Search and Rescue) team landed and recovered the team members and the air crew, several of whom were wounded, before placing demolition charges to destroy the stricken helicopter. The ODA was ferried back to Kuwait by the CSAR where it reconfigured its loads and later successfully inserted outside Nasiriyah to conduct a Special Reconnaissance mission on the bridges leading into the city ahead of the Marine advance.

The Green Berets had several contacts with Fedayeen Saddam before linking up and escorting the lead Army and Marine units into the city. The team went to work developing a local informer network to identify and track local Ba'athists and Fedayeen. Four other 5th Special Forces Group ODAs were busy training the so-called Free Iraqi Forces, who had been ferried into Kurdistan and then flown into the recently captured Talil airfield outside Nasiriyah. Predictably, they were a mixed bag with some units performing well and others proving a liability.

An armed M1078 Light Medium Tactical Vehicle (LMTV) modified into "War Pig" mother ship configuration, supporting 5th Special Forces Group ODAs in the western desert. (CROSSSUD)

TASK FORCES 7 AND 64

On March 18, B and D Squadrons of the British SAS had infiltrated by both ground and air-headed for the H-2 and H-3 airbases in the western desert along with 1 Squadron of the Australian SASR. The mobility patrols set up covert observation posts around the airbases and called in airstrikes that defeated the minimal Iraqi resistance. The combined British and Australian squadrons drove straight on to H-2, virtually unopposed. A company of Rangers and Marines from 45 Commando flew in from Jordan to secure the sites. Handing

over to the follow-on forces, the SAS teams moved on to their next objective – the intersection of the two main highways linking Baghdad with Syria and Jordan.

Other SASR patrols were hunting Scud-B TELs. On March 22, an apparent Scud command and control site was raided by a large SASR fighting patrol. As the surprised Iraqis withdrew under the withering fire from the SASR's six-wheeled LRPV, one escaping truck was disabled while a second escaped, but in flames. The facility proved to be the principal communications node for all Iraqi forces in the western desert. It was destroyed by Coalition strike aircraft vectored in by the patrol. A second communications site was also successfully raided, although Fedayeen Saddam in armed technicals, evidently a roving anti-Special Forces unit, arrived soon after and engaged the Australian patrol with DShK heavy machine gun and RPG fire.

Australian SASR operators mounted on a Perentie LRRV at the gates of Al Asad Air Base in western Iraq, April 2003. (Sergeant W. Guthrie; Australian DOD)

Australian operators from the 4th Battalion, Royal Australian Regiment (Commando) – now 2 Commando Regiment – conduct clearance operations at Al Asad Air Base, western Iraq. (Australian DOD)

The Australian operators returned fire. With both sides trading rounds, the battle was at an impasse until the Iraqis attempted to flank the patrol. In its first combat use by the Australians, one of the armed technicals of the Fedayeen was successfully destroyed by a Javelin missile, which saw the Iraqis hastily retreat back to the communications facility the SASR had just raided. As an Iraqi mortar team attempted to set up its base plate and a truck full of Iraqi Army reinforcements arrived, the attached US Combat Controller called in a pair of nearby A-10A ground attack aircraft that soon ended hostilities.

Several days later, six SASR operators in two LRPV trucks were carrying out a mounted reconnaissance near the border with Jordan when they were confronted by an Iraqi Army force of infantry supported by two armed technicals. The Australians suppressed the infantry with their .50cal heavy machine guns and 40mm Mk19 grenade launchers before again destroying the technicals with a Javelin. An estimated dozen Iraqis were killed in the action. By the end of March, a half squadron SASR mobility patrol was estimated to be just 80km from Baghdad itself and closing.

Early April saw Australian patrols moving toward al Asad Airbase, 200km northwest of Baghdad. South of al Asad was a concrete production facility, which

Special Boat Service

Often viewed as the naval equivalent of the SAS, the Special Boat Service also began life during the early days of World War II. Raised in 1940 as a covert sabotage and raiding unit that would infiltrate enemy harbours by means of a folding canoe named the Folboat, the SBS was initially called the Folboat Section. It was renamed the Special Boat Section in 1941 and served in the Middle East and Mediterranean theaters before being subsumed into the fledgling SAS.

In 1943 a new unit of SBS was raised from a combined force of SAS and Royal Marine Commandos and saw action in the Mediterranean and Baltic while other SBS served in Burma. The only Victoria Cross recipient from the British Special Forces was awarded to Maj Anders Lassen of the SBS. After the war the SBS, like its SAS

cousin, was involved in numerous "small wars," generally in a covert capacity. The section was renamed the Special Boat Squadron in the late 1970s before serving with distinction in the Falklands, conducting vital long-range reconnaissance missions in often appalling weather conditions.

In 1987 the SBS was renamed the Special Boat Service and served in Northern Ireland, the Gulf War, the Balkans, East Timor, Sierra Leone, and Afghanistan. The SBS is now organized along SAS lines with four squadrons divided into 16-man troops. Like the better-known US Navy SEALs, the SBS retains both its traditional maritime reconnaissance, sabotage, and raiding roles as well as an increasingly full spectrum of land-based special operations tasks.

the SASR soon learned was defended by some 40 Iraqi Army troops and some civilian workers. Wanting to avoid any civilian casualties if possible, the SASR commander blocked off all exits to the site and requested an orbiting Navy F-14 Tomcat to carry out a Show-of-Force over the concrete plant. The plan worked and the garrison was quickly convinced to surrender. The SASR used similar tactics to capture the air base itself. Using their recently issued SR-25 sniper rifles, the operators dropped rounds close to Iraqi soldiers to erode their morale. Precision airstrikes were conducted by RAAF F/A-18 Hornets to destroy fighting positions on the outskirts of the base. Once the Australians had occupied the control tower, they engaged in several short contacts both with remnants of the garrison force and looters. By mid-April, the SASR were reinforced by a company of Commandos from 4RAR who were employed clearing the base and securing the 50-odd Iraqi jet aircraft and helicopters the SASR had captured there.

SBS AMBUSH

While operations were proceeding very well for the British and Australian SAS units in the west, in the north M Squadron was finding itself mired in an incredibly dangerous situation. The squadron had deployed a small reconnaissance team mounted on Honda All Terrain Vehicles (ATV) into Iraq from Jordan in early March, its first mission being a reconnaissance of an Iraqi air base at al Sahara. The team was compromised by an anti-Special Forces Fedayeen Saddam unit and

Unknown British Special Forces – most likely SBS – conducting a mounted patrol in Iraq. The Land Rovers are not standard SAS Desert Patrol Vehicles as they lack a number of their normal features, such as smoke dischargers. (Photographer unknown)

barely escaped, thanks to an American F-15E that flew air cover for the team during its escape and the brave pilots of the RAF who brought in an extraction Chinook under the Fedayeen's noses. Although the SBS operators didn't know it, the mission was a shadow of things to come.

A second, larger SBS operation was launched into northern Iraq from Jordan via the recently captured H-2. The objective was twofold: locate an Iraqi Army Corps and make contact to take its surrender, and to survey and mark viable temporary landing zones for follow-on forces. The full squadron deployed in over 30 vehicles – a mix of Land Rover Pinkies and Honda ATVs – flown into western Iraq. From there the squadron group set off, heading for the Kurdish north to locate the elusive 5th Army Corps. Somewhere past Tikrit, the squadron was compromised by a goat herder.

The SBS still managed to drive for several days, unaware that another of the anti-Special Forces Fedayeen Saddam units was tailing them. At an overnight position somewhere near Mosul, the trap was sprung. Initially the squadron was engaged by multiple DShK heavy machine guns followed by RPGs. As the SBS returned fire, it began taking incoming fire from something larger – it appeared that an Iraqi Army armored unit equipped with the local variant of the T-72 had joined the fight alongside the Fedayeen. The squadron patrol scattered, managing to race past Iraqi Army dismounted infantry that was closing in on them – it was a well-constructed trap.

A number of Pinkies became bogged in swampy ground in a nearby wadi and had to be abandoned. Bar mines were placed on the vehicles to deny them to the enemy. However, it appears several did not detonate for whatever reason and two Pinkies, at least one ATV, and a dirt bike were captured by the Iraqis and later exhibited on Iraqi television as proof of a great battle success over Western Special Forces. The SBS was in three distinct groups: one, with several operational Pinkies, was being pursued by the Iraqi hunter force; a second, mainly equipped with ATVs, was hunkered down in a hide site while it tried to arrange an extraction; the third, of just two operators perched on an ATV, raced for the Syrian border.

The main group in the Pinkies managed to transmit their emergency brevity code "Battleaxe," which brought Coalition strike aircraft overhead. The problem was that the aircraft could not identify the friendlies on the ground from the numerous pursuing Iraqi vehicles. It has never been explained why the SBS were apparently not equipped with infra-red strobes, although their vehicles did mount Blue Force Tracker units. Eventually, the second group were located and extracted by a RAF Chinook. The first group made it to an emergency rendezvous point with strike aircraft flying low level Show-of-Force sorties over the pursuing Iraqis. A RAF Chinook managed to fly in and extract the group. Remarkably, there had been no SBS casualties.

Some two weeks later, the fate of the third group became known when Syria admitted to holding the two SBS operators. The pair had made it across the border before crashing their ATV. They were captured by Syrian troops as they tried to restart it. Their release was negotiated and the final chapter in the sorry saga was closed. It was also the end of any major SBS operations in Iraq. At the end of initial hostilities, G Squadron of the SAS flew in to replace B and D squadrons which rotated home.

UMM QASR

The Naval Task Group launched its operations on the night of March 20. Two offshore platforms for loading oil tankers were among its initial targets – the Mina al Bakr Oil Terminal (MABOT) would be seized by SEALs from SEAL Team 8 and 10 while the Khor al Amaya Oil Terminal (KAAOT) would be secured by Poland's special operations unit, the GROM. SEALs from the SDV (Swimmer Delivery Vehicle) teams had successfully carried out a covert reconnaissance of both sites several days earlier using their Mk8 mini submersible.

Thirty-one SEALs, two Navy EOD operators (in case the rig was wired for demolition), an Air Force Combat Controller and several Iraqi interpreters were involved in the seizure of the MABOT platform. A similar number of GROM operators struck the offshore KAAOT platform. Both were quickly seized with zero resistance, although explosives were found and made safe by the GROM operators.

The shore-based pumping station for each platform at Umm Qasr and the al Faw was also seized by a mixed unit of SEALs and Royal Marines. The operation was tragically delayed by the crash of a Marine CH-46 Sea Knight as it launched from Kuwait carrying seven members of 3 Commando's Brigade Reconnaissance

A famous image of Polish GROM special operators pulling security at Umm Qasr at the commencement of hostilities. (US SOCOM)

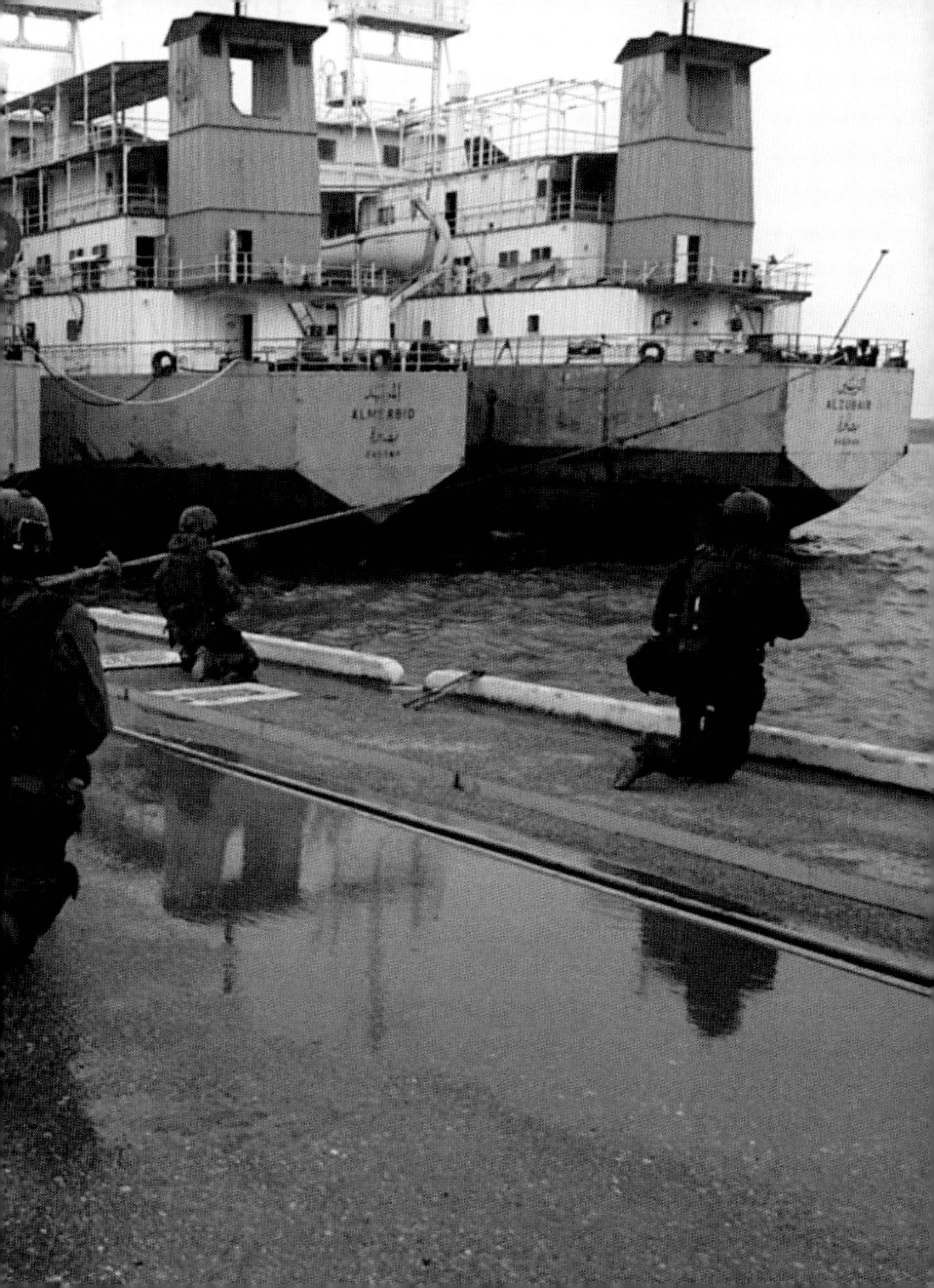
ALMERBID
ALZUBAIR

A SEAL Team One Desert Patrol Vehicle (DPV) on exercises in Kuwait just prior to the invasion. (PH1 (SW) Arlo K. Abrahamson; US Navy)

Force and a member of 29 Commando Royal Artillery. Sadly all were killed along with four US Marine aviators.

The Umm Qasr site was prepared by an AC-130 Spectre strike and a flight of A-10As engaged a nearby SAM installation and a responding Iraqi mechanized unit before the SEALs and Royal Marines eventually landed. They cleared two Iraqi bunkers, killing several Iraqi soldiers with the SEALs securing the facility itself and the Royal Marines establishing a defensive cordon. The attached Combat Controller called in one of the A-10As to engage an Iraqi Army vehicle, which later approached the site. Royal Marines and SEALs also infiltrated into the al Faw pumping station, quickly seizing the site after engaging and destroying an Iraqi Army truck carrying infantry. Members of 40 and 42 Commando, Royal Marines were flown in to reinforce and secure the sites.

Other Naval Task Group operations included elements of three SEAL platoons in GMV trucks and their distinctive dune buggy Desert Patrol Vehicles seizing the al Zubayr metering station while the 1st Marine Expeditionary Force attacked through the Rumaylah Oil Fields north of al Faw. Captain Robert Harward, the SEAL who had commanded Task Force K-Bar in Afghanistan, commented that there were more SEALs deployed during the Iraqi invasion than at any one time during the Vietnam War.

Another SEAL-led operation, this time with operators from SEAL Team 5 and GROM, was the seizure of the Mukarayin Dam, 57 miles northeast of Baghdad to prevent any opportunity for Iraqi forces to flood the capital as a last-ditch defensive measure. Six MH-53J transport helicopters were earmarked for the infiltration – the lead helicopter carried the SEAL command and control element along with six SEAL snipers; the second carried 20 SEAL assaulters and two attached EOD operators; the third carried some 35 GROM; the fourth and fifth carried a Desert Patrol Vehicle, each with a SEAL crew; and the sixth was tasked as the dedicated CSAR helicopter should things go wrong.

The lead Pave Low touched down on the roof of a three-storey power generator building and the snipers deployed into overwatch positions. The GROM and SEAL assaulters fast roped to the ground with one Polish operator breaking a leg. The Desert Patrol Vehicle crews were dropped off at either end of the dam, one supported by six SEAL operators, the other with four SEALs. The DPVs with their mounted .50 and M60E4s machine guns took up blocking positions covering the access roads on to the dam. The combined SEAL and GROM unit held the dam for five days until relieved by the Marines.

The SEALs and GROM continued their highly successful partnership throughout the rest of the invasion phase with raids and antisniper operations conducted in Baghdad. SEALs and Special Boat Teams also secured the waterways around Umm Qasr. They were also involved in various VBSS (Visit Board Search Seizure) missions (known in SEAL terminology as "underways") to seize Iraqi craft carrying seaborne mines, a task they were assisted in by the "Bubblies" of Royal Australian Navy Clearance Diving Team 3 (a unit with responsibilities for both naval EOD and beach and littoral reconnaissance).

THE WOLVERINES

The men of B Squadron of Delta Force, known as the "Wolverines," became the first United States SOF unit to enter western Iraq as it rolled across the border from Ar'ar in western Saudi Arabia. The unit was transported in 15 customized Pinzgauer 6x6 Special Operations Vehicles and several armed Toyota Hilux pickup trucks. Accompanying the squadron of operators were Air Force Special Tactics teams, a Delta intelligence and targeting cell, several Military Working Dog teams and two American Iraqis who had volunteered to serve as interpreters. Task Force 20's formal role was to conduct selected high-priority SSEs on suspected chemical weapon facilities before heading for the Haditha Dam complex.

Along the way, Delta supported Coalition SOF in seizing the H-3 airfield. They also conducted numerous deception operations to confuse the Iraqis as to

Another rare image of Delta Force in the western desert operating alongside Little Birds of the 160th Special Operations Aviation Regiment. (Photographer unknown)

the true disposition of Coalition Forces in the west. Meanwhile, Rangers from 3rd Battalion of the 75th Ranger Regiment conducted a combat drop into H-1 airfield located between Haditha and Ar Rutba on March 24, securing the site as a staging area for operations in the west.

For several nights, Delta Recce operators drove through Iraqi lines around Haditha Dam on their custom blacked-out ATVs, marking targets for Coalition airstrikes resulting in the eventual destruction of a large number of Iraqi armored vehicles and antiaircraft systems. Delta's reconnaissance of the dam indicated that a much bigger force would be needed to seize it, so a request was made and approved for a second Delta squadron from Fort Bragg to be dispatched along with a further battalion of Rangers. Task Force 20 also requested, and received, an attached company of M1A1 Abrams main battle tanks from C Company, 2/70th Armor. The tanks, soon to be termed 'Team Tank', were flown in by C-17 transport aircraft from Talil to H-1 and then on to Mission Support Site (MSS) Grizzly, a desert strip established by Delta Force located between Haditha and Tikrit. The additional Delta operators of C Squadron flew directly into Grizzly from the United States.

April 1 saw the Delta squadron and 3/75th Rangers conduct a night-time ground assault in their Pinzgauers and GMV trucks against the Haditha Dam complex. Three platoons of Rangers seized the dam's main administrative buildings with little initial opposition, while a pair of AH-6M Six Guns orbited overhead. Soon after daybreak, a Ranger sniper shot and killed three Iraqis with RPGs on the western side of the dam and Rangers on the eastern side engaged a truck carrying infantry, which led to an hour-long contact.

South of the dam itself, another Ranger platoon was busy securing the dam's power station and electricity transformer against sabotage. Another platoon was occupied establishing blocking positions on the main road into the dam complex. The blocking positions came under sporadic mortar fire, resulting in the AH-6Ms flying multiple gun runs to silence the mortar positions. Another mortar team soon opened fire from a small island that was quickly engaged and silenced by a Ranger Javelin team.

For five days after the seizure of Haditha Dam, Iraqi forces continued to harass the Rangers. The harassment principally consisted of episodic artillery and mortar fire along with several infantry counterattacks against the blocking positions. The HIMARS rocket system saw its first combat deployment at the dam, firing counter-battery missions. Three Rangers were tragically killed on April 3 by a Vehicle-Borne Improvised Explosive Device (VBIED) at one of the blocking positions. The car was driven by a distressed pregnant Iraqi woman who asked the Rangers for water before detonating the car killing herself, another female in the vehicle, and the three Rangers. It is assumed the women were perhaps fanatical Ba'athists or perhaps members of Ansar al-Islam that had escaped Operation *Viking Hammer*.

At one point, an Iraqi forward observer in civilian dress took to the waters of the dam in a kayak. The kayak was engaged and sunk by .50cal fire and the spotter captured with sketch maps of the Ranger positions. Another more pressing problem occurred when an Iraqi artillery round struck an electricity transformer, shutting down power to the dam. After the transformer was repaired, it was discovered only one turbine was operating out of the five at the dam. Additionally, the dam's seals were now leaking. A former Special Forces engineer with Civil Affairs was flown in by MH-47E who, along with the Iraqi civilian staff of the dam, managed to jury-rig fixes that would ward off catastrophe in the short term. An Army Engineer unit was later brought in to stabilize the facility. Ironically it appeared that the Iraqis had not been planning to destroy the dam and flood the 3rd Infantry Division as it advanced through Karbala, although the Task Force 20 mission to prevent it almost resulted in that unintended result.

Delta had handed over to the Rangers at Haditha and headed north to conduct ambushes along the highway above Tikrit, tying up Iraqi forces in the region and

Rangers seen through night vision clearing Objective Cobalt, Haditha Dam, April 2003. (USASOC)

Humor from B Company, 3rd Battalion, 75th Ranger Regiment at Haditha Dam. (USASOC)

attempting to capture fleeing high-value targets trying to escape to Syria. Team Tank convinced Iraqi Generals that the Coalition's Main Effort might be coming from the west after all. It was in a contact near Tikrit on April 2 that tragedy struck Delta. It had been shadowed by what may have been elements of the same anti-Special Forces Fedayeen Saddam units that the SBS had encountered in roughly the same area.

Contacted by half a dozen armed technicals, two Delta operators were wounded, one seriously. The squadron requested an urgent aero medical evacuation and immediate close-air support as Iraqi reinforcements in the form of a company of truck-borne infantry arrived. The Nightstalkers of the 160th SOAR answered the call and two MH-60K Blackhawks carrying a Para Jumper medical team and two armed MH-60L DAPs lifted off immediately and were over the besieged operators' positions some 90 minutes later. The DAPs began engaging ground targets, which allowed the Delta operators to move their casualties back to an emergency HLZ, enabling the Blackhawks to land. One of the operators, Master Sergeant George "Andy" Fernandez, who had already passed away from blood loss, was loaded on to the second helicopter wrapped in a US flag. The MH-60s lifted off and raced back toward H-1 escorted by a pair of A-10As. The DAPs stayed on-station, destroying a truck carrying an Iraqi mortar and several infantry squads. As the aircraft passed overhead, Iraqi infantry began firing small arms up at the DAPs until they were silenced by Delta snipers.

Another pair of A-10As soon arrived and were guided on to targets by the DAPs. One airburst 500lb bomb sprayed fragments within 20m of Delta positions, but killed a large number of enemy infantry gathering in a wadi. The DAPs handed off to the A-10As to cover the Delta squadron as it prepared to advance further north. Low on fuel, the DAPs flew ahead of the ground callsigns and spotted several enemy units that they engaged with 30mm cannon and minigun until, dangerously low on fuel, they finally turned back for H-1.

Staging out of MSS Grizzly, Delta mounted operations to interdict Ba'ath Party high-value targets on Highway 1 (Highways 2 and 4 through the western desert had been secured by British and Australian SAS teams). April 9 saw the combined team seizing yet another airfield near Tikrit. During that night attack one of Team Tank's M1A1s had driven into a 40ft deep hole, flipping the Abrams tank over and injuring one of the crew. The disabled tank was later destroyed by two 120mm rounds from one of its sister tanks to deny it to the enemy. By mid-April, Delta had advanced into Baghdad and the men of Team Tank returned to their parent unit.

SAVING PRIVATE LYNCH

The initial intelligence that led to the rescue of 19-year-old Private First Class Jessica Lynch of the US Army's 507th Maintenance Company was provided by an informer who had approached ODA 553 when it was working in Nasiriyah. Lynch had been captured after her support convoy became lost and was ambushed in Nasiriyah. The intelligence was passed up the line through attached Special Forces liaison officers and on to Task Force 20. Planning for a rescue operation was immediately begun.

The concept of operations called for a multi-service effort to support the black SOF assault elements that would carry out the POW (Prisoner of War) recovery mission. Launching from the recently captured Iraqi airfield at Talil, the operation included more than 290 Rangers from both the 1st and 2nd Battalions; 60 or so special operators from DEVGRU – along with PJs (Para Rescue Jumpers) and Combat Controllers from the 24th Special Tactics Squadron; conventional Marines from Task Force Tarawa then currently fighting through the city and aviators from the Army, Marines and Air Force.

The plan called for the Task Force Tarawa Marines to conduct a deception operation by launching a mission to seize the bridges across the Euphrates to draw attention away from the hospital. An air strike by Marine Air AV-8 Harrier strike aircraft would then be conducted against one of the bridges to confuse the opposition further and a pair of orbiting Marine AH-1W Cobra attack helicopters were tasked to over-fly the area to conceal the sounds of incoming SOF helicopters. Air cover was provided by an AC-130 Spectre fixed-wing gunship and a Marine EA-6 Prowler to jam any enemy SAM systems that might be present.

With the deception operation underway, the SEAL and selected Ranger elements would be inserted by four MH-60K Blackhawks and four MH-6 Little Birds. They would be supported by four AH-6 attack helicopters and two of the stars of the war's opening night, the MH-60L DAPs. The Rangers would be flown in by Marine CH-46s and CH-53 transport helicopters to establish a cordon around the hospital grounds and man-blocking positions on surrounding roads. The main assault force of SEALS would arrive by a ground convoy comprised of AGMS Pandur armored vehicles and GMV trucks while the hostage rescue element landed directly on the objective in MH-6 Little Birds.

At 0100hr on April 1, 2003, the Marines commenced their deception plan, timed to coincide with the launch of the rescue force. CIA elements cut the city's power as the helicopters approached their objective, ensuring the aviators could clearly identify their HLZs and confusing any nearby opposition by plunging the city into darkness. The AH-6s led the way, ready to suppress any opposition with their miniguns, while immediately behind flew the MH-6s to drop off their Task Force 20 sniper teams at strategic locations around and on the hospital to cover the approach by the assaulters. The DAPs and AH-6s covered the MH-60Ks as they dropped off assault teams on the hospital roof and another by the front door. The ground assault convoy arrived on cue and the assaulters raced inside, making their way to the second floor where Lynch was located. Shotguns were used to blow in locked doors and flashbang stun grenades reverberated through the night. A final MH-60K touched down near the entrance with a team of PJs and SOAR medics on board to transport Lynch to safety.

The Ranger blocking teams were brought in by an initial flight of three Marine CH-46s which landed outside the hospital grounds to block the main roads and cut off any potential reinforcements along with any squirters from the hospital itself. A second wave of CH-46s and CH-53s arrived minutes after the first lift was completed and heading back to Talil. Despite some sporadic fire directed at the Ranger-blocking positions, the hospital itself was devoid of gunmen, although evidence suggested Fedayeen Saddam had been using parts of the hospital as a base.

Thirteen minutes after the first assaulters entered the hospital, a team of PJs and SOF medics carried Lynch from the hospital's main entrance on a folding litter and secured her in the waiting MH-60K which quickly lifted off to rendezvous with a standby medical flight at Talil and then onward to Kuwait and finally the United States. The job for the SEALs and the Rangers was not yet over, however, as they eventually recovered the remains of eight members of Lynch's unit that had been killed or died from their wounds. The bodies were placed in the SOF vehicles and returned to the airfield along with the assault teams, AH-6s flying escort above them as the Ranger blocking teams collapsed their cordons and exfiltrated in the Marine helicopters.

Despite cynical accusations of a public relations stunt by elements of the media, there was no denying the fact that Task Force 20 had carried out the first successful United States POW rescue mission since World War II. Such accusations also seem to forget that it is the military's role to attempt to rescue prisoners if they can be located. Luckily, Lynch was and the mission was launched. It also reassured all soldiers and Marines that their government would indeed never leave a man, or in this case a woman, behind.

An unmarked but armed Hughes 500 Little Bird helicopter believed to be operated by the CIA SAD Air Branch, western Iraq, picking up a captured Iraqi general. (CROSSSUD)

HUNTING THE WMDS

Intelligence indicating that chemical and biological weapons stocks may have been located at a complex known as the al Qadisiyah Research Centre, north of Haditha, led to another Task Force 20 operation being launched on the evening of March 26, 2003. B Company of the 2nd Battalion of the Rangers would support a DEVGRU SEAL assault element.

The target of the operation, codenamed Objective Beaver, was one of the regime's palaces, nestled along the shore of the al Qadisiyah Reservoir, which had been outfitted as a research laboratory nestled among both residential and governmental buildings. The assault package that lifted off that night included two AH-6M attack helicopters and a pair of MH-60L DAPs along with a pair of MH-6Ms carrying DEVGRU aerial sniper teams riding on the external pods.

The Rangers would insert first from four MH-60Ks into blocking positions around the site followed minutes later by a pair of MH-47Es that would insert the main DEVGRU assault force beside Objective Beaver, the target building. A second pair of MH-47Es would orbit nearby carrying a Ranger QRF and the dedicated CSAR element in the event of a helicopter crashing. The operation itself went smoothly and according to plan until the first MH-60K landed near its assigned blocking position and was engaged by enemy small arms fire from a nearby building. An AH-6 spotted the muzzle flashes and fired a 2.75in rocket into the location, silencing the small arms fire. The second MH-60K was also struck by small arms fire as it touched down, which was rapidly suppressed by its door gunner's minigun. It was quickly becoming clear that the site was becoming a "cherry" or contested HLZ.

Air Force A-10As engaged nearby electricity transformers in an attempt to black out the area that was successful, but it also resulted in a series of explosions and a resulting fire at the transformer stations that dramatically lit the sky, now pinpointing the orbiting helicopters for enemy gunmen. Small arms fire increased as the final two Blackhawks inserted their blocking teams, and a Ranger suffered the first wounding of the battle with a through and through gunshot wound to his back, puncturing a lung.

The helicopter carrying the wounded Ranger deposited its passengers and immediately departed with 160th aircrew and a SEAL medic working to stabilize the casualty. The MH-60K sped to a staging site where the Ranger was transferred to a waiting field surgical team on board an idling HH-130 transport aircraft that had been specially outfitted for medical emergencies.

The AH-6s and DAPs continued to suppress targets as the MH-47Es carrying the main assault force closed on the target. The snipers sitting on the external pods of the MH-6s engaged numerous gunmen and vehicles. The MH-47Es nonetheless landed under heavy enemy small arms fire with rounds punching through the thin-skinned aircraft. Remarkably, both managed to insert their assaulters safely in one piece. However, as they lifted off a Nightstalker crew member was shot in the head, the round striking him in the jaw. The crew chief and door gunners applied immediate first aid to attempt to staunch the blood loss. The MH-47E immediately set out for the staging area at the best possible speed.

Midway to the airstrip, and the waiting HH-130, the wounded airman stopped breathing. The Nightstalker aviators immediately began CPR and, after five long minutes, the wounded man began to breathe again. The MH-47E landed soon after and the gravely wounded aviator was transferred to the HH-130, which took off with both wounded now on board and the full field surgical team working on them. Happily, both men survived their wounds.

Back at the objective, the SEALs conducted a hasty SSE while the blocking positions continued to receive and return fire. The SSE took longer than usual owing to the size and maze-like structure of the building. The AH-6s and the snipers continued to engage enemy gunmen while the DAPs pushed out further to ensure no reinforcements approached the blocking positions. The DAPs engaged and destroyed numerous Fedayeen Saddam armed technicals heading for the facility.

Finally, the "objective complete" call was broadcast and the two back-up MH-47Es landed to extract the SEALs while the MH-60Ks returned to pick up the Rangers from their blocking positions. In total, the assault teams had been on the ground for some 45 minutes. Apart from the two casualties, the teams escaped unscathed except that most of their helicopters now sported new bullet holes. Later tests conducted on the material recovered by the assaulters showed no evidence of chemical or biological weapons at Objective Beaver.

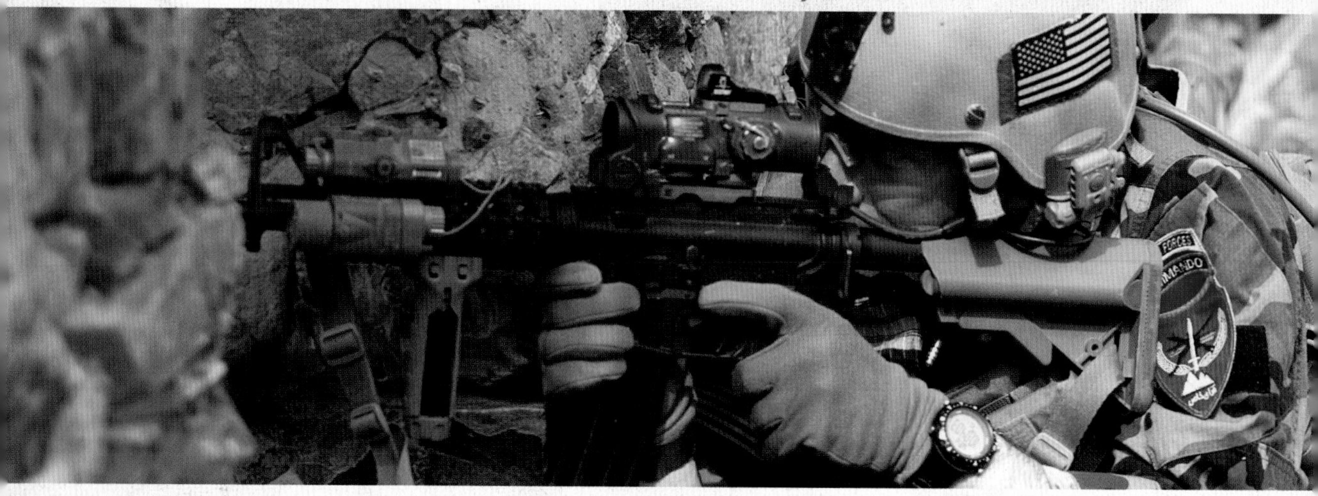
FORCES

CHAPTER 4
COUNTERING INSURGENCY
AFGHANISTAN 2002-2009, IRAQ 2003-2011, AND THE PHILIPPINES 2002 ONWARD

Although the focus for the United States and its close allies was now firmly on Iraq, operations continued in Afghanistan, albeit at a reduced pace and at a reduced level of support. The US Combined Joint Special Operations Task Force began to see National Guard Special Forces Groups (NGSFG) replacing the full-time units that were earmarked for Iraq. (Many who have worked with the NGSFP and the full-time units rate them both equally highly.) SOF helicopter and ISR (Intelligence Surveillance and Reconnaissance) support dwindled. The black SOF elements were also reduced as they and their CIA brethren prepared for the new theater of war.

What SOF remained was scattered throughout the Afghan Provinces in a largely uncoordinated effort at counterinsurgency. Much of this effort was concerned with hunting down enemy individuals of interest and lower-tier high-value targets in a war of attrition against the local Taliban. Until the arrival of General Stanley McChrystal in 2009, much of the work of SOF in Afghanistan had focused on Direct Action against insurgent groups; counterguerrilla rather than counterinsurgency.

As acclaimed author Linda Robinson explains in her book *One Hundred Victories*:

> Until 2009, the entire US military effort was overly focused on hunting down individuals considered to be problematic. This was a diversion from doctrine, in which counter guerrilla operations are merely a subset of activity, something to be nested within a wider approach that, depending on the circumstances, is termed "counter insurgency", "foreign internal defense" or "stability operations."

US Army Special Forces operators firing on insurgents during a compound clearance. (US DOD)

What traditional counterinsurgency was occurring was generally on a very localized level and often led by Green Beret teams recruiting and training Afghan Militia Forces to provide security in their area of operations. Other militias were recruited and retained almost purely as strike forces, harking back to Vietnam days when the Green Berets would raise local "indig" (indigenous) forces to target the Viet Cong. Indeed the CIA SAD developed several of these units that could have been directly inspired by their Phoenix Program in Vietnam known as Counterterrorist Pursuit Teams.

The Special Forces ODAs were assigned either an offensive, direct-action role, which would entail them operating in far-flung provinces with locally recruited militias as

A US Air Force Para Rescue Jumper secures a HLZ at Bagram, 2010, a green smoke grenade marking the landing zone in the background. He is armed with a camouflage-painted M4A1 carbine with a Spectre sight. Note his aides-mémoire on his left wrist, listing aircraft call signs and similar information. (Staff Sergeant Christopher Boitz; US Air Force)

hunter-killer forces, or they would be assigned a Foreign Internal Defense (FID) detail which saw them partnered with Afghan Army Kandaks (battalions) in a training and mentoring role. This FID role did see successes – for instance, the first two Afghan Commando units were raised in 2007 thanks to the Green Berets. Not surprisingly though, the Direct Action tasking was far more popular than the FID role.

SOF in general had become too enamored with Direct Action. The perception of Special Forces and SEALs in particular as highly trained door-kickers filtered down from the Bush-era White House to CENTCOM and consequently into the perceptions of the SOF operators themselves. Particularly in the immediate post-9/11 years, Direct Action was seen as the preferred option in the newly declared Global War on Terror. Psy Ops, Civil Affairs and Foreign Internal Defense – the key components of counterinsurgency – would be finally recognized as equally if not more important to the war effort, but it took a number of years and the ascendance of those such as General Petraeus before the situation changed. In that time, the counterinsurgency in Afghanistan suffered from the focus on Direct Action missions and "killing our way to victory," as Petraeus later termed it.

It wasn't just the Direct Action focus that was harming the Afghan mission. Reconstruction funds were still available and Provincial Reconstruction Teams

A Green Beret Major (complete with Afghan Commando patch) on a partnered patrol returns fire during a contact in Kunar Province. What sets this Green Beret apart is that he lost one of his legs during a firefight in Iraq in 2007. Now operating with a prosthesis, he served in Afghanistan with the 3rd Special Forces Group in 2012. (Mass Communication Specialist Second Class Clay Weis; US Navy)

(PRTs) did all that they could, but Iraq was receiving the lion's share of resources. It was not until the success of the so-called "Iraqi Surge," again under General Petraeus, and his literal rewriting of the counterinsurgency handbook, and the movement of conventional forces into the volatile southern provinces of Afghanistan, that more attention became focused on what was sometimes considered the "Forgotten War."

ISAF PARTNERS

From 2002, ISAF member states contributed troop commitments to the NATO-led stabilization force. Among these were special operations forces. Many ISAF SOF units operated under their particular country's Rules of Engagement (ROE), which were often markedly more restrictive than some of their allies. They also

were restricted by national caveats that placed conditions on when and where a nation's forces could be deployed. Many of the European partner nations only contributed forces with the caveat that they would be given responsibility for safer Provinces to the north and west of Afghanistan. America's closest allies – the British and the Canadians, for example – were sent into the south and experienced conditions that resembled conventional war fighting rather than any localized insurgency.

CZECHOSLOVAKIA

Since April 2007, a 35-man deployment of the Special Operations Group (SOG) of the Czech Military Police was deployed supporting the British in Helmand under ISAF command in a variety of force protection and Direct Action tasks. The Czech commitment increased in 2011 as the Czech Republic deployed a full Special Operations Task Group, including the Czech Army's 601st Special Forces Group under the newly formed ISAF SOF command.

FRANCE

French special operators had served in Afghanistan since the beginning of ISAF and 150 COS operators were later deployed to replace the Italian ISAF SOF contingent in 2003 – again primarily conducting reconnaissance and close-protection tasks. A 200-man COS unit operated under the direct command of OEF-A between 2003 and 2007, although according to authors David Auerswald and Stephen Saideman in *NATO in Afghanistan: Fighting Together, Fighting Alone*, their tasks were restricted to "short-term counter terrorism and counterinsurgency raids" rather than longer Special Reconnaissance missions. Incredibly, nor were they apparently allowed to conduct partnered operations.

Despite these restrictions, the French SOF operators were responsible for a large number of successful Direct Action missions, often in joint operations with American and sometimes British SOF. Sadly one of their better-known operations (French SOF being notoriously secretive) involved the brutal deaths of two operators from the 1st RPIMA (1er Régiment de Parachutistes d'Infanterie de Marine, or 1st Marine Parachute Infantry Regiment) who were involved in a reaction force to assist an ambushed engineer convoy in Helmand. While attempting to evacuate the wounded, the French operators were captured along with a number of ANA (Afghan National Army) soldiers. They were executed in front of the captured Afghans.

The French SOF contribution to OEF-A ended in 2007 after disputes over its role. A 150-man task group returned in 2009 operating directly for the French ISAF contribution and also conducted significant mentoring of Afghan security forces. All French forces were withdrawn in 2012.

GERMANY

Although nominally under OEF command, operationally the KSK had worked for ISAF since 2005, carrying out numerous operations in the vicinity of the German presence in Kabul including a successful raid on an al-Qaeda safe house for suicide bombers in October 2006. KSK operators have commented in the German media about the restrictions placed upon them by their national caveats and stated a preference for working directly for the Americans as they had done in the days of Task Force K-Bar.

Germany's elite counterterrorist border police unit, Grenzschutztruppe 9 (GSG 9) was also deployed to the Kabul area, providing specialist close protection to German officials and facilities. It carried out a similar mission in Iraq.

ITALY

Italy deployed SOF in the form of the Composite Incursiori Company of the 9th Parachute Assault Regiment, known internationally as Col Moschin (named after the site of a famous battle between the Italians and Austrians in World War I), and from the Navy's Gruppo Operational Incursiori. Italian SOF was not placed under US-led OEF-A command, instead it deployed directly in support of the Italian ISAF Task Force-Nibbio where they carried out local force protection and reconnaissance tasks. However, Col Moschin operators did work alongside the British SBS to attempt to rescue two Italian agents in September 2007.

Rangers return to their Stryker Infantry Fighting Vehicles after a daylight raid in Helmand's Nad-e-Ali District during the 2010 fighting season. The Rangers have been operating a small number of Strykers since 2005 in both Iraq and Afghanistan as a means to infiltrate and exfiltrate a target under armored protection. Note the Rangers are wearing a dump pouch on the left-hand side to drop empty magazines into rather than discard them on the battlefield. (SPC Joseph Wilson; US Army)

OPERATION *ENDURING FREEDOM*-AFGHANISTAN,
SPECIAL OPERATIONS TASK FORCES AREAS OF RESPONSIBILITY 2010-2014

TURKMENISTAN

UZBEKISTAN

TAJIKISTAN

CHINA

N

Amu Darya

Mazar-e-Sharif

⑦

AN

Harirud

⑤

Herat

Harirud

Kabul

Jalalabad

Kabul

Helmand

Tora Bora△

AFGHANISTAN

INDIA

Gardez

Khost

Shah-I-Kot-Valley

△

①

Zhawa

②

④

RAN

Lashkar Gar

Kandahar

⑥

Helmand

③

**Operation *Enduring Freedom–Afghanistan*,
Special Operations Task Forces
Areas of Responsibility 2010–2014**
1) The West — Marine Special Operations Command
2) Helmand Province — Marine Special Operations
   Command
3) The South West — Marine Special Operations
   Command and Army Special Forces
4) The South East — Navy SEALs
5) The East — Army Special Forces
6) The South — Army Special Forces
7) The North — 82nd Airborne Division

LITHUANIA

LITHSOF first deployed a 40-man group in November 2002. It was involved in Special Reconnaissance taskings and the recovery of a downed MQ-1 Predator UAV. Since 2006 LITHSOF has been in action in the south with British forces.

NETHERLANDS

The Korps Commandotroepen (KCT) Viper Teams deployed directly under the command of OEF-A in 2005 with 165 KCT operators backed by four Dutch Chinooks. Under the ISAF mandate, KCT deployed to Tarin Kowt in Uruzgan

Norwegian FSK special operators firing on Taliban insurgents during the April 2012 attacks in Kabul. The FSK had only recently relieved a New Zealand SAS detachment, which had been mentoring the Kabul Crisis Response Unit, an Afghan counter-terrorist SWAT team. The number of spent LAW rockets is impressive as are the empty ammunition tins. (Photographer unknown)

Province in 2006 to work alongside the Australians. KCT conducted long-range reconnaissance and specialist intelligence gathering for both the Dutch Battle Group and the ISAF SOF command.

NORWAY

Norwegian SOF, commanded by ISAF, has been involved since the very beginning in Afghanistan in 2001. Although a very small detachment, it lost an Army HJK (Haerens Jegerkommando) officer in July 2007 to enemy fire in Logar Province. The Norwegian counterterrorist unit FSK (Forsvarets Spesialkommando) carried out a successful hostage rescue of Christina Meier, a pregnant German NGO worker in Kabul in August 2007. No shots were fired and the hostage takers were believed to be a criminal gang rather than insurgents.

ROMANIA

Around 40 operators from the 1st Special Operations Battalion "Eagles" were deployed to Afghanistan in 2006 under the direct command of OEF-A. They transitioned to ISAF command the following year and were heavily involved in mentoring Afghan National Army units. The Romanian commitment eventually grew to a full Special Operations Task Group comprising of three ODA-sized elements. They often operated closely with Green Beret ODAs on joint patrols, even deploying hybrid ODAs of both Romanian and American operators.

POLAND

GROM (Operational Mobile Reaction Group) enjoys very close ties to SOCOM and a 40-man element deployed to Afghanistan in early 2002. Poland deployed both the 1st Special Commando Regiment and GROM during 2007 to

OPPOSITE A rare image of Australian SASR troopers clearing a target compound somewhere in Uruzgan Province, 2009. Note the varied headgear and that only one man is wearing his helmet. The yellow cooking oil containers to the left are often used by the insurgents to hide IEDs. (Australian SOCOMD)

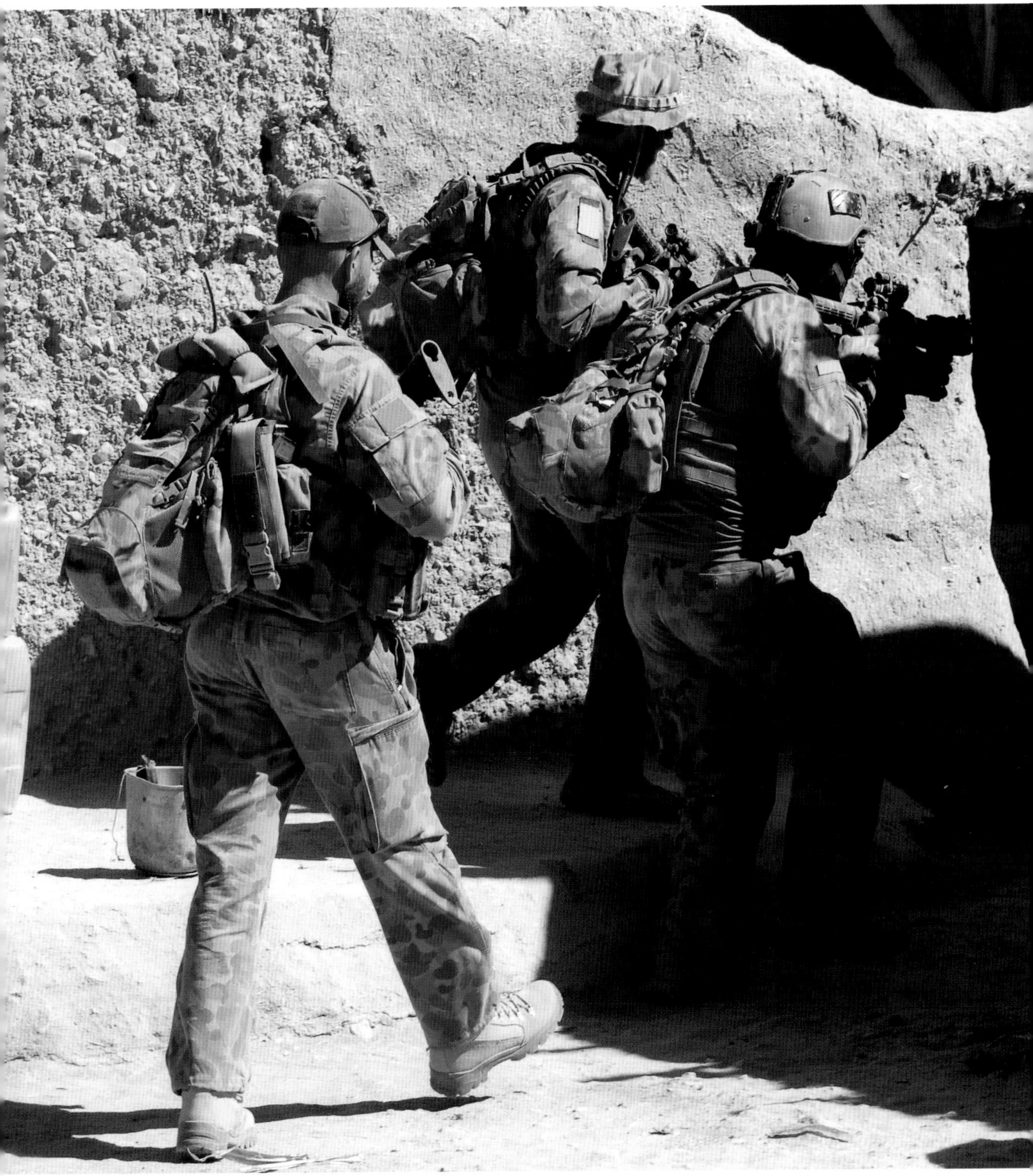

Kandahar, after successful earlier tours in Iraq operating alongside the SEALs. This deployment was under direct US command. They were restricted by no national caveats – the only restriction placed on them was regarding cross-border operations into Pakistan. Along with their Direct Action successes, the Poles were considered very effective in training and mentoring their partnered Afghan National Police units.

UNITED KINGDOM SPECIAL FORCES

UK Special Forces continued to operate both under OEF-A direction and conduct unilateral operations. Known as Task Force 42, the unit was primarily manned by an SBS squadron, supported by teams from the Special Reconnaissance Regiment (SRR) and the Special Forces Support Group (SFSG). From 2005, Afghanistan was largely the preserve of the SBS while their Army counterparts fought in Iraq.

Along with training and mentoring Afghan Provincial Response Companies, Afghan police tactical units that operate jointly with Coalition SOF, Task Force 42 conducted operations in direct support of the British Battle Group deployed to Helmand Province from 2006, and for ISAF SOF Command and operations directly for the Americans in pursuit of high-value targets (detailed in Chapter 6).

A joint Afghan Police and US Army Special Forces patrol prepares to set off. The Green Berets favour the ATVs, with pintle-mounted Mk46 machine guns, as they can go places larger vehicles cannot. By avoiding known trails and tracks, the Special Forces also argue they avoid the majority of IEDs. (Technical Sergeant Carmen A. Cheney; US Air Force)

MOWING THE GRASS

Many of the operations conducted by CJSOTF forces in Afghanistan from 2002 to 2008/9 revolved around seizing munitions and clearing Taliban-controlled villages. Many of these operations were colloquially referred to as "mowing the grass" of insurgents. The use of Improvised Explosive Devices (IEDs) increased as insurgents began to understand they could not challenge ISAF forces in a conventional fight, so the SOF's focus moved toward raiding IED factories or IED facilitators – those who brought in the fertilizer to use in explosives, those who sourced the crude wiring, clocks and timers, and those who built them. By 2008, IED cells had become the new high-value target.

A typical Green Beret raid in this period was explained to the author by a US Army special operator with multiple tours in Afghanistan:

> There would be a couple of trucks of SF with ANA. There may be support elements like Intel types or Psy Op. Sometimes we had Predator [armed UAV] or Spectre [fixed-wing gunship] overwatch. We'd set up a standard perimeter: overwatch (crew served and DM [designated marksman] positions), command and control, casualty collection, a holding/screening area for PUCs [Persons Under Control], and maybe a broadcast position for the Psy Op loudspeaker.
>
> Sometimes the Afghans would just knock but the more fun raids had the 18C [Green

US Army Green Berets return fire against an insurgent sniper position during a joint operation with the Afghan 6th Commando Kandak in Wardak Province. Note the short barrel on his carbine which will limit his fire to only 200m–300m. (Staff Sergeant Kaily Brown; US Army)

The Afghan 8th Commando Kandak conducting a night raid under the mentoring of Western SOF. Note the Afghan Commando carries a US M4 carbine mounting an M203 grenade launcher, ACOG sight and AN/PEQ-2 laser pointer; equipment which is very similar to that carried by American units. (MCCS Robert Fluegel; US DOD)

Beret demolition specialist] putting a water charge on the door and blowing it. Then the Afghans would make entry, sort of a rule about that. The SF guys would follow. After that it was a standard site exploitation and screening of people in the courtyard.

One time we had a raid on a high walled compound in the city with the standard outer courtyard and metal gates. We used the [Mercedes] G Wagens to pull up next to the wall then we put a ladder on top and sent some Afghans and a couple of US over the wall to open the gate, rather daring I thought. On another occasion, the guys were setting up demo (to blow the door) and a bad guy on the roof woke up or somehow saw us coming. He was crawling to the edge of the compound roof over the door with his AK, and as he began to point it down at the entry team, the DM [designated marksman] took him out.

Raids were sometimes accomplished by a helicopter assault force while others were conducted by a ground assault force. Some included both components. An Army special operator who worked numerous raids in Afghanistan explained how a raid in the early years would be accomplished:

A typical team consisted of Army Rangers (10 to 15 with a Lieutenant in charge), one to three OGA [Other Government Agency – CIA] for obvious reasons, two to five Army SF for high level commo [communications], explosives, linguistics et cetera and, depending on the mission, five to eight AMF [Afghan Militia Forces]. We choppered out with the 160th [Special Operations Aviation Regiment] to where the high value target suspect was, made the hit and choppered back or made the hit and called in more Rangers to secure the area [as no AMF were allowed on chopper missions].

Or we took Hilux Toyotas and drove out to the AO [area of operations] without the Rangers (they only rode in HMMWVs but the HMMWVs were too wide to make it down many of the roads in the north). We fattened the teams with SF and/or CAG [Combat Applications Group, more commonly known as Delta Force] guys and more AMF to ensure we had enough guns in these cases.

Sometimes the assault force would be ambushed either on the way to or, more commonly, returning from a raid. A Green Beret commented on his "actions on" in the event of a Taliban ambush: "The Mk19 was used to shock them so we could break contact. The SOP [Standard Operating Procedure] for us was to shock them and get out of the kill zone. Dismounting and engaging was not allowed unless absolutely necessary. There just weren't enough of us to sustain a firefight for long so we got the hell out and called the Rangers on QRF [Quick Reaction Force] or called in a gunship!"

CIA AMBUSH

The CIA's Special Activities Division (SAD) was also heavily involved in the war. A team of SAD officers based at a remote Forward Operating Base in Shkin, just over the border from Pakistan, were among those at the tip of the spear. In October 2003, a team comprised of a former Navy SEAL and a legendary former Delta operator, William 'Chief' Carlson, set out with a force of Afghan militia (the genesis of the CIA's Counterterrorist Pursuit Teams). Their mixed convoy of soft-skinned HMMWVs and Toyota Hilux trucks was three hours into the mission when on a winding mountain trail, they were ambushed.

US Army Rangers from 1st Battalion, 75th Ranger Regiment watch their arcs as a CH-47D Chinook lands to extract them, Ghazni Province, 2012. (Private First Class Pedro Amador; US Army)

RURAL HIGH-VALUE TARGET RAID
SOMEWHERE IN AFGHANISTAN

This illustrative scenario shows how Coalition SOF might conduct a typical raid on a high-value target in a compound in rural Afghanistan. Note however that most such operations are conducted at night to maximize both surprise and the technological advantage in night vision enjoyed by the Coalition units.

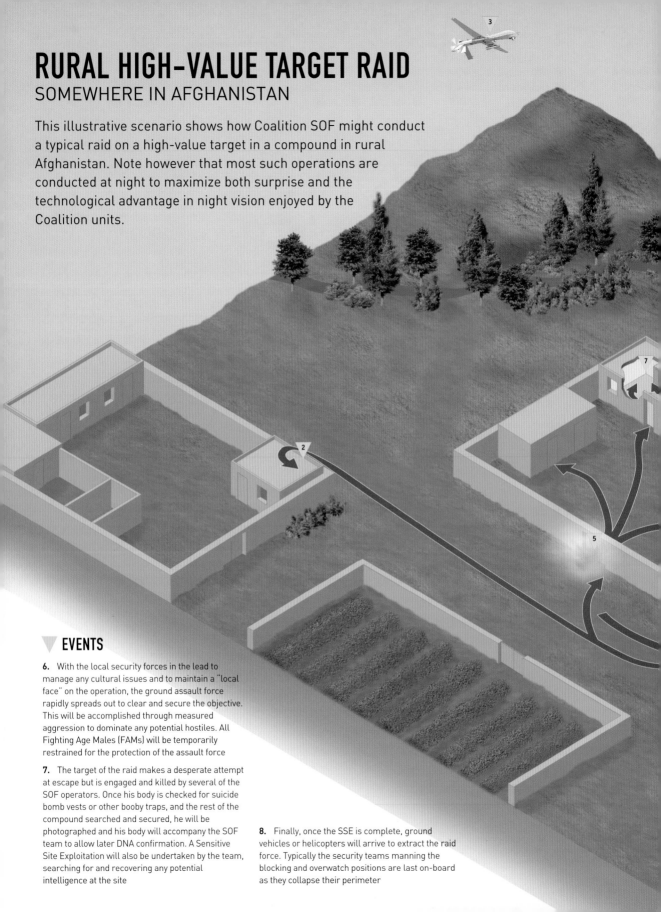

▼ EVENTS

6. With the local security forces in the lead to manage any cultural issues and to maintain a "local face" on the operation, the ground assault force rapidly spreads out to clear and secure the objective. This will be accomplished through measured aggression to dominate any potential hostiles. All Fighting Age Males (FAMs) will be temporarily restrained for the protection of the assault force

7. The target of the raid makes a desperate attempt at escape but is engaged and killed by several of the SOF operators. Once his body is checked for suicide bomb vests or other booby traps, and the rest of the compound searched and secured, he will be photographed and his body will accompany the SOF team to allow later DNA confirmation. A Sensitive Site Exploitation will also be undertaken by the team, searching for and recovering any potential intelligence at the site

8. Finally, once the SSE is complete, ground vehicles or helicopters will arrive to extract the raid force. Typically the security teams manning the blocking and overwatch positions are last on-board as they collapse their perimeter

▼ EVENTS

1. A blocking and overwatch position is established to guard against "squirters" or enemy reinforcement. A machine-gun team commanded by a junior NCO and a Designated Marksman would be deployed here. All members of the security and assault teams will wear intra-team radios allowing constant communication

2. Another security position is established on the northern corner of this compound to guard this side of the target site. It is similarly armed and equipped as the first

3. Orbiting above are both an armed UAV and an MH-60L Direct Action Penetrator, ready to engage any enemy reinforcements or if bunkers or similar strongpoints are encountered. Aerial sniper teams are also commonly employed to act as cut-off groups

4. A C3 (Command, Control and Communications point) has been established here on a compound roof. The C3 group includes the officer commanding the ground assault force, his radio operator, an attached Joint Tactical Air Controller, a Special Forces medic and a two-man security element. The C3 group will coordinate all elements of the ground operation, serve as a casualty collection point and will designate an area where persons under control (detainees) will be held until processed. Human Exploitation or Female Engagement Teams may also be standing by to question the occupants of the target compound

5. The SOF team have breached the compound's main gates with a water charge – a common non-pyrotechnic breaching option. A two-man security element are covering the entry point. Both would carry further Method of Entry (MOE) tools which can be brought forward if required. This was most likely conducted after an interpreter attempted to talk out the HVT via a bullhorn

US Air Force Technical Sergeant Kevin Whalen, a Joint Terminal Attack Controller attached to an Army Special Forces patrol, is sitting next to the Mk19 automatic grenade launcher, in the notorious Gayan Valley in eastern Afghanistan, 2003. Not long after this photograph was taken, his patrol was caught in a well-coordinated ambush. Whalen engaged numerous enemy firing points with the Mk19 until the weapon was disabled by enemy gunfire, being struck no less than six times. While attempting to recover the Mk19, Whalen himself was shot three times; one bullet hit him in the left arm, but the others thankfully hit his body armor plate and his Gerber multi-tool. Dropping down into the GMV to bandage his wound, he reverted to his principal role and called in close air support, which broke the ambush. He refused to be evacuated until other wounded were extracted; he managed orbiting close air support until the patrol was safe. For his actions, Sergeant Whalen was awarded the Silver Star. (US Air Force)

Under fire from RPGs and PKM machine guns, and with one Afghan Toyota immediately disabled by an RPG, Chief Carlson's HMMWV was peppered with fragments from an RPG airburst. The HMMWV was pouring smoke when it was engaged by enemy machine gun fire. Carlson managed to maneuver the truck around so that his passengers, including the former SEAL medic, could exit the vehicle with some cover. Unfortunately in doing so, Carlson exposed himself to machine gun fire and was shot and killed.

The convoy was now separated and a number of Afghans were seriously wounded. The SEAL managed to organize the Afghans into returning fire at the enemy firing points before he ran into the maelstrom to rescue several wounded Afghans. The SEAL, former Lieutenant Mark Donald, then organized the Afghans to break contact with their wounded and extract back several hundred meters in their still operable trucks to a position that offered some cover from the enemy.

A QRF composed of infantry soldiers from the 10th Mountain Division and more Afghan militia, led by another former SEAL SAD officer, Christopher Mueller, soon arrived and joined the fight as Apache attack helicopters swept in to engage enemy positions on the ridgelines. The QRF advanced further up the trail to clear it and allow the wounded to be evacuated, but again contacted the enemy. Their former SEAL commander was sadly killed in the firefight. Eventually, under the cover of Air Force A-10A ground attack aircraft, the combined Afghan/

US force broke contact and withdrew back to Shkin. Except for one man, everyone had been wounded and two were dead. Mark Donald was later awarded the Navy Cross for his actions during the ambush.

OPERATION *RED WINGS*

The SEALs were also rotating through Afghanistan, sometimes co-locating with Special Forces ODAs but often deploying to remote patrol bases to conduct patrolling, intelligence gathering, and limited counterinsurgency among the local inhabitants. They also often conducted operations at the request or in support of conventional ground-holding units. One such operation, now famously retold in both the book and film, *Lone Survivor*, was Operation *Red Wings*.

As part of a larger Marine Corps operation targeting insurgent elements in the Korengal and Matin Valleys in eastern Afghanistan, *Red Wings'* objective was to identify an insurgent commander to allow follow-on forces to kill or capture him. To identify the target, a four-man SEAL reconnaissance element from SEAL Team 10 was inserted into the area. The SEALs' mission was originally going to

Marcus Luttrell, the sole survivor (fourth from left), and the fallen SEALs of Operation *Red Wings* – a mixed unit from SEAL Team 10 and SEAL Delivery Vehicle 1 and 2. All of the men in this photograph, apart from Luttrell, perished either on the ground as part of the initial four-man reconnaissance team or when the QRF helicopter, Turbine 33, was shot down by an insurgent RPG. (US Navy)

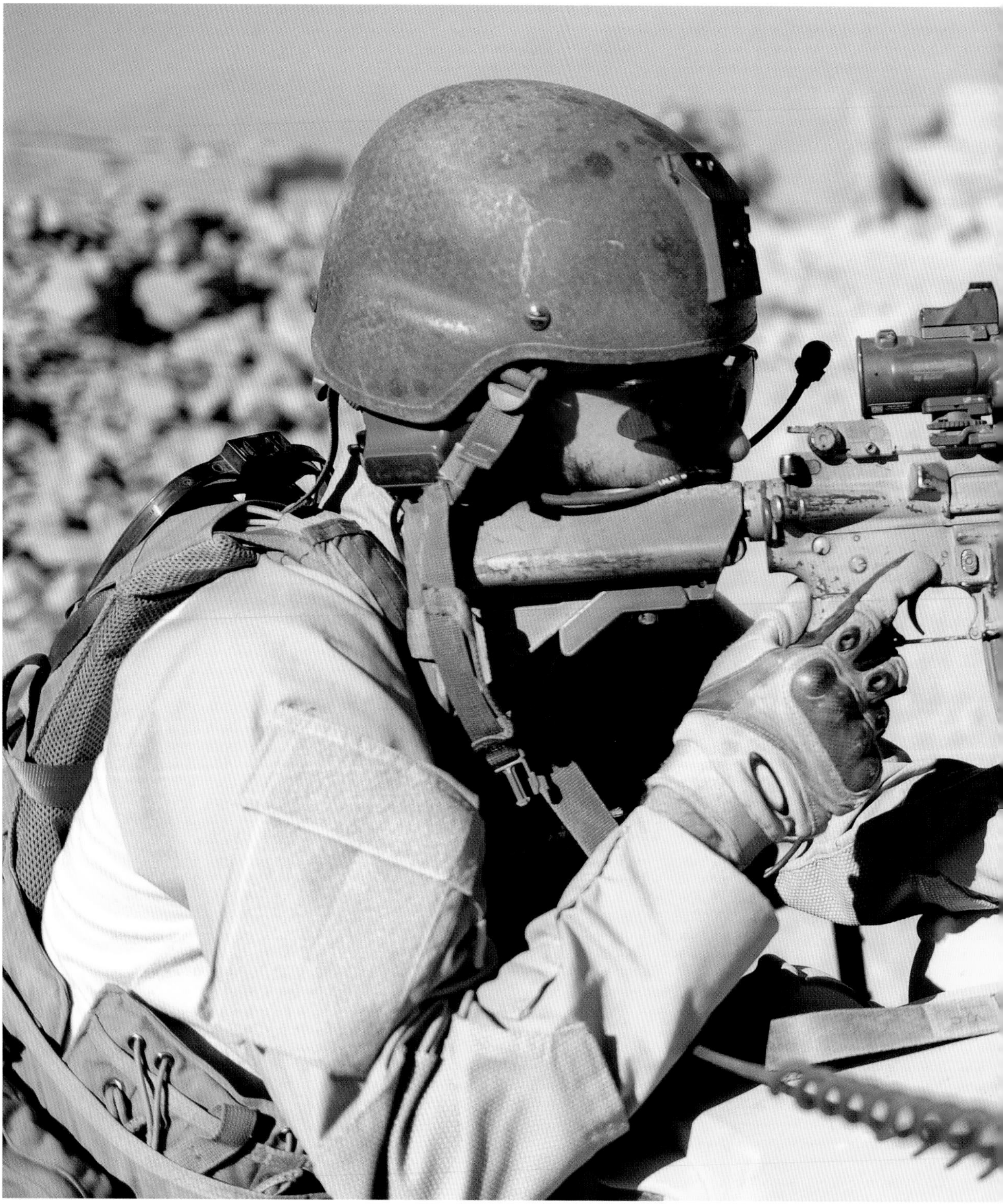

A US Army Green Beret provides overwatch with his M4A1 carbine as a new Afghan Police checkpoint is built. (Staff Sergeant Joseph Swafford; ISAF)

be conducted by the Marines, however, the Marine planners wanted access to 160th SOAR MH-47Es. To receive such access, the mission needed an SOF ground component, so the SEALs were added to the operation.

The team was compromised by an Afghan goat herder almost immediately after it infiltrated into the area, and was soon contacted by a numerically superior force of insurgents. The Navy After Action Report (AAR) mentions 20 to 30 insurgents (the film version indicates more than 50, while the book mentions anywhere between 140 and 200, but the original AAR seems most likely for a number of reasons). A protracted firefight sees the SEALs trying to hold off their attackers who are bracketing them with RPG and PKM machine gun fire.

Carrying only M4 carbines and Mk12 special-purpose rifles, the team was both outnumbered and outgunned. Team leader, Lieutenant Michael Murphy (posthumously awarded the Medal of Honor for his actions), already badly wounded, broke cover in an attempt to get to high ground to call in the SEAL QRF on his satellite phone. The call got through, but Murphy paid for it with his life. Two other members of the team were also killed in the brutal firefight, leaving one remaining SEAL unconscious and knocked down a gulley from an RPG near miss.

The QRF, eight SEALs and eight Army aviators from the 160th SOAR raced to the area in an MH-47E, call sign Turbine 33, arriving at the initial infiltration site only to be caught in an insurgent ambush. An RPG round entered through the open rear ramp as the helicopter descended to land, blowing several operators clear out of the Chinook. The 160th pilots courageously tried to keep the helicopter aloft, but it was a losing battle. The MH-47E plowed into a mountainside and exploded, killing all on board. It was, at that time, the largest single combat loss for US Naval Special Warfare since the Normandy landings. The total has now sadly been eclipsed by the downing of Extortion 17, a CH-47 Chinook, in 2011.

The surviving SEAL managed to evade his pursuers until he was eventually taken in by a sympathetic local villager who cared for his wounds and hid him from the Taliban, an act which put both his and his family's lives in danger. An Army Ranger patrol found him five days later, homing in on the beacon on his PRC-148 emergency radio. A HH-60G Pave Hawk rescue helicopter was brought in by the Rangers to fly the lone survivor to safety.

VILLAGE STABILITY OPERATIONS

In 2008 and 2009 General Stanley McChrystal, now commander of the Afghan theater, began to reorganize and reprioritize SOF in Afghanistan. For the first time, an integrated counterinsurgency initiative, led by the Special Forces, was

implemented. The Combined Joint Special Operations Task Force-Afghanistan (CJSOTF-Afghanistan) was given two key tasks: the Community Defense Initiative which later became the Village Stability Operations (VSO); and Foreign Internal Defense (FID) partnering with Afghan security forces. In broad terms, it meant that the Green Berets were given the focus to concentrate on developing an "Afghan solution" by establishing local police and militias to defend villages from insurgent influence and to train and mentor the Afghan National Army (ANA) to be able to plan and conduct operations on their own without recourse to Western forces.

Direct Action operations were now either Afghan led at the local level or prosecuted by black SOF at the theater level. The focus was firmly back on Unconventional Warfare and Foreign Internal Defense – the bread and butter of Army Special Forces. Given the number of tasks performed by the Green Berets, other SOF were brought in to assist. Chief among these were the SEALs, not traditionally considered an organization that prides itself on the softer skills, and the Marines of the Marine Special Operations Battalions (later renamed in 2014 as the 1st Marine Raider Battalion in honor of their World War II forefathers).

A US Army Special Forces M-ATV (MRAP-All Terrain Vehicle) negotiates a rare paved mountain road during joint operations with Afghan Commandos in Kapisa Province, 2014. The M-ATV was designed as a replacement for the up-armored M1114 HMMWV and as a more agile and manoeuvrable MRAP. This Green Beret version carries a CROWS remote weapon station mounting a .50cal M2 heavy machine gun. (Specialist Connor Mendez; US Army)

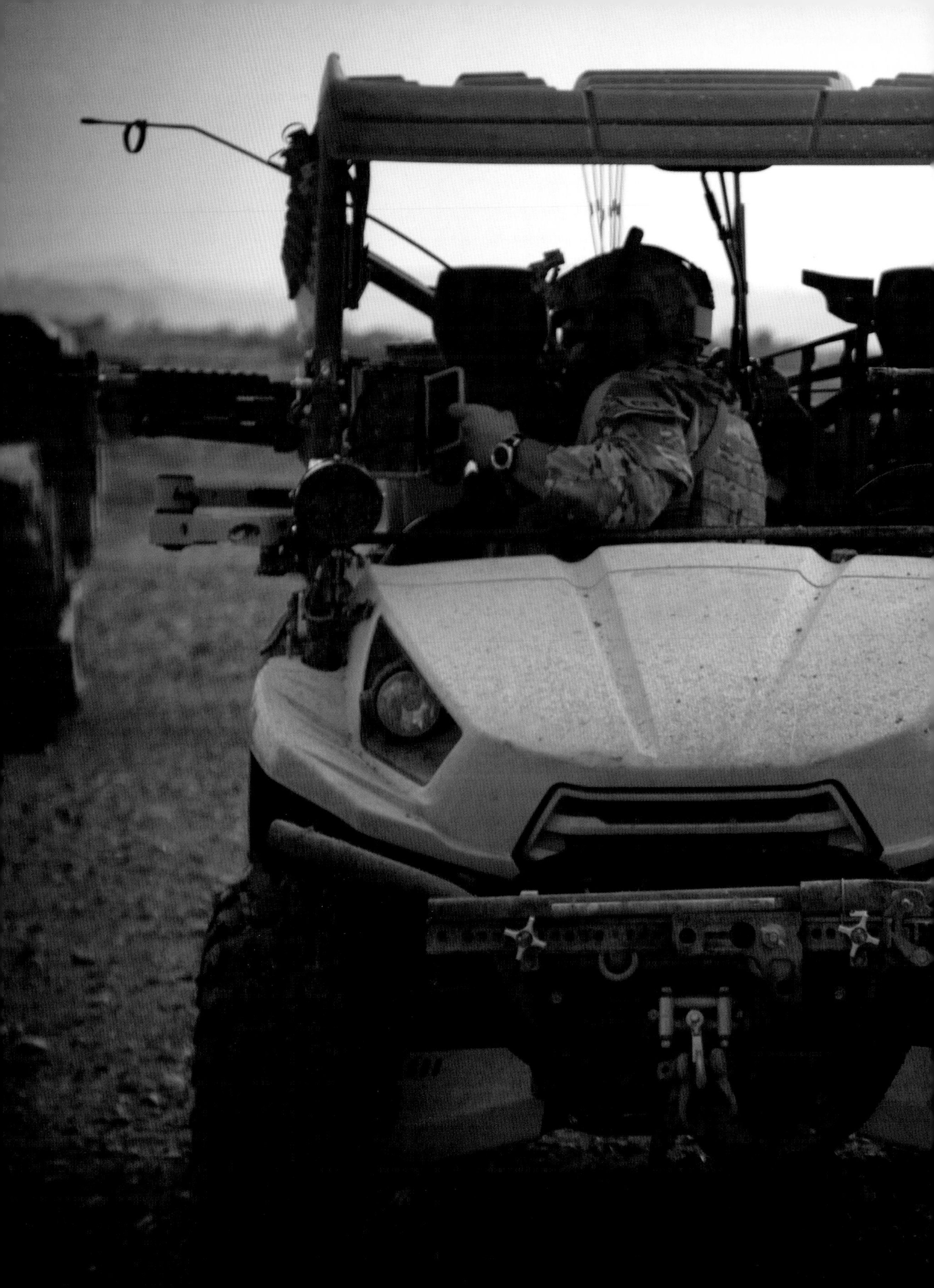

MARSOC Marines of Special Operations Task Force-West engaging Taliban firing points during a patrol halt in Farah Province, 2012. Like the Green Berets, MARSOC has favoured the Kawasaki All-Terrain Vehicles with mounted machine guns for their ability to access even the roughest terrain. Note that the patrol also comprises an M-ATV MRAP (to the right) and an up-armored GMV (just visible to the left). (Sergeant Pete Thibodeau; USMC)

Former SEAL and author Dick Couch explains in his excellent account of the SEALs in the Anbar Province of Iraq, *The Sheriff of Ramadi*, that "Even today, with their numbers on the rise, the Army Special Forces are hard-pressed to keep more than a thousand specialists in Iraq. There are simply too few of them, and Iraq is not the only place where their talents are needed."

Until this re-alignment, most counterinsurgency efforts in Afghanistan were local programs. Larger programs, such as the Afghan Public Protection Program, although initially successful, would inevitably be hampered by corruption and falling standards as programs were handed over to conventional units to manage. Equally, many localized anti-Taliban initiatives often descended into age-old inter-tribal conflicts over land and political influence.

Noted journalist Kevin Maurer in his insightful account of his time embedded with a Green Beret ODA, *Gentlemen Bastards*, explained it succinctly:

> Until the war in Iraq, Special Forces were the military's counterinsurgency experts. They spent years training foreign armies and toppled the Taliban by mentoring Northern Alliance fighters. But in the … years since, Special Forces units have instead focused on raids. Now, with time running out in Afghanistan, Special Forces are once again going back to their roots and have started to focus on training Afghan security forces and building the Afghan government one village at a time.

A pair of Green Berets riding a rather uniquely armed Polaris All-Terrain Vehicle in Jalrez, 2009. The weapon in front of the rider is the Mk47 Stryker automatic grenade launcher, while the operator perched on the back next to the 40mm ammunition box carries the Mk11/SR-25 designated marksman rifle adopted by the regular US Army, in a slightly revised form, as the M110. (Sergeant Teddy Wade; US Army)

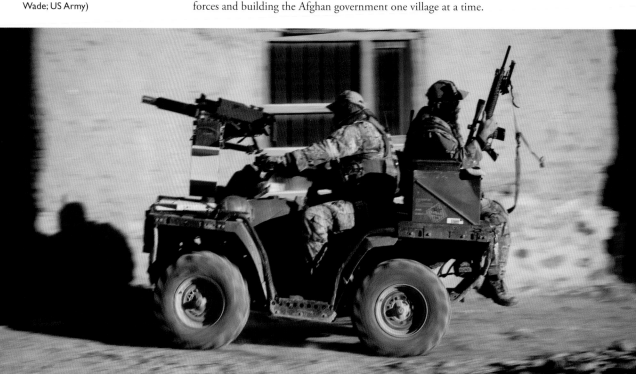

A Green Beret from Special Operations Task Force-South moves to take up a firing position while on a partnered patrol with Afghan Commandos in Kandahar Province, 2011. He wears an Afghan Commando patch on his right shoulder and a Garmin GPS strapped to his right wrist. (Sergeant Ben Watson; US Army)

McChrystal's former deputy from Delta, Brigadier General Scott Miller, deployed to Afghanistan in early 2010 to head up the CJSOTF-Afghanistan. Miller, with McChrystal's support, took the controversial step to assign virtually all SOF in the theater to a new counterinsurgency role. This would become known as the ALP/VSO Program (Afghan Local Police/Village Stability Operations). The only units exempt were certain partnered training teams working with Afghan forces and the JSOC Task Force.

After McChrystal's unfortunate resignation in light of a questionable article by a *Rolling Stone* reporter, General Petraeus took over command of the Afghan theater, continuing the support for the ALP/VSO Program. SOF in Afghanistan was now task-organized into battalion level Special Operations Task Forces (SOTF), each with a geographic area of responsibility. Marine Special Operations Command (MARSOC) would have the west of Afghanistan and Helmand, and with the 1st Special Forces Group, the southwest. The SEALs would have the southeast, while the Green Berets would take the south and the volatile east. Finally the north was assigned to the conventional forces of the 82nd Airborne Division.

Each of these regional SOTFs was given the mission of selecting likely villages within their assigned area for the program. The objective was twofold: one, to push the special operators out into the villages to raise local defense forces, and two, to grow an ever-increasing security zone or bubble around each of the selected towns. The operators would also conduct Civil Affairs projects while training and mentoring the local militia. These projects included road building, the digging of wells, medical clinics and the construction of schools.

The ALP/VSO program was successful in many areas. According to journalist Linda Robinson the initiative passed or failed based on the following factors: the amount of Taliban influence in the targeted village; engaging the correct elders

A joint Afghan Commando and American Special Forces patrol in Nangarhar Province heads out from a patrol base, mounted in a mixture of ATVs, pick-up trucks and MRAP (Mine Resistant Ambush Protected) vehicles, 2010. (Sergeant Patricia Ballou; US Army)

(the British early on in the Helmand campaign aligned themselves with elders whom the majority of the province distrusted and disliked with predictable results); and the nature of the SOF deployment needed to be seen as temporary to ensure the locals would contribute to their own defense rather than rely on the Americans. When these factors came together, and particularly in areas where Afghan Army Special Forces were deployed alongside the Americans, success would often follow.

Some units developed innovative ways to increase security within their areas of responsibility. A SEAL Platoon in the Chora District in Uruzgan Province copied a successful initiative from Baghdad and built a wall constructed of 500m of HESCO barriers to divert insurgent movements away from their assigned VSO village. The wall was a resounding success with the Afghan villagers themselves eventually taking ownership of it. The SEALs and other SOTFs still conducted Direct Action operations, but always now partnered with Afghan forces. These operations were not without losses. The SEALs in Uruzgan conducted a joint operation into the notorious Shah Wali Kot Valley where they suffered the loss of a Black Hawk, which was struck by an insurgent RPG. The crash killed 11, seven US and four Afghans.

The special operators were not immune to the phenomenon of Green on Blue (murders of Coalition Forces by Afghan security force members) attacks either. MARSOC teams suffered several casualties as did a Green Beret ODA in March 2012. Even the partnered forces suffered such incidents, for example in Paktika Province, as journalist Linda Robinson recounted, a "turned" Taliban who had joined the local ALP drugged his colleagues and shot and killed all nine of them. In the majority of partnered situations, with two to three US personnel attached to every 30-man Afghan platoon, there were thankfully few such issues.

ISAF SOF was also heavily involved in the program. Most Coalition Forces trained and deployed with partner units, such as the Australian SASR with their Uruzgan Provincial Response Company. The US Army Rangers, although typically assigned the kill or capture mission, also developed a fledgling national counterterrorist unit known initially, and rather euphemistically, as the Afghan Partner Unit (it was renamed the Kteh Kas meaning Special Force in Dari). The

unit was a JSOC-style command made up of four squadrons with its own intelligence function. The fact that, by the end of 2012, more than three quarters of operations in southern Afghanistan were fully Afghan planned, led, and conducted speaks volumes to the success of the SOF training.

Admiral William McRaven, former head of JSOC and SOCOM explained the importance of the SOF COIN effort in Afghanistan in a 2013 interview: "The preponderance of SOF's efforts in Afghanistan is currently applied toward protecting the population and increasing local capacity through village-stability operations and developing the Afghan Local Police. This includes training Afghan security forces to protect the population and the improvements that have been made in the villages." He further added that Direct Action, kill or capture raids, had a direct relationship to the success of local COIN efforts: "… our lethal operations are valuable and complementary to our VSO/ALP efforts as they create chaos within the enemy's network. This chaos buys the space and time … to support the expansion of VSO/ALP in Afghanistan."

The vast majority of operations was approved and conducted at a local level with only night raids requiring higher clearance – both to allow de-confliction with black SOF and to meet any requirements of the Afghan government, such as

A wonderful image of an Australian SASR mounted patrol in its overnight hide site in Uruzgan Province, 2009. A SASR operator on sentry duty wears night vision goggles while visible in the background are a Perentie LRPV and a Bushmaster Infantry Mobility Vehicle (IMV), suggesting this may be a joint Commando and SASR mission. (L.S. Paul Berry; SOCOMD)

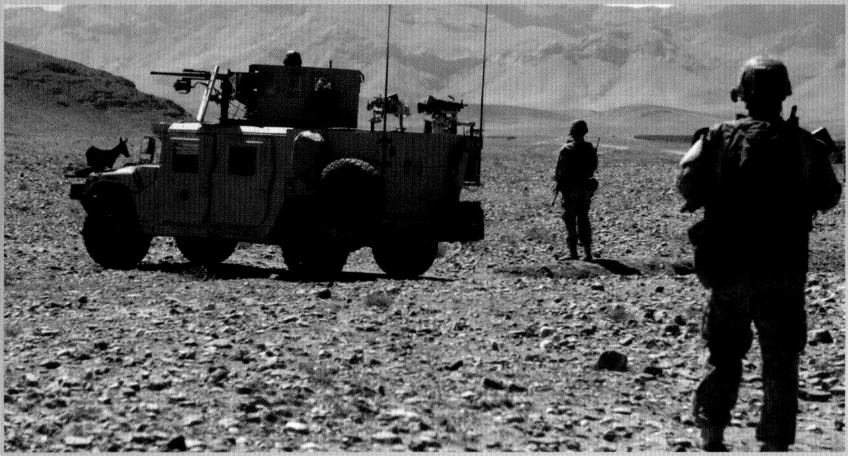
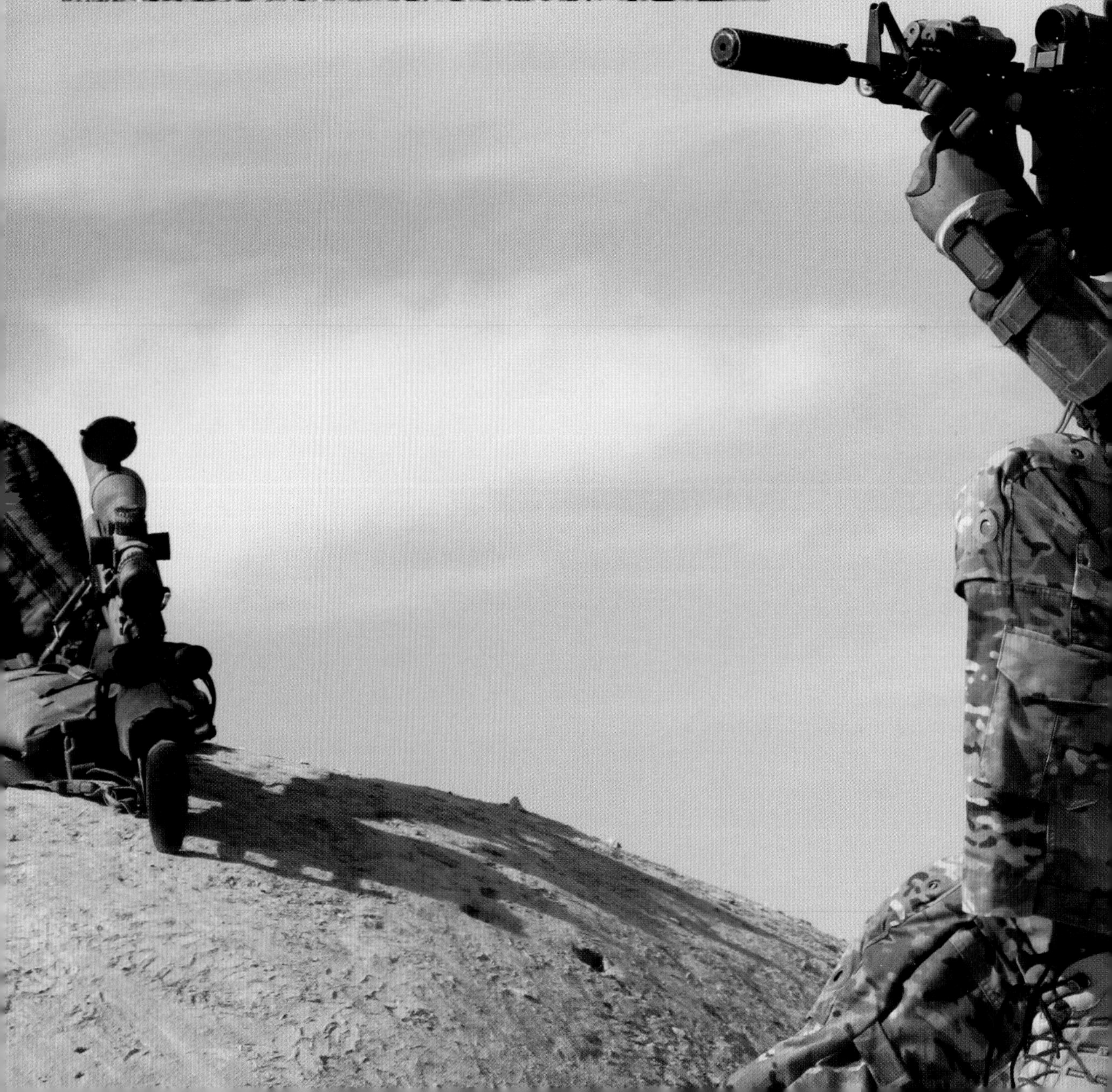

MAIN MARSOC Marines conducting overwatch from an Afghan rooftop. Note the sniper rifle resting nearby for targets beyond the range of their M4A1 carbines. (US SOCOM)

INSET A MARSOC patrol somewhere in Afghanistan, 2010. The up-armored GMV features a .50cal M2 in the O-GPK turret and a pair of M249s on swing arm mounts in the rear bed, unlike the Green Beret version that generally mounts a single M240 in the rear. (Sergeant Brian Kester; US Marines)

MARSOC

The Marine Corps long distrusted elite units and resisted joining the Special Operations Command until almost ten years after its formation. Politically, SOF was the future and that was where the budgets where being allocated. The Marines also saw that they could offer some already finely honed capabilities to the joint command.

Three battalions of Marines make up the core of MARSOC, supported by specialist dog handlers, tactical intelligence and EOD teams. These battalions are divided into four companies, each comprising four Marine Raider Teams. These 14-man Marine Raider Teams (MRTs) are further sub-divided into two seven-man Tactical Elements. The MRTs were designed with the Army's Special Forces in mind – units that could conduct Direct Action and Special Reconnaissance along with possessing the language, teaching and cultural skills to conduct Foreign Internal Defense.

MARSOC's initial deployment to Afghanistan in 2007 was mired in controversy when the unit's Fox Company was sent back to the United States, and its commander was relieved from duty after a shooting that led to as many as 19 civilians killed after the Marines were involved in a complex ambush by insurgents that included a suicide VBIED and small arms fire. It was alleged that the MARSOC Marines killed the civilians while attempting to suppress the enemy firing points.

Since those early days, MARSOC has become a strong partner in SOCOM and proven itself able to conduct full-spectrum special operations. They have successfully conducted both long-term counterinsurgency under the VSO program and carried out complex Direct Action tasks sometimes while trying to bring stability to a village.

the issue of court warrants. The so-called Night Raids had long caused disharmony between ISAF and the Afghan government. President Hamid Karzai, particularly in the latter years of his rule, would often rail against these operations as an affront to the Afghan people. When civilians were inadvertently killed on JSOC raids, and these deaths were still a relatively rare occurrence, Karzai would ramp up the rhetoric for purely domestic political reasons. He needed to tread a very fine line between supporting ISAF and the Americans and being seen to put Afghanistan's needs first.

The Afghan Security Forces training teams accompany their charges out into the field on operations. Sometimes these are partnered operations in which the Western SOF will conduct much of the planning or, increasingly they became Afghan led with Western advisers only along to provide tactical input as required. It was for acts conducted on one such operation in July 2012, in Bagdhis Province, that one MARSOC Gunnery Sergeant was posthumously awarded the Navy Cross, the second highest US award for valor.

A patrol led by Afghan Army Commandos was ambushed by insurgents in the hard cover of a number of buildings. With three Afghans hit by small arms fire, two Marines, Gunnery Sergeants Jonathan Gifford and Daniel Price, raced

A US Navy SEAL wearing the distinctive AOR2 camouflage uniform, assigned to Special Operations Task Force-South East greets village children in Uruzgan Province. (Mass Communication Specialist Third Class James Ginther; US Navy)

forward on an ATV to retrieve the wounded under direct fire from the enemy. Gifford and Price evacuated the wounded to an emergency HLZ from where they could be safely extracted, and then went back to the fight.

Other Afghan Commandos were pinned down by heavy fire, so Gifford and Price led an immediate assault against the enemy positions. During the fierce close-quarter battle, the pair managed to climb on to the roof of an insurgent-occupied building, allowing Gifford post a grenade down the chimney. It was soon after that he and Price were struck and killed by enemy PKM fire. Price was awarded the Silver Star for his actions that day (several years earlier, Price had been awarded the Bronze Star for continuing to man the Mark 19 on his GMV for several hours after the vehicle itself was destroyed in a firefight in Farah Province).

REBUILDING IRAQ

The Combined Joint Special Operations Task Force-Arabian Peninsula (CJSOTF-AP) was established in May 2003 and replaced the two CJSOTFs and the Naval Task Group that had commanded SOF during the invasion. Around 80 percent of SOF assets were rotated out of theater at the conclusion of major combat operations.

A US Army Ranger watches his arc while a CH-47D Chinook lands in the background, Balkh Province, Afghanistan, 2012. (Specialist Stephen Cline; US Army)

An MH-60L Direct Action Penetrator (DAP) from the US Army's 160th Special Operations Aviation Regiment looses off a volley of unguided 70mm Hydra rockets at a distant target. The Hydras are supremely effective, particularly with the anti-personnel fletchette variant, but scatter across a wide area, making them unsafe to use around friendly troops. A laser-guided variant is currently under development. (US SOCOM)

Elements of Task Force 20 remained and transitioned to hunting high-value former Ba'athists under direct JSOC command. Since 2003, the CJSOTF-AP has been based around the 5th and 10th Special Forces Groups, which deploy for seven-month rotations, often supported by elements from a number of other Special Forces Groups. As an indication of numbers, at the height of the Iraqi Surge in 2008, there were some 5,500 United States SOF in-theater including both those assigned to CJSOTF-AP and to the JSOC Task Force.

Much of CJSOTF-AP was focused on the core Special Forces skill set of training and advising local Iraqi forces. These units eventually included the ICTF (Iraqi Counterterrorism Force) developed as a Direct Action national SOF unit akin to Delta Force, and the ISOF (Iraqi Special Operations Forces) that was closer to Rangers, of which there were three battalions raised. The ICTF even had an Operator Training Course based on the Delta model – 90 days with training initially carried out in Jordan, but based in Iraq since 2006. The ICTF conducted several successful complex hostage rescues and was involved in virtually every major operation since Fallujah in 2004.

A retrospective by CWO3 Kevin Wells in the SOCOM journal *Special Warfare* explained the duality of the Foreign Internal Defense (FID) and Unconventional

Warfare (UW) missions for Army Green Berets: "On the surface, UW might seem to be almost the opposite of FID, but the FID mission is enhanced by UW training and mentality. What disrupts and terrifies the insurgent most are other insurgents hunting them, disrupting his plans and turning the populace against him. Large conventional forces ... will not be the insurgents' principal threat; it will be someone who operates in their backyard." In Iraq, Wells states that "Each ODA hit the ground, picked up whatever ISF [Iraqi Security Forces] they could find, simultaneously trained them while developing and prosecuting targets," a process he termed "Combat FID."

An Iraqi Commando from the 9th Regional Commando Battalion, Iraqi Special Operations Forces is mentored in close-quarter battle shooting by Navy SEALs in Anbar Province, 2006. His weapon is an American M4A1 mounting an EO Tech holographic sight. The Commando patch affixed to the top of his helmet is a curious addition – the Velcro attachment point is normally used to affix an infra-red "glint" marker to allow friendly forces to be identified at night from the air. (Sergeant Brandon Pomrenke; US Army)

As part of much-needed wider stability operations in the chaos following the fall of Hussein's regime, the Special Forces began to train local Iraqi forces in what was largely an initially uncoordinated effort to develop some sort of security forces that could assist in stabilizing the country. US forces had been caught at a distinct disadvantage in the immediate post-warfighting aftermath; conventional or unconventional, American and British soldiers were not trained in law enforcement or the type of civil reconstruction that the country desperately needed. The patently ridiculous decision by the Coalition Provisional Authority (CPA) to dissolve the Iraqi military and security apparatus only drove malcontents toward the burgeoning insurgency groups and denied the Iraqi people a police force to maintain order.

Operators from SEAL Team 4 protecting Air Force One on a brief visit to Iraq, 2007. Note the additional armor plating added to the rear cargo area on this SEAL GMV-Navy variant. (Staff Sergeant Cherie A. Thurlby; US Air Force)

The Green Beret-trained Iraqi Counter Terrorist Force conduct a simulated hostage rescue in 2009. Unlike many Iraqi soldiers, these ICTF operators look virtually indistinguishable from Western SOF in both their manner and tactics. Not surprisingly, the ICTF have fought well against Islamic State following the Coalition withdrawal. (Captain Thomas Avilucea; US Army)

The opposition to Coalition Forces began as a mixed bag of what became known as Former Regime Elements (FRE) comprised of Fedayeen Saddam die-hards, Iraqi Army officers, criminal gangs (who later cottoned on to the lucrative market in kidnapping) and disaffected military age males. Ironically, there were no foreign fighters or al-Qaeda elements in Iraq until later in 2003 when they began to filter in from Syria and Iran (apart from those of Ansar al-Islam who had been largely destroyed and routed in Operation *Viking Hammer*).

The stability plan called for the raising of three light Iraqi Army divisions, primarily for external defense. The Iraqi Police, fragmented and poorly supported, were to be the frontline against any insurgency. Police training was often conducted by contractors whose skills and enthusiasm varied. Special Forces ODAs were paired with local Iraqi Police SWAT units to teach them tactical skills. The ICTF began training soon after the end of conventional hostilities. A multi-ethnic force, the ICTF was envisioned as a national counterterrorism unit that could conduct unilateral actions against terrorist threats. The ICTF was under the operational control of CJSOTF-AP until 2006 when command and control for the unit was handed over to the Iraqis under the newly established Iraqi Counterterrorism Service (CTS).

Other Iraqi SOF were established with the assistance of the Green Berets, including an SOCOM-style command. The 1st Iraqi Special Operations Force (ISOF) Brigade would eventually be formed to command the ICTF, the 36th Commando Battalion, Recce Battalion, the Iraqi Special Warfare School and a Support Battalion. Similarly, an Iraqi Police special operations command, the Emergency Response Brigade, was raised from local Iraqi Police SWAT elements and comprised of six SWAT Battalions.

Sectarianism and corruption within both the Iraqi Army and Iraqi Police were still major obstacles. Major Dave Butler of the US Army interviewed one Special Forces officer who stated that "If the target is a Shia, unless he is a low-level guy, they're [the Counter Terrorism Service] not going to action it." Butler also noted the development of a warrant system, similar to the one eventually adopted in Afghanistan after Karzai's protests against Night Raids, which required independent judicial approval aimed at addressing corruption in the targeting process. Unfortunately, the warrant process itself facilitated corruption as targets were turned down for political, tribal or ethnic reasons. It also often comprised operational security with tribal members tipping off targets known to them.

PHANTOM FURY

All manner of United States SOF were involved in the two major offensive operations into the Iraqi city of Fallujah in 2004. Fallujah, always considered something of a dangerous backwater by most urbane Iraqis, was a traditional smuggling route into Syria, Saudi Arabia and Jordan and was ruled by rural tribes, all still keenly loyal to Saddam Hussein. The dictator had always treated Fallujah well, allowing it a kind of semi-autonomy and in response, Fallujahans made up a strong proportion of key positions within Hussein's military and intelligence services. It was also considered a hotspot of Sunni religious conservatism.

The city was largely bypassed during Operation *Iraqi Freedom* and in the immediate post-invasion security vacuum. The city had appointed its own city council after the collapse of Saddam's regime and was not considered a priority by Coalition Forces. Trouble only began when elements of the 82nd Airborne were dispatched to the city at the end of April 2003. The paratroopers took over a primary school as a temporary patrol base. This led to nearly immediate conflict with the civilian population which wanted the school reopened. In still murky

Iraqi Police SWAT, mentored by US Army Special Forces Operational Detachment Alpha 9522, conduct a patrol searching for insurgent weapons caches in western Ninewah, Iraq, 2008. Note the homemade armored cage and gun shield for the PKM on the lead vehicle. (Mass Communication Specialist Second Class Todd Frantom; US Navy)

circumstances, the paratroopers were fired upon by gunmen hiding within the chanting crowd and returned fire, killing 17 demonstrators and wounding a significant number. Adding further fuel to the fire, no US servicemen were wounded in the altercation.

A resulting protest several days later also ended in tragedy when members of an armored cavalry unit returned fire on insurgent gunmen using the crowd for cover and killed three further demonstrators. The fledgling local nationalist insurgents and former Ba'ath Party members were soon whipping up further dissent, which ended in the first US death in the city when a convoy of HMMWVs was ambushed. The situation further degenerated as attacks against American patrols and Iraqi police increased.

Due to its proximity to the "rat-lines" that brought foreign fighters into Iraq, Fallujah had also become a home for al-Qaeda and its leader, the Jordanian former criminal, Abu Musab al Zarqawi. Zarqawi had established links with the local Fallujahan insurgency and his foreign fighters used safe houses within the city for both transiting fighters into Iraq and into other provinces, and as a logistics hub. Their presence fuelled the local insurgency as they passed on skills and equipment, including advice on IED construction.

Zarqawi was already a key high-value target for the JSOC Task Force which had conducted numerous operations into Fallujah in its hunt for him and his lieutenants. It was also believed that foreign hostages taken by Zarqawi's group may have been held in the city (it is now suspected that the decapitation murders of both American journalist Nick Berg and British civil engineer Kenneth Bigley may have been committed in Fallujah). In late March 2004, a Delta Force ground assault force was ambushed as it exfiltrated from a target site in the city with the operators having to use their Pandur armored vehicles for cover against the heavy fire. In the chaos, one of the insurgent detainees had even managed to escape.

Responsibility for Fallujah had been transferred to the US Marines who took a conscious decision to distance themselves from the actions of their Army counterparts in a last-ditch effort to avoid Fallujah falling under insurgent control. They attempted to pay belated recompense for the earlier deaths of the demonstrators and planned to wear Woodland pattern camouflage uniforms and patrol wearing soft caps to differentiate themselves from the 82nd Airborne, but the seeds of the insurgency were already flowering and such efforts were considered too little, too late by much of the civilian population.

The final straw was the ambush and murder of four private military contractors from the Blackwater firm which were escorting a civilian contractor. Apparently dismissing the simmering tensions in the city, the four were ambushed in their unarmored Mitsubishi Pajero SUVs, and their bodies were set alight and grotesquely hung from the Old Bridge, one of two bridges over the Euphrates.

FOREIGN FIGHTER INFILTRATION ROUTES (RATLINES), IRAQ, 2005

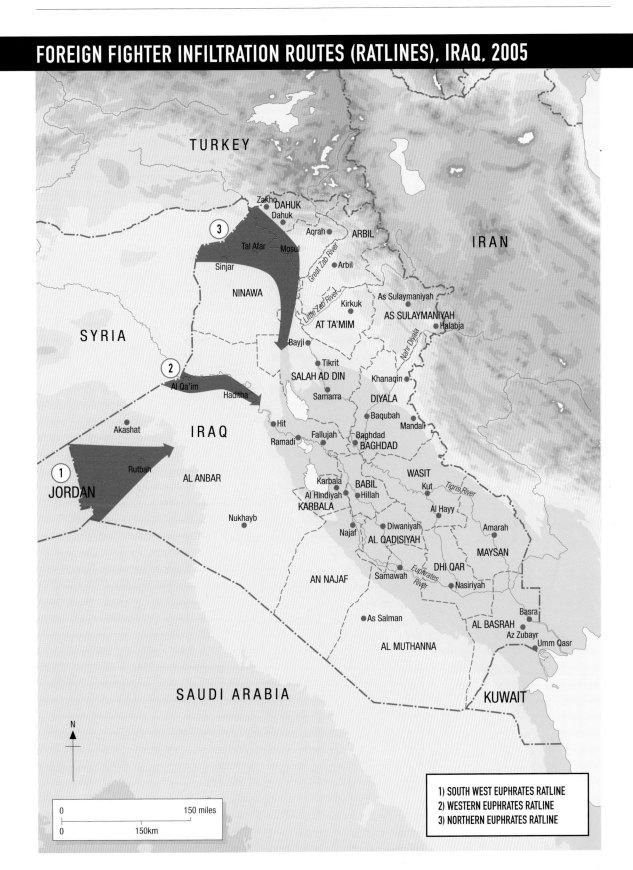

1) SOUTH WEST EUPHRATES RATLINE
2) WESTERN EUPHRATES RATLINE
3) NORTHERN EUPHRATES RATLINE

US Army Special Forces from Special Operations Task Force-West prepare their GMVs prior to an operation in Haditha, 2007. The operators wear a mix of ACU and three-color desert pattern uniforms. (Mass Communication Specialist Second Class Eli J. Medellin; US Navy)

The fact that the murdered contractors were all former members of the Rangers and SEALs added to the sense of outrage, eerily reminiscent of the grisly fate of the bodies of the Delta snipers in Mogadishu, Somalia back in 1993.

An immediate response was required and the Marines were ordered into Fallujah against their better judgement. SOF was quickly brought into the fight. Marine Force Recon led the reconnaissance effort while Delta embedded operators singly or in pairs within the Marine platoons to provide communications, assault, and sniping expertise to the younger, less experienced Marines. The operation known as *Vigilant Resolve* was hastily planned and its consequences were not well considered. It became a rallying cry for insurgents across Iraq and across the Sunni–Shia divide. News media repeated insurgent disinformation that the Marines were shelling mosques (in fact the Marines fired no artillery during the battle), further inflaming passions.

Amid this, both Coalition and Iraqi politicians begged for the offensive to be halted, to which President George W. Bush was eventually forced to agree. The Marines halted offensive operations and planned to extract back out of the city. Security would be handed to an organization known as the Fallujah Brigade – a locally recruited militia that included suspected insurgents. In late April, just prior to the total withdrawal from the city, a small Delta Force element was co-located with a Marine platoon manning a pair of houses they were using as an observation post. The Delta operators were there to instruct the Marines on the use of a new antistructural version of the AT-4 (M136) rocket.

However, the location of the Americans was quickly identified, and soon large numbers of insurgents were arriving in the vicinity. Sniper fire lead to RPG fire as the insurgents probed the American positions. The insurgent grapevine was reporting that this was the beginning of a second offensive into Fallujah instead of just an isolated Marine platoon and several special operators. The RPGs were soon joined by PKM fire and the assaults on the two buildings began from an estimated 300 insurgents.

As Marines went down wounded, a Delta medic, Staff Sergeant Dan Briggs, crossed the street between the houses on no fewer than six separate occasions, exposing himself to withering small arms fire each time he did so to treat badly wounded Marines. Of the 37 men, 25 were eventually wounded and one killed. Two Delta operators, Master Sergeant Don Hollenbaugh and Sergeant Major Larry Boivin, positioned themselves on the rooftop of a three-storey building with a pair of Marines and held back the onslaught until a grenade landed on the roof, seriously wounding the two Marines and Boivin, who already had fragmentation wounds. As the wounded were evacuated, Hollenbaugh was the only one left on the rooftop.

Hollenbaugh ran from position to position, firing rounds at each or pitching grenades down upon his attackers. A heavy machine gun opened up on him at one point, which he suppressed, temporarily at least, with a few well-placed rounds from his M4. Later when the PKM started up again, he fired his last AT-4 rocket at it, which put it out of commission permanently. Hollenbaugh kept the fire up as HMMWVs ferried the wounded out. Eventually, a Marine Captain ran up the stairs and told Hollenbaugh he was the only one left and it was time to leave. The Delta Sergeant had just one magazine left in his rifle.

For their efforts at keeping the young Marines alive, the three Delta operators received decorations: Boivin was awarded the Silver Star while Hollenbaugh and Briggs, the courageous medic, were awarded the Distinguished Service Cross, second only to the Medal of Honor. Tragically, Sergeant Major Boivin died in a freak accident on a railroad crossing in 2012 back in the United States after retiring from Delta.

Delta and the JSOC Task Force continued to hunt Zarqawi and his lieutenants in the interim period between Operation *Vigilant Resolve* and what would become known as Operation *Phantom Fury* (or al-Fajr in Arabic meaning New Dawn) beginning in October 2004. The Task Force was prosecuting a target every few days within the city, mainly via precision air strikes as the risk to ground assault forces was often too high to contemplate. The insurgents in Fallujah knew that a Coalition assault was inevitable, and under the guidance of the influx of foreign fighters, began to build defensive networks throughout the city.

Three veteran Delta operators including Master Sergeant Don Hollenbaugh and the late Sergeant Major Larry Boivin (and an unidentified Marine) pictured on a Fallujah rooftop in 2004 just before the battle that would earn Hollenbaugh the Distinguished Service Cross, second only to the Medal of Honor; and the late Sergeant Major Boivin the Silver Star. (Photographer unknown)

An exceedingly rare shot of Delta operators in combat on a rooftop in Fallujah. The operator firing the AT-4 (M136) is probably the late Sergeant Major Boivin while the operator in the foreground is probably Master Sergeant Don Hollenbaugh. The operators and a small unit of Marines were surrounded by upwards of 300 insurgents during the April 2004 battle. (Photographer unknown)

SOF Weapons

Special operators have always used the weapons best suited for their particular needs; from the De Lisle suppressed carbines and FP-45 Liberator pistols of World War II through to today's custom-built rifles. It is perhaps surprising then that the most common SOF weapon is also on general issue to much of the United States military – the M4 carbine.

The M4, or its selective fire version the M4A1, is carried by all branches of SOCOM and many Coalition Forces such as SASR, the French COS and the New Zealand SAS. The British use a Canadian version of the same weapon, the Diemaco C8. Even Delta Force and DEVGRU use a weapon based on the M4 – the Heckler & Koch 416 – essentially a piston-driven enhancement of the M4.

The carbine has evolved with the addition of ultra short barrels for CQB (close quarters battle), a range of electronic sights and devices that emit both invisible infra-red and visible laser beams. Many operators also mount grenade launchers such as the 40mm M320 on to the carbine. Some units, such as DEVGRU, still use the aging M79, although often shortened to resemble an over-large pistol.

In a similar way to 5.56mm carbines, most units also use the same submachine guns (SMGs) namely Heckler & Koch MP5s and MP7s – most often equipped with sound suppressors and used for CQB situations. SMGs were once a distinctive tool of SOF, but with the advent of compact 5.56mm carbines and specialist ammunition that can account for the loss in terminal effect of a rifle round being fired from such a short barrel, SMGs now see relatively rare use. Suppressed and in an urban environment, DEVGRU SEALs still swear by their MP7A1s.

Pistols too are remarkably similar, with the field dominated by Glocks and SIG Sauers. Three calibres also dominate: the traditional 9mm, the emergent .40 and the .45. The .40 was first used by Delta in Iraq as operators discovered their custom .45s were not coping well with the fine Iraqi sand. Field trials found the Glock performed flawlessly despite the environment, so most of the unit transitioned to Glocks. Many Green Berets also carried Glock 19s in preference to their elderly issue Berettas.

A US Air Force Combat Controller from the 321st Special Tactics Squadron, attached to an Army Green Beret ODA, provides aerial overwatch from a Blackhawk with his 5.56mm Mk12 Special Purpose Rifle. Note his locally produced team patch – Task Force Kapisa, named for the Afghan province he operated in. The patch features the ubiquitous Punisher skull and not clearly visible in the photograph, the number of the ODA he is attached to – ODA 0115 in this case. (Technical Sergeant Kevin Wallace; US Air Force)

These ranged from fortified buildings, trench lines and berms to hinder armored vehicles, strategically placed car bombs, and 'daisy chained' IEDs, some buried under paved roads that the insurgents resealed with bitumen to disguise their presence. The insurgents also began wiring certain houses in the city with massive IEDs with martyrs prepared to act as bait to draw in US troops and then detonate the building around them.

SEALs conducting reconnaissance near the berms tested out reports that the insurgents were equipped with night vision by throwing an infra-red chemical light out into the street which immediately drew small arms fire, proving that at least some of their adversaries were equipped with some form of night vision. It also later became clear that the foreign fighters included experienced Chechens who wore older US chocolate chip-patterned fatigues in an effort to disguise themselves as Iraqi Army. Liquid amphetamines were also discovered in many of the insurgent positions and stories emerged of drugged insurgents taking huge amounts of firepower to kill.

The final Marine Corps threat assessment prior to the launch of *Phantom Fury* documented some "three hundred and six well-constructed defensive positions ... many of which were laced with improvised explosive devices (IEDs)" within the city. "Intelligence also identified 33 of 72 mosques in Fallujah being used by insurgents to conduct meetings, store weapons and ammunition, interrogate and torture kidnap victims, and conduct illegal Sharia court sessions."

JSOC elements, SEALs, the 5th Special Forces Group and Marine Force Recon were heavily involved in shaping operations prior to the November 7 D-Day when Coalition conventional forces fought their way into the city. The SOF shaping operations included sophisticated feints conducted with the Marines aimed at keeping the insurgents in the dark as to the direction of the final assault; close-target reconnaissance to develop the clearest possible picture of insurgent strengths and direct-action missions where a logistics node or IED factory was targeted. Finally, on the night of November 7, the berms were breached and Coalition Forces entered the city.

TOP A mixed Polish GROM and US Army Special Forces patrol engage insurgents during Operation *Jackal* in Diwaniyah, Iraq, 2007. (Sergeant Rob Summitt; US Army)

ABOVE Polish GROM and Green Berets use a GMV as cover as they advance on an insurgent position in Diwaniyah, Iraq, 2007. Note this GMV has been fitted with a FRAG up-armor kit and had extra armor plate and ballistic glass added to the cargo area for urban combat. (Sergeant Rob Summitt; US Army)

Attached to many of the Marines companies were SEAL sniper teams, mainly from SEAL Teams 3, 5, and 10. As one Marine Lieutenant Colonel explained:

> We had done the same thing down in Najaf and it worked really well in Fallujah as well. These sniper teams come with a real good capability because they're all Joint Tactical Air Controller (JTAC) qualified and can call fires also. So we put them with our companies and when we got to a key piece of terrain – an extra tall building or a real good field of fire – we'd dismount them and put them in there. We'd use that cover to get them into position and secure them. We'd give them Quick Reaction Force (QRF) capability, so if they had to break contact, they could get back to you.

Among those SEAL sniper teams was the legendary Chris Kyle of *American Sniper* fame. Kyle was fast on his way to achieving the most sniper kills of any serving sniper in the US military and added to his count in Fallujah by 19. (Kyle recorded 160 confirmed kills from the total of 255 kills he personally claimed before he retired from the Navy. He was tragically murdered in the United States in 2013.) Kyle and the other SEALs operated in small teams of two snipers and two observers along with a security element.

Operators from Delta and the Green Berets of the 5th Special Forces were also parcelled out in small teams, most comprising just three or four operators, to embed with Marine and Army infantry units. These teams followed the earlier model established during Operation *Vigilant Resolve* by providing advanced communications, sniping and assault experience and mentoring to the soldiers and Marines fighting house to house through the city. Force Recon Marines had infiltrated into the city to establish hide sites several days before operations began to call in artillery fire missions and airstrikes. Fallujah was also one of the first battles involving the Marines of the recently raised Detachment One of MARSOC.

SEALS IN IRAQ

Following the invasion, SEAL platoons rotated through Iraq, conducting overwatch for US and Iraqi patrols and directly mentoring local Iraqi forces. They also conducted surveillance and sniping missions into known trouble spots. In September 2004, a SEAL sniper element was tasked with establishing an overwatch and surveillance position overlooking the notorious Haifa Street in Baghdad. Using a technique first pioneered by the British SAS in Northern Ireland, they secreted themselves within a battalion-sized mechanized unit that would actually deliver them to their location. The idea was that while everyone concentrated on the conventional forces in their Bradley IFVs, the snipers could unobtrusively enter a nearby building and establish its hide site.

On this particular occasion, it didn't quite pan out as planned. Within minutes of the Bradleys moving off, the SEALs were contacted. Someone had seen them enter the building and word was spreading of their presence. The SEALs notified the 9th Cavalry unit that had inserted them and began firing back. The Bradleys turned around and drove back to the hide location. The Cavalry troopers had only just arrived and established security around their vehicles when a

civilian car sped around the corner and crashed into the rear of a Bradley, detonating in a massive explosion. One soldier received the Silver Star for climbing into the Bradley to assist his comrades. Remarkably, there were no casualties and the SEALs extracted under the cover of the other Bradleys.

Navy SEALs mentoring Iraqi Army Scouts in Fallujah in 2007. (Mass Communication Specialist Second Class Eli J. Medellin; US Navy)

From 2005, the SEALs were heavily committed in the west of Iraq in Anbar Province. There are two major cities in Anbar: Fallujah and Ramadi. While the situation in Fallujah had forced two large-scale offensives to win back the city, the Marines also had their hands full in Ramadi. Already a major trouble spot, the city descended into further chaos as AQI (Al Qaeda in Iraq) fighters vacating Fallujah escaped to Ramadi. A SEAL Task Unit was co-located with the Marines

Iraqi Army Scouts trained by Navy SEALs conduct live fire close-quarter battle training in 2008. He wears the older US three-color desert pattern uniform, and just visible is a skull bandana covering his face (another common SEAL affectation). His compatriots both wear masks – a common practice as the soldiers' families were often targeted for retribution by insurgents. (Sergeant Daniel T. West; US Army)

at Al-Asad Air Base and pushed out elements into Ramadi and Habbaniyah. The SEALs were initially tasked with developing targeting for the Marines and providing sniper overwatch for their patrols. The SEALs were already training an Iraqi Army Unit in Habbaniyah, although Foreign Internal Defense was their main focus until later that year.

A SEAL Task Unit generally comprised two individual SEAL Platoons. Each Platoon was made up of a pair of seven-man Squad elements commanded by a Junior Officer. Three of these Task Units (although a fourth is often added) along with a Special Boat Team detachment and a Headquarters Team made up a Naval Special Warfare Squadron. The Headquarters Team included integral intelligence, targeting and EOD personnel.

According to veteran SEAL and author Dick Couch, when the SEALs began FID in earnest it was with two Iraqi units – the Army Scouts who conducted conventional reconnaissance missions, and the Special Missions Platoon (SMP), a locally formed unit that would later fight alongside the SEALs. The training focussed on basic infantry skills such as patrolling and small unit tactics. The SEALs shied away from advanced topics such as sniping and counter-IED techniques as the ultimate loyalty of their charges could never be fully known. Along with low baseline skills, the SEALs struggled with the lack of a strong NCO class within the Iraqi military and officers who were often little more than political appointees.

A SEAL Lieutenant in Iraq quoted by Couch commented on the SEALs' initial feelings toward the training mission:

[the SEALs had] a mind-set on the part of the operators that if it wasn't DA, or direct action, it wasn't worth doing. When we were assigned to training duty, it led to a big mismatch between the expectation and the reality. Yet there it was; we were trainers. And if we were going to get into the battlespace, it would be with the Iraqis we trained. Once that sunk in, the guys became a little more diligent about their training responsibilities.

Despite these challenges, the SEALs were soon conducting joint operations with both partnered units. A Special Reconnaissance mission for example, would be manned by a team of two Americans and eight Iraqis. In the early days they would focus on the surveillance portion of the mission and use conventional US Army or Marine units to conduct the raids and arrests. As the SEALs were beginning to make headway in Ramadi, AQI was starting to infiltrate the area by targeting local Sheikhs and convincing them to allow the jihadists to marry into the local tribes, thus cementing their powerbase. As a result, Sheikhs that resisted these advances were met with typical al-Qaeda brutality: they were beheaded and their bodies dumped in their communities. Al-Qaeda's efforts to install a Sharia-style local shadow government in Ramadi, much like those presided over by the Taliban in disputed provinces in Afghanistan, would later lead to AQI's downfall.

During the first half of 2006, the SEALs increasingly partnered with the conventional forces of the 1st Brigade Combat Team of the 1st Armored Division which was planning a large-scale conventional offensive in Ramadi. The SEALs,

along with the Scouts and the SMP, would conduct reconnaissance, surveillance, and sniper overwatch tasks. With their own targeting cell, they also began raids on local insurgent leaders. When the 1st Brigade Combat Team began the concerted offensive to clear Ramadi of AQI fighters, some 1,100 insurgents were eventually killed, a third by attached SEAL snipers.

During this time, two SEAL operators were killed in action – their first losses in Ramadi. Petty Officer Mike Monsoor died after leaping upon an enemy

SEALs from SEAL Team 10 kit up for an operation targeting an al-Qaeda foreign fighter cell in Fallujah, Iraq, 2007. Note the frog emblem painted on the rear of the left operator's body armor – a common SEAL affectation along with the ever popular Punisher skull. (Mass Communication Specialist Second Class Eli J. Medellin; US Navy)

US Navy SEAL PO2 Michael A. Monsoor, pictured here carrying the Mk46 SAW during a patrol in Ramadi. Monsoor died after throwing himself upon an enemy grenade, saving his team mates – an act for which he was posthumously awarded the Medal of Honor. (US Navy)

grenade during a rooftop firefight. Two of his fellow SEALs were badly wounded from the grenade fragments and their Iraqi Scouts routed and ran back into the cover of the building. The fourth SEAL, only slightly wounded, managed to radio to his colleagues and get the reluctant Scouts to return fire. A SEAL element in a second overwatch position immediately ran through a fusillade of fire to reach the dying Monsoor and his team mates. A Bradley IFV evacuated the wounded SEALs, but Monsoor was sadly beyond help. Along with a Silver Star he had received for rescuing a wounded SEAL in an earlier battle in the city, he was also awarded the Medal of Honor.

The advances made by conventional forces and the SEALs in Ramadi, combined with the brutal tactics of AQI, helped to increase recruitment in a local police initiative. The program was designed to bring the local Sheikhs' militias into the fold as uniformed Iraqi Security Forces, and volunteers from these would serve locally in their communities to defend them against al-Qaeda. The Sheikhs also received generous grants and opportunities for US contracts to entice them to join. The kidnapping and murder of Sheikh Khalid in August 2006 proved to be the tipping point. A month later the Sheikhs signed a declaration agreeing to fight AQI and by the close of 2006, even former insurgents were joining the fledgling local police. What would later become known as the "Anbar Awakening" had begun.

In neighbouring Fallujah, the SEAL Task Unit were also heavily involved in the fight. One joint operation to capture an AQI leader resulted in the first Iraqi Scout through the door being killed. The SEAL with him was severely wounded. The next two SEALs in the stack returned fire and immediately made entry, one going left and one going right. In the left-hand room, Senior Chief Matt Dale ran into three insurgents who opened fire at point-blank range, his SEAL team mate across the hall was struck in the head by one of their AK rounds and was killed instantly. Another round had taken the top off Dale's thumb and smashed his Mk18 carbine. The operator immediately transitioned to his SIG Sauer P226 pistol and engaged the insurgents. Senior Chief Dale was struck an incredible 27 times – 11 being stopped by the ceramic trauma plates in his vest. He fired until his P226 was empty and all three insurgents were dead. Senior Chief Dale made a complete recovery and returned to service with the SEALs.

STATUS OF FORCE

Army Special Forces eventually became more focused on Direct Action once again as General McChrystal's methods with his JSOC Task Force were apparently working. He pushed for, and received, greater integration of white SOF into his Task Force operations. Additionally he raised Task Force 17; a Counter Iranian

Influence SOF unit comprised principally of Army Special Forces ODAs and initially commanded by a Green Beret officer (until clashes for resources resulted in his replacement with an officer from Delta). The Green Berets' mentoring success with ISOF meant that their days of traditional counterinsurgency in Iraq were numbered as they became embedded with ISOF units, living alongside and accompanying them on missions – practically forming hybrid Iraqi–US special operations teams. Army Special Forces continued to operate alongside their Iraqi counterparts until the end of the Status of Forces Agreement and the final withdrawal of American forces from Iraq.

OPERATION *ENDURING FREEDOM–PHILIPPINES*

Since the beginning of the Global War on Terror, there has been another, much lesser-known, operation. Operation *Enduring Freedom-Philippines* (OEF-P), as its name suggests, was set up to combat terrorism in the Philippines. The country has suffered a long-term Islamic insurgency in Mindanao with the Moro National Liberation Front. The Moros maintained training camps that hosted a large number of jihadists throughout the 1980s who were intent on joining the jihad in Afghanistan. This contact with the Afghan Arabs resulted in links being forged with individuals who would later become key players in al-Qaeda.

Operators from Marine Special Operations Command conduct small arms training as part of Foreign Internal Defence assistance to the Philippines Army as part of Operation *Enduring Freedom-Philippines*. (Mass Communication Specialist First Class Troy Latham; US Navy)

A Special Boat Team fast boat operating in support of SEALs deployed as part of Operation *Enduring Freedom-Philippines*. The boats carry a fearsome amount of firepower including multiple twin M240 machine guns and an M134 minigun. These boats featured in the recent Hollywood movie, *Act of Valor*.

Two terrorist groups were formed, initially from jihadists who had returned from the Soviet–Afghan War: the Abu Sayyaf Group (ASG), and Jemaah Islamiyah (JI). Both organizations began conducting terrorist attacks across the region against Western and Asian targets. After the events of 9/11, and the activities of Khalid Sheikh Mohammad and JI, the United States extended an offer of military support to the Philippine government, which was gratefully accepted.

OEF-P was established in 2002 to conduct what one SOCOM history terms "full spectrum embedding and engagement." In more direct terms, OEF-P has focused on long-term partnered operations with both Philippine police and Army special operations and intelligence units. OEF-P has also offered professional development to these local units, particularly the skills necessary to counter ASG and JI, which included training helicopter aircrew to fly using night-vision goggles, tactical intelligence gathering and exploitation and close quarter battle skills.

Much of the work has fallen on the shoulders of the US Army Green Berets and specifically the 1st Special Forces Group. The SEALs and US Air Force Special

Operations have also had a long-term presence in the Philippines (the Philippine Air Force has developed the capability to drop guided munitions from their aging OV-10 ground attack aircraft thanks to the CIA's SAD Air Branch and the USAF). All American SOFs now operate under the Joint Special Operations Task Force-Philippines in a similar fashion to their organization in Afghanistan or the Horn of Africa. Along with mentoring and joint exercises, the Special Forces also conduct numerous counterinsurgency activities such as medical clinics in outlying villages to counterterrorist propaganda efforts.

Operationally, there are few confirmed details about the Green Berets and SEALs conducting partnered operations, although elements from both units are partnered with the Philippine Army and Police SOF. Rumors have abounded for years about Australian SASR involvement in direct-action missions, but sadly these have never been substantiated. One particular rumor mentions a SASR Troop conducting partnered operations to hunt two of the terrorists responsible for the Bali nightclub bombings.

Officially, the special operations task force "does not engage in combat operations and does not operate from independent locations." They must at all times be accompanied by local SOF and only defensive fire is permitted, and only then under extreme conditions. Another rumor concerns the hostage rescue of an American missionary couple kidnapped by Abu Sayyaf. The bungled rescue attempt in June 2002, in which one of the missionaries and another hostage were killed in the cross-fire, was carried out by a local paramilitary force rather than any of the Philippine SOF units. Also standing by, according to rumor, was Gold Squadron of DEVGRU which was forward deployed to either assist the local SOF or carry out the operation unilaterally if required. If true, it was unfortunate the SEALs weren't given the go-ahead.

One Green Beret was killed in a terrorist bombing in the southern city of Zamboanga and there have been mentions of wounded Special Forces and SEALs over the years, which would indicate they sometimes get close to the action. One operation which did see foreign involvement was the ambush of Abu Sabaya, the leader of the Abu Sayyaf gang that seized the American hostages. Soon after the bungled rescue, US ISR assets located the terrorist leader. The Philippine Naval Special Operations Group, supported by US Navy SEALs in high-speed RIBs (rigid inflatable boats) were waiting for him.

An American Predator UAV had "lased" the target as he tried to escape in a smuggler's boat; marking the target for the Philippine special operators (the infra-red laser is only visible through night-vision goggles). US Army Nightstalker MH-47Es were also involved in the operation, using searchlights mounted on the helicopters to pinpoint the target's boat while the Philippine operators opened fire. The terrorist leader was killed, and four other terrorists were captured with him.

CHAPTER 5
INDUSTRIAL COUNTERTERRORISM
HUNTING AL-QAEDA IN IRAQ 2003–2012

"A lot of guys obviously hate the place. But in the early mornings when the sun came up, the temperature got just right and the sky looked lovely… I can't tell you about the people. My only interactions with them is in their house at 2AM, usually scared shitless" US Army Ranger, Iraq.

Since the invasion of Iraq, JSOC's Task Force 20 progressed through a large number of designation changes as its designation at the time became too well known and was published by the media. There were initially two distinct but related task forces operating in both Afghanistan and Iraq: Task Force 5 (formerly Task Force 11) and Task Force 20 respectively. They were amalgamated in July 2003 and renamed Task Force 21, later renamed Task Force 121.

The task force names lasted anywhere from a few months to a year or more. Task Force 121 became Task Force 6-26, Task Force 145 became Task Force 88. In CENTCOM media briefings that sometimes announced the results of Task Force operations, their involvement was disguised and they were obliquely referred to as "OCF" or "Other Coalition Forces." Conventional forces in Iraq, and even other SOF, knew them simply as the enigmatic "Task Force."

The Task Force's headquarters and support teams were initially based at Baghdad International Airport (BIAP) in a location known as Camp Nama before relocating to the airbase at Balad's Camp Anaconda. The operational components were deployed in four distinct geographically based elements (a fifth was added in February 2006 and known as Task Force East); all were manned by US Army and US Navy SOF units apart from one.

Task Force Central was structured around a Delta Force squadron with a platoon of Rangers as both a force protection and a reaction force, and was based in central Baghdad. Task Force West was comprised of a DEVGRU SEAL squadron and was once again supported by a reinforced Ranger platoon, based in

A rare shot of British Special Forces Support Group (SFSG) operators, c. 2006. The SFSG conducted both Direct Action missions and training of local security forces. They wear the then unusual Crye MultiCam pattern uniforms and carry a mix of L85A2 assault rifles, modified L110A2 Minimi Para light machine guns and suppressed H&K 417 marksman rifles. Soon after the L85A2s were replaced by Diemaco C8 carbines in line with other British Special Forces. (Photographer unknown)

Tikrit. Task Force North was Ranger led with a small Delta outstation and based out of the northern city of Mosul. All of the geographic task forces were supported by the Nightstalker helicopter crews of the 160th SOAR.

The sole non-US element was Task Force Black which was comprised of a rotational British SAS Sabre squadron and a platoon of paratroopers from the Special Forces Support Group (SFSG, also known as Task Force Maroon). A small team from the Joint Support Group (JSG) operated alongside them – the highly secretive JSG ran a human intelligence

Unidentified US Special Operations Forces, most likely Green Berets, on an operation in Iraq. Intriguingly, note the undercover operator behind them. (Photographer unknown)

network for the Special Forces, along with tasking a group of local nationals known as the Apostles (as there were initially 12 of them) who were trained by the JSG and the SAS in surveillance and urban reconnaissance techniques. The Apostles could reconnoiter locations that even the specialists from the JSG or Special Reconnaissance Regiment (SRR) could only dream of.

The UK Special Forces presence was headquartered right next door to Delta in Baghdad in a building referred to as the Station House (to make commuting between the two units even easier, a wall was knocked down between the Delta and SAS compounds). The Task Force Central location where the SAS was based was code-named Mission Support Site (MSS) Fernandez after the fallen Delta Master Sergeant who had been killed on operations near Tikrit with Task Force Wolverine. The helicopters of 160th SOAR could land on an improvised landing pad located at the front of the mansions to pick up the assault teams for their nightly raids.

Although they were often shuttled to their targets by American 160th SOAR helicopters, the SAS were supported by RAF Special Forces Flight Chinooks and Army Air Corps 657 Squadron flying the versatile Lynx helicopter. Later in the campaign the SAS would receive support from the RAF's Puma fleet.

The American units working for the JSOC Task Force generally served three-month rotations because of the extremely high tempo and hazardous nature of their operations; as explained by a Ranger who served several tours with the Task Force: "I don't know what the regular grunts are doing on a daily basis, but definitely doing what we do for twelve months straight would get exhausting. I think we'd get worn out and complacent and start losing lives." The SAS served four-month tours for the first two years of the Task Force's existence before their tours were extended to six months. Although mentally and physically challenging, this allowed the British operators to develop a greater understanding of their enemy and had the added benefit of extending the period of downtime between combat deployments for each squadron.

TOP British SAS operators assigned to Task Force Black, c. 2005. Note the subdued Union Flag patches worn on their Paraclete body armor, chest-mounted pistol holsters and a mix of camouflage uniforms. The SAS would soon change to MultiCam along with Delta Force. (Photographer unknown)

ABOVE Delta Force launching on a rare daylight raid, c. 2003–2004. Note the M4A1 carbines, which have yet to be replaced by the H&K 416, the lack of "zap numbers" (number and letter combinations normally worn as a patch that identifies an individual operator) and older Woodland pattern pouches. (Photographer unknown)

The mission of the Task Force in Iraq was to defeat the rapidly expanding Sunni insurgency. At its inception, the Task Force targeted former Ba'ath Party members (Saddam Hussein's political party), who were organizing fledgling armed resistance groups against Coalition Forces, and what became known as Former Regime Elements (FRE). A deck of cards was issued to operatives that showed the top generals and officials from Saddam Hussein's regime that were still unaccounted for. As the Sunni insurgency gathered pace, the American units began to target the Sunni insurgents and foreign fighters that were entering Iraq. The British were largely relegated to the FRE target list and complained of chasing down "old men."

The Rangers planned and conducted their own raids as well as providing force protection for the special mission units such as Delta, as explained by one Ranger veteran: "Raids are primarily what we do. There are also a couple of squads tasked out to CSAR [Combat Search and Rescue] operations [to protect the Air Force Special Tactics teams], and of course we also support the big tier one SOF i.e. CAG [Delta] and DEVGRU. We've also run joint task forces with the SEALs, since we have a similar mission overseas [direct action], where we took turns pulling isolation/security, and doing the actual hit."

The Task Force chalked up several early successes including the capture of Palestinian terrorist leader Mohammed Abbas in Baghdad on April 19, 2003 and the Iraqi deputy Prime Minister, Tariq Aziz, captured on April 25. The Task Force also carried out several unusual one-off missions, including the recovery of a Mi-17 Hip helicopter for use in later covert operations. It also continued to raid suspected WMD sites throughout April, sometimes only hours ahead of the official Army WMD SSE team – the 75th Exploitation Task Force.

It was also tasked with the interdiction (the delaying, disrupting, or destroying of enemy forces or supplies en route to the battle area) of fleeing Ba'athists and notched up some notable successes in this area. On the night of June 18, 2003 near the Syrian border, AC-130 Spectre fixed-wing gunships, guided in by Task Force 20 operators, struck a convoy of Ba'ath Party members escaping to Syria. Intelligence indicated that the convoy may have included Hussein and/or his sons, Uday and Qusay. Other reports claim the convoy was comprised of oil smugglers.

Once the convoy was destroyed by the guns of the AC-130s, Task Force 20 conducted a heliborne assault into a nearby compound that proved to be a

TOW II anti-tank guided missiles are fired from HMMWVs of the 101st Airborne Division at the safe house sheltering Uday and Qusay Hussein, the sons of Saddam Hussein, in Mosul after the brothers fought off an initial Delta Force assault. (US SOCOM)

TOW II missiles strike the Mosul safe house of Uday and Qusay Hussein. The Delta operators are distinguishable by their olive-drab helmets. Their interpreter can be seen in the brown tee shirt on the right, his discarded megaphone on the ground nearby. (US SOCOM)

Ba'athist safe house for ferrying former regime elements across the border. The Task Force also came under fire from Syrian border guards leading to an uneven firefight that left several Syrians dead. Some 17 Syrian border guards were captured and immediately released; among them five wounded who were treated by Delta medics before repatriation. The British Special Forces of Task Force Black conducted their first operation alongside Delta's B Squadron with a combined helicopter and ground assault against a target in Tikrit. Delta also captured number four on the deck of cards, Iraqi General Abid al-Hamid Mahmud al-Tikriti, in a June raid on the safe house in which he was hiding. Delta's next public success would be Hussein's two sons, Uday and Qusay.

UDAY AND QUSAY

With a $15 million reward on each of their heads, it didn't take long for a former regime member to sell out Hussein's murderous sons. The intelligence was initially passed by an informer to the 101st Airborne Division, which passed it to its

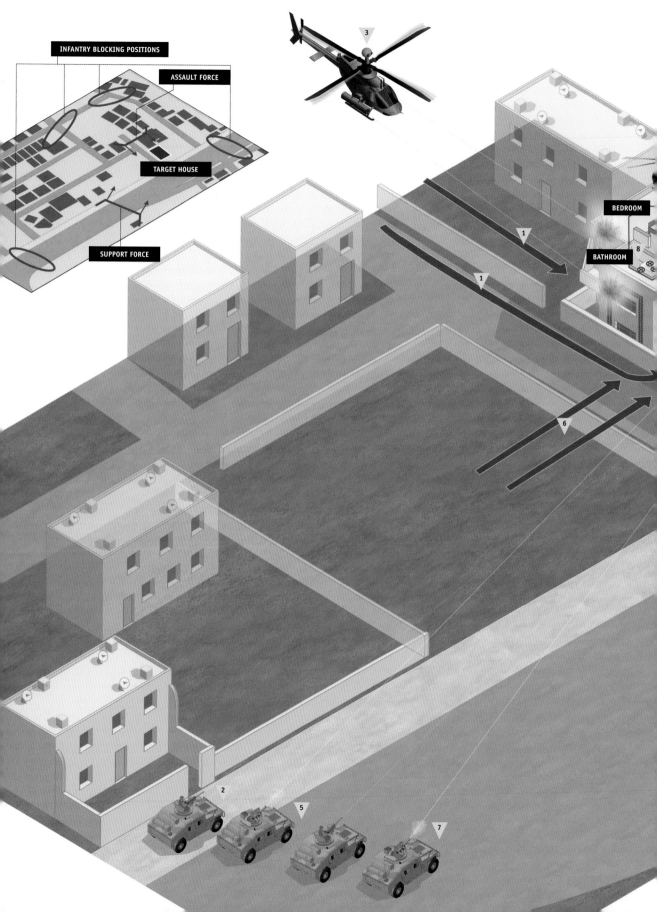

INFANTRY BLOCKING POSITIONS

ASSAULT FORCE

TARGET HOUSE

SUPPORT FORCE

BEDROOM

BATHROOM

THE KILLING OF USAY AND QUSAY HUSSEIN
JULY 22, 2003

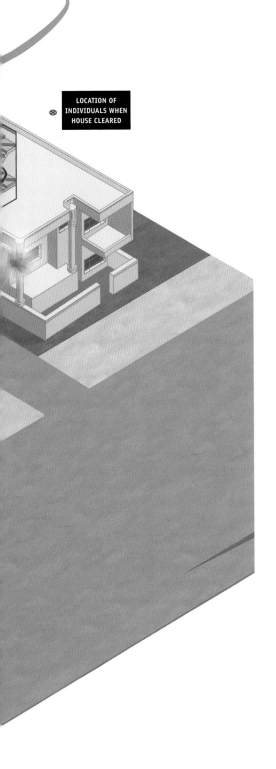

LOCATION OF
INDIVIDUALS WHEN
HOUSE CLEARED

▼ EVENTS

1. A Delta Force ground assault team arrive in unmarked vehicles and use an interpreter to "call-out" the occupants of the house. The owner (rumored to be the man who sold out the Hussein brothers) and his sons leave the building. The Delta assaulters attempt an entry but are beaten back by small-arms fire and grenades, with several operators wounded in the attempt

2. Conventional forces forming part of the outer cordon around the target house are instructed to "soften up" the occupants of the house before another entry is attempted and a fusillade of TOW 2 antitank missiles and .50cal machine-gun fire peppers the building

3. Kiowa armed reconnaissance helicopters also strafe the building from the air with rockets and machine-gun fire

4. An MH-6 Little Bird briefly lands on the flat roof of the target house to insert another Delta assault team which attempts to make entry from the roof, but again finds their way barred

5. The HMMWVs of the cordon force again fire upon the house in preparation for another street-level entry attempt

6. A third entry attempt by Delta is yet again beaten back under a hail of gunfire

7. Yet more preparatory fire is directed into the building with even more TOW missiles being launched

8. Finally, a Delta team manages to successfully breach into the house, killing the survivors

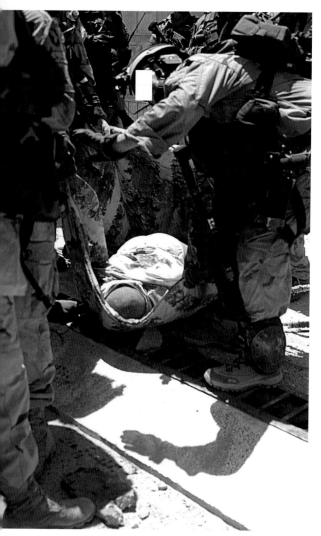

The body of Uday Hussein, the eldest son of Saddam Hussein, being carried from his safe house by Delta Force operators, July 2003. During the battle, several Delta operators were wounded and a Delta combat assault dog was killed. (Photographer unknown)

divisional Special Forces liaison, which in turn contacted Task Force 20. Apparently, Uday and Qusay were hiding in the informer's home along with Qusay's 14-year-old son and a bodyguard in the suburb of Al Falah in Mosul.

On July 22, 2003 several platoons from the 101st Airborne set up an outer cordon around the target house. A Delta assault team stacked near the entrance to the mansion while the occupants of the house were called upon via loudspeaker to surrender via a Delta interpreter. The informer and his two sons walked out, arms raised as previously agreed, but there was no response from the Hussein brothers. The assaulters breached the front door with explosives and threw in flashbang stun grenades before entering cautiously. They were immediately engaged by a fusillade of small arms fire as they entered the ground-floor hallway.

One operative received a gunshot wound to the hip and had to be dragged back into cover. Several others were lightly wounded by grenade fragments as they withdrew from the house – the occupants were posting grenades over a second-floor internal balcony down on the assaulters. A second entry attempt was again met by gunfire and grenades. The team discovered that the interior stairs to the second floor where the brothers were believed to be hiding had been blocked by furniture and other obstacles to impede any rapid assault.

Another group of assaulters fast roped to the roof of the building from a hovering MH-6 Little Bird to examine the possibility of conducting an explosive breach directly down through the roof. While they were moving around the assaulters were almost engaged by an orbiting OH-58 Kiowa-armed reconnaissance helicopter which took them for insurgents. Finally a decision was made to soften up the target with heavy weapons fire before another entry was attempted; the 101st Airborne was ordered to engage the building with its .50cal heavy machine guns and M136 disposable antitank rockets. A third entry was then attempted, but the assaulters were again driven back by gunfire from inside. The brothers were proving to be hard nuts to crack.

The conventional forces were then asked to deploy their HMMWV-mounted TOW II antitank guided missiles. Some ten TOW missiles were launched into the house followed by repeated gun runs from OH-58s, hosing the premises with both .50cal machine guns and 2.75in unguided rockets. Finally, Delta successfully made entry to the residence and, climbing up to the second floor, discovered Qusay and the bodyguard already dead from the TOWs or helicopter barrage. Qusay's teenage son, Mustapha, was hiding under a bed and opened fire as the operators entered his room. They had no choice but to return fire and he was killed. Uday was discovered last, gravely wounded but still armed and moving around in a bathroom. A Delta operator shot and killed him, finally ending the dreadful business.

As the Sunni insurgency continued to gather pace, the SAS in a joint operation with Delta targeted its first terrorist in a step away from the FRE target list, although all did not go according to plan. Operation *Abalone* in October 2003 targeted a Sudanese jihadist facilitator based in the western city of Ramadi – he and his associates were believed to be staying in four neighboring houses. Two assault elements from A Squadron stacked up on two of the target houses while Delta stacked up on the other pair. The outer cordon was manned by the local ground-holding unit equipped with M2A3 Bradley IFVs.

As the SAS breachers detonated their frame charges, they were taken under fire from insurgents within their target houses – all the members of one entry team were hit in the initial fusillade. One of them was an attached SBS Corporal, who was tragically killed. The other wounded SAS operators were recovered under heavy fire and the Bradleys were brought forward to suppress the terrorists firing from the target house. A Delta element then successfully assaulted the house, killing several terrorists inside. After the SAS secured its final objective, an aero medical evacuation was conducted for the wounded SAS operators, and the assault teams collapsed their cordon as they began receiving sporadic small arms fire from the neighborhood (something that would become all too common. The cordon teams on all raids were as concerned about ad hoc reinforcements from the neighborhood as squirters from within the target location).

RED DAWN

Although the Task Force continued to target successfully former regime members, one of its primary targets still eluded capture – the dictator Saddam Hussein himself. Intelligence from detained former members of the Ba'ath Party, supported by signals intelligence from ISA, finally pinpointed the fugitive at a remote farm compound south of Tikrit. On the evening of December 14, 2003, Operation *Red Dawn* was launched, apparently named after the action film of the same name.

Conventional forces of the 1st Brigade Combat Team of the 4th Infantry Division provided the outer cordon while operators from Delta's C Squadron

Intelligence Support Activity

The Intelligence Support Activity (ISA) is the most secretive of the JSOC units. It is known by various names that are changed regularly to maintain operational security. It is believed ISA have been recently known as the Mission Support Activity. Previously they have garnered such exotic code names as Torn Victor, Centra Spike, Intrepid Spear, and Grey Fox. Within JSOC they are normally termed Task Force Orange or simply, the Activity.

Along with the most Hollywood of code names, the ISA also carries out some of the most Hollywood of special missions. Originally conceived as a small US Army Intelligence and Security Command unit to gather actionable intelligence in denied areas, the ISA was transferred to direct JSOC command in 2003 after frequently acting in support of JSOC missions in the Balkans, Somalia and Colombia.

Its members are trained and equipped to gather tactical intelligence principally through classified electronic and signals interception methods as well as more traditional human intelligence methods of developing local national assets – in Somalia in the late 2000s ISA had established an extensive network of informers and years earlier had done similar to support Task Force Ranger in 1993.

The ISA has a fleet of aircraft available to it, leased or purchased by JSOC and SOCOM, that allows it to conduct manned reconnaissance and interception missions over countries where al-Qaeda and their affiliates are active. ISA teams will often deploy alongside a JSOC Task Force to generate live targeting intelligence. They can track miniature bugs hidden in a terrorist's clothing or listen in on satellite telephone calls. They can even track insurgents through invisible dyes that can be applied to a suspect's clothing or vehicle.

searched two locations in the area codenamed, somewhat fittingly, Wolverine 1 and 2 (in the film *Red Dawn*, the Wolverines are the heroic teenage partisan fighters). An initial sweep of the area found nothing unusual and the site was declared a "dry hole." As the operators were finishing up and the helicopters had been called, one assaulter randomly noticed a piece of flooring material that he kicked to the side, exposing a spider hole dug into the ground. The operator turned on his weapon-mounted light but could see nothing, so he prepared to drop a fragmentation grenade into the hole to clear it in case it led to an insurgent tunnel system.

Suddenly a disheveled and bearded figure appeared in the spider hole. He was quickly buttstroked by a Delta operator (struck with the stock of his M4 carbine)

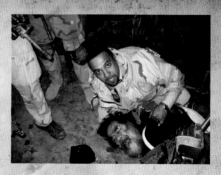

The infamous *Time Magazine* cover shot of Saddam Hussein dragged from his spider hole by members of Delta Force and the Intelligence Support Activity, Iraq, 2003. The man holding Hussein was an interpreter. (US DOD)

and disarmed of an unloaded but fully functioning selective fire Glock 18C, which was later presented to President George W. Bush by the operators. It was a move that disappointed General McChrystal, according to his autobiography, as he felt it looked too much like "currying favor" with the President. Hussein was dragged out of the hole and the famous image was taken at the feet of a number of Delta and ISA operators. Along with the Glock, an AK-47 and $750,000 in US bank notes was recovered from the hole.

The capture of the dictator seemed somewhat anti-climactic after the months the Task Force had spent searching for him. Hussein surrendered rather meekly and offered no real resistance in comparison to his two sons who had put up such a bloody fight. He was exfiltrated on a 160th SOAR MH-6 Little Bird and taken into formal custody at Baghdad International Airport before being handed over to the Iraqis who infamously hanged the dictator after two separate trials.

ZARQAWI

The Task Force's most high-profile target since Saddam Hussein was the Jordanian terrorist Abu Musab al Zarqawi. Zarqawi graduated from street gangs and drug dealing in his native Jordan, via a stint in prison, to Palestinian terrorist organizations and finally to Ansar al-Islam in northern Iraq where he narrowly escaped Operation *Viking Hammer* in the early days of Operation *Iraqi Freedom*.

A thoroughly detestable thug, his murderous skills eventually saw him become the nominal leader of al-Qaeda in the Land of the Two Rivers, better known as al-Qaeda in Iraq or simply AQI. He was responsible for attempting to incite a genocidal civil war between Sunni and Shia with the stated aim of destroying the Shia as a people. He also followed Khalid Sheikh Mohammed's grisly example in

TOP LEFT Delta Force operators, c. 2005 in Iraq. They wear standard three-color desert BDUs and MICH helmets with Paraclete vests. Although at least one operator wears a drop holster, others can be seen with the holster attached to their plate carriers. (Photographer unknown)

TOP RIGHT A trio of Delta operators pause after securing an objective during a building assault, c. 2007. All carry the Heckler & Koch 416 assault rifle jointly developed by H&K and Delta Force. Each operator wears an individual mix of MultiCam and three-color desert pattern uniforms and their own highly personalised body armor and first line gear. (Photographer unknown)

US Army Rangers assigned to Task Force Central conducting training with 160th Special Operations Aviation Regiment. Although the Little Birds look like they are painted black, in reality they are a very dark olive-drab. (Photographer unknown)

popularizing the trend for beheading Western hostages and releasing the videotape of the murder to a clutch of jihadist websites. This kind of behavior continues today with IS (Islamic State) in Syria and Iraq, AQI's latest manifestation and certainly an organization that Zarqawi would have supported wholeheartedly.

In fact, his psychopathic outrages, including the bombing of Muslim civilian targets and the gruesome murders of Shia worshippers, made the central al-Qaeda leadership wary of the former drug dealer. Bin Laden sent a letter to Zarqawi asking him to concentrate his violence on more legitimate targets, as his excesses were damaging the al-Qaeda brand. A $25 million reward was posted for the Jordanian, matching that offered for bin Laden himself; certainly another factor that no doubt did little to relieve the tensions between Zarqawi and al-Qaeda high command. Despite this, in October 2004, the Jordanian pledged formal allegiance to bin Laden and his organization, receiving the Saudi's blessing to use the al-Qaeda name.

While hunting for Zarqawi and his thugs, and targeting nationalist Shia and Sunni insurgent cells, the Task Force was also responsible for conducting any planned hostage rescue missions in Iraq. A multinational team had been stood up in Baghdad known as the Joint Hostage Working Group. It was both a reporting and planning cell composed of law enforcement and intelligence agency investigators as well as Special Forces liaison officers.

Its role was to act as a sort of intelligence fusion cell working to release hostages seized by nationalist insurgents, criminal gangs or al-Qaeda. With vast sums of money being offered by al-Qaeda for Western hostages, particularly for Americans or British nationals, many criminals got in on the act, selling their hostages up the line to the jihadists. In fact, intelligence indicating a criminal gang was planning to sell its hostage would be enough to launch an assault, as once the hostage was in terrorist hands, his fate was virtually decided.

OBJECTIVE MEDFORD

The Task Force's first hostage rescue was conducted in June 2004. Four Italian security contractors had been seized in April. Soon after, one was graphically murdered while being filmed by his insurgent captors. Another hostage was added to their number when a Polish contractor was snatched at the start of June. Their abductors passed on a statement that the other hostages would be executed unless

US Army Rangers from Task Force Central practice fast roping from an MH-6 Little Bird at MSS Fernandez in Baghdad. (Photographer unknown)

Italy withdrew its contribution from the Coalition. Instead, intelligence recovered from raids and solid detective work resulted in a dramatic daylight raid launched by elements of A Squadron of Delta Force against an isolated compound near Ramadi codenamed Objective Medford. The operation included four MH-60L Blackhawks and four MH-6 Little Birds carrying the assault elements and aerial sniper teams.

Touching down at 1100hr, one MH-60L was slightly damaged when its tail struck the target compound's wall. The Delta operators stormed inside, capturing several of the kidnappers who surrendered immediately with raised hands. The four hostages were rapidly located in an adjacent room, and bolt cutters were used to cut their restraints before they were flown out on the Blackhawks. A grainy helmet camera video exists of the operation which highlighted two things: the speed and aggression of the operators as they cleared the house and the incredible relief shown on the faces of the hostages when they realized they were being rescued.

As was shown in Chapter 4, Fallujah saw JSOC operating alongside conventional Army and Marine units during both Operation *Vigilant Resolve* and Operation *Phantom Fury*. The Task Force's shaping operations were instrumental in the success of the latter operation. In particular, its movement analysis from its ISR-manned and unmanned aircraft was praised as it allowed targeting of known terrorist nodes such as IED factories. Closely supporting conventional forces, which was also a good public relations exercise by the sometimes aloof special operators, further strengthened the bonds with units that they would probably work with in the future.

ISR

ISR stands for Intelligence Surveillance and Reconnaissance. The British version is ISTAR, for Intelligence Surveillance, Target Acquisition, and Reconnaissance. Both relate to information-gathering techniques and platforms. In terms of ISR techniques, most centre on technological means, such as signals intercepts or video surveillance. In terms of ISR platforms this can include any number of ground-based or aerial assets that collect information ranging from UAVs and manned reconnaissance aircraft such as the U-28A or RC-12, to ground-based sensors and surveillance equipment. Special reconnaissance teams can also be considered as an ISR asset.

The massive growth in ISR has been largely driven by the wars in Iraq and Afghanistan. SOF in particular has been at the forefront of ISR development, including many of the classified practices developed for JSOC. For the on-the-ground commander, the advantage of ISR is a greatly enhanced level of situational awareness of the battlefield. He can make decisions after viewing the terrain or after being informed that there are insurgents in that house you are about to enter.

ISR has also come into its own in the sphere of kill or capture missions. So-called long-loiter UAVs such as the Global Hawk or Sentinel allow a target to be covertly tracked for extended periods. The target's conversations and e-mails can be intercepted by ISR platforms. When the opportunity arises to launch an assault team against the target, manned ISR can give the assaulters another set of eyes and inform them of any squirters or reinforcements that may be approaching the target area.

According to veteran BBC reporter Mark Urban in his excellent account of UK Special Forces in Iraq, *Task Force Black*, while JSOC focused all of its attention on Fallujah, the British SAS were forbidden from becoming involved as their political masters at Whitehall feared that *Phantom Fury* would become another media disaster with doctored accounts of civilian deaths dominating Arab media channels. Although generally still relegated to hunting Ba'athists, the SAS had its own near miss with Zarqawi in February 2004 when a strike team hit a safe house in Baghdad. Later intelligence indicated that it had only just missed the Jordanian terrorist.

The treatment of detainees by the Task Force at its Baghdad and later Balad detainee sites became a matter of conflict with the British. McChrystal had instituted an investigation into claims that a number of prisoners had been mistreated at the sites and disciplinary action was taken against a number of operators. The allegations centred on physical violence (the use of a Taser on an al-Qaeda prisoner, according to McChrystal) and intimidation of detainees rather than organized torture. Some viewed it simply as a means of extending the "shock of capture" (the period immediately following capture in which a prisoner is most likely to reveal information). It did mean that the British government was not comfortable with the SAS handing over detainees to the Americans unless conditions at the facility were improved.

The SAS had captured a pair of Pakistani nationals in a February raid that also saw two other jihadists shot dead by the assaulters and an SAS Sergeant shot in

OPERATION *IRAQI FREEDOM*
JOINT SPECIAL OPERATIONS COMMAND TASK FORCE AREAS OF RESPONSIBILITY 2006–2007

TURKEY

Zakho • DAHUK
• Dahuk

Aqrah • ARBIL

IRAN

Tal Afar • • Mosul
Sinjar • ④ • Arbil

NINAWA

Kirkuk • As Sulaymaniyah •

SYRIA

AS SULAYMANIYAH
• Halabja

AT TA'MIM

Bayji •

⑤ • Tikrit

Al Qa'im • SALAH AD DIN

Khanaqin •

Haditha • Samarra •

DIYALA

• Baqubah
Akashat • Hit •

Mandali •

IRAQ Fallujah • Baghdad
Ramadi • BAGHDAD
Rutbah •

① ②

Karbala • BABIL WASIT
Al Hindiyah • Hillah Kut • Tigris River
JORDAN AL ANBAR KARBALA ③
• Al Hayy

Nukhayb •

Najaf • Diwaniyah •
AL QADISIYAH Amarah •

MAYSAN

DHI QAR

AN NAJAF Samawah • Euphrates River
• Nasiriyah

⑥ • Basra

As Salman •
AL BASRAH
Az Zubayr •
AL MUTHANNA • Umm Qasr

SAUDI ARABIA KUWAIT

N

0 ———— 150 miles
0 ———— 150km

1) TASK FORCE CENTRAL (DELTA FORCE)
2) TASK FORCE BLACK/KNIGHT (SAS)
3) TASK FORCE EAST (DELTA FORCE)
4) TASK FORCE NORTH (RANGERS)
5) TASK FORCE WEST (DEVGRU)
6) TASK FORCE SPARTAN (SAS)

An unfortunately low-resolution shot of Task Force Knight (formerly Task Force Black) posing for a team photograph under the notorious Assassin's Gate in Baghdad. Intriguingly there is a mix of MultiCam and civilian clothing, the Toyota pick-up trucks and the combat assault dog. (Photographer unknown)

the face with an AK-47 – remarkably, it proved to be only a light wound and he returned to active duty with the squadron. Dangerous raids such as that also highlighted another major difference between the British and the Americans – that of the Rules of Engagement (ROE). As Mark Urban explained, "The Americans, after some costly setbacks assaulting houses, were quite ready to drop a bomb … or strafe a car from a helicopter gunship if their intelligence told them that the person inside had a history of taking life and could be about to do so again." British ROEs were later changed to be somewhat more in line with Delta, but they never allowed the same kind of flexibility afforded the Americans.

As well as casualties from the incessant raids the Task Force conducted, it also lost one of its own to a terrorist bombing. In December 2004, a Saudi-born Ansar al-Sunnah terrorist dressed in an Iraqi Army uniform detonated a suicide bomb vest packed with ball bearings inside a dining facility at a Forward Operating Base (FOB) in Mosul. The blast killed 22 American servicemen; among them was an operator from the ISA.

RAIDS

American Roy Hallums was another held hostage by insurgents – his captivity lasted for an incredible 311 days after being seized in November 2004. After intelligence obtained from a detainee interrogation, a Delta assault force landed in Little Birds at an isolated farmhouse outside of Baghdad. The assaulters cleared the building, realizing that the hostage takers had taken flight at the first sound of helicopters. As assaulters searched the building they moved a piece of furniture concealing a trap door to the basement cell where Hallums and his fellow hostage were being held. A Delta operator asked him if he was Roy Hallums and when he

answered in the affirmative, the operator gave the "Jackpot" brevity code to signal to all members of the team and HQ in Balad that he had been rescued.

A special operator described how many of these raids were conducted;

> You have what they call landing on the X, the Y and then an offset landing. Landing on the X is literally right on top of the target, the Y is within like 500 meters or so, and an offset is a hike, say three to six kilometers typically, to mask the presence of helicopters. You'll usually post some sort of overwatch, rear security, and then a squad will clear the actual house.
>
> It's not (necessarily) a loud thing. We have ICOM radios [commercial walkie-talkie style radios also popular with the Taliban] as well as MBITRs [Multi-Band Intra Team Radios] for everybody, so we've cleared entire houses and not awakened the occupants. No need for "sounding off" and yelling. We call it "soft knock," but you pan across the doorway and peek through windows before entering the room to clear as much as possible before you even go in. After that, it's like typical CQB [Close Quarter Battle] where you clear corners and such. My guys were pretty big on this, but others are bigger on the door breaches and flashbangs.

"Objective secure" would be announced across the radio net as the target location was systematically cleared of hostiles and secured for the Sensitive Site Exploitation (SSE) stage to begin. The helicopters or ground assault force would then call back for pick-up. Once the SSE was complete, the evidence and any detainees would

US Army Special Forces soldiers conducting joint raids with ISOF's 8th Regional Commando Battalion in Baqubah, Iraq. Note just visible the operators spread out along either side of the street to provide security while the assaulters complete their mission. (Petty Officer Second Class Emmanuel Rios; US Navy)

Task Force Red Rangers conducting a raid in Iraq targeting al-Qaeda elements, 2006. (US SOCOM)

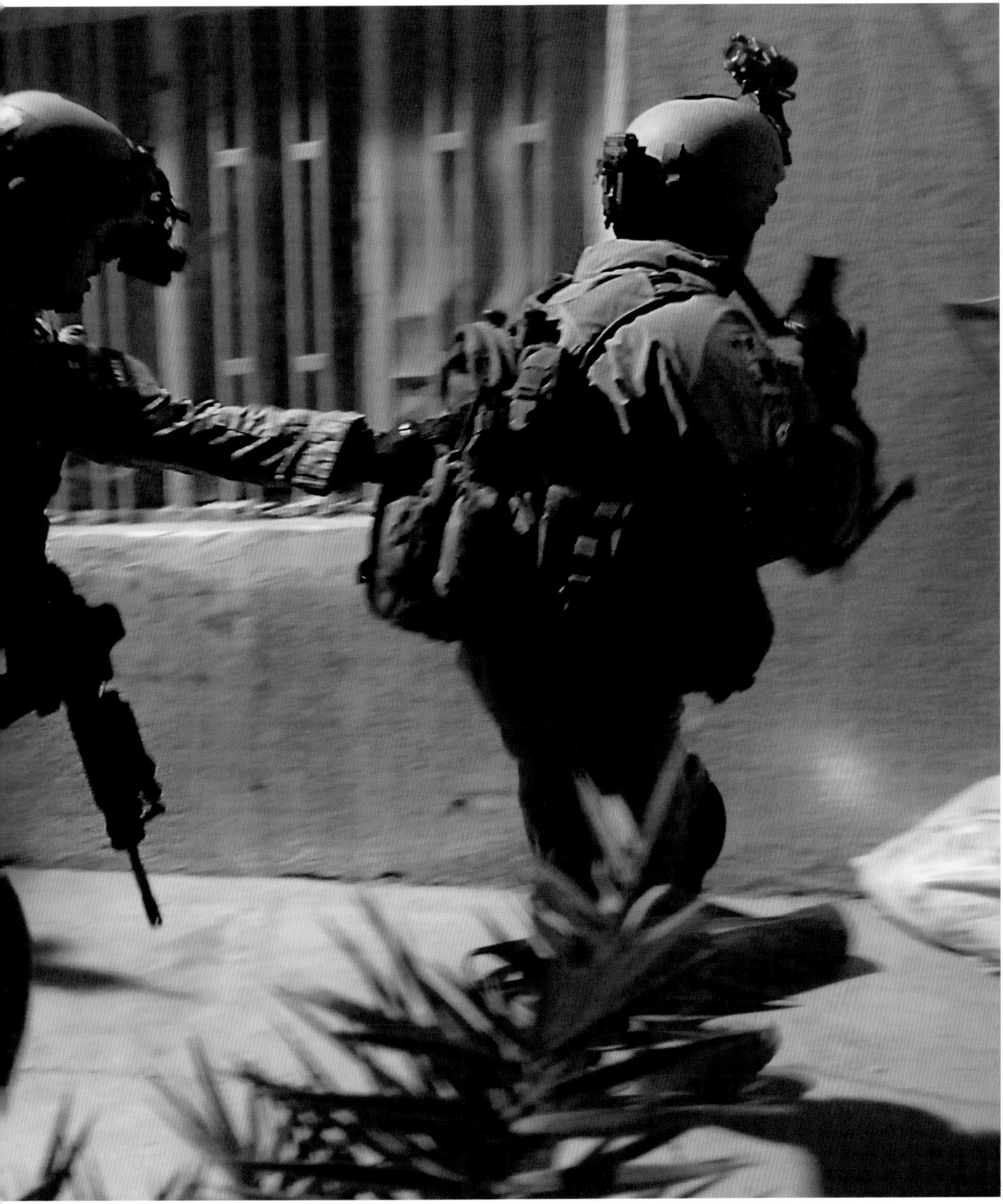

Rangers collapsing a security cordon somewhere in Iraq, c. 2007. Note the ACU pattern uniforms and the MultiCam assault pack carried by the Ranger on the left. (US SOCOM)

be loaded into the helicopters or vehicles before the inner cordon around the target would be collapsed and the assault force would head for home.

> After you clear it, you'll have security out to isolate the target, probably get machineguns on the roof top, and then start SSEing the house, interrogating occupants, etc. After that you'll call the birds, move to exfil [exfiltration] with prisoners and evidence, and take off. We do both helo and ground insertions. We almost always have air overwatch. Usually a DAP [MH-60L Direct Action Penetrator], sometimes AH-6s [armed Little Birds] and on occasion, if they are expecting something big, a Spectre gunship.

In February 2005, Zarqawi again narrowly escaped death or capture after he fled from a building being targeted by a JSOC helicopter assault force. His vehicle bypassed a Ranger blocking position as the camera of a Predator UAV overhead, which had been following Zarqawi's escape and feeding the intelligence down to the ground elements, decided at that exact moment to malfunction, meaning that the Task Force lost sight of the target.

THE WESTERN EUPHRATES RATLINE

The city of Al Qaim sat on what Coalition Forces termed the Western Euphrates Ratline, which facilitated the movement of foreign fighters into Iraq from the border with Syria. With a massive increase in the number of suicide bombings carried out by foreign jihadists in Baghdad, Delta redeployed to shut down the bombers' highway in to Iraq. To do that, General McChrystal needed more operators and more enablers such as helicopter crews, intelligence analysts, and so on. He brought in another Delta squadron from Fort Bragg and small teams of SEAL reinforcements from DEVGRU.

The operation into Al Qaim was codenamed Snake Eyes. The enemy there were trained jihadists who had a thorough understanding of SOF tactics and techniques, and were prepared for the inevitable showdown with Coalition Forces. Zarqawi's fingerprints were all over the area. Two hugely experienced Delta operators were killed in an early Snake Eyes raid on a fortified AQI safe house. This followed the death of another veteran operator only weeks before, also in Al Qaim.

The two Delta operators had breached the target house only to find it fortified with sandbags – a bunker built within the building, much like those constructed by insurgents in Fallujah the preceding year. The team extracted the fatally wounded operators, pulled back to a safe distance, and dropped a JDAM (Joint Direct Attack Munition) on the house, flattening it. As more raids went in, the fighting began to resemble Fallujah in other ways too – diehard jihadists who often wore suicide bomb vests or had wired their safe houses as massive IEDs. The operators were facing an adaptive and skilled enemy, which would stand and fight even against overwhelming firepower.

More operators were tragically lost in the struggle to shut down the Western Euphrates Ratline and stop Iraq descending into civil war. Three more Delta soldiers and a Ranger died when an antitank mine destroyed their Pandur near the border town of Husaybah. However, the operational fury was starting to hurt Zarqawi's organization. The net was tightening, but it would take another year before the JSOC Task Force zeroed in on Zarqawi himself.

OPERATION *MARLBOROUGH*

Task Force Black was no less busy, with the SAS taking up the slack in Baghdad as Delta focused on western Iraq. The SBS had also rotated a squadron through Baghdad and was seeing significant action. Like their American counterparts in DEVGRU, the SBS was predominantly deployed to Afghanistan. A significant SAS presence would not be seen in Afghanistan until after the withdrawal of

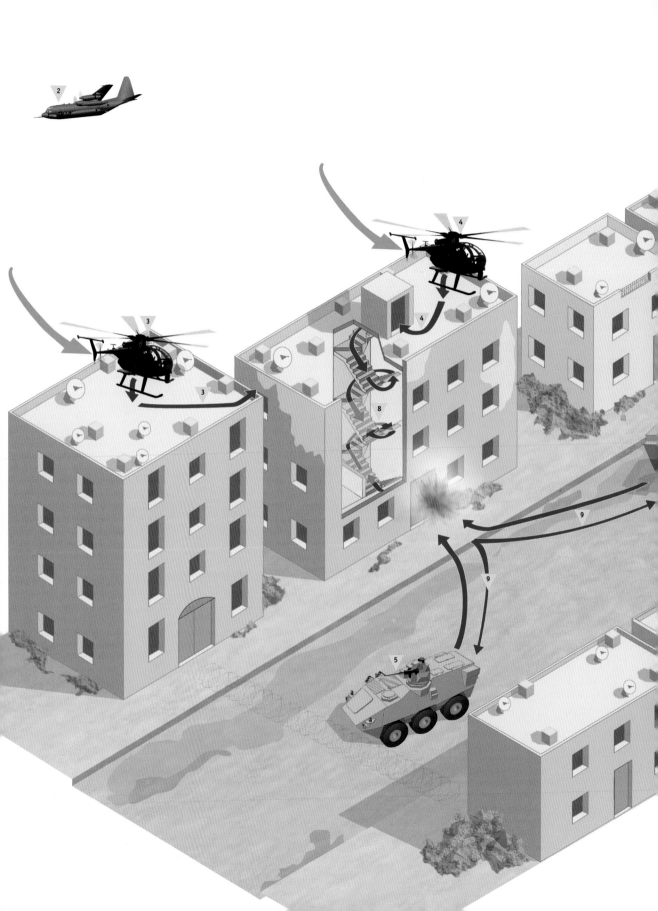

URBAN HIGH-VALUE TARGET RAID
SOMEWHERE IN IRAQ

This illustrative scenario shows a typical raid against a high-value target in Iraq. Here, a combined ground and helicopter assault force is raiding a three-story city building in a major built-up area such as Baghdad or Mosul. Most such operations are conducted at night to give all possible advantages to the special operations units.

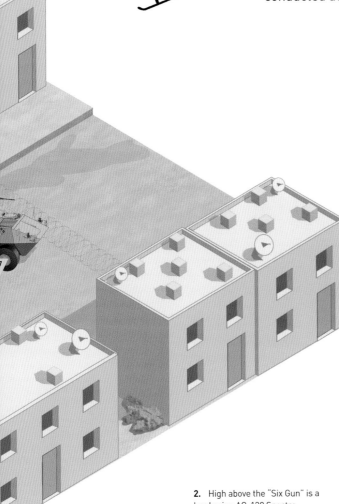

3. An MH-6 "Six Pax" Little Bird has just dropped off a four-man sniper overwatch team on the roof of the tallest building in the area. The two-man sniper team will engage any "squirters" escaping the building or engage any reinforcements. They are protected by a two-man security team which will maintain full 360-degree security while the sniper team are on the scope

4. An MH-6 "Six Pax" inserts a four-man roof assault team onto the rooftop of the target building. These operators will breach down onto the top floor and begin clearing the target as the ground assault force breaches and clears upward. They will meet somewhere in the middle

5. On the street, the ground assault force have arrived and blocking positions have been established to keep out any local foot or vehicle traffic while the operation is conducted. The blocking position teams will use razor wire, luminous signs in Arabic, flashing lights and loudspeakers manned by an interpreter to warn off curious civilians. Flashbang stun grenades can be used if anyone continues to approach, and warning shots are authorized if individuals are attempting to breach the cordon. Finally, suspect vehicles or individuals will be engaged once they have become a threat

6. A second blocking position is established, also featuring a two-man machine gun team manning a 7.62mm Mk48 medium machine gun

7. These six-wheeled armoured vehicles, known as Pandurs, are used by Delta Force to approach a target location under heavy armored protection. With the IED threat, these vehicles are essential. The gunners stay with the Pandurs ready to provide suppressive fire

8. The ground assault force have breached the front door and are clearing into the ground floor after first dispatching their Combat Assault Dog to search for booby traps or hidden terrorists. The dog can transmit live video to the handler and the ground force commander from a video camera mounted on his back. He is also trained to attack armed terrorists. The ground assault force will methodically clear each room encountered, blowing in locked doors with shotguns and posting flashbang grenades into each room before entering. The team will eventually link up with the roof assault team to secure the objective

9. Any casualties or detainees will be brought out to a covered position between the armored vehicles to allow them to be stabilized or questioned respectively. Urgent casualties can be loaded directly into one of the Pandurs and driven off at high speed with gunship cover overhead, or the tiny MH-6 can land in the street to evacuate the casualty. Once the SSE is completed, the assault teams will climb aboard the Pandurs for the extraction and the blocking positions rolled up. Rooftop security teams will often be picked up by MH-6s. A typical operation can be over within minutes

▼ EVENTS

1. An AH-6 Little Bird "Six Gun" arrives first to overfly the target and ensure no enemy are waiting to ambush the unarmed MH-6 troop-carrying Little Birds. The AH-6 is armed with both rockets and miniguns should a threat appear

2. High above the "Six Gun" is a lumbering AC-130 Spectre fixed-wing gunship, ready to engage any enemy reinforcements with its 40mm cannons and 105mm howitzer. Additionally it can "glint" a large area with its infra-red searchlight, visible only to operators wearing night vision goggles. It will also be using its sensors to watch any suspicious vehicles or individuals in the immediate area around the target location.

An MH-6 Little Bird drops a Ranger roof team into position during a training exercise. Little Birds often inserted assault or overwatch teams on to rooftops in Iraq. (US DOD)

British conventional forces from Iraq in 2009, although small teams did deploy to support specific operations.

In July 2005, M Squadron of the SBS and a US Army Ranger platoon conducted an operation against an al-Qaeda safe house full of suicide bombers known as Operation *Marlborough*. Time sensitive intelligence indicated three suicide bombers at the location were planning an imminent strike on a civilian target in Baghdad. Using GMV trucks borrowed from Delta, an SBS ground assault force drove up on the target location while RAF Puma helicopters carrying aerial sniper teams orbited above.

As the SBS assaulters approached, a suicide bomber ran toward them from the house. Before he could be engaged he detonated his vest, blowing himself up in a huge explosion. The blast almost hit a Puma that was passing low overhead at the time. As this was happening at the front of the house, another suicide bomber made a run for it out the back. He was spotted by a UAV and an SBS sniper in a Puma engaged and killed the bomber in his tracks. The primary assault team breached into the compound and began to clear the target location methodically. The final third suicide bomber emerged as they were doing so, only to be rapidly engaged and killed by an SBS operator at close range before he could detonate his explosive-packed vest.

BASRA

The SAS also maintained an Operation *Hathor* detachment – a handful of operators based with UK forces in Basra. Hathor's primary role was to protect SIS (MI6) officers and to conduct surveillance and reconnaissance for the British Battle Group. This role led to the SAS finding itself in the curious position of having to rescue two of their own in September 2005.

An SAS team, part of the Hathor Detachment, kitted up prior to an operation in Basra, Iraq. (Photographer unknown)

The operators from A Squadron had been captured in Basra by the Iraqi Police (IP), or at least men wearing IP uniforms (the Iraqi Police, particularly in the south, were notorious for being infiltrated by the insurgency). At the time the SAS operators were conducting surveillance on a senior Iraqi Police officer who was believed to be highly placed within the Shia insurgency. Something went wrong at an Iraqi Police checkpoint and the SAS operators ended up shooting one Iraqi before racing through the checkpoint with the "police" in pursuit.

Their vehicle broke down and not wishing to make a bad situation worse, the two SAS operators surrendered. They were immediately bustled away to a central Basra police station where they were beaten. As news reached the Task Force, McChrystal offered the services of Delta's D Squadron and dispatched a JSOC Predator to Basra. Twenty operators from the SAS's A Squadron and a platoon from the Special Forces Support Group immediately flew from Baghdad to Basra.

The British Battle Group had placed a cordon around the police station and held back baying mobs of civilians, some of whom began throwing rocks and later petrol bombs. The gunmen holding the SAS operators knew they had to move their hostages before the British attacked the police station to free them. As they dragged their prisoners outside, the operators deliberately began a scuffle with their captors, knowing the longer they were in the open, the better chance an overhead ISR asset would have of spotting them.

Luck was indeed with them and the crew of a Broadsword ISR Sea King which was hovering over the area saw them and subsequently tracked the gunmen's car carrying the two SAS hostages. It drove to a house in central Basra and the operators were dragged inside. Overhead signals intelligence indicated the prisoners were to be handed over to an insurgent group if that had not already occurred. There was no time to lose.

A Squadron assaulters arrived at the target house and conducted a textbook explosive entry through multiple breach points and rapidly cleared the house. To their surprise, the kidnappers had fled – perhaps at the sound of the British helicopters. Both SAS soldiers were recovered, bruised and battered, but alive to

US Army Rangers of Task Force Red landing on a rooftop somewhere in Iraq, courtesy of an MH-6 Little Bird flown by the 160th Special Operations Aviation Regiment. (Photographer unknown)

03/28/200

tell the tale. Publicity from the rescue also forced a name change for Task Force Black. They were now known as Task Force Knight and were soon hunting for another kidnap gang – this time of controversial British peace campaigner, Norman Kember.

Along with a small team from Canada's counterterrorism unit JTF2, the Task Force began raiding properties linked to the insurgents who had abducted Kember and his colleagues – two Canadians, James Loney and Harmeet Singh Sooden, and an American, Tom Fox. The kidnappers demanded the release of insurgent prisoners and sent a number of video tapes showing the hostages in Guantanamo-style orange jumpsuits styled like Zarqawi execution videos. In March, several months after they were first seized, the American hostage, Tom Fox, was brutally murdered.

The successful detainee interrogation of a recently captured insurgent who knew the kidnap gang finally revealed the location of the surviving hostages. Wary of an ambush, the hostage takers were telephoned by the SAS moments before a strike team from B Squadron approached. The kidnappers were warned that they had better leave quickly. Having evidently taken the SAS's advice, the three hostages were recovered unharmed and without a shot being fired as B Squadron burst into the house. There was no sign of the hostage takers. Years later when the kidnappers were arrested by the Iraqi Police, Kember refused to testify against them.

On New Year's Day 2006, a Task Force Red assault team came across a surprise when it raided a remote farmhouse outside Baghdad. One of a large number of raids that were planned that night, the Ranger operation was one of the last and almost didn't launch as mechanical problems plagued one of its helicopters. When the Rangers eventually reached the target and breached into the farmhouse, they captured several gunmen without a fight and recovered a freelance British journalist, Phillip Sands, who had been kidnapped a week earlier. As the journalist wasn't working for a particular network, his kidnapping hadn't been reported and the Joint Hostage Working Group was unaware of his plight. His rescue was purely by chance.

THE BAGHDAD BELTS

Delta and the SAS were now focusing their attentions on the so-called "Baghdad Belts," a concentric zone around the capital. The phrase had been first used by AQI and a diagram representing it was recovered during a raid. The belts included such notorious trouble spots as Fallujah to the west, Baqubah to the north, and Latifiyah and Yusufiyah to the south. Increasingly, intelligence developed by the Task Force was pointing at these cities as regional staging areas for al-Qaeda in Iraq.

As General McChrystal explained in *My Share of the Task*:

[AQI] used the ratlines from Syria, west along the Euphrates and southwest through Ar Rutba, to move foreign fighters. A third ratline ran north into Mosul, which AQI used as a rear support area, raising money and building cells but committing relatively fewer operations there. While al-Qaeda never tried to hold terrain in Baghdad itself, it increasingly sought to control the belts around the city – more sparsely populated, with less Coalition troop density. It aimed to funnel violence into Baghdad … in order to demonstrate the futility of MNF-I's [Multi National Forces-Iraq's] efforts, paralyze the government, and help spur civil war.

A concerted campaign was required to weed out the terrorists in the Baghdad Belts. April 2005 saw the first shots fired of the campaign when a Delta element supported by the Rangers assaulted an AQI safe house in Yusufiyah, capturing five terrorists and killing another five. The SAS ran into concerted resistance at one of its targets in Yusufiyah. This time it was targeting an al-Qaeda suicide bomber cell. A helicopter assault force deployed four teams of assaulters at an off-set HLZ to avoid warning their targets. Above, aerial sniper teams in Lynx helicopters and an AC-130 fixed-wing gunship covered the teams' advance while ISR aircraft monitored the location, feeding back streaming video to the TOCs (Tactical Operations Centres) in Balad and Baghdad.

The teams discovered an unlocked rear door and the plan for an explosive breach rapidly changed to a silent entry, as described by the Ranger earlier. As the first team entered the building, the stillness of the night was broken by AK-47 fire and three of the SAS assaulters fell badly wounded. The other teams rapidly

A Green Beret provides perimeter security from his GMV on a joint ISOF and US Army Special Forces operation in Baghdad, 2007. Note the infra-red laser visible from his AN/PEQ-2 infra-red illuminator mounted on his M4A1 carbine. (Mass Communication Specialist Second Class Brett Cote; US Navy)

dragged the wounded back out as the cordon team from the SFSG attempted to suppress the enemy fire from the house. A second assault was attempted but was again driven back by small arms fire and grenades, resulting in another two wounded SAS operators. During the battle, one of the suicide bombers managed to escape from the rear of the house and took cover under a car while a sniper in a Lynx tried to hit him.

Eventually the assaulters made it into the residence and cleared it, killing three more terrorists inside. One terrorist, wearing a suicide bomb vest, raced away from the assault team up a central staircase to the roof, pursued by an SAS Sergeant. As they reached the flat roof of the building, the terrorist turned and detonated his vest, killing himself and blowing the British operator back down the stairs. Luckily he survived with only minor injuries. The second suicide bomber hiding under the car was eventually shot and killed by the SFSG.

Delta launched yet another operation the next month in Yusufiyah, this time in broad daylight – a significant departure from Task Force standard operating practice. Daylight operations were only launched against what were termed time-sensitive targets – a hostage who was about to be moved, or a car bomber about to set off on his mission. In Ramadi, the Rangers of Task Force Red were often forced to launch daylight raids despite the risks, as they were finding that their targets were moving out of the city at night to avoid their raids.

British Special Forces pictured at MSS Fernandez in Baghdad. The operator to the right looks British however he wears an American "Fuck al-Qaeda" patch that was conceived and worn by Delta. A British version with the Union Flag replacing the Stars and Stripes was later distributed among the SAS squadrons. The pistol holsters mounted to the chest of their plate carriers continued to be the fashion for a number of years. In Afghanistan, as little as possible was worn on the front of the vest as it reduced the amount of flying hazards should an operator come into contact with an IED. (Photographer unknown)

The operation on May 14 was conducted by Delta's B Squadron and was aimed at disrupting a number of al-Qaeda safe houses in the city. As soon as the 160th SOAR Blackhawks touched down, the assaulters began receiving small arms fire, which soon escalated to include mortars and at least one DShK heavy machine gun. The Blackhawks did what they could from the air while a pair of AH-6M attack helicopters flew multiple gun runs to suppress enemy firing points. Delta now had five wounded, several seriously, and in desperate need of evacuation.

One of the Little Birds, from B Company, 1/160th SOAR, was shot down over the battle with both pilot and co-pilot killed in the crash. The Delta operators fought their way through to secure the crash site, but sadly there was little they could do. Despite continuing heavy opposition – which resulted in a number of helicopters being forced to return to base due to heavy damage – Delta managed to reach the objective and four terrorists were captured.

Even as an aero-medical evacuation flight landed to whisk several wounded civilians and operators out, it was taken under fire. The assault force eventually collapsed their cordon and pulled back to allow several JDAMs to be dropped on the enemy positions, finally allowing the assaulters to break contact and withdraw. An estimated 25 al-Qaeda fighters had been killed on the operation.

US Army Rangers display a Soviet-made RPK light machine gun and Kalashnikov-pattern rifle recovered during a Task Force raid. (US SOCOM)

THE JORDANIAN

The key, however, was still Zarqawi. His central role in the insurgency in Iraq had ensured that his death or capture was JSOC's number one priority. On June 7, 2006, they found him. Years of effort had led the Task Force to the most wanted man in Iraq. Ultimately it was Zarqawi's spiritual adviser, Sheikh Abd al Rahman, who led JSOC to its target. The connection between the two men had been made through long loiter surveillance and nodal analysis, and the efforts of some of the

A Ranger assault team moves into place outside a target location. Note the battering ram and assault ladder carried by the Rangers. All wear AN/PVS-14 monocular night vision devices. Note also the uniform set-up of their M4A1 carbines compared to Delta Force or the Green Berets. (US SOCOM)

best interrogators in the US military. US Army Major General Bill Caldwell said the operation was the culmination of "a very long, painstaking, deliberate exploitation of intelligence, information-gathering, human sources, electronic (and) signal intelligence."

A MQ-1 Predator was watching when Zarqawi finally stepped from the shadows – he was staying at an AQI safe house northeast of Baqubah and outside the small town of Hibhib. An assault troop from the Delta squadron in Baghdad immediately prepared to launch, but as it climbed aboard a pair of MH-6 Little Birds, one of the helicopters lost engine power and wouldn't restart. A replacement MH-6 was dispatched from Balad, but it would take 30 minutes before it arrived as MSS Fernandez.

Worried that they would lose their quarry, General McChrystal's team ordered a pair of nearby F-16C Fighting Falcons into action – they would bomb the AQI safe house rather than run the risk of losing Zarqawi again. The Delta assaulters would have faced a difficult operation as the height and number of trees around the house, and the considerable distance to the nearest cleared area to use as a HLZ, would have forced them to fast rope down on to the target house. While they fast roped, their Little Birds would be vulnerable to any ground fire. The Task Force couldn't wait for the back-up helicopter to arrive from Balad and ordered the one operational MH-6 to launch with its Delta assaulters perched on its external pods. They would be needed to secure the site after the bombing and confirm Zarqawi's presence.

A final problem arose when it became apparent that only one F-16C was available, the other was in the midst of refuelling from an airborne tanker. The lone F-16C was ordered to deliver its ordnance on to the AQI safe house. After a false start owing to a miscommunication that saw the F-16C make a low attack pass over the house, a collective breath was held by those watching the Predator feed as the F-16 turned and came back around, hopefully this time to deliver its ordnance.

Finally the F-16C dropped a laser-guided 500lb bomb right on top of Zarqawi's safe house, with a delayed fuse to allow it to penetrate into the building before exploding. As a massive smoke cloud rose into the sky, the F-16C dropped a second 500lb bomb on the house to make sure no one escaped. Soon after, the first Delta element arrived by Little Bird to confront Iraqi police, who were already loading Zarqawi into a waiting ambulance.

They claimed not to know who the Jordanian was, but the operators disarmed them and took charge of Zarqawi who, incredibly, was still alive. The Delta medic worked to save him as the other operators cleared the site of the bombing, recovering the bodies of the spiritual advisor al Rahman, three adults and a female child – all inadvertently killed because of Zarqawi's murderous efforts to start a civil war in Iraq.

With Zarqawi's death, the work of the Task Force did not stop, and there was little time for celebration, That very night, 14 high-priority targets were added to the already-scheduled raids – each was a target that had been uncovered as part of Zarqawi's and al Rahman's network and would need to be hit before word got out that they were dead. Soon the hunt began again, now searching for Zarqawi's successor, his former second in command, Abu Ayyub al Masri.

INDUSTRIAL COUNTERTERRORISM

JSOC in Iraq was at the pinnacle of what was later termed industrial counterterrorism. General McChrystal had constructed the most sophisticated and effective man-hunting organization in the history of warfare. He had taken the unusual step of handing Iraq to Delta in 2003 as the insurgency first began to stir, promising that no other unit would come in to take over – Delta were there for the duration and it was its fight and its war. At the same time, McChrystal gave Afghanistan to a rotating command of the Rangers and DEVGRU.

It effectively meant that the Delta squadron commander was in charge of all JSOC resources in Iraq. Squadrons which rotated out stayed abreast of developments to ensure institutional knowledge was retained across the organization, and McChrystal built an agile, learning organization that could adapt quickly to a cunning and merciless enemy. Their operational tempo had also increased dramatically. In April 2004, Delta was running about ten operations a month. Four months later that had increased to 18. By 2006, they were averaging 300 raids a month. Assaulters were hitting one location, exploiting it and moving on to the next – often the teams were raiding three or four targets a night.

The intelligence product recovered from these raids, known as pocket litter as it included everything that was turned out from the pockets and wallets of dead or captured terrorists, was fed to the Task Force's own intelligence fusion cells. Two had been established as the Joint Interagency Task Force-East (JIATF-East) based in Bagram, Afghanistan and JIATF-West based in Balad, Iraq. The fusion cells were designed to support McChrystal's mantra: "F3EA – Find, Fix, Finish, Exploit, Analyze."

Firmly believing that it "took a network to destroy a network," the JSOC commander brought in intelligence and imagery analysts from the CIA and DIA, the National Security Agency (NSA), and the National Geospatial Intelligence Agency (NGA), to work with his team. Bringing together specialist areas of expertise, JSOC hoped to eliminate the "blinks" – operational delays caused by time spent contacting and requesting data, or expertise from other agencies. McChrystal felt that if he could get as many of the key agencies in one room and talking on the same network, he could dramatically decrease the blinks and increase the responsiveness of his targeting intelligence, and thus the output of his assault teams.

His objective was the creation of what he called the "unblinking eye" – the ability to find and continually track a target until it could be destroyed or captured. Reducing the blinks meant that all assets could be aimed at a particular target, and with the advent of new technologies and partner agencies working with JSOC, the unblinking eye concept became a reality. These new technologies included an NGA element that studied patterns of terrorist behavior in Iraq with the aim of predicting it (and which proved very useful against the al-Qaeda car-bombers).

The Task Force also instigated the technical development of a "magic wand" that could track the signals from specific cell phones – including from the air. Reports indicate a version was later developed that could be worn by assaulters, allowing them to track individual cell phones while at a target site. Software was developed to map the relationships between cell phones captured on the raids and those that

US Army Rangers seated on the external pods of an MH-6 Little Bird somewhere in Iraq as seen through a night vision camera. (Photographer unknown)

were being targeted. The technology was further refined over the years with NSA support from a team known as the Geo Cell, which geo-located targets in real-time via their cell phones (this technology was further refined and deployed years later to direct UAV strikes by JSOC against targets in the Pakistan tribal areas).

SENSOR TO SHOOTER

General McChrystal also needed to shorten the "sensor to shooter" cycle. He wanted the Task Force operating like narcotics police: hitting one target, and based on the intelligence found there, moving on to the next in a series of rolling raids. This required his analyst team to be able to exploit quickly any pocket litter, hard drives, or other intelligence recovered at a target location. The team could then use nodal analysis and database tools to make the connections that would lead to a fresh target that could be transmitted to the assaulters while they were still on the ground.

To do all of this, the analysts needed the pocket litter as an important first step. By and large, assault teams had been bagging everything found on or around their targets and placing it all together in black plastic rubbish bags. This inevitably meant that evidence was cross-contaminated and increased the time it took to understand exactly who they had and who their connections were. The assaulters were soon issued with digital cameras and instructed to photograph everything and everyone at the location and upload this to the analyst team. They were also schooled in evidence chain procedures, and pocket litter began being tagged in separate bags.

A DEVGRU SEAL writing under the pen name of Mark Owen described these Sensitive Site Exploitations in Afghanistan in 2009: "Basically, we shot pictures of the dead, gathered up any weapons and explosives, and collected thumb drives, computers, and papers. SSE had evolved over the years. It had become a way to rebut false accusations that the fighters we killed were innocent farmers … The more SSE we provided, the more proof we had that everyone we shot was guilty."

With the images the assaulters were uploading, the analysts could use facial recognition software, first pioneered by the British in Northern Ireland, to test for matches against known terrorists whose faces had been captured by surveillance or UAV cameras. The facial recognition also allowed the analysts to map connections between individuals and their cell phones. The Task Force needed surveillance assets to track all of these targets. So after increasing frustration at delays in acquiring their own Predator UAVs, SOCOM, JSOC's parent organization, purchased six ISR propeller planes that were custom-fitted for JSOC from the ground up. The planes could provide both aerial surveillance and signals intercept capability, while SOCOM waited for the Predators. Later in 2005, SOCOM raised its first Predator squadron with 24 aircraft – many of these were parceled out to JSOC, armed with Hellfire missiles and controlled-effect 250lb GPS-guided bombs.

The FBI was also an early supporter. The Bureau's Hostage Rescue Team (HRT) – the domestic law enforcement unit responsible for counterterrorism operations on American soil and ironically created with the assistance of Delta operators – joined JSOC in Iraq and Afghanistan. Its purpose was to offer its investigative experience to the assaulters after McChrystal specifically requested FBI expertise. These agents came along with Delta on their raids and were involved in numerous firefights, including killing terrorists.

THE LONG GAME

General McChrystal had to be careful to protect his precious resources. Owing to the grueling selection, normal attrition, increased liaison taskings, and the shocking number of casualties JSOC was incurring, Delta squadrons were often reduced to 30 or fewer healthy shooters. These operators could all expect to be deployed for a minimum of four months to Iraq conducting extremely dangerous

An Army Ranger pulling security outside a target site somewhere in Iraq, c. 2006. He wears a Protective Combat Uniform cold weather jacket and on his lower forearms are strapped plastic-covered aides-mémoires that provide important call signs and brevity codes at a glance. Snipers have been seen using a similar system for their rifle DOPE (Data-On-Previous-Engagements). (US SOCOM)

Assault Tactics

The Delta assaulters often raided a location by landing from Little Birds either directly on to the often flat Iraqi roofs or by fast roping straight down from the helicopters. Blocking teams, who established an outer cordon, would do likewise. The helicopter assault force would then fight its way down through the target building. A ground assault force, often arriving in armored six-wheeled Pandurs, would simultaneously hit the target from the ground floor up with the teams meeting somewhere in between. The extraction would also often be by armored vehicle, as experience showed that if a raid went "kinetic" (meaning it turned into a firefight), other insurgent gunmen, and often just anyone with an AK-47 in the immediate area, would show up to take a pot shot at the raiding party.

The Pandur was officially known as the Advanced Ground Mobility System (AGMS) and had been purchased for Delta in the wake of their experiences in Somalia during Operation *Gothic Serpent* in 1993. The unit realized it needed its own integral light armoured capability and an initial purchase of a dozen modified 6x6 Pandur armored personnel carriers was made. The JSOC Pandurs featured an advanced Israeli appliqué armor package, blast seating, a ballistic glass-enclosed

driver's compartment allowing full 360 degree situational awareness, and an advanced electronic countermeasures suite to defeat radio- and cell-phone detonated IEDs. It could also be sealed to operate in an NBC environment.

The SAS were also keen to purchase a number of the Pandurs for strike operations as the IED threat increased in Iraq. The manufacturer could not provide the Pandurs in the short time required, so instead the SAS purchased the Australian Bushmaster in a custom model known as the Escapade. It also featured an appliqué armor package to defeat RPGs and a Remote Weapons System mounting a .50cal heavy machine gun, among other technical enhancements. The upgraded Bushmasters arrived in Iraq in 2007. They were also deployed to Afghanistan after the SAS left Iraq in 2009.

The Little Bird helicopters of the 160th SOAR also proved ideal for Iraq. Compact and extremely agile, they could land in alleyways or on rooftops that larger helicopters such as the MH-60L simply could not. Their speed and size was their principal protection from ground fire. The AH-6M Six Gun gunship version would often be the first over a target, ready to suppress any enemy firing positions with its miniguns and rockets before the transport MH-6Ms arrived with the operators strapped on to the external pods. Air cover for the extraction back to base was provided by both AH-6Ms and aerial sniper teams perched on the pods of the MH-6M.

A rare shot of a Pandur Armored Ground Mobility System (AGMS) in use by Delta Force in Iraq. The AGMS was fitted with an Israeli passive appliqué armor package that bolted on to the chassis. This image is from about 2004; later versions featured improved gunner protection rather than the basic ASK shield seen here. (Photographer unknown)

and high-tempo operations every year as the squadrons rotated through. The remainder of the year was spent with four months as the on-call squadron to respond to emergencies or reinforce at short notice or on extended training, often overseas, and four months either doing build-up training for or resting after an Iraq deployment.

A much greater effort was also being made with local ground-holding units when Task Force assaults were conducted in their area of operations. The Task Force and SOF in general had long been criticized by conventional forces for poor communication and coordination. The same criticism was commonly heard in Afghanistan. The assault teams would arrive unannounced, conduct their operation and fly out, leaving the local units to deal with community anger and pick up the pieces of any counterinsurgency programs they had been attempting.

SOF argued that they needed to maintain operational security to avoid tipping off their targets. McChrystal's team worked hard to change this perception. The Task Force began to use "ops boxes" which would advise all Coalition Forces that an SOF operation was underway in a particular area. It also assigned liaison officers who would be attached to the local TOC while the operation was conducted. This allowed any questions or clarifications to be addressed directly to a representative of the Task Force.

The success of the Task Force was beginning to be seen at the tactical level as al-Qaeda terrorists began to fortify their safe houses and IED-making factories in response to the night raids. On one particular operation, six terrorists blockaded themselves on the second floor of a target building. After a Delta operator was wounded, the decision was made to bring up a pair of Bradleys with their deadly

A Ranger squad providing security on an objective. The lead man wears a PCU cold-weather jacket, MICH helmet with AN/PVS-14 monocular NOD and carries the then recently issued Mk46 squad automatic weapon – a modified version of the standard Army M249 SAW. (US SOCOM)

25mm cannons to level the second floor. Even after both Bradleys exhausted their ammunition and set fire to the building, the jihadists fought on, firing from the windows. Eventually a thermobaric demolition charge was placed by a Delta EOD operator that finally brought the building down around the jihadists' heads.

An AH-6M Little Bird was shot down in November 2006 while escorting in a 20-man Delta assault helicopter force riding on two MH-6s and two MH-60Ls on their way to a time-sensitive daylight raid to target a foreign fighter facilitator. En route to the target, an RPG fired skyward by an opportunistic insurgent as they flew over Talil struck the AH-6 in the tail, blowing away the rotor. With consummate skill, the pilots managed to land the helicopter in one piece in a nearby field. The assault force quickly landed and the operators set up a defensive cordon around the downed aircraft while the two pilots, both injured in the crash, were evacuated by the MH-60L.

While they awaited a Downed Aircraft Recovery Team (DART), a number of technicals (armed trucks) were identified closing in about a kilometre from the crash site. The surviving AH-6M Six Gun took off to intercept. As he flew low over the technicals to ensure they were not Iraqi security forces, he saw that each of the six trucks had a twin-barrel 14.5mm ZPU-2 antiaircraft cannon mounted on its flat bed. Moments later, he had his answer as the ZPUs began to engage the ground force. The AH-6M immediately rolled in and opened up on the technicals with its miniguns followed by its 2.75in unguided rockets.

The antiaircraft fire was joined by a large number of insurgents in houses below who began firing small arms and RPGs up at the little helicopter. These gunmen, numbering around 20, were also within line of sight of the crash site. The AH-6 pilot made gun runs on the trucks and launched rockets at the houses to keep their heads down (his co-pilot even began firing his M4 carbine out of the helicopter's open door at the insurgents). The pilot, CWO5 David Cooper, remarked in an interview, "Varying altitude and airspeeds, banking left and right, again I'm just acting like a crazy man in that helicopter so they cannot get a bead on us."

A QRF from the Task Force had been launched, but it would take time to get there. The lone AH-6 kept up the gun runs on the technicals and the insurgents in the buildings. Running low on ammunition, it landed several times to rearm from the munitions carried on the downed Little Bird. The pilot kept the insurgents at bay until the QRF arrived led by two AH-6Ms (one flown by the original crew of the shot down Little Bird). The three Little Bird Six Guns joined forces and opened up on the remaining technicals before the insurgents broke contact and retreated.

The AH-6s orbited over the crash site to protect the Delta operators while a pair of F-16C Fighting Falcons arrived to hunt down the two trucks, which had managed to escape. They destroyed the first, but as they swung in to line up the last one, the lead F-16C came in too low and hit the ground, exploding in a massive fireball, tragically killing the pilot – the only US casualty of the day.

THE IRANIANS

In 2007 General McChrystal established Task Force 17 as the Counter-Iranian-Influence unit, targeting the Iranian-supported Special Groups of Shia insurgents and their al Quds Force trainers. Al Quds is a covert unit of the Iranian Revolutionary Guards that was long suspected of supporting Shia insurgents with training and technology, including the deadly EFP (Explosively Formed Projectile) IEDs. Delta had captured five Iranians from the al Quds in Irbil, northern Iraq – the first solid evidence of direct involvement with the insurgency.

The capture of the five al Quds members may have led to a later Iranian-backed operation against US forces at a Joint Security Station in Karbala. Gunmen dressed in American ACU camouflage uniforms and carrying M4 carbines arrived at the base in a number of black SUVs. The Iraqi gate guards had waved the SUVs through assuming they were Americans. Instead the occupants of the SUVs shot and killed one US serviceman and wounded three others. They grabbed four American soldiers at gunpoint and bundled them into the SUVs before speeding away. The SUVs were later found dumped and all four Americans shot dead, three in the vehicles and one at a local hospital. Based on intelligence recovered from an SAS raid in Basra, Delta Force later killed the alleged mastermind of that operation in a raid in Sadr City when the target attempted to grab one of the operators' H&K 416 rifles. The SAS also captured a Lebanese Hezbollah facilitator who was working for the Iranians as a trainer for the Shia insurgents. He was later handed over to the Iraqis who released him in 2012, much to the disgust of the Americans.

The British were also losing helicopters. In April 2007, a pair of Pumas conducting the insertion of an SAS raiding party collided with each other. Two SAS operators were killed in the crash and another badly wounded. This and a second fatal Puma crash in November, which left a further two SAS soldiers dead, resulted in an RAF Board of Inquiry that suggested that the special operators were forcing the pilots, and the elderly Puma airframes, to conduct maneuvers that were considered unsafe and beyond the scope of what the aircraft were designed to do.

Another SAS soldier was killed in Tikrit in 2008 in an operation targeting a two-man car bomb cell that went badly wrong. After using a loudspeaker to call on the occupants to surrender and sending in a Combat Assault Dog, who was killed by the building's occupants, an SAS assault team explosively breached into the target house and was immediately ambushed as it entered. Four SAS operators were seriously wounded by small arms fire and an SAS Sergeant killed. The terrorists fired out at the operators as they attempted to withdraw with their wounded until an orbiting AC-130 opened fire on the house, allowing the operators to break contact and pull back.

Residents in a neighboring house then opened fire on the assault team. The AC-130 switched targets and engaged the second house with its 40mm Bofors cannon. Terrorists escaping from the neighboring house as the roof collapsed used several civilians as human shields, who were unfortunately engaged and killed from the air by the AC-130 which couldn't distinguish the terrorists from the hostages. Eventually the objective was secured and the assaulters confirmed both targets had been killed.

The Task Force conducted a rare cross-border raid in October 2008, some of which was filmed by Syrian civilians on their cell phones. The target of the raid was Abu Ghadiya, an Iraqi facilitator for al-Qaeda in Iraq. He facilitated the crossing of foreign jihadists from the Syrian border into Iraq by providing false passports, weapons, and cash along with access to a network of al-Qaeda fixers in Iraq who would ensure the jihadists reached the front line. He was believed to be shipping as many as 100 jihadists into Iraq every month.

The target was near the infamous city of Al Qaim where Delta Force and the Marines had long been battling foreign fighters entering the country via the Western Euphrates Ratline. This time however, the target was situated just over the border in Syria itself, in the village of Al Sukariya. With its position confirmed by ISR, a helicopter assault force was launched on a late afternoon raid from a Task Force forward-operating location in Tikrit. It was apparently composed of four MH-60L Blackhawks and a pair of AH-6M Six Gun attack helicopters.

The assault package landed on top of the target location – a farm building under construction that Abu Ghadiya was using as his temporary headquarters. Two MH-60s stayed aloft, carrying cut-off groups and snipers, while the other two landed the assault team on the target. From the cell phone footage, it is apparent that some resistance was encountered as the distinctive sound of miniguns firing can be heard, either from the AH-6s or the doorgunners on the MH-60Ls. The target, his brother and a number of gunmen were killed by the Delta operators on the ground. The body of Abu Ghadiya was bagged up by the assaulters and placed aboard one of the helicopters for later DNA matching before the whole assault force extracted back across the border to Iraq. Total time on the ground had reportedly been less than 15 minutes.

A Green Beret assigned to the counter-Iranian-influence Task Force 17 maintains security during an operation in Baghdad in 2008. (Senior Airman Clay Lancaster; US Air Force)

A Ranger carrying an M4A1 carbine with underslung M203 grenade launcher and M68 Aimpoint sight, 2004. Just visible by his right leg is a pistol-grip Remington entry shotgun loaded with specialist frangible shells to blow locks on doors. Note also his abseil gloves hanging from his armor. (US SOCOM)

One of the last SAS operations in Iraq saw a troop from B Squadron conduct a combat parachute drop into Anbar Province targeting an al-Qaeda counterfeiter who financed AQI operations. For the SAS, their war ended in April 2009 as UK forces withdrew from Iraq. The main British base in southern Iraq had been controversially closed in late 2007 in a deal with the Shia militias, and Special Forces operations in the south were significantly curtailed to avoid aggravating the situation. The last SAS operators left Iraq in May 2009.

In the rest of Iraq, operations for the Task Force were also beginning to reduce as the Sons of Iraq initiative continued to gain momentum and more and more districts were handed over to Iraqi Security Forces. Iraqi SOF was also increasingly taking the lead in raids against al-Qaeda targets. Zarqawi's successor, the Egyptian Abu Ayyub al Masri was finally tracked down and killed by Iraqi SOF in April 2010 southwest of Tikrit.

The night-time raid killed al Masri; Abu Omar al Baghdadi, the leader of the al-Qaeda affiliate Islamic State of Iraq (later known as ISIL, ISIS, and IS, and at the time of writing headed by another terrorist calling himself al Baghdadi); al Baghdadi's son and al Masri's assistant. The assaulters surrounded a remote building where the targets were sheltering. They were ordered to come out by the Iraqi SOF but instead opened fire. The joint unit returned fire and entered the building. Al Masri detonated his suicide bomb vest, killing himself.

A UH-60 Blackhawk supporting the operation crashed sadly killing a Ranger Sergeant and injuring the American aircrew. Two days later al-Qaeda's northern commander was killed in a joint raid in Mosul – no doubt targeted thanks to intelligence recovered from the earlier operation in Tikrit. These operations

DELTA FORCE RAID,
AL SUKARIYAH, SYRIA, OCTOBER 2008

demonstrated the dramatic new skills of Iraqi Special Operations Forces, developed by intensive mentoring by Army Green Berets and SEALs.

The war in Iraq officially ended for the United States on December 31, 2011 when the Iraqi government failed to agree a new Status of Force Agreement with the United States government. JSOC in Iraq, with the British Special Forces by their side, had killed an estimated 3,000 insurgents over the nine years of the relentless campaign.

They captured upwards of 9,000.

The Task Force was widely credited with both drastically reducing the operational effectiveness of the insurgency as its leaders and bomb makers were routinely captured or killed; enabling the counterinsurgency surge and the Sons of Iraq initiative to succeed by eliminating what General Petraeus termed the "irreconcilables." JSOC and the SAS also saved the lives and limbs of many Coalition soldiers, Marines and Iraqi civilians who otherwise would have fallen victim to al-Qaeda's increasingly sophisticated IEDs and car bombs.

CHAPTER 6
KILL OR CAPTURE
AFGHANISTAN 2006–2014

The SOF campaign in Afghanistan was focused to a large degree, particularly before 2009, on targeting the "irreconcilable elements" within the insurgency – the leaders who would never be swayed to sit at the negotiating table, their subcommanders, and their key bomb makers and logisticians. The United States and ISAF felt that, like in Iraq, precisely targeted SOF capture or kill missions against such individuals would positively shape the battlefield.

Intractable Taliban leaders could be replaced by more moderate or at least less competent replacements, or the time-honed skills of the master bomb maker would vanish with his death, meaning IEDs facing the troops on the ground may be easier to detect and to disarm. General McChrystal and his replacement Admiral Bill McRaven talked about "degrading capabilities," and the capture or kill missions were aimed at doing exactly that.

At the strategic level, the black SOF conducted such operations against high-value targets whose death or capture would have theater-level impact – principally senior figures in the Taliban and al-Qaeda-related targets. White SOF carried out operations in support of both local and national objectives – they would target the leaders of the Taliban shadow government within a province, for example, and also target local bomb makers and IED cells which were causing problems for local ground-holding units. They would also be involved in supporting conventional operations such as large-scale offensives by targeting local leadership to degrade the insurgency's response to such operations.

Although NATO figures suggest around 90 percent of these operations were resolved without a shot being fired, they were viewed with suspicion by some segments of the media who argued they were akin to death squads. When civilians

A US Army Ranger Military Working Dog team maintaining perimeter security during a kill or capture night raid, Afghanistan, 2012. The green glow comes from the Rangers' night vision goggles. (Sergeant Brian Kohl; US Army)

were hurt or killed on these raids, Afghan political figures from President Karzai down would issue strongly worded calls for an end to such night raids and for ISAF forces to be barred from entering Afghan homes. Much of Karzai's spite was for the domestic political audience, although his calls did eventually result in tactical change on the battlefield – a particularly dangerous precedent.

From 2012, ISAF forces were no longer allowed to enter Afghan residences – all entries would have to be conducted by Afghan Security Forces apart from in narrowly defined "exceptional circumstances" – normally based on the type of target that was being pursued. Additionally, each operation would have to be pre-approved by an Afghan judicial body. However, the caveat was that these approvals and restrictions only applied when an Afghan civilian home was to be searched; there was a reasonable chance of Afghan prisoners being detained; and if the targets were not an "immediate threat." Under these caveats, unilateral operations could still be launched.

A Navy SEAL Military Working Dog handler and his dog providing overwatch for his team. The SEAL carries the Mk18 CQB-R carbine, a weapon developed for Naval Special Warfare. Note also the dog has goggles available to shield his eyes from dust or during fast rope insertions. (Lance Corporal Ryan Rholes; US Marines)

THE TASK FORCE

As has been said earlier, Task Force Sword became Task Force 11 in January 2002. Manned by a DEVGRU squadron and a Ranger company and supported by a company of helicopters from the 160th SOAR, the Task Force had many notable successes while its higher-profile counterparts in Iraq received most of the precious surveillance and reconnaissance assets. Years later, in an unclassified SOCOM release in 2013, the role of the JSOC Task Force in Afghanistan was graphically spelled out: "Conducts offensive operations in Afghanistan to degrade Taliban, al-Qaeda, and the Haqqani Networks in order to prevent them from establishing operationally significant safe havens which threaten the stability and sovereignty of GIRoA (Government of the Islamic Republic of Afghanistan) and the United States." For many years, its primary targets remained al-Qaeda and al-Qaeda-related groups such as Haqqani.

In 2003, the SEALs of DEVGRU conducted a cross-border operation to transfer captured high-value target and 9/11 planner Khalid Sheikh Mohammed from Pakistan to southern Afghanistan. The terrorist mastermind had been arrested in a joint Pakistani ISI and CIA operation and was now heading to a US black site prison in an undisclosed country – most likely Poland or Romania. But first he needed to be brought back to Afghanistan.

Seen through a night vision camera, an unknown US SOF operator, most likely a Ranger or Green Beret, provides overwatch from a compound roof during a night raid in Afghanistan, 2012. (Specialist Stephen Cline; US Army)

Under Operation *Noble Venture*, companies from the Rangers and 82nd Airborne secured an improvised desert strip in a dry river bed near the Pakistani border. An MC-130 Combat Talon cargo plane landed, taxied to a halt and lowered its ramp, its engines spinning. A SEAL Desert Patrol Vehicle appeared carrying several DEVGRU operators and their captive strapped in the rear seat with a hood over his head. The little dune buggy raced down into the dry riverbed and up the MC-130's ramp. As quickly as it had arrived, the Combat Talon raised the ramp, taxied and lifted off, taking the SEALs and their high-value target with it.

VIGILANT HARVEST

DEVGRU and the Rangers also crossed into Pakistani territory in their hunt for al-Qaeda leaders allegedly under the codename *Vigilant Harvest*. Although the CIA's Counterterrorist Pursuit Teams have long strayed across the ill-defined border with Pakistan, the first generally acknowledged cross-border operation involving the American military was conducted in March 2006 when a DEVGRU and Ranger element, flown in by the 160th SOAR, struck an al-Qaeda training camp in northern Waziristan. Although falsely credited to the Pakistani Special

Service Group, the operation killed as many as 30 terrorists including the infamous Chechen camp commandant Imam Asad.

The teams had "spun up" (been ready to go, onboard their helos with rotors spinning) before for cross-border operations, but they had never been given the green light. In late 2005, an operation was planned into Pakistan after CIA intelligence was received that indicated al Zawahiri, al-Qaeda's spiritual leader, was attending a meeting in a compound close to the border. The plan called for a DEVGRU troop to parachute in from MC-130s while in Afghan airspace, use directional chutes to steer across the Pakistani border, land, proceed to the target, and capture or kill the leadership targets before being exfiltrated by MH-53 transport helicopters that would fly low and fast across the border, staying under Pakistani air defense radar.

A SEAL DEVGRU team kitting up prior to an operation. They wear Naval Special Warfare specific Crye AOR1 camouflage pattern (visually similar to Marine desert MARPAT) and Crye plate carriers, also in AOR1 pattern. Their rifles are HK416s. (Photographer unknown)

The political leadership in the US administration was wary of any operation that would give jihadist elements in Pakistan ammunition against the increasingly frail Pakistani government. It wanted reassurances that the SEALs would not be caught and paraded in front of television cameras in Lahore or Islamabad. JSOC offered to add a company of Rangers to the assault package to provide force protection for the assaulters and an Immediate Reaction Force if needed on the target.

The Pentagon was not convinced that the single source for the intelligence was to be trusted (and doubtless fearing the possibility of a baited ambush similar to that which occurred years later with the al-Qaeda double agent turned suicide bomber at Forward Operating Base Chapman who killed seven CIA personnel in 2009).

As the size of the assault force grew so did the trepidation felt in certain parts of the Pentagon and White House, even after the operation was officially authorized. Frustratingly for the operators, the MC-130 carrying the raiders was in the air and closing on the Pakistani border when the operation was aborted. A 2006 strike by a CIA Predator UAV in the same area narrowly missed killing al Zawahiri.

In 2007, a Task Force kill or capture operation was almost launched to target bin Laden himself. A CIA source had reported seeing bin Laden in Tora Bora. A significant proportion of the ISR assets available in the theater converged on the remote area, searching for corroborating intelligence. Like the 2005 operation,

US Army Rangers from the 3rd Battalion of the 75th conducting a clearance operation, 2012. Note the radio operator using a satellite array to transmit while his colleagues maintain 360-degree security. (Sergeant Brian Kohl; US DOD)

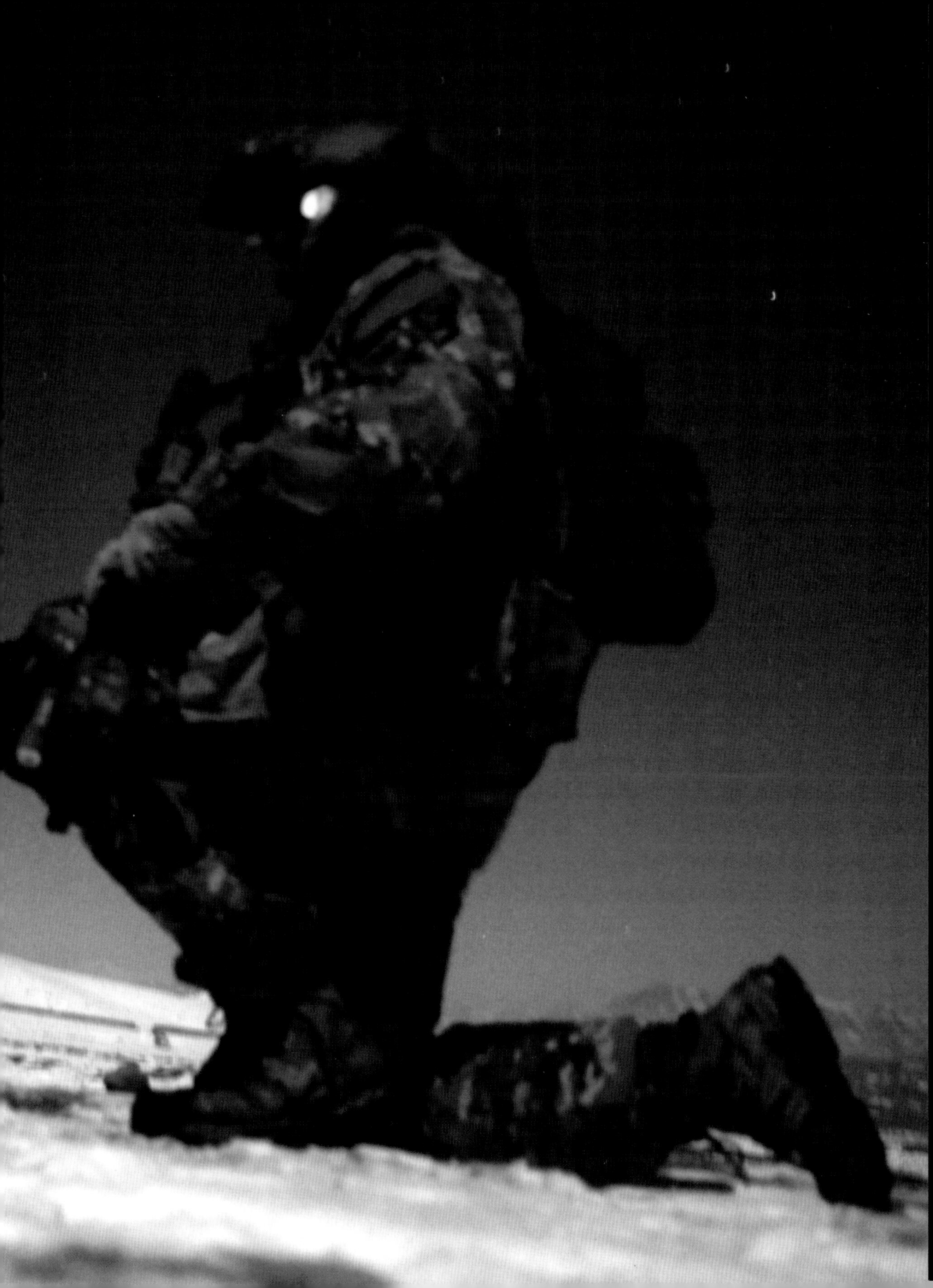

An impressive image of an US Army Blackhawk dropping off a small SOF reconnaissance team somewhere high in the Afghan mountains. The SOF team are unknown, but it could be Army Special Forces or Ranger Reconnaissance Company or even Coalition SOF such as the British SAS. (US SOCOM)

the initial plan, based around a small helicopter assault force landing at the target site, soon ballooned in size to include Special Forces ODAs as cut-off groups and a Ranger element to provide a cordon for the SEALs.

Eventually the operation was launched under the cover of Air Force bombing, but after a week of fruitless searching through the mountains, there was no sign of high-value target number one. Another operation was launched a year later into Angoor Adda in southern Waziristan, targeting unspecified al-Qaeda leadership targets. A number of terrorists were killed by the SEALs but no high-value targets were identified at the site.

The CIA also maintained a cross-border capability in the form of the indigenous militia of the Counter Terrorist Pursuit Teams. The CTPTs employed former SOF contractors working for the Special Activities Division to mentor, train, and deploy alongside the locally recruited militia in a program similar to the Vietnam era Civilian Irregular Defense Groups which conducted border surveillance operations for the CIA and Special Forces (some of the CTPTs wear Vietnam-style Tiger Stripe camouflage uniforms in perhaps an ironic tip of the hat to their heritage). The first CTPT was established in Kabul but deployed extensively in the east to conduct cross-border intelligence gathering, reconnaissance, and ambushing. The largest CTPT was based at Firebase Lilley in Shkin.

Along with deniable cross-border operations hunting al-Qaeda, the JSOC Task Force was also targeting Taliban leadership in Afghanistan and conducting the occasional hostage rescue. In September 2005, a British security contractor was kidnapped by Taliban insurgents in Farah Province. The JSOC Task Force managed to locate where he was being held – in a mountainous region of Bala Boluk – and, according to a later coroner's inquest, attempted a hostage rescue operation. Tragically, his Taliban captors apparently slashed the hostage's throat and fled as a DEVGRU team arrived on an early morning raid.

In July 2006 a joint operation mounted by the Rangers and DEVGRU was eerily both reminiscent of the Operation *Red Wings* shoot-down of Turbine 33 a year earlier and prescient of the future downing of Extortion 17 in August 2011. A pair of MH-47Es attempted to insert a combined strike element of Rangers, SEALs, and Afghan Commandos on to a target compound in Helmand Province, but it was ambushed by a large insurgent force. With some elements already on the ground and both helicopters being struck by small arms fire, one MH-47 pilot banked away and bravely put himself and his aircraft directly in the line of fire between it and its partner, which was still on the ground disembarking its cargo of special operators.

The MH-47 was hit by an RPG which caused enough damage to force the helicopter to crash-land. The skill of the Nightstalker pilots saved the operators and aircrew on board. Miraculously no one was seriously wounded in the crash. The Ranger mission commander and an attached Australian Commando organized an all-round defense while its sister MH-47 stayed on-station and held back advancing insurgents until its miniguns ran dry. High above them, an AC-130 Spectre fixed-wing gunship joined in the battle and kept the downed aircrew and passengers safe until a British Immediate Response Team helicopter successfully recovered them. The AC-130 then opened up on the downed MH-47, destroying the wreck and denying it to the Taliban.

The actions of the pilots of the 160th SOAR were not the only heroics being displayed. Ranger Master Sergeant Leroy Petry was awarded the Medal of Honor for his actions in Paktia Province on May 26, 2006 during a daylight high-value target raid. Clearing a compound, Petry and a fellow Ranger were struck by small arms fire, wounding them both. Finding cover behind an animal enclosure, a Ranger Sergeant ran forward to treat their wounds. As he was doing so, an insurgent grenade detonated nearby wounding the newly arrived Sergeant and Petry's colleague who had already suffered multiple gunshot wounds.

Moments later a second insurgent grenade landed right next to the trio. Before it could detonate, Petry made a split-second decision to save his comrades' lives and grabbed the grenade and threw it back toward the insurgents. Just as it left his hand, the grenade exploded, taking Petry's right hand with it. He remained conscious and even managed to apply a tourniquet to his wrist to stem the blood loss and assist his wounded team-mates until the insurgents were eliminated and the objective secured.

A US Army Ranger from 1st Battalion, 75th Ranger Regiment provides overwatch for his team-mates during a raid in Paktia Province, 2013. He is one of his platoon's designated marksmen and carries the 7.62mm Mk17 SCAR mounting a Spectre variable magnification sight. (Specialist Codie M. Mendenhall; US Army)

Rangers secure an entrance during a joint raid with Afghan Commandos, 2009. The Ranger on the right carries a hydraulic Hurst Rabbit Tool to force open doors. The Ranger on the left appears to be a medic, based on the pack he is carrying. (Sergeant Matthew Friberg; US Army)

A Ranger assault team moves into a target location – smoke is just visible probably from a flashbang distraction device. The Ranger on the right carries a short-barrelled M4A1 with an EO Tech close-quarter battle sight – Ranger units often equip their assault fire teams with such specialist CQB weapons. (Sergeant Matthew Friberg; US Army)

Another 2006 mission highlighted the incredible work conducted by the 75th Ranger Regiment's highly secretive Ranger Reconnaissance Detachment (RRD). A six-man RRD team attached to the JSOC Task Force inserted into the Hindu Kush mountain range after intelligence indicated insurgent chief Haqqani would be entering Afghanistan from Pakistan. Establishing an observation post at a position almost 4,000m above sea level, the RRD team waited and watched for their target. As insurgents streamed into the area, indicating something big was indeed about to occur, the Ranger team was spotted and fired upon. In response, the RRD's attached JTAC called in an orbiting B-1B strategic bomber to pummel the insurgents. Although an estimated 100 insurgents were killed in the airstrikes, Haqqani was unfortunately not among them.

UK SPECIAL FORCES

Coalition Forces were also conducting kill or capture missions at the behest of JSOC and ISAF. In Helmand Province, British Special Forces from the SBS and SRR were heavily engaged in degrading the local Taliban's ability to attack Task Force Helmand, the British Battle Group in the province. One of the earliest was Operation *Ilios* on June 27, 2006.

An Australian SASR soldier training Uruzgan Provincial Response Company police in close-quarter battle tactics. Note their distinctive Bulgarian AMD-65s fitted with Aimpoints and laser pointers. (Corporal Chris Moore; Australian DOD)

BELOW British Special Forces Support Group operators aboard a Marine CH-53 on a joint operation in Helmand. The All-Terrain Vehicles sometimes with trailers, as shown here, are often brought on heliborne SOF operations thanks to their compact size – they are primarily used to carry ammunition and water resupplies or to evacuate casualties. (US DOD)

An exceedingly rare image of the Special Forces Support Group (SFSG) in Afghanistan, c. 2008. To either side are a pair of Menacity OAV/SRV vehicles – a version of which became the British Army's Jackal platform. The operators wear Crye MultiCam and Paraclete plate carriers in Ranger Green. (Photographer unknown)

The operation targeted four Taliban leaders on the outskirts of Sangin. Sadly it ended in disaster. The team was a mixed, 16-man unit from C Squadron of the SBS and the recently raised SRR. Disembarking from their Land Rovers some distance from the targets, the team made their way silently into the target compounds and quietly snatched their suspects. As they made their way back to their vehicles, they were contacted by a number of insurgents and a firefight broke out. With one of their vehicles disabled by RPG fire, the team took cover in an irrigation ditch and dispatched a desperate request for assistance while holding off an estimated 60 insurgents.

The Helmand Battle Group had not been informed of the operation until things went wrong and a Quick Reaction Force was requested by the Special Forces liaison officer attached to Battle Group HQ. A Gurkha QRF was rapidly dispatched only to run into an insurgent ambush. After an hour-long gunfight, and under the protective gaze of a pair of Apache attack helicopters, the combined Gurkha and SOF force managed to break contact and withdraw to the closest FOB. There they discovered that two of the SOF operators, an officer from the SRR and an SBS Sergeant, were missing.

A British Parachute Regiment company was immediately lifted into the area by RAF Chinook to conduct a search for the missing men. One operator had made an attempt to reach the SOF vehicles in an effort to evacuate their wounded but was shot in the process. His team mates witnessed the shooting and saw his unresponsive body and assumed he was dead. The second operator went missing during the chaos of the firefight, his fate unknown. A pair of Apaches spotted two heat sources and guided in the ground troops to recover both bodies from a nearby field. An account that the men's bodies had been mutilated by the Taliban has never been confirmed. Of the four Taliban commanders seized in the operation, two were killed in the ambush crossfire, while the two others escaped in the chaos.

Other later operations were far more successful, including the killings of Mullah Dadullah and Mullah Abdul Matin by the SBS. The one-legged Mullah Dadullah was the Taliban's military commander and a member of its leadership council. He spent much of his time in Pakistan, fully aware that he would be on American targeting lists. After a controversial prisoner exchange of two senior Taliban commanders, including Mullah Shah Mansoor, Dadullah's brother, for a captured Italian journalist and his Afghan interpreters in March 2007, an ISA team tracked the pair by classified means, hoping they would reveal the location of Dadullah.

By May, the two senior Taliban leaders had led JSOC to a compound near Bahram Chah in southern Helmand. ISA confirmed that their target was in the compound, having crossed the border from Pakistan for an important Shura. An SBS reconnaissance element in Menacity Surveillance and Reconnaissance

A group of unknown British Special Forces – most likely a combined element of SBS (in the mixed camouflage patterns) and SFSG – somewhere in Afghanistan. Based on their equipment the image probably dates from 2005–2006. (Photographer unknown)

Vehicles conducted a close-target reconnaissance of the compound, parking up in camouflaged hides and watching through long-range cameras. It appeared that there were around 20 insurgents protecting Dadullah. An airstrike was considered but decided against as there was no guarantee Dadullah would be killed. A night-time helicopter-borne raid would be the only way to make sure.

With the ISA monitoring its target, the majority of C Squadron of the SBS kitted up and boarded a pair of RAF CH-47D Chinooks which landed at an off-set HLZ. The SBS operators, under overhead Apache cover, dashed down the ramps and into the darkness. Moments later they breached the compound and a lengthy but one-sided firefight erupted as small groups of Taliban were hunted down and killed. During the one long contact, four SBS operators were hit and wounded, one seriously. Finally, Dadullah himself was cornered and shot in the chest and head. Digital imagery was taken and a quick SSE conducted before the helicopters returned to pick up the strike force.

As a postscript to the operation, Dadullah's brother, Mullah Shah Mansoor, freed by the Afghan government in the earlier prisoner exchange, along with Mullah Abdul Rahim, the Taliban's Shadow Governor of Helmand, were both killed in an airstrike on a Taliban leadership meeting several months later, leading to informed speculation that Mansoor had been continually and technically tracked by ISA until his eventual demise.

Mullah Abdul Matin, the Shadow Governor of Musa Qalah in Helmand Province, was killed a year later in February 2008 in Gereshk. Matin, his sub-commander, and several bodyguards were travelling by motorcycle when an SBS team was inserted in their path by Chinook. Matin and his colleagues were ambushed by the SBS operators and all were shot dead.

The SBS have also been involved in hostage rescues in Afghanistan. In September 2007, a joint mission with Italian Col Moschin SOF was launched to recover two Italian intelligence agents who had been captured by the Taliban. The plan was for Col Moschin to take the lead, parachuting into an off-set drop zone and marching overnight to surround the target compound. Once in place, the Italian assaulters would storm the compound and release the hostages. Several teams from C Squadron of the SBS were standing by several kilometers away in a number of Lynx and Chinook helicopters to provide cut-off groups in case the insurgents attempted to escape. Overhead, an American Predator fed real-time video to the British and Italian teams.

It has never been disclosed if the Italian operators were compromised as they moved in or whether chance intervened in their plans, but the insurgents brought the hostages out of the compound and loaded them into a number of four-wheel drive vehicles before the Italian SOF were in a position to stop them. The SBS were notified and took up the chase, closing in on the speeding vehicles. Aerial snipers engaged the vehicles' engine blocks with .50cal Barrett M82A1 antimaterial rifles, forcing the vehicles to stop. A Chinook had dropped off more than a dozen SBS operators ahead of the vehicles. As the Taliban leapt from their trucks they were engaged in a brief firefight. All eight insurgents were shot dead. However, they had managed to shoot both hostages – one was shot in the head and chest and later died of his wounds.

In September 2009, the SBS and the SFSG conducted a hostage rescue mission in Kunduz Province. A *New York Times* journalist, Stephen Farrell, and his Afghan interpreter, Sultan Munadi, had been investigating the controversial ISAF bombing of a pair of hijacked petrol tankers, which had killed a large number of civilians when they were seized by Taliban insurgents. ISR confirmed they were being held in a Taliban safe house in the Char Dara District. Senior Taliban leaders were picked up on signals intercepts discussing moving the hostages across the border into Pakistan, so British Special Forces were forced to act.

With JSOC UAV support, the target house was confirmed and kept under constant surveillance while an operation was launched to rescue the pair. Inserted by 160th SOAR helicopters directly on to the target, the SBS team assaulted the building while the SFSG established blocking positions, ensuring that no Taliban could escape and no enemy reinforcements could cause difficulties for the rescue team. In the pre-dawn operation, the Afghan interpreter was shot and killed as was an SFSG soldier from 1st Battalion, the Parachute Regiment. Two civilians were also killed by the explosive breach the assaulters used to gain entry to the main house. The journalist was rescued unharmed.

AUSTRALIAN SOF

Among Coalition SOF, one of the largest deployments after the Americans and the British was the Australians. After a number of SASR (Special Air Service Regiment) Special Forces Task Group rotations in 2001 and 2002, a larger

A British Special Forces Support Group operator caught exiting a US Marine CH-53E at Camp Bastion after a joint operation in Helmand, August 2013. The SFSG operator carries a 7.62mm HK417 indicating his role as a marksman or sniper. (Sergeant Gabriela Garcia; US Marines)

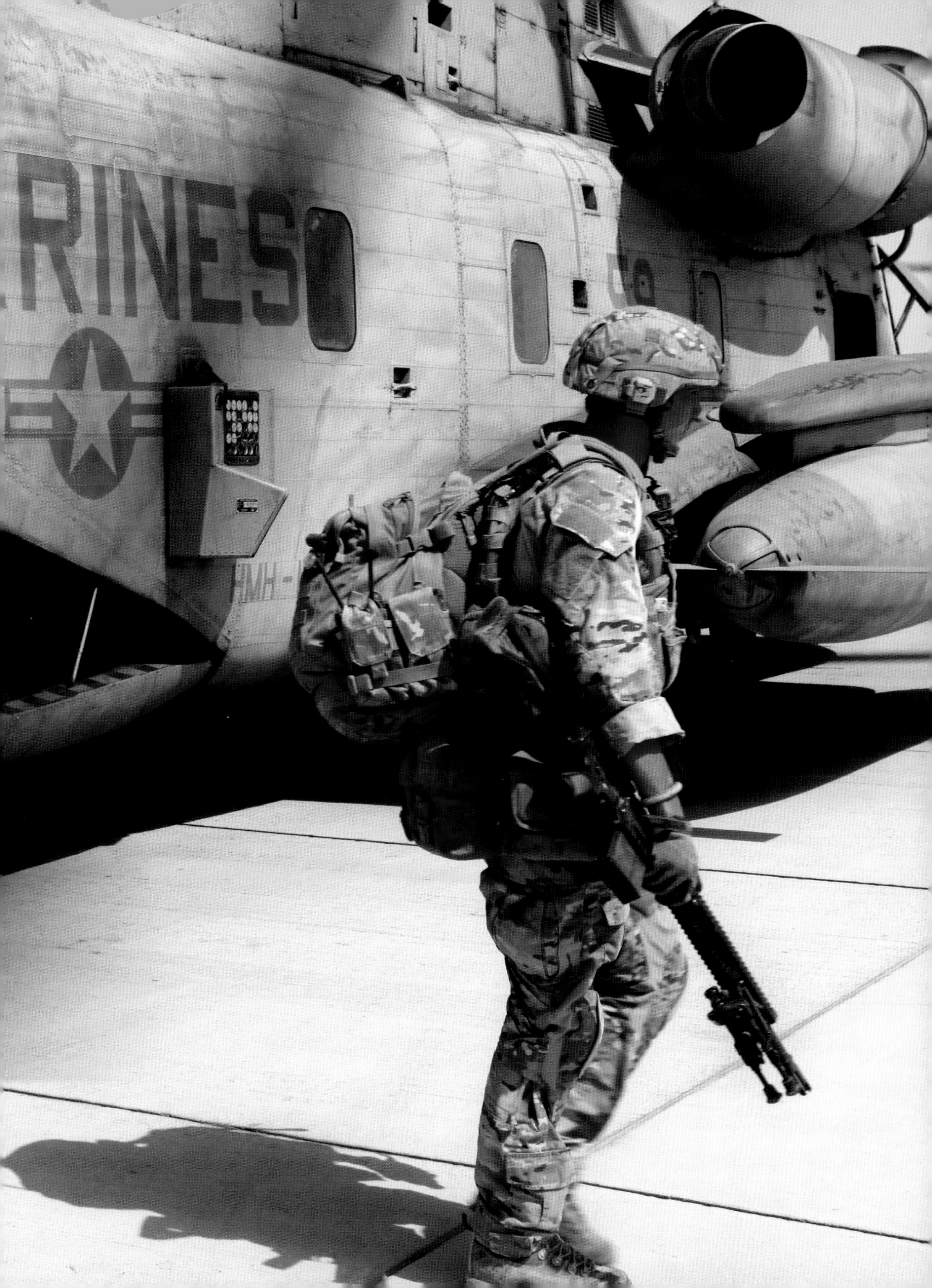
RINES

SASR

The Australian Special Air Service Regiment was founded in 1957 based on a number of World War II special operations unit. Closely aligned to its British counterparts in 22 SAS, the SASR was organized in a similar fashion – there are currently three Sabre squadrons and one covert squadron that does not appear on its formal structure.

In the early years, the SASR deployed with the British SAS to Borneo where its legendary reconnaissance and jungle fighting skills were first honed. Ten years in Vietnam saw the SASR called Ma Rung by the enemy – the phantoms of the jungle. Small SASR patrols of five men would silently operate in the Viet Cong's backyard,

conducting intelligence-gathering operations or snap ambushes aimed at snatching a prisoner or simply unsettling the opposition.

After Vietnam, SASR sometimes struggled to find a role until it was given the national counterterrorism mission in the late 1970s. The SASR also deployed on covert missions to Papua New Guinea in the 1980s and later to Somalia. In 2000, the SASR and 4RAR Commando (now 2 Commando Regiment) provided reconnaissance and surveillance capabilities for the UN-mandated INTERFET intervention into East Timor. Along with the British, the SASR were one of the first units to deploy in support of Operation *Enduring Freedom-Afghanistan*.

An Australian SASR patrol is extracted by a UH-60 Blackhawk from the 101st Airborne Division somewhere in Uruzgan Province. (Australian DOD)

commitment followed in August 2005 with the deployment of the first Special Operations Task Group (SOTG). This was built around an SASR squadron operating in the troubled Uruzgan province where the Australians also ran a Provincial Reconstruction Team. A second SOTG was again deployed in April 2007. This was the first time a company from 4RAR (4th Battalion, the Royal Australian Regiment; now 2 Commando Regiment) – an elite light infantry unit comparable to the Rangers – deployed with the SASR.

These later deployments were more focused on direct action operations, with the SASR taking the fight to the Taliban and acting as offensive force protection for the conventional forces Reconstruction Task Force. It also carried out operations in direct support of the various US-led SOF Task Forces. Indeed, the SASR's first casualty from enemy fire occurred with the death of Sergeant Matthew Locke on 25 October 2007 from Taliban small arms fire while on a mounted patrol in support of a larger ISAF operation. Soon after, the 4RAR Commandos lost their first man in a direct action operation against a Taliban bomb-making facility near Tarin Kowt.

A reconnaissance patrol into the inhospitable Kush Khadir Valley, in November 2007, north of its base at Tarin Kowt is a good example of the type of operations in which the newly arrived 4RAR component was engaged. The operation required a small team to climb through the snow-tipped ridges on the hunt for a Taliban group that was reported to be operating in the area.

Climbing at dark wearing night-vision goggles, the lead Australians almost ran into a Taliban commander who appeared from behind some rocks, a much-prized AK-74 in his hands. Firing simultaneously, the Australian rounds found their

Personnel from the Australian Special Operations Engineer Regiment conduct a controlled explosion of an IED uncovered ahead of a Special Operations Task Group mounted patrol. Incredibly, the rear air hatch gunner of the second Bushmaster is still manning his MAG58 medium machine gun while the detonations occur. Notice also the huge amounts of stowage carried externally and the 84mm Carl Gustav rounds in their green plastic casings at the left rear of the closest Bushmaster. (Sergeant Neil Ruskin; Australian DOD)

mark, killing the Taliban leader. Two more insurgents appeared, one carrying an RPG. A PKM opened fire on the Commando section from a ridge above them. Below them they could now make out a large cave, swarming with insurgents – they had stumbled across an insurgent base camp.

The Commandos fired 40mm grenades down at the cave entrance while one man launched a LAW rocket at the PKM position that was pinning down his colleagues. The rocket hit home, silencing the machine gun. More 40mm rounds were launched into the cave mouth, which eventually collapsed. Other insurgents were now beginning to encircle the Commandos. As the first hints of dawn broke, the Australians knew they needed to escape before sunrise allowed the insurgents to surround them fully. As they broke contact, a Commando 81mm mortar battery covered their withdrawal before close-air support arrived to bomb the ridgelines.

The Commandos also served as a Quick Reaction Force to assist SASR patrols or other Coalition Forces that got into trouble. In July 2006, a Canadian JTF2 assault team became pinned down by a numerically larger Taliban force on a mission targeting an insurgent leadership target. One JTF2 operator was dead and two seriously wounded. The Australian Commandos launched a ground QRF to secure an emergency HLZ to allow the wounded to be extracted. The

Two Australian Commandos from the Special Operations Task Group in the middle of a firefight with insurgents. The operator in the foreground lays down suppressive fire with his M4A5 carbine while his mate prepares to post a grenade at the opposition. (Australian DOD)

American aero-medical evacuation helicopter was engaged as it landed as the Commandos tried to suppress numerous enemy firing points.

After the Canadian wounded were safely extracted, the Commandos collapsed their perimeter and moved out in their own vehicles only to run into a number of insurgent ambushes on their return route, which the Commandos fought through, sometimes dismounting to assault enemy gun positions. Incredibly, the platoon made it out without any serious injuries.

THE VICTORIA CROSS

At the time of writing three Australian Special Force soldiers have been awarded their nation's highest honor, the Victoria Cross, for actions in Afghanistan. The first was Trooper (now Corporal) Mark Donaldson of 1 Troop, 3 Squadron SASR who was part of a joint operation with a US Army Green Beret ODA in September 2008 in the northwest of Uruzgan Province. The operation was designed to lure the insurgents into a trap using a ground convoy of five Special Forces GMV trucks as the bait.

SASR sniper teams had inserted on foot the night before as part of two cut-off groups to overwatch the mounted patrol. The plan worked and soon a small group of insurgents appeared, intent on ambushing the convoy. Instead, they

An Australian SASR patrol pauses to interact with local children during a long-range patrol, 2009. By this stage, the IED and mine threat was becoming so severe that the SASR began to rely heavily on the Bushmaster Infantry Mobility Vehicles – a Class I MRAP in American terms – rather than their traditional six-wheel Perenties (although the Perentie had seen several upgrades including the provision of under floor armor). (Sergeant Neil Ruskin; Australian DOD)

were engaged by the SASR snipers. Minutes later, a Toyota Hilux carrying a number of armed insurgents arrived to investigate what had happened to their colleagues, and they were likewise engaged and killed.

A second vehicle arrived, this time a van. Three insurgents were engaged by the sniper teams until they spotted a female non-combatant inside the vehicle. A surviving insurgent used the woman as a human shield, knowing that ISAF ROEs would not allow the SASR operators to fire. The insurgent was eventually killed by a sniper without harm to the woman. A motorbike arrived to pick her up and was allowed to pass unchallenged. The SASR operators had so far killed 13 insurgents.

A similar ruse on September 2 in the Ana Kalay Valley was also successful, resulting in seven enemy dead. It was mid-afternoon when the joint patrol decided to return to the American Patrol Base. With 39 assorted Green Berets, SASR operators and Afghan Police on five GMVs, the patrol headed back. Moments later they were engaged by RPG and small arms fire from at least four firing points, including fire from above them on a parallel ridgeline. A vicious firefight erupted.

Trooper Donaldson managed to suppress one enemy position with an 84mm Carl Gustav recoilless rifle as the vehicles got slowly moving, watching for IEDs with their gunners firing in every direction. SASR operators ran alongside, using the vehicles as cover as they returned fire. One Green Beret was already seriously wounded. The American JTAC managed to call in a flight of F/A-18 Hornets that conducted gun runs against insurgents on the ridgeline. The aircraft returned later to drop a 500lb JDAM on a particularly troublesome group of enemy.

Despite suppressive fire from the vehicle gunners and close-air support, there were only brief lulls between enemy fusillades. As the vehicles crawled along the valley, more patrol members were getting hit. This slowed the convoy further as each casualty

had to be patched up before he could be moved. The JTAC attempted to get a pair of Dutch Apaches to provide support, but owing to their more restrictive ROEs, they refused to fire as they could not positively identify the enemy positions. Minutes later, the JTAC himself was shot. Getting the convoy moving again, with RPGs still exploding around them, the SASR operators continued their "Mogadishu Mile" running alongside. (The Mogadishu Mile referred to the actions of American Rangers and Delta operators during the famous Black Hawk Down battle in Somalia when they were forced to run, under fire, alongside already overloaded vehicles.)

As the patrol neared the end of the valley and the American base came into view, an RPG airburst wounded an SASR dog handler (his explosive detection dog, Sarbi, bolted and disappeared only to be found a year later, relatively healthy after a year in the Afghan wilds, by an American Green Beret patrol) and blew an Afghan interpreter out of one of the trucks. The interpreter, seriously wounded, was lying out in the open as more RPGs swept in.

Donaldson decided to act, running the 80m to the wounded man through a barrage of fire and carried him back to the vehicles in a fireman's carry with enemy rounds striking all around him. Eventually Donaldson got the wounded man inside one of the GMVs and he and another operator climbed into the back of the truck, Donaldson manning the rear swing-arm-mounted M240 machine gun until it was struck by an enemy bullet and disabled. Eventually they got back to the Patrol Base, the vehicles smoking, scarred hulks. They had survived a 3½ hour 4km rolling ambush. Thirteen members of the joint patrol were badly wounded, seven of them SASR and one Green Beret had been killed. Donaldson was awarded the Victoria Cross for the "most conspicuous acts of gallantry in action in a circumstance of great peril in Afghanistan."

TOP LEFT US Army Green Berets firing an M3 Carl Gustav recoilless rifle on a range in Helmand Province. Note the second operator, only just visible behind the first, braces the firer as he fires the round. The backblast is suitably impressive and the Taliban understandably fear the Charlie G. (Sergeant Benjamin Tuck; US Army)

ABOVE The famous Sarbi, a SASR EDD (Explosive Detection Dog), who was declared missing in action during the ambush that saw Tpr Mark Donaldson win the Victoria Cross. Sarbi survived for almost a year in the wilds of Helmand until she was spotted and recovered by a US Army Green Beret patrol that remembered the incident. Donaldson was promoted to Corporal in 2010. (Australian SOCOMD)

OPPOSITE Cpl Mark Donaldson VC of the SASR stands in full assault kit carrying a 7.62mm Mk14 Enhanced Battle Rifle, an upgraded SOF version of the venerable M14. (Sergeant Paul Evans; Australian DOD)

A MARSOC up-armored HMMWV patrol in southern Helmand Province, 2008. Note the Afghan flag on the lead HMMWV and that the trucks are off-road – a far safer proposition in IED-ridden Helmand. From 2008, most non-SOF units were barred from deploying HMMWVs and other relatively light vehicles "beyond the wire," relying instead on MRAPs. (Staff Sergeant Luis P. Valdespino Jr; USMC)

OPPOSITE Corporal Ben Roberts-Smith of the SASR immediately prior the kill or capture operation into the Shah Wali Kot which would earn him a Victoria Cross. He carries the Mk14 Enhanced Battle Rifle – note the EO Tech close-quarter sight and folding Aimpoint magnifier behind it. (Sergeant Paul Evans; Australian DOD)

THE EAST SHAH WALI KOT OFFENSIVE

In June 2010, a five-day operation was planned by the Special Operations Task Group based in Tarin Kowt. The aim of the operation was to stem the tide of an insurgent supply line which brought fighters, munitions and IED components from Pakistan into Uruzgan via Kandahar City to the south and Helmand to the west. The Shah Wali Kot Valley in Kandahar Province was a ratline for this insurgent smuggling route.

Shaping operations had begun the previous month with a series of lightning helicopter raids and mounted reconnaissance into insurgent-held areas to both map the FLET (forward line of enemy troops) and to discover how the insurgents would react when pressured in specific geographical areas. It also allowed ISR or "special reporting" as it was known by the Australians, to begin to tag the electronic emissions of enemy leadership targets. During these shaping operations, several Bushmaster Protected Mobility Vehicles were struck by IEDs, but thankfully without serious casualties.

Early on June 10, 2010, a large-scale disruption operation was launched to both draw out and destroy the insurgents the Australians now knew were hiding in the Shah Wali Kot. A secondary objective was to identify where their leaders were located and to capture or kill them. Alpha Company of 2 Commando Regiment inserted into an off-set HLZ early in the morning and moved through the villages in the valley on foot, meeting locals and holding Shuras with village elders. The Commandos would effectively act as the bait. Once contact was made, the Commandos would fix the insurgents in place and destroy them with organic weapons systems or by close-air support. A separate SASR force stood by at Tarin Kowt to launch against any leadership targets that appeared.

First contact was made against a 2 Commando sniper team which was providing overwatch above the village of Chenartu. The snipers fired first, killing three insurgents who were attempting to flank them. A sporadic firefight erupted with three further insurgents killed by the snipers. Two years later, a D Company sniper officially made the longest range sniper kill in history on April 2, 2012 in the Kajaki District of Helmand. In a still classified joint operation, a Commando sniper firing the Barrett M82A1M .50cal sniper rifle hit and killed an insurgent at a recorded distance of 2,815m.

In Chenartu, the civilians soon began leaving the village in droves – a clear "combat indicator" that the Australians had seen many times before. Once the women and children started to leave, they knew the enemy was close. In fact, a large enemy force had moved into position, surrounding the Australians and began to probe the Commando positions. Isolated gunfights occurred all around the Commando perimeter. By the afternoon, a coordinated insurgent attack began in earnest now that they knew where the Australians were located. The level of fire was ferocious: "every single Commando position was pinned down pretty much by heavy machine guns or rocket propelled grenades," explained the SOTG commander.

Close-air support, including A-10As and Apache attack helicopters, was vectored into the valley to suppress the enemy firing points – the trap had now been sprung. In between the gun and bomb runs of the close-air support, the Commando's 81mm mortars kept up a constant rate of fire. In the middle of the battle, ISR received intelligence on the location of a number of their leadership targets – evidently they had retreated to another village in the area. The SOTG commander stated:

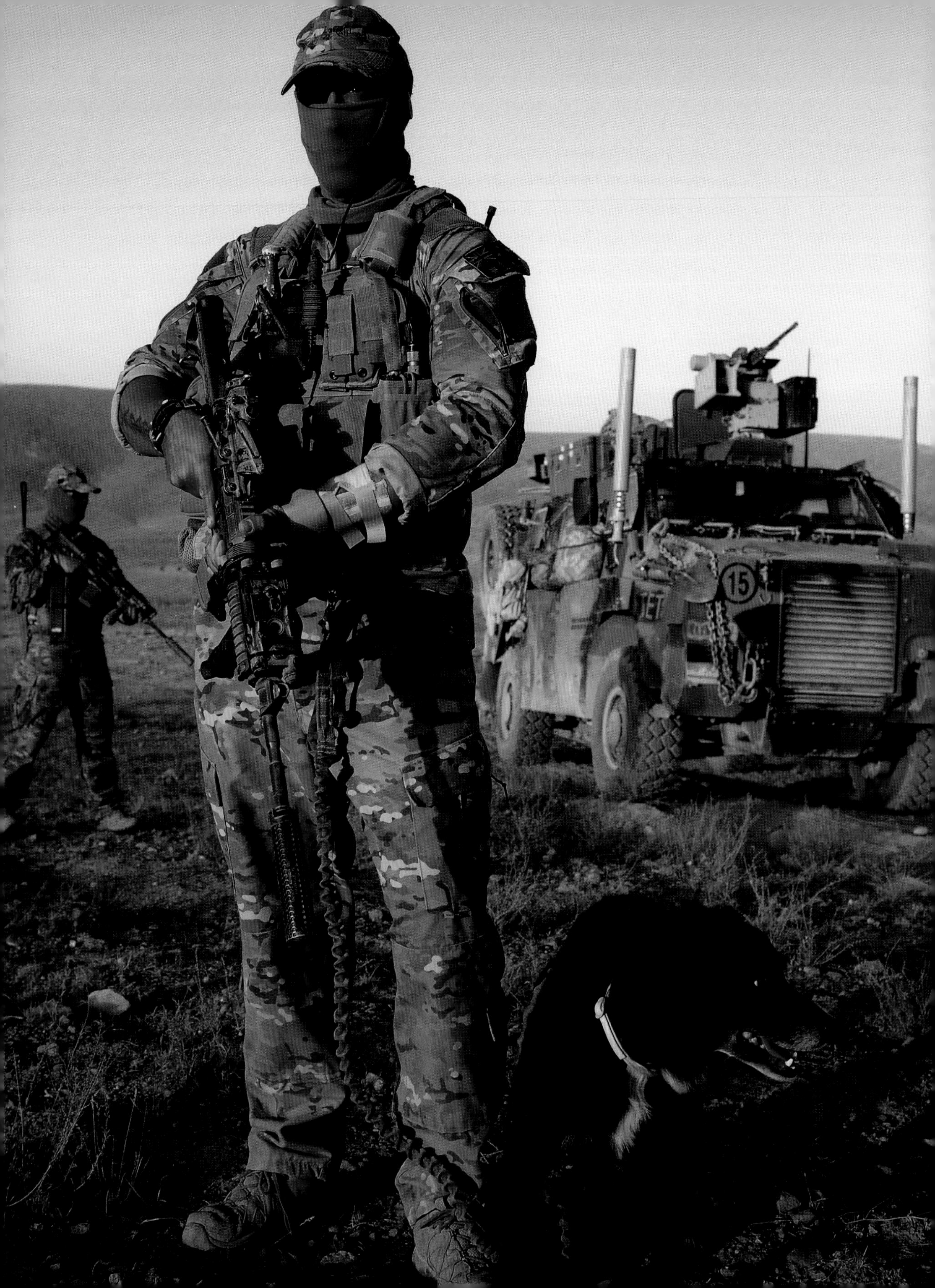
15

"We got some indications that there were a couple of key Taliban leaders in that area. It was at that point that I launched 2 Squadron soldiers to go and do a capture-or-kill mission on those commanders."

At his order, E Troop of 2 Squadron SASR launched from Tarin Kowt in four Blackhawk helicopters from the US Army's 101st Airborne Division. Accompanying them were a pair of Apaches to escort the Blackhawks on to the target and provide close-air support to the SASR operators once they were on the ground. Their target was an insurgent-held village called Tizak, 5km to the west of the Commandos' fight in Chenartu.

Two Blackhawks carried the assault element and five members of their partnered Provincial Police Response Company. A third carried an SASR cut-off group to manage any squirters, and the fourth carried the "aerial fire support team," as one participant explained, a six-man SASR patrol that could provide precision sniper fire from the air or reinforce the primary assault teams. In total, there were 25 SASR operators on the helicopters inbound to the target.

The Blackhawks received ground fire even before they landed as they over-flew the target to see if the arrival of the helicopters induced any insurgents to attempt to escape. As the lead helicopters landed to drop off their passengers, the assaulters were contacted on the HLZ from numerous, well-sited enemy firing points. The retreating Blackhawks were hit numerous times as was one of the escorting Apaches. The assault team, caught on the HLZ, took cover where they could in "shell scrapes" in the earth or behind small dirt mounds and attempted to return fire and win back the initiative.

Meanwhile, the aerial snipers had been sent to orbit the battle space at one end of the valley, keeping clear while the escorting Apaches were talked on to insurgent positions by the cut-off group which had landed on a ridge overlooking the village.

When the aerial sniper team's Blackhawk flew over a rocky hill, it was engaged from below. Corporal Ben Roberts-Smith explained in a later interview:

The peak was about 50 meters below us so when an insurgent with an RPG popped up from the rocks we saw him straight away. Our patrol commander, Sergeant P, screamed 'RPG, right, three o'clock' but a sniper and I were already firing.

We were sitting in the open door of the helicopter with our legs dangling over the side. The insurgent got the RPG away, and it passed just under my feet. At the same time, two more insurgents opened up with a PKM machine gun and rounds began tearing through the cockpit and belly of the Blackhawk.

OPPOSITE An Australian dismounted patrol conducted by 2 Commando Regiment. The central figure is a Military Working Dog handler and his EDD hound. Dogs, including Combat Assault Dogs, have been increasingly integrated into Australian SOF tactics since 2007 after their success in Iraq with both British and American Special Forces. Behind the handler is an Australian Bushmaster IMV used by both the Australians and the British SAS. (Corporal Chris Moore; Australian DOD)

US Army Rangers from the 75th Ranger Regiment dash across a vulnerable point one by one to reduce the chances of more than one man being hit during a raid in Afghanistan. (US DOD)

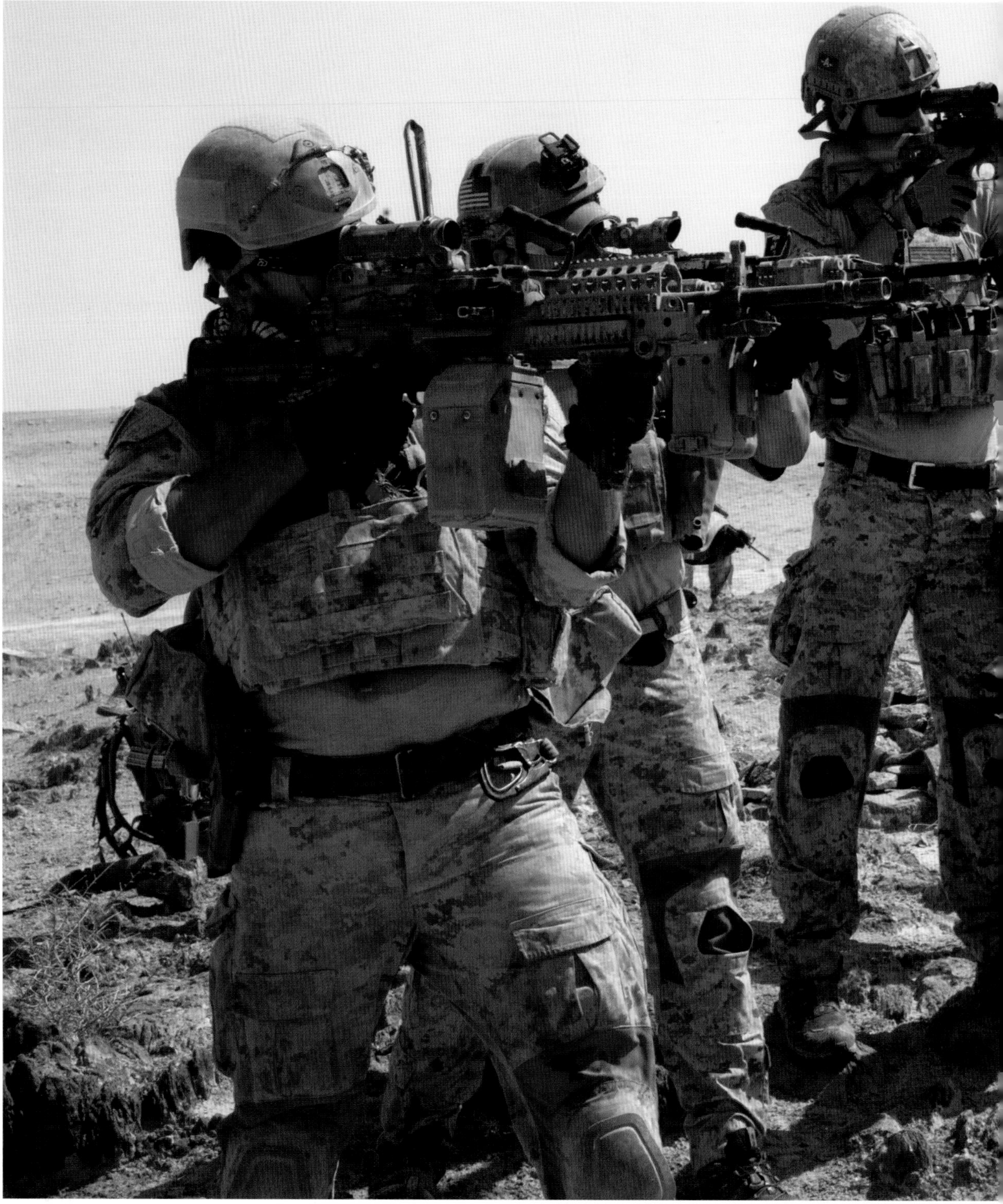

A US Navy SEAL fire team watches for insurgent threats as a Blackhawk lands in the background in the Shah Wali Kot Valley. The SEALs wear AOR1 pattern camouflage and carry a mix of Mk48 medium machine guns and an Mk18 CQB-R carbine. Their working dog watches on. (Petty Officer First Class Martine Cuaron; US DOD)

The coolness under fire of the American pilots saved the day, as they brought the helicopter around broadsides to provide a stable firing platform so that Roberts-Smith and the sniper could engage and kill the insurgents. After briefly landing to collect the insurgent weapons and any intelligence on the bodies, the team was ordered back to the other end of the valley. The assaulters were still pinned down on the landing zone.

As they approached the target area, the helicopter was again engaged by PKM fire. Forced to land near the village due to the weight of enemy fire, the shot-up Blackhawk finally limped away to its base at Tarin Kowt. The newly arrived SASR team managed to direct the fire of the Apaches on to several insurgent positions, allowing another Blackhawk to land to evacuate a wounded Afghan policeman and an SASR operator who had been shot through the shoulder. As the helicopter lifted away with the casualties on board, at least two RPGs narrowly missed it.

Roberts-Smith and his five fellow operators set off to flank the main enemy positions. They maneuvered under intense fire from a trio of PKM machine gun teams and numerous RPG gunners until Roberts-Smith could make it to a small grape-drying hut adjacent to the compound wall where most of the enemy fire was coming from. As he reached cover, an insurgent with an RPG in his hands appeared at the window, but the SASR operator quickly killed him.

An SASR Sergeant managed to post a grenade at the machine guns, temporarily stunning them and giving Roberts-Smith the opportunity he needed. Moving quickly forward, the big Australian shot and killed two PKM gunners before assaulting into the compound where several more insurgents

Afghan National Army Commandos from the 3rd Special Operations Kandak on a partnered operation with Navy SEALs wait for the rotor wash to dissipate after being inserted by CH-47D into the Shah Wali Kot. (Mass Communication Specialist First Class Martin Cuaron; US Navy)

were shot and killed. A third PKM gunner and his loader were shot at the rear of the compound as they attempted to ambush the SASR operators. As the patrol cleared through the battlefield and linked up with the assault team, Roberts-Smith shot and killed another insurgent he heard using his cell phone to direct enemy fire from a brush-covered spider hole. The final enemy casualty of the day was an insurgent who had hidden in some rocks and waited patiently for some time to kill an Australian. As he leapt out, his AK raised, he was shot and killed by the operators at point-blank range.

The SASR force had killed over 70 insurgents including ten of their named leadership targets. The primary high-value target had been wounded in the battle and managed to escape, only to later die of his wounds. In Chenartu, the Commandos had accounted for two dozen insurgents themselves – the two contacts had lasted some 13 hours and several of the SASR soldiers were down to their last magazine. Only two Australians had been wounded and miraculously none killed.

2 Squadron SASR and Alpha Company, 2 Commando were later awarded a new battle honor for "extraordinary heroism, exemplary combat performance and the relentless destruction of a highly trained and fanatical Taliban enemy of numerical superiority." Thirteen soldiers were awarded decorations for valour, while Corporal Ben Roberts-Smith was awarded the Victoria Cross.

A dramatic shot of Australian SASR operators engaged in combat with insurgents at an undisclosed location in southern Afghanistan, 2011. The weapon the operator is firing is the 7.62mm FN Maximi medium machine gun, similar to the Mk48 in American service. Both operators wear MultiCam trousers but US Navy AOR1 shirts. At the machine gunner's feet are a .338 Lapua Magnum Blaser R93 Tactical 2 sniper rifle and a suppressed M4A5 carbine. (Australian SOCOMD)

SOF Snipers

The wars in Iraq and particularly Afghanistan have once again proven the value of the sniper. Both in direct engagement of enemy personnel and in providing overwatch security and intelligence gathering from their hide sites, snipers are an important force multiplier. As importantly, snipers provide a precision option to SOF commanders that virtually eliminate any danger of collateral damage, a core consideration in counterinsurgency warfare.

The ways snipers have deployed have evolved as the wars have progressed. Gone are the days of snipers deploying in isolated pairs. Today, a sniper team is likely to comprise at least two sniper pairs and a security element to guard their backs, a harsh lesson learnt after two US Marine sniper teams were killed in Ramadi and Haditha after insurgents crept up on them. Snipers on sniper ambush missions, such as to interdict insurgent IED cells, also now deploy more commonly at night, particularly in Afghanistan where it is difficult to establish a hide site without being compromised by the locals who actively watch for Coalition troops.

Another change has been the widespread adoption of the concept of aerial sniper support, which sees the sniper team stationed in a helicopter to provide overwatch for an assault force as it hits its target. Snipers are also now used in disabling or destroying IEDs at range. The sniper has become a potent psychological warfare tool with the mere rumor of his presence limiting insurgent freedom of movement – in Fallujah, the SOF and conventional snipers were so feared that one of the first requests made in ceasefire talks was for the snipers to be withdrawn.

Their intelligence-gathering role has also increased as commanders see the value of establishing snipers in

A US Army Ranger sniper team firing the .50cal Barrett M107 anti-material sniper rifle in Afghanistan. Note the expended casing in the air and the significant dust cloud from the muzzle blast. (US SOCOM)

a covert observation post to conduct pattern of life surveillance on an area. Delta snipers are often used in this role, deployed in small two- or three-man recce/sniper teams to watch a target for days or even weeks at a time. Once the intelligence required is gathered, the snipers will quietly exfiltrate without a shot fired and with the enemy none the wiser as to their presence.

The weapons have also changed. Iraq has necessitated a move away from the traditional bolt action sniper rifle to the semi-automatic sniper rifle generally based on the M16 series (such as the SR-25 or the HK417). In the urban maze of Iraqi cities, fast follow-up shots are often needed with multiple targets presenting themselves. The semi-automatic also allows the rifle to be used to clear rooms or to defend a compromised hide site. Pistols have also seen a renaissance with snipers as their long-barreled, bolt-action rifles were less than ideal when moving through buildings or compounds where insurgents could lurk behind any door.

Sniper rifles have also increased in caliber, mainly due to the extended ranges encountered in both Afghanistan and Iraq. Many SOF sniper rifles are now chambered for the .300 Winchester Magnum cartridge – such as the Mk13 famously used by the US Navy SEALs – or the .338 Lapua Magnum employed by UK and Australian Special Forces in a range of platforms including the Blaser R93 Tac 2 and the Accuracy International L115A3. Also prominent has been the resurgence of the 12.7mm or .50cal antimaterial rifles such as the McMillan TAC-50 (used by a Canadian sniper to make a shot at 2,430m during Operation *Anaconda*) or the Barrett M82A1 (deployed by Delta Company 2 Commando snipers who made, to date, the world's longest-range shot in Afghanistan – 2,815m).

A MARSOC partnered patrol crossing a winter stream, Afghanistan, 2014. Note the newly adopted suppressed Mk21 Precision Sniper Rifle carried by the lead operator – available in 7.62mm, .300, or .338, the Mk21 is set to replace all SOCOM sniper rifles in service. Just visible behind the wall in the background are other operators providing security. (US SOCOM)

An SASR dog handler training in Uruzgan with his Combat Assault Dog. The CAD wears a ballistic vest with a camera unit attached to allow operators to see what he or she sees on a handheld unit. (Corporal Chris Moore; Australian DOD)

Australia's third Victoria Cross to a Special Forces operator was awarded to Corporal Cameron Baird, who was sadly killed in action on June 22, 2013. Baird was an assault team leader on an operation targeting an insurgent group in the Uruzgan village of Ghawchak. A Commando platoon and a team from the Afghan Provincial Police Response Company were inserted outside the village by Chinook. As they exited the helicopters they were fired upon.

The Commandos raced to get clear of the exposed HLZ. One of the other team leaders was shot twice, one being stopped by the trauma plate in his vest. Baird moved his team up to cover them while they evacuated the wounded Corporal back to cover. At that point they were engaged by a tremendous amount of small arms, PKM and RPG fire from a compound with a commanding view of the area. Baird and his team made it over an irrigation ditch to the wall of the compound, under fire at every step. Once there they realized there was only one way into the compound – through an arched entrance. The problem was that several insurgents, including a PKM gunner, were firing from inside the compound out through the entranceway.

Corporal Baird knew that the other team leader, who had a shattered femur, needed an aero medical evacuation, and to bring the helicopter in, the insurgent fire needed to be stopped. An airstrike was not an option as there were too many civilians in the area. Baird attempted an entry on the compound, but was driven back by the weight of fire. He tried again moments later but was forced to retreat when his M4A5

suffered a stoppage. Finally on a third attempt he managed to make it into the entrance way and engage one of the insurgents. In the return fire, Corporal Baird was shot and killed instantly. Another Commando managed to post a fragmentation grenade through the entranceway, allowing Baird's body to be dragged back as other Commandos stormed into the compound and killed the remaining insurgents, allowing the aero medical evacuation helicopter to be brought in.

HOSTAGE RESCUES

In October 2010, a reinforced Troop of Red Squadron from DEVGRU along with two squads of Rangers launched on a mission to rescue a British aid worker, Linda Norgrove, who had been seized by insurgents in a mountainous region of Kunar Province, some 16km from the border with Pakistan.

Signals intercepts and aerial ISR assets had found Norgrove was being held in one of two hillside compounds deep in the notorious Korengal Valley (known to many from the award-winning documentary, *Restrepo*) by at least six insurgents. With UK Special Forces fully committed to operations in the south of the country, the SEALs were given the mission and dispatched toward the objective at 0300hr in a pair of MH-47Es with AC-130 and armed Predator UAV cover overhead.

Due to the rocky terrain and the lack of a covered approach to the target compounds, the assaulters were forced to land on the X – directly on top of the

A rare image of a pair of US Army Rangers clearing a room during a night raid in Helmand Province, 2012. Both wear night vision goggles and carry M4A1 carbines fitted with full length Daniel Defense Picatinny rails, Spectre sights, SU233 weapon lights and AN/PEQ-15 infra-red illuminators. (Specialist Justin Young; US Army)

target. The Rangers were dropped nearby to establish blocking and support by fire positions overlooking the compound. The lead MH-47E flared over the first compound and the assaulters quickly fast roped to the ground. Snipers in the second helicopter, watching for squirters who were attempting to escape with the hostage, shot and killed two guards with their suppressed HK417 rifles.

As the assaulters landed in the compound, insurgents appeared from several small buildings and were immediately engaged. Two who made a run for it were shot and killed by the AC-130 orbiting above. The assaulters were then fired upon by an insurgent coming out of one of the buildings. Fire was returned and the insurgent killed. Unknown to the team at that point, the insurgent had been dragging the hostage out of the building at the time. Norgrove sustained a non-fatal gunshot wound to the leg, which may have occurred at that point in the operation.

Fearing more insurgents were in an area between two buildings, a fragmentation grenade was posted toward the area by a SEAL operator. The SEALs cleared the buildings, confirming all six insurgents were dead. The entire operation had taken an incredible 60 seconds. Norgrove was then discovered, fatally wounded, lying next to the blown-apart body of one of the insurgents. Initially it was thought she had been killed by the insurgent detonating a suicide bomb vest. Only later did it emerge that the cause of her death was probably the SEAL grenade.

The operator who posted the fragmentation grenade apparently did not admit to it in after-action reviews until helmet camera footage was reviewed by the squadron commander. A fragmentation grenade and a flashbang stun grenade are demonstrably different shapes and weights and could not have been confused,

LINDA NORGROVE RESCUE ATTEMPT, OCTOBER 2010

1) DEVGRU operators fast rope outside two hillside compounds
2) Ranger blocking and sniper overwatch positions are established
3) A casualty collection and command and control point is established with Ranger security
4) DEVGRU breaches the first compound and engages several insurgents
5) DEVGRU breaches the second compound, also killing a number of insurgents and, tragically, Linda Norgrove with a fragmentation grenade

Linda Norgrove Rescue Attempt, October 2010
1) A reinforced troop from DEVGRU and two reinforced squads of Rangers launch from Bagram in two MH-47Es, headed for the notorious Korengal Valley
2) They insert directly onto the X with operators fast-roping to the ground

particularly by such an experienced operator. Three operators were eventually dismissed from the unit.

Operation *Jubilee* was another hostage rescue mission, this time conducted in Badakhshan, eastern Afghanistan. A British aid worker, Helen Johnston, and her female colleague, a Kenyan NGO worker, and two Afghan guides had been kidnapped by bandits who offered their release in exchange for a ransom that included the release of a notorious drug dealer. With the very real fear that the kidnappers may sell on the hostages to the Taliban, with whom they had already been in contact, Coalition Forces worked around the clock to locate them.

Signals intercept teams got a fix on the kidnappers' location and long-loiter high altitude UAVs soon began constant pattern of life surveillance in an effort to establish exactly where the hostages were being held, the numbers of kidnappers and their daily routines. Such pattern of life surveillance can inform everything from the approach routes an SOF team might take (for example whether a

A massive haul of insurgent RPG warheads, artillery shells, mortar bombs, and sundry other explosive munitions being prepared for demolition by Australian Special Operations Engineer Regiment operators. (Australian SOCOMD)

particular road was subject to insurgent checkpoints or if a mountain trail was too narrow for Humvees) through to the way the SOF team will gain entry to the target location (such as the height of the walls, the location of windows, or the availability of covered avenues of approach to the target).

This type of surveillance is carried out by UAVs, as in the case of Operation *Jubilee*; manned reconnaissance overflights; local human intelligence assets; or physical surveillance by SOF operators. The most risky, but also potentially the most rewarding, is having physical eyes on the target itself by experienced operators, although such missions can go disastrously wrong, as demonstrated in the book and now movie *Lone Survivor*. It was soon established that the hostages had been split up and were being held in two caves within a heavily wooded valley in the Koh-e-Laram forest. A joint British–US hostage rescue mission was planned.

Two teams – one from the SAS and one from DEVGRU – would insert 2km from the target location at an off-set LZ to maintain the element of surprise, flown to the area by 160th SOAR Blackhawks. The assaulters would then advance on foot through the forest and establish a security cordon before assaulting into the caves simultaneously. The operation went like clockwork, and the assault teams stormed the caves in a flurry of flashbang stun grenades.

The SEALs cleared their cave, killing all seven gunmen, but reported no sign of the hostages. The SAS team assaulted into their cave, killing a further four gunmen and thankfully rescuing all four of the hostages. None of the hostages or the assaulters was wounded in the brief firefights. The hostages were quickly checked by SAS medics before the helicopters returned to pick up the combined assault teams and their charges.

A December 2012 hostage rescue operation was again carried out by DEVGRU. A US citizen working for an NGO, Doctor Dilip Joseph, and two local Afghan associates were kidnapped by a bandit gang in the east of Afghanistan. A DEVGRU assault successfully rescued the three hostages and killed all seven hostage takers, but the assault team lost one of its operators, who was shot in the head during the assault.

OPERATION *JUBILEE*, MAY 2012

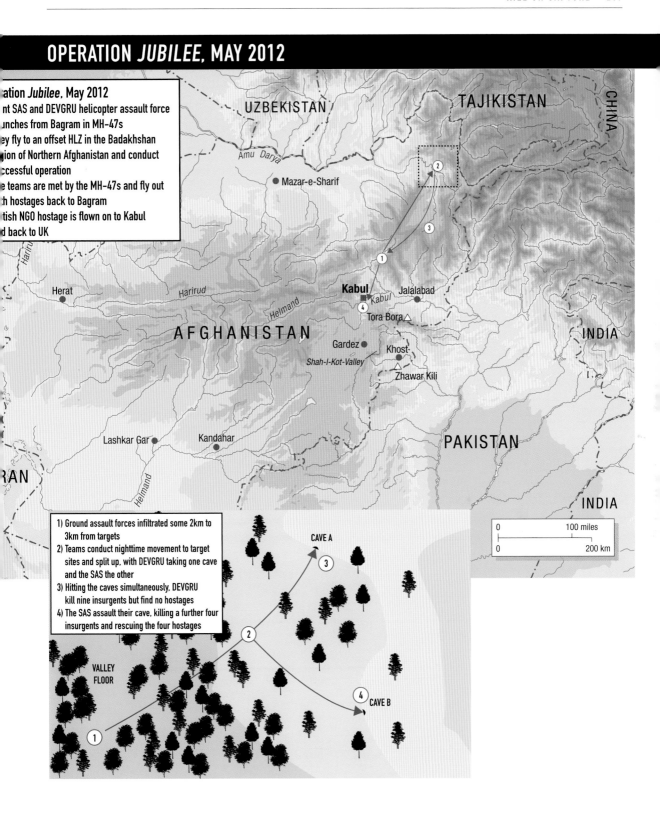

...ation *Jubilee*, May 2012
...nt SAS and DEVGRU helicopter assault force
...unches from Bagram in MH–47s
...ey fly to an offset HLZ in the Badakhshan
...gion of Northern Afghanistan and conduct
...ccessful operation
...e teams are met by the MH–47s and fly out
...h hostages back to Bagram
...tish NGO hostage is flown on to Kabul
...d back to UK

UZBEKISTAN

TAJIKISTAN

CHINA

Amu Darya

● Mazar-e-Sharif

2

3

1

Harirud

● Herat

Harirud

Kabul
■ Kabul ● Jalalabad

Helmand

4

● Tora Bora △

AFGHANISTAN

INDIA

Gardez ●

Shah-I-Kot-Valley

Khost ●

△ Zhawar Kili

Lashkar Gar ●

Kandahar ●

PAKISTAN

Helmand

INDIA

| 0 | 100 miles |
| 0 | 200 km |

1) Ground assault forces infiltrated some 2km to
   3km from targets
2) Teams conduct nighttime movement to target
   sites and split up, with DEVGRU taking one cave
   and the SAS the other
3) Hitting the caves simultaneously, DEVGRU
   kill nine insurgents but find no hostages
4) The SAS assault their cave, killing a further four
   insurgents and rescuing the four hostages

CAVE A

3

2

4 CAVE B

VALLEY
FLOOR

1

Rangers maintaining security outside a target site at an undisclosed location in Afghanistan. The two Rangers to the right carry 5.56mm M4A1 carbines with SOPMOD Block 2 rails while the Ranger to the left is armed with the 7.62mm Mk17 SCAR serving as a designated marksman rifle. The 5.56mm Mk16 SCAR was trialled by the Rangers, but was not felt to offer any significant advantage over their M4s. (Private First Class Coty M. Kuhn; US Army)

ABBOTTABAD

The ultimate kill or capture raid was the May 2011 Operation *Neptune Spear*, the cross-border raid targeting al-Qaeda leader Usama bin Laden. After years of painstaking investigative work, it emerged that bin Laden may have finally been located, living in a custom-made compound in the Pakistani city of Abbottabad. Several options were presented by the CIA to President Obama: an airstrike by a B-2 stealth bomber, a UAV strike, or a helicopter assault force of SEALs. Each option had its advantages and disadvantages in terms of potential collateral damage and the ability to ascertain whether bin Laden had actually been killed by the strike.

Eventually, President Obama agreed that the SEALs were the best option available to him. He made sure that if the worst did happen and the assaulters were left stranded, they would have the capability to, in the President's words, "fight their way out of Pakistan." This direction led to the addition of a pair of MH-47Es to the strike force, which landed at a staging point outside of Abbottabad, ready to be brought forward as a QRF if needed. Inside these helicopters were additional SEALs and a Ranger element along with a Combat Search and Rescue team (a Ranger squad is often assigned as force protection for CSAR teams).

The ground assault force itself was composed of 22 hand-picked senior members of Red Squadron, an EOD operator, a CIA interpreter and a Combat Assault Dog named Cairo, a Belgian Malinois. They would be transported to the objective in a pair of very crowded but very advanced Blackhawks, flown by Nightstalker aviators. The Blackhawks, termed Silent Hawks by some, were right out of Area 51 – specially designed stealth versions that benefited from both a reduced radar profile and were significantly quieter than their more conventional brethren.

The mission called for the force to launch from Jalalabad where the JSOC Task Force maintained its own secure staging area. The two Blackhawks would cross the border and proceed directly to Abbottabad, while the two MH-47s headed north. The MH-47s would carry fuel bladders for a FARP (Forward Armament and Refuelling Point) site which would be established north of Abbottabad and protected by the Ranger element. The modified Blackhawks would need to refuel in Pakistan before heading back to Afghanistan.

The plan was for one Blackhawk to hover over the courtyard while the assaulters fast roped down – snipers in the second Blackhawk would cover their descent. From there they would split up into smaller teams to clear a guest house and establish a sniper overwatch position while a larger team conducted a breach into the main house, assaulting and clearing up through the three-storey structure.

At the same time, the second Blackhawk would land to drop off a five-man team, two of whom would patrol the outer wall with the Malinois and three, including a SAW gunner, who would establish a blocking position to dissuade any locals from becoming involved. The CIA interpreter would announce to any curious onlookers that the raid was a Pakistani police operation. After dropping off these teams, the Blackhawk would then hover over the main building while the remaining assaulters would fast rope on to the roof and begin assaulting downward through the building.

The operation launched on the night of May 1, 2011 and all went according to plan until the first Blackhawk levelled out to fast rope the assaulters into the compound. The helicopter was caught in a state called settling with power. This occurs when a helicopter hovers close to the ground after a fast approach and is forced to land through its own downwash. Only the remarkable skills of the Nightstalker pilots kept the helicopter reasonably level as it rapidly descended and crashed against an inner courtyard wall. The pilots had managed to keep the rotors clear of obstacles to avoid a catastrophic separation, which could have seen the helicopter roll or operators injured or killed by rotor fragments.

The second Blackhawk, unsure of exactly what had just occurred with the first, wisely landed to drop off its teams instead of hovering over the main target house to deploy the fast rope. From that point on, the assaulters quickly followed their rehearsed roles and converged on the main house after shooting dead bin Laden's courier who attempted to engage the assault team with his AK-47. The teams explosively breached into the main house and methodically cleared each floor, killing bin Laden's son Khalid as they did so. Finally they made it to the third floor and the point man shot and killed bin Laden as he poked his head out from his bedroom to find out what was going on.

The SEALs immediately went into SSE mode and began bagging up laptops, hard drives and paper files – anything that could be of intelligence value. Once completed, they placed bin Laden in a body bag and moved out to rendezvous with the helicopters. The EOD operator placed charges on the downed Blackhawk to deny it to the enemy after all sensitive material had been recovered or destroyed.

The charges exploded just before an MH-47 arrived to pick up the remaining assaulters. The MH-47 flew directly for Jalalabad, while the remaining Blackhawk flew first to the FARP in Pakistan before heading for home with the second MH-47 in trail. The entire operation had taken just 40 minutes on the ground; the SEALs had trained for 30 minutes with 10 minutes available for contingencies such as a helicopter crash – time that they had needed.

An RQ-170 Sentinel capable of both capturing streaming surveillance footage through cloud cover and jamming local Pakistani air defense radars had been overhead during the operation. Officials at Bagram and the White House had

OPERATION *NEPTUNE SPEAR*, MAY 2011

NEPTUNE SPEAR TIMELINE

1 Assault Element of two MH-X Black Hawks and assaulters takes off from Jalalabad and flies toward Pakistan border

2 Contingency Force is carried on two MH-47E Chinooks to wait at a secure staging area inside the borders of Afghanistan

3 Quick Reaction Force (QRF) follows the Assault Element on two MH-47E Chinooks and lands several miles from Abbottabad to set up a "Forward Area Refueling Point" (FARP) at Kala Dhaka for the Black Hawks' return flight

4 Assault Element reaches Abbottabad in two MH-X Black Hawks undetected; in the raid on his compound bin Laden is killed and one MH-X destroyed

5 Surviving MH-X departs to FARP with bin Laden's corpse and one SEAL team

6 One QRF Chinook picks up remaining SEALs and captured materials and returns direct to Jalalabad special operations force (SOF) base

7 Once refueled, surviving MH-X departs FARP, with Chinook following, and they return to Jalalabad SOF base

8 Two C-130s fly bin Laden's body and SEAL teams to Bagram Air Base

9 Bin Laden's corpse flown to USS Carl Vinson in the northern Arabian Sea, where he is buried at sea at an undisclosed location

A night-vision image of another partnered night raid – this time conducted by the Afghan 3rd Commando Kandak and US Navy SEALs who can be seen using an assault ladder to establish a rooftop overwatch position in Kandahar Province, 2011. Three suspected insurgents were detained and an amount of Taliban propaganda material recovered during the SSE. (Specialist Daniel P. Shook; US Army)

watched the mission unfold in real time, including the helicopter crash. Bin Laden's body was transferred by a Ranger team to the USS *Carl Vinson* for burial at sea after the Saudi authorities declined to take his body back to his birthplace. After ten long years, the hunt for bin Laden was over.

EXTORTION 17

Only a few months after Abbottabad, DEVGRU suffered its greatest losses to date in August 2011 when a mission in the Tangi Valley in Wardak Province to kill or capture an insurgent leader went terribly wrong. A reinforced platoon of Rangers had inserted at an off-set HLZ and marched in to the target area before conducting a surprise raid on the targeted compound. Although there was no sign of the quarry, the Rangers were soon in heavy contact with insurgents. It was some three hours before an urgent request was made for the IRF (Immediate Reaction Force).

An IRF is a team which stands by in the general area of an operation or on alert at a nearby FOB to be brought forward when reinforcements are needed – typically when things have gone wrong, such as a helicopter crash or when assaulters suffer large numbers of casualties. On this mission, the IRF was requested to intercept a number of insurgent squirters and establish a blocking position several kilometers from the Rangers' raid location in an effort to capture them. The IRF launched in an Army National Guard CH-47D Chinook.

As the Chinook, callsign Extortion 17, made its final approach to the HLZ, a number of insurgents positioned about 200m away fired RPGs at the helicopter. One RPG warhead struck the rear rotor of the Chinook, shearing off 10ft of rotor and causing the aircraft to crash immediately to the ground. The Chinook was consumed by a massive fireball only moments later. The Apaches that had escorted the Rangers into their target immediately suppressed the RPG firing points with

A US Army Ranger squad awaits a CH-47D Chinook landing to extract them, Afghanistan, 2008. (US SOCOM)

their 30mm cannons and a "Fallen Angel" was declared with CSAR scrambled. Rangers rushed to the crash site on foot while the Apaches and AC-130 maintained a protective vigil overhead.

Thirty-eight people perished in the crash. Twenty-two were from Naval Special Warfare including 15 operators from DEVGRU's Gold Squadron. The other Navy personnel killed were SOF support personnel, including a signal intercept technician and a dog handler with his dog, Bart. An Air Force special operations team of PJs and a Combat Controller, a partnered Afghan Commando element, and the Army National Guard aircrew of the CH-47D were also killed.

Numerous factors appeared to have contributed to the tragedy. An MQ-1 Predator, which was orbiting overhead, stayed locked on to the squirters and did not clear the intended HLZ of Extortion 17. An AC-130 illuminated the landing zone with its infra-red searchlight and it was declared "ice" or clear upon the final approach of Extortion 17. The Chinook did not have its own accompanying Apaches. Those that were supporting the Rangers only became involved in the arrival of Extortion 17 when it was approximately three minutes from its HLZ. One Apache crew member later commented that he felt the landing zone needed to be secured by ground elements.

Perhaps most tellingly, Extortion 17 was a "plain vanilla" CH-47D Chinook without the specialist avionics or RPG threat detection systems that are now standard on 160th SOAR MH-47s. It was flown by an experienced National Guard pilot. However, the aircrew was not trained in the SOF tactics typically used by the Nightstalkers, including landing techniques to minimize time on the ground and advanced evasive maneuvers.

HAQQANI

Following the Iraq drawdown and since the Afghan Surge of 2008 and 2009, Delta Force has returned to conducting operations in Afghanistan. Apparently, the country was carved up, with the SEALs taking the north and the east while Delta took the south and the west. One of Delta's largest operations occurred in the southeast in Paktika Province.

Based on information provided by a highly placed detainee, Delta Force conducted a July 2011 operation targeting a foreign fighter staging area, allegedly facilitated by the Haqqani Network. The Nightstalkers inserted a helicopter assault force element from A Squadron supported by Ranger and Afghan SOF elements into the Sar Rowzah District on July 20. The assaulters were engaged in

an immediate contact with the enemy which was heavily armed with RPGs and DShK heavy machine guns. During the night-time fighting, ISAF estimated approximately 30 insurgents were killed.

As the sun rose, so did dozens of remaining insurgents who had been hiding in crude but effective bunkers and caves in the mountainous region. An armed UAV, AH-6s and DAPs flew in close support for the ground forces, as did ground attack aircraft. Fighting continued into a second day as the bunkers and fighting positions were systematically cleared, some by use of the recently issued thermobaric Mk14 Antistructural Grenades. An estimated 80 to 100 Haqqani and foreign fighters were killed in the two-day battle. A Delta Master Sergeant was sadly killed by insurgent small arms fire late during the action.

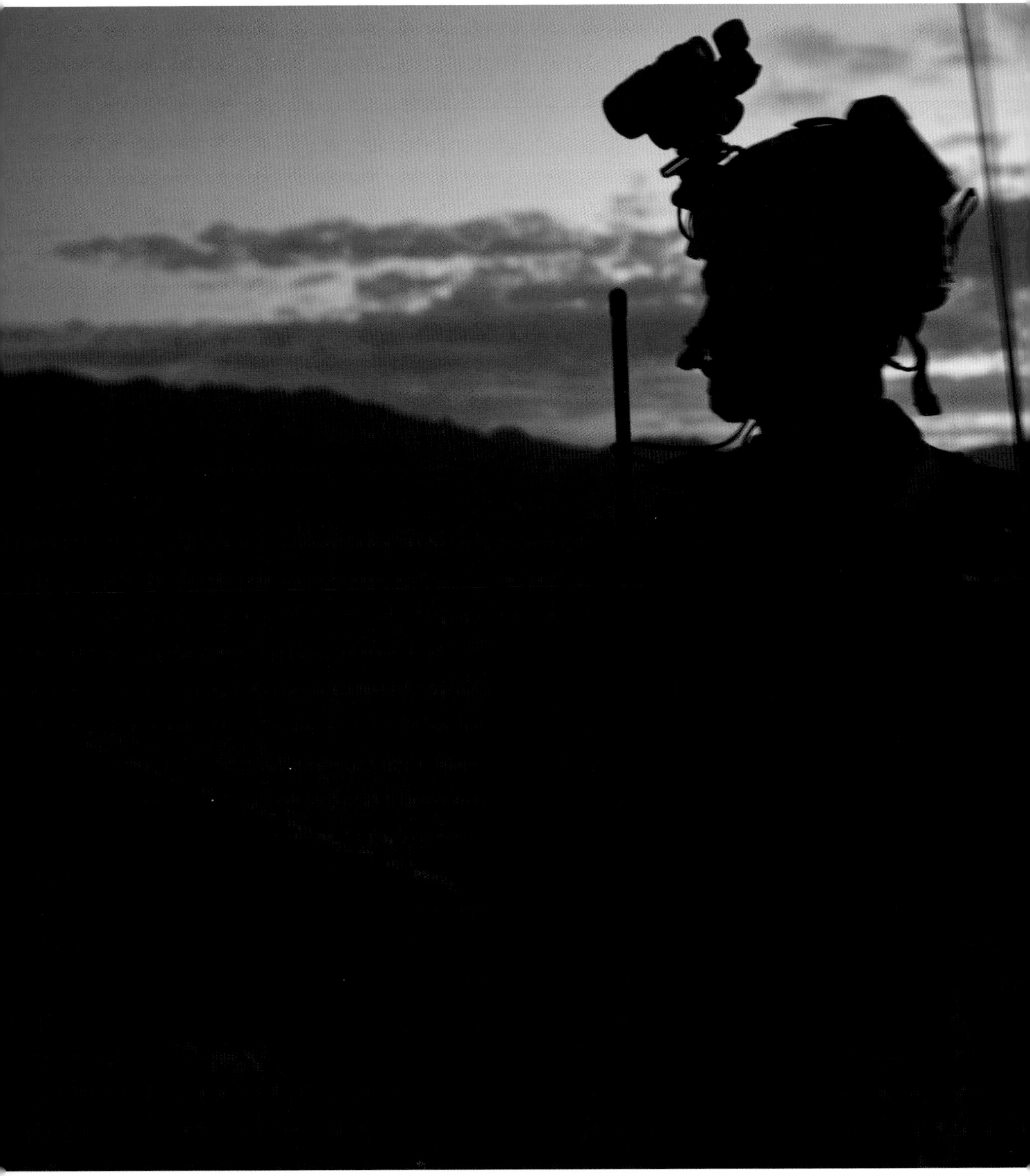

Delta was briefly in the spotlight again when the Taliban filmed the release of Army Sergeant Bowe Bergdahl, the only prisoner of war of the Afghan insurgency. Bergdahl had been held by the Haqqani Network in Pakistan for five years after disappearing from his FOB under mysterious circumstances. DEVGRU and the Rangers had "spun up" on several operations to rescue him over that time, but each resulted in a "dry hole," including one operation south of Kabul in July 2009 that resulted in one SEAL seriously wounded and a Combat Assault Dog killed. After years of stalled negotiations, a deal was struck trading Bergdahl for five Taliban leaders held in Guantanamo Bay.

On the appointed day of the transfer, at least two MH-60M Blackhawks and a U-28A surveillance aircraft arrived over the agreed location – a desolate valley somewhere on the border near Khost – to meet with an estimated 18 insurgents. One Blackhawk orbited overhead carrying a sniper element with rifles trained on the insurgents below, who had arrived in Toyota pick-up trucks with their prisoner in tow. The second MH-60M touched down, yards from the insurgents.

Inside the helicopter were several Delta operators dressed in full MultiCam assault kit, ready to respond to any hint of a double cross. Two operators in civilian clothing – their appearance masked by baseball caps, sunglasses and shemaghs – and an interpreter strode from the Blackhawk to meet the insurgent representatives, who appeared with Bergdahl. After a few brief words, the POW was escorted by the operators back to the helicopter where he was thoroughly searched for explosive devices before the team and Bergdahl climbed aboard the Blackhawk and departed.

In Afghanistan, General McChrystal's concept of the unblinking eye of human intelligence – real time and long-loiter surveillance, signals intercepts and expert analysis – led to targeting that was reckoned to result in 50 percent of all operations killing or capturing their primary targets and of the remainder, 80 to 90 percent resulting in the killing or capture of a secondary target or associate of the primary target.

Kill or capture missions helped give ISAF counterinsurgency initiatives like the Village Stability Operations program the room to succeed. Like similar operations in Iraq, they have also saved many lives – both among ISAF forces and the civilian population. They have also severely degraded the capabilities of the insurgency and blunted many planned operations including mass suicide bombings. They may also, in the long run, help bring the Taliban to the negotiating table.

OPPOSITE An Air Force Special Tactics JTAC attached to Special Operations Task Force-South during a partnered night raid in Kandahar Province that recovered a large amount of HME (homemade explosive – typically constructed using cheap Pakistani fertiliser that has now been outlawed in Afghanistan), a pair of Chinese 107mm unguided rockets the Taliban use to fire at FOBs and a quantity of small arms. (Specialist Daniel P. Shook; US Army)

CHAPTER 7
NEW THEATERS

As we have seen, the global jihadist threat did not confine itself purely to Afghanistan and Iraq. With many of their former sanctuaries destroyed, jihadists looked for new bases and new recruitment centres. Their ideal conditions included a weak to non-functioning central government, a large Sunni population, and a geographical location that offered some protection from counterterrorist operations in terms of either the pure inaccessibility of the area itself or a sympathetic civilian population in which to hide.

In 2009, the US Defense Department changed the name of the Global War on Terror to the distinctly less glamorous Overseas Contingency Operations (OCO). These contingency operations have occurred in numerous failed and failing states across the globe in a never-ending attempt to stop the jihadists gaining "another Afghanistan." At the same time, the JSOC Task Force hunts wanted jihadists across the globe, not just in Iraq and Afghanistan but in Madagascar, Iran, Peru, Mali, Yemen, Libya, Somalia, Nigeria, and Lebanon. (Not long after 9/11, an ISA operator, who was following a target in Beirut, was kidnapped. He eventually broke free, shot and killed his kidnappers and thankfully escaped unharmed.)

These contingency operations are conducted under the authority of two executive orders – 2004's al Qaeda Network Execute Order, which allowed JSOC to operate in over a dozen countries with which the United States was not currently at war; and 2009's Joint Unconventional Warfare Task Force Execute Order which gave JSOC permission to conduct advance force, reconnaissance, and human intelligence operations in nations where there may be a need for a US military presence. In effect, this allowed units like ISA to enter a country, develop a network of sources and begin to track targets – all before any formal operation was authorized by the White House.

DJIBOUTI

In the Horn of Africa, much of the counterterrorist operations there are organised from the Djibouti, the former French colony of French Somaliland. Camp Lemonnier, once a French Foreign Legion base, has become the hub for both black and white SOF operations into nations such as Somalia and Yemen. Officially a US Naval Expeditionary Base assigned to the Combined Joint Task Force-Horn of Africa (CJTF-HOA), Camp Lemonnier houses conventional *and* special operations units. The company-sized US Army East Africa Response Force is based out of the camp, and is primed to reinforce US diplomatic outposts in the region if they come under threat.

Special Operations Command and Control Element-Horn of Africa (SOCCE-HOA) is also based at Lemonnier. SOCCE-HOA commands all SOCOM units

assigned to training or operational missions in the region, including elements of the Joint Special Operations Task Force-Trans Sahara (JSOTF-TS) and Naval Special Warfare Unit 10. It also coordinates a rotational detachment of US Army Special Forces which conducts Foreign Internal Defense training in counterinsurgency in both Djibouti and in countries such as Mali.

Hidden in a separate secure compound within the camp, much like the SOF enclaves at Bagram, are an estimated 300 JSOC personnel. These personnel comprise special operators, intelligence and imagery analysts, and a dedicated UAV cell. The UAV cell is commanded by a JSOC Major and tasks a flight of eight MQ-1 Predators conducting operations over Somalia, Mali, and Yemen. The Predators have been carrying out strike and surveillance missions from Camp Lemonnier since late 2010. Prior to that, both the CIA and JSOC had used the base as a temporary forward location for Predator and Reaper sorties into the

Navy SEALs fast rope from hovering MV-22 Osprey VTOL aircraft during a training exercise. Note the incredible amount of dust kicked up by the downdraft. Several SEALs were seriously wounded from enemy small arms fire on-board an Osprey during a non-combatant evacuation in South Sudan in December 2013. (Senior Airman Sheila DeVera; US Air Force)

region. In 2013, they were moved to a remote desert airstrip, which increased operational security and allayed local fears after a UAV and its live Hellfire missile crashed in a Djibouti suburb.

Since October 2011, a squadron of USAF F-15Es has bolstered the offensive strength of the base. The F-15Es have flown numerous combat missions into Yemen in support of both Yemeni government forces and unilateral strikes directed by JSOC and CIA targeting cells. Along with the UAVs and F-15Es, surveillance flights are conducted by Air Force Special Operations Command U-28As, modified Pilatus PC-12s, that are outfitted with sophisticated signals intercept equipment and optical sensors, which can provide real-time intelligence for ground operators.

Special operations in the African theater are conducted under a range of code words. Somalia is apparently referred to under the code word Octave while Yemen falls under Copper. Offensive operations are referenced by the code word Dune, thus SEAL operations in Somalia would be known as Octave Dune, or in Yemen as Copper Dune. The overall effort in Somalia is known as Octave Shield while US operations in North and West Africa are known as Juniper Shield.

OPERATION *CELESTIAL BALANCE*

Before Djibouti became the epicentre of counterterrorism operations in Africa, unilateral operations were launched from temporary forward locations in friendly host nations, such as Kenya, or from US Navy ships. The 2009 Operation *Celestial Balance* was one example of the latter. The target was the facilitator between al-Qaeda and al-Shabaab, and a member of the East African al-Qaeda cell responsible for the 1998 bombings of the US embassies in Kenya and Tanzania. He was also involved in the deadly bombing of a Kenyan holiday resort and the attempted shooting down of an Israeli airliner in Kenya.

A long-running CIA CTC/SAD operation had hunted for the individual for a number of years, recruiting a network of Somali agents and paying off Somali warlords for information on the whereabouts of the al-Qaeda planner and his associates. A team brought in from the ISA began piecing together the target's location from cell phone intercepts and surveillance from both short-range Navy Scan Eagle UAVs and the longer-range CIA Predators.

Eventually the target was located and an option to strike while he travelled to visit al-Shabaab members was developed. CIA and JSOC planners presented President Obama with four options: a Tomahawk cruise missile strike, an airstrike, an attack by Little Bird helicopter gunships, or to attempt to capture the target by a helicopter assault force of SEALs.

The President chose the second option as it limited any potential collateral damage and the chances of US casualties. However, on the day of the operation,

UNITED STATES SPECIAL OPERATIONS FORCES IN AFRICA 2013–2014

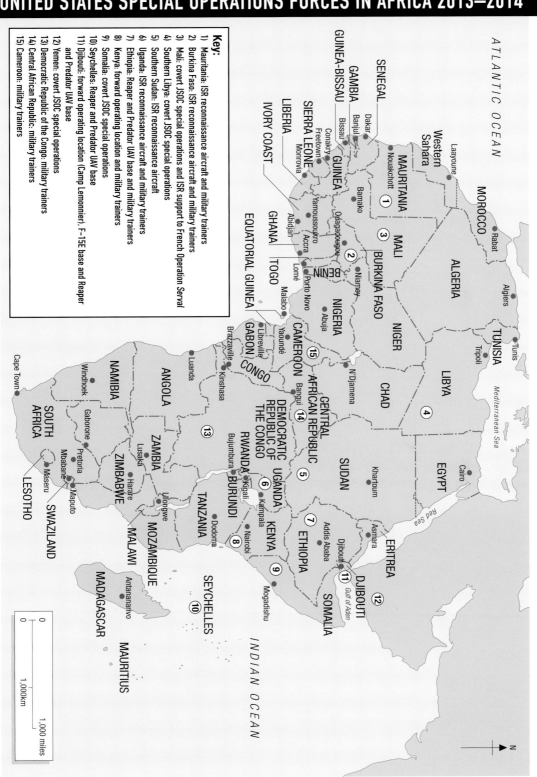

Key:

1) Mauritania: ISR reconnaissance aircraft and military trainers
2) Burkina Faso: ISR reconnaissance aircraft and military trainers
3) Mali: covert JSOC special operations and ISR support to French Operation *Serval*
4) Southern Libya: covert JSOC special operations
5) Southern Sudan: ISR reconnaissance aircraft
6) Uganda: ISR reconnaissance aircraft and military trainers
7) Ethiopia: Reaper and Predator UAV base and military trainers
8) Kenya: forward operating location and military trainers
9) Somalia: covert JSOC special operations
10) Seychelles: Reaper and Predator UAV base
11) Djibouti: forward operating location (Camp Lemonnier); F–15E base and Reaper and Predator UAV base
12) Yemen: covert JSOC special operations
13) Democratic Republic of the Congo: military trainers
14) Central African Republic: military trainers
15) Cameroon: military trainers

as the Marine Air AV-8B Harrier approached its release point, it reported a malfunction in its targeting system, most likely a problem with its SNIPER sensor pod. So the emergency back-up plan swung into action: eight helicopters, piloted by members of the 160th Special Operations Aviation Regiment, launched from a Navy ship sitting just off-shore. The helicopters included four AH-6M Little Birds equipped with miniguns and rocket pods and four MH-60L Blackhawks carrying a team of Navy DEVGRU operators.

The AH-6s struck first, strafing the two-vehicle convoy as it barrelled along the remote country road, killing the target and three al-Shabaab insurgents. After disabling the vehicles, the AH-6s orbited overhead in overwatch as the MH-60s landed, dropping off the DEVGRU operators, who cleared the vehicles and recovered the body of their target in order to take DNA swabs to positively confirm his identity.

This wasn't the first or the last JSOC operation in Somalia. The Intelligence Support Activity and SAD Ground Branch had been running a number of operations since 2003, including widespread cell phone intercepts. They used their local–national agent network to purchase any surface-to-air missiles that came on to the market (a similar SAD mission in Libya occurred years later) and to track and monitor al-Qaeda and al-Shebaab targets.

The Combined Joint Special Operations Task Force-Horn of Africa (CJSOTF-HOA) even had a rescue plan in place if ISA or SAD operators were captured, known as Operation *Mystic Talon*. It was built around a Special Forces CIF Company (Commander's In-Extremis Force – a dedicated direct action and hostage rescue unit within each regional Special Force Command), a SEAL Platoon and Air Force Special Operations assets. If necessary, they would fight their way into Somalia, recover the prisoners, and fight their way back out should a mission be needed to be launched before a dedicated JSOC hostage rescue Task Force could be deployed to the region.

An Mk5 Special Operations Craft of the type that ferried DEVGRU ashore in Somalia in their aborted raid to kill or capture an al-Shabaab high-value target, October 2013. (MCSA Anthony Harding; US Navy)

Two SEALs in combat swimmer attire moments after leaving the surf. The SEAL in the background carries the 7.62mm Mk48 medium machine gun while the SEAL in the foreground carries the FN SCAR Mk17 battle rifle, also in 7.62mm. (US SOCOM)

The earliest known of these Somali operations was conducted under Operation *Cobalt Blue* in 2003 and involved SEALs using SEAL Swimmer Delivery Vehicles (mini-submarines) to swim ashore along the Somali coastline and emplace covert surveillance cameras. These cameras, known as Cardinals, were designed to watch likely target locations for wanted terrorists as al-Qaeda and its affiliates began to regroup in Somalia. Unfortunately, due to the technology of the day, these cameras captured little as they only took one image a day. It is not known whether they were ever retrieved or still sit undisturbed along the Somali coast.

The 2006 Ethiopian invasion of Somalia provided JSOC and the CIA with the perfect opportunity to conduct covert offensive actions against al-Qaeda and al-Shabaab targets. Alongside Ethiopian troops were a number of camera-shy Caucasians in civilian garb who called in deadly strikes from AC-130 fixed-wing gunships. The US had also assisted the Ethiopians with satellite imagery and even established a temporary staging location in eastern Somalia. ISA teams used their signals intercepts and NSA technology to geo-locate leadership targets that were then struck by the AC-130s. Although large numbers of low-level fighters perished, no senior leaders were confirmed killed in the airstrikes. The heavy-handed Ethiopian invasion also proved to be a recruitment windfall for al-Shabaab.

OCTAVE FUSION

A hostage rescue in January 2012 again saw American boots on the ground in Somalia. Under Operation *Octave Fusion*, a DEVGRU element from Red Squadron launched a daring rescue mission to recover American NGO worker Jessica

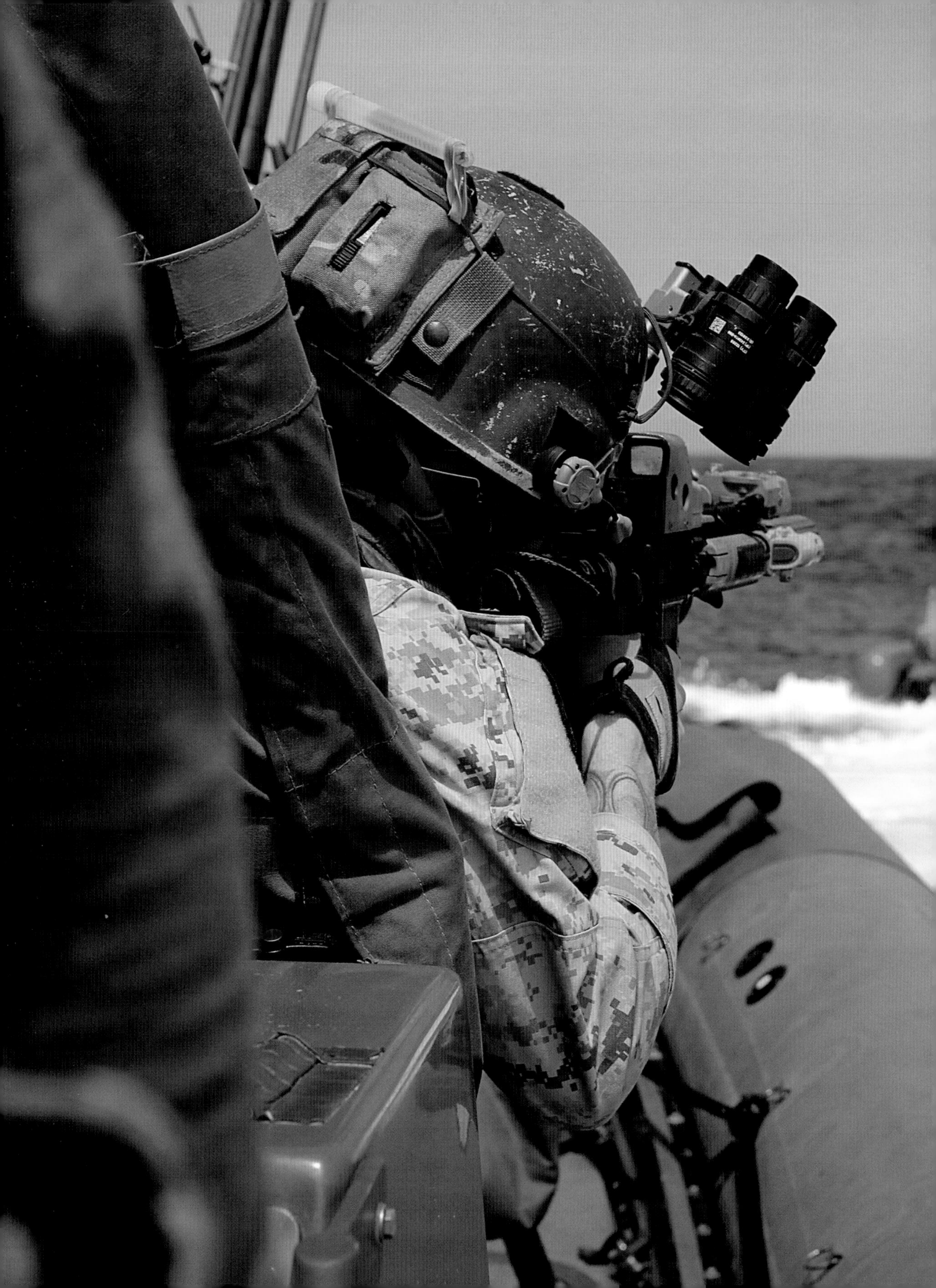

A MARSOC Marine provides overwatch as an assault team clambers aboard a suspect vessel during a VBSS (Visit-Board-Search-Seizure) training mission. The operator is equipped with a suppressed M4A1 carbine with EO Tech sight. (Staff Sergeant Robert Storm; US Marine Corps)

French SOF training for operations in Mali. Seen here are members of the Army's airborne reconnaissance unit 13e RDP; the parachutists of the French SAS 1er RPIMa; and the Air Force CPA10 special tactics unit. They carry an interesting mix of 9mm Heckler & Koch MP5 sub-machine guns and 5.56mm Colt M4A1 and HK416 carbines. (Adjudant Lefeuvre Wilfried; French COS)

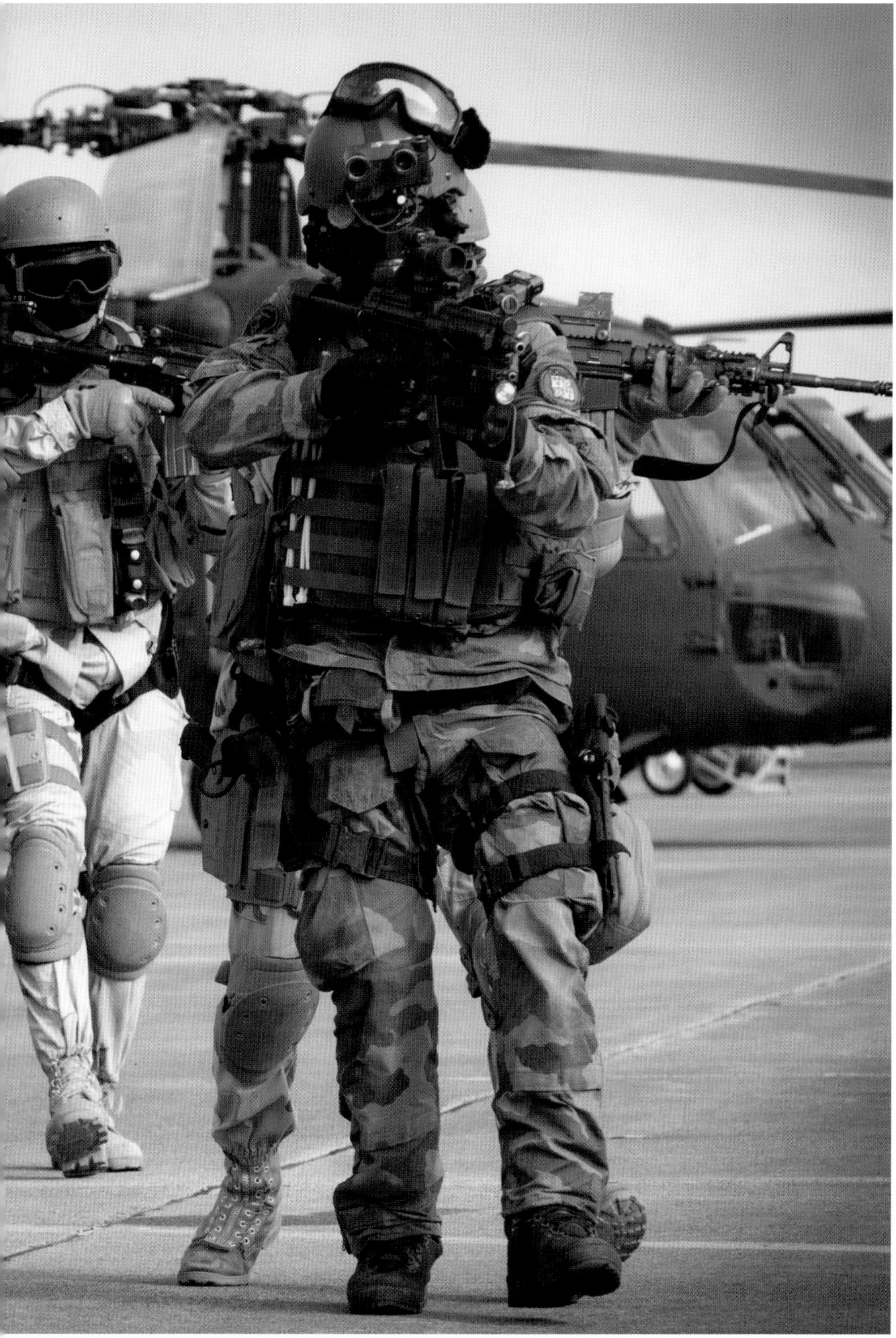

US Navy SEALs pulling security while teams fast rope to the deck of a warship during a VBSS training exercise – note the SEALs carrying the Heckler & Koch MP5 Navy which has been largely superseded by the Mk18 CQB-R carbine. (Petty Officer Second Class George R. Kusner; US Navy)

Buchanan and her Danish colleague, who had been captured by Somali bandits and held for several months. With fears the hostages could be sold on to al-Shabaab and with Buchanan's health failing, it became a time-sensitive operation.

A troop of SEALs conducted a night-time combat HAHO (High-Altitude High-Opening) parachute jump to an off-set drop zone. The team then conducted a night march to advance on the objective – a Somali pirate camp. The SEALs silently established a cordon with sniper overwatch while the assaulters attacked the camp, throwing flashbang stun grenades to disorient the hostage takers. Several managed to fire back before they were engaged and killed by the SEALs.

With the nine gunmen dead, the assaulters identified the two hostages and quickly established a security position, several SEALs covering the hostages with their own bodies when it appeared more gunmen might be on their way. After some 45 minutes on the ground, a pair of MH-60s arrived at a landing zone marked by infra-red strobes to pick up the assaulters and the hostages. Further SEALs and a QRF were on standby, should they be needed. The Blackhawks, with an AC-130 flying high above, lifted off and left Somali airspace, heading for Camp Lemonnier in Djibouti.

The SEALs of DEVGRU had also famously carried out a similar hostage rescue in 2009 off the Somali coast when pirates kidnapped the captain of the container ship *Maersk Alabama*. The story was filmed as *Captain Phillips*. After being held for five days on a small lifeboat, one of the pirates pointed his AK-47 at the hostage, prompting three DEVGRU snipers deployed on a nearby US Navy destroyer to fire. With three near simultaneous headshots, the pirates were killed before they could

OPERATIONS IN SOMALIA, 2009–2013

YEMEN

Gulf of Aden

DJIBOUTI

● Djibouti

AWDA L

● Berbera

**WOQOO YI
G ALBEED**

● Burao

Hargeysa

TOGDHEER

SANAAG

SOOL

● Garoowe

ETHIOPIA

100   200   300km

50   100   150   200 miles

MUDU

● Galcaio

● Dusa Marreb

GALGUDUUD

PROVISIONAL ADMINISTRATIVE LINE

BAKOOL

● Oddur

● Beledweyne

HIIRAAN

Jalalaqsi

● Baidoa

GEDO

● Balli Doogle

BAY

**SHABEELLAH A
DHEXE**

● Baardheere

Webi Shabeelle

YA

**JUBBAD A
DHEXE**

Merca ●

Mogadishu

BANAADIR

Webi Jubba

**SHABEELLAH A
HOOS E**

**JUBBAD A
HOOS E**

Kismayo ●

Indian Ocean

Inset 1 (top right)

DJIBOUTI   *Gulf of Aden*

● Djibouti

AWDAL   ④

**WOQOOYI
GALBEED**

Hargeysa

SOOL

G
N

ETHIOPIA

MUDUG

① Galcaio

● Dusa Marreb

GALGUDUUD

PROVISIONAL ADMINISTRATIVE LINE

③   ②

Operation *Octave Fusion*, Somalia, January 2012
1) Hostages seized near Galcaio
2) Hostages moved close to Ethiopian border
   near Galguduud
3) DEVGRU launch operation from neighboring
   Ethiopia, parachuting into Somalia and walking
   several kilometers to insurgent camp. Nine gunmen
   are killed in a brief firefight. Both hostages are
   recovered. MH-60s land to extract assault force.
4) After successful rescue, hostages and assaulters
   flown to Camp Lemonnier, Djibouti

Inset 2 (middle right)

ETHIOPIA

PROV

● Dusa Marreb

GALGUDUUD

BAKOOL

● Oddur

● Beledweyne

HIIRAAN

Jalalaqsi

● Baidoa

● Balli Doogle

BAY

Webi Shabeelle

**SHABEELLAHA
DHEXE**

**SHABEELLAHA
HOOSE**

BANAADIR

② Merca ①   **Mogadishu**

Webi Jubba

③

Indian Ocean

Navy SEAL High Value Target Raid,
Barawe, Somalia, October 2013
1) DEVGRU Troop inserted by Special Operations Craft
2) Conduct unsuccessful raid and fallback to boats
3) Boats link up with US Navy ships in the Indian Ocean

Inset 3 (bottom right)

● Baidoa

● Balli Doogle

BAY

● Merca

Mogadishu

BANAADIR

SHAB

Webi Shabeelle

②

**SHABEELLAHA
HOOSE** ◄—

①

③

Indian Ocean

7.6 Operation *Celestial Balance*, Somalia,
September 2009
1) After failed airstrike, DEVGRU team launch in Little
   Birds to intercept al Shabaab target on road to Barawe
2) The insurgent convoy is attacked by AH-6
   gunships firing miniguns and rockets
3) DEVGRU operators land and recover target's
   body for later DNA confirmation

NB This operation was repeated to an extent in September 2014
when the leader of al Shabaab was killed in a combined Reaper UAV
and AC-130 strike. DEVGRU operators again landed by helicopter, and
after a brief firefight, extracted with the body for DNA comparison,
flown to Camp Lemonnier, Djibouti

harm the hostage. A DEVGRU assault team standing by in a RIB boarded the lifeboat and, unsure if the snipers had made all of their shots, shot each hostage taker several more times before safely securing the hostage.

The French conducted their own hostage rescue operation in Somalia, unfortunately with tragic results. An undercover agent of the French DGSE (Directorate General for External Security) operating under the name of Denis Allex was captured by al-Shabaab insurgents in July 2009 in the Somali capital Mogadishu. The 47-year-old former COS Special Forces soldier was conducting an undisclosed counterterrorist mission in the war-torn country with a fellow DGSE operator, who managed to escape the kidnapping.

Both US and French technical and human intelligence teams, including an ISA team and U-28A surveillance flights out of Djibouti, were immediately deployed in an exhaustive effort to locate the hostage. Somali assets on the ground recruited by DGSE identified several locations where the agent had been held, but they were always one step behind the hostage takers who continually moved Allex. As al-Shabaab were caught up in the bitter fighting for the capital against African Union troops at the time, Allex was moved to a small village, 110km south of Mogadishu, called Bulo Marer.

US and French satellites and unmanned reconnaissance flights monitored the hostage's location for several months as operators of the DGSE's Division Action

A wonderful shot of a joint VBSS (Visit-Board-Search-Seizure) exercise between the US Navy and the Jordanian Navy. The fast boats are crewed by Special Boat Teams while the assaulters are made up of SEALs, Jordanian and Iraqi Special Forces. Note the Jordanian Little Bird and the mix of Jordanian Blackhawks and US Navy Seahawks. (Sergeant Melissa C Parrish; US DOD)

unit planned for a hostage rescue, should the opportunity arise. The unit is similar to the CIA's Special Activities Division and is composed of former French Special Forces soldiers and Marines who conduct covert counterterrorist missions. As news of the deteriorating health of the hostage reached them in December 2012, the 50-man Close Quarter Battle Group of Division Action, also known as CPIS, was ordered by French President Hollande to prepare to conduct an opposed hostage rescue into Somalia.

Initial preparations were conducted at the CPIS base in France before the team was forward deployed to Camp Lemonnier, Djibouti where replicas of the target house were built and the teams drilled endlessly, using the latest intelligence supplied by Somali agents on the ground. Their rehearsals in Djibouti were aided by a small team of SEAL operators from DEVGRU's Red Squadron. The US also provided surveillance assets, including the JSOC Predator UAVs based at Camp Lemonnier and air cover in the form of both AC-130 Spectres and an RQ-4 Global Hawk UAV during the mission itself.

At midnight on January 11, five EC-725 Caracal helicopters of the COS Special Forces Flight lifted off from a French Navy ship, escorted by two COS Tiger attack helicopters. The Caracals flew to the coast blacked-out under night-vision conditions and inserted the operators 9km from the target location at an off-set LZ to ensure the sound of the helicopters did not tip off al-Shabaab. The insertion went according to plan with the operators making good progress on foot. (Some accounts mention the operators encountering gunmen during the infiltration, but this hasn't been confirmed. If true, the hostiles were quickly and quietly dealt with.) Once the team arrived at the target location, they stacked up to prepare for an explosive breach of the main gates. It was at that time that their luck ran out.

Depending on sources, an insurgent either walked out to urinate and let out a cry as he was shot, or an insurgent sleeping in the courtyard, concealed from view under a pile of rubbish, was inadvertently bypassed and raised the alarm before being killed. Either way, the alarm was raised and the rescue team found itself in the middle of a vicious firefight. The leader of the CQB Group was severely wounded as an insurgent fired through a wall and a popular Sergeant was killed as the operators attempted to breach the target house. It is believed that the hostage, Denis Allex, was executed by his captors at this time. The sounds of battle brought al-Shabaab reinforcements and the DGSE cordon teams, manning blocking positions around the target, were engaged in a heavy firefight.

The difficult order to break contact and withdraw back to the HLZ was finally given and the teams began to fall back, collapsing the cordon and carrying their badly wounded Captain. Unfortunately, they were unable to retrieve the body of their fallen Sergeant. Five other operators had also been wounded. The Tiger attack helicopters were called in and they flew cover for the special operators as they escaped on foot toward their emergency HLZ. With the Tigers holding the advancing insurgents at bay, the assault force managed to board the Caracals safely and head back to the Mistral without further casualties. Tragically, their wounded Captain died on the flight back despite the best efforts of their medics. The mission was far from a success: two DGSE operators killed, five wounded and the target of the rescue, Denis Allex, murdered by his kidnappers. Some 17 insurgents were killed by the CQB Group operators, while the Tiger gunships accounted for dozens more.

Later that year, DEVGRU would have its own disappointment in Somalia when an operation to seize a wanted al-Shabaab leader linked to the Westgate shopping mall massacre in Kenya (and an associate of the terrorist killed by DEVGRU in 2009 on Operation *Celestial Balance*) ended in the SEALs retreating without their prize. Infiltrating in apparently a single MK V Special Operations Craft (with several other Special Operations Craft in support close to the shoreline), the SEALs closed in on a fortified beachside residence, known to be an al-Shabaab safe house, in the town of Barawe.

Using their night vision, the team managed to reach the target location safely and deploy an outer cordon while an assault team stealthily prepared to conduct a breach. Unfortunately, the assaulters were spotted by a restless al-Shabaab fighter who walked outside for a cigarette. A gunfight erupted between the operators and al-Shabaab militiamen as the assaulters conducted the breach and stormed into the safe house. As they methodically cleared each room using flashbang stun grenades, the assault team began to encounter heavy resistance and a large number of civilians in and around the target building. The firing and explosions had also attracted a large number of militiamen from the surrounding area who engaged the SEALs manning the outer cordon in running gun battles. With civilians interspersed with the gunmen, the SEALs couldn't call in an orbiting AC-130 for fear of killing innocents.

When it became obvious that there was little chance of reaching their target and an ever-increasing chance they would be swamped and overrun, the commander gave the order to break contact and the team withdrew some 200m back to the beach where they were successfully extracted by the special operations boats. The SEALs allegedly suffered no casualties, although traces of blood and discarded equipment recovered by al-Shabaab at the beach may point to at least one operator being wounded.

LIBYA

Following the Arab Springs in Tunisia and Morocco, there was a popular uprising in Libya. Western nations watched cautiously to see if the rebels stood any real

A MH-47E of the US Army's 160th Special Operations Aviation Regiment hovers over a warship as Romanian and Croatian SOF fast rope to the deck during a VBSS training mission. (US SOCOM)

chance of deposing President Gaddafi's regime. With the US declaring there would be no American military boots on the ground, the job of supporting the rebels fell to the CIA and specifically SAD Ground Branch. Eventually NATO combat aircraft joined the fight, conducting airstrikes on regime targets. On the ground small numbers of SAD, Saudi and Qatari Special Forces helped guide in those strikes.

Alongside them were members of E Squadron, a UK Special Forces unit established several years earlier, which is akin to SAD Ground Branch. E Squadron is comprised of selected members of 22 SAS, the SBS, and the SRR and is tasked by the Director of UKSF to support Secret Intelligence Service (SIS, better known as MI6) operations. It is not a formal squadron within the establishment of any individual UK Special Forces unit. Previously, SIS relied primarily upon contractor personnel.

An early covert operation in Libya involving E Squadron went wrong when SIS decided to make contact with some of the key rebel leaders. Flown in by an RAF Special Forces Flight Chinook, six E Squadron members and the two SIS officers they were escorting were briefly detained by rebel forces until it was established who they were. Regular UK Special Forces were also deployed under

Operation *Ellamy* to Libya, including a Troop from D Squadron that worked alongside the Qataris to mentor the Libyan rebels and coordinate NATO close air support. When Gaddafi later attempted to flee, his convoy was ambushed by a CIA Predator that engaged several vehicles with its Hellfire missiles, which allowed the dictator to be captured, and brutally executed, by Libyan rebel fighters.

On September 11, 2012, the US Consulate in Benghazi was overrun by militants. The US Ambassador and an Information Officer were murdered along with members of a CIA security team, former SEAL contract security officers. A low-profile security posture had been adopted – there was no rescue force (such as the Marine Fleet Antiterrorism Security Team later deployed) immediately available. Small teams from SAD and JSOC were both conducting operations in Libya at the time – most probably advance work on the later snatch missions conducted by Delta Force.

A seven-man team of CIA personnel, which included two Delta operators, were the closest and flew by commandeered jet from the Libyan capital, Tripoli, to Benghazi once the alarm had been raised. After a delay organizing transport through the areas controlled by rival militias, the team arrived at the CIA section of the Consulate known as the Annex, which was still under concerted attack. Mortar rounds killed the two former SEALs as they defended the location and seriously wounded a State Department security contractor. The Delta operators evacuated the wounded, maintained the defense and organized for a vehicle convoy to extract the Consulate staff. One of the Delta operators, a Marine who had passed the grueling Delta selection and conducted a rare lateral transfer, won the Navy Cross for his actions. The other, an Army Sergeant, won the Distinguished Service Cross.

With confusion still reigning on the ground, and with the strong possibility the US Ambassador had been seized, a Delta squadron was forward deployed from Afghanistan to conduct any possible rescue, but ultimately was not required. After the Benghazi tragedy, those responsible were targeted by JSOC, working in close cooperation with the CIA and FBI. Libya had become a safe haven for other terrorists as well, including some of those responsible for the 1998 bombings of the US embassies in Tanzania and Kenya.

In October 2013, a dramatic snatch operation was conducted in the early morning darkness in Tripoli. An al-Qaeda planner was in his car, returning to his home after morning prayers. Suddenly a nondescript white van pulled in alongside him while a second car pulled in ahead of him to block any escape. Operators in civilian clothes, carrying suppressed sidearms and what appears to be at least one suppressed MP7A1, raced from their vehicles and quickly disarmed, cuffed and hooded the target before bundling him into the waiting van. A third vehicle was stationed further up the road covering the team in case anyone attempted to intervene.

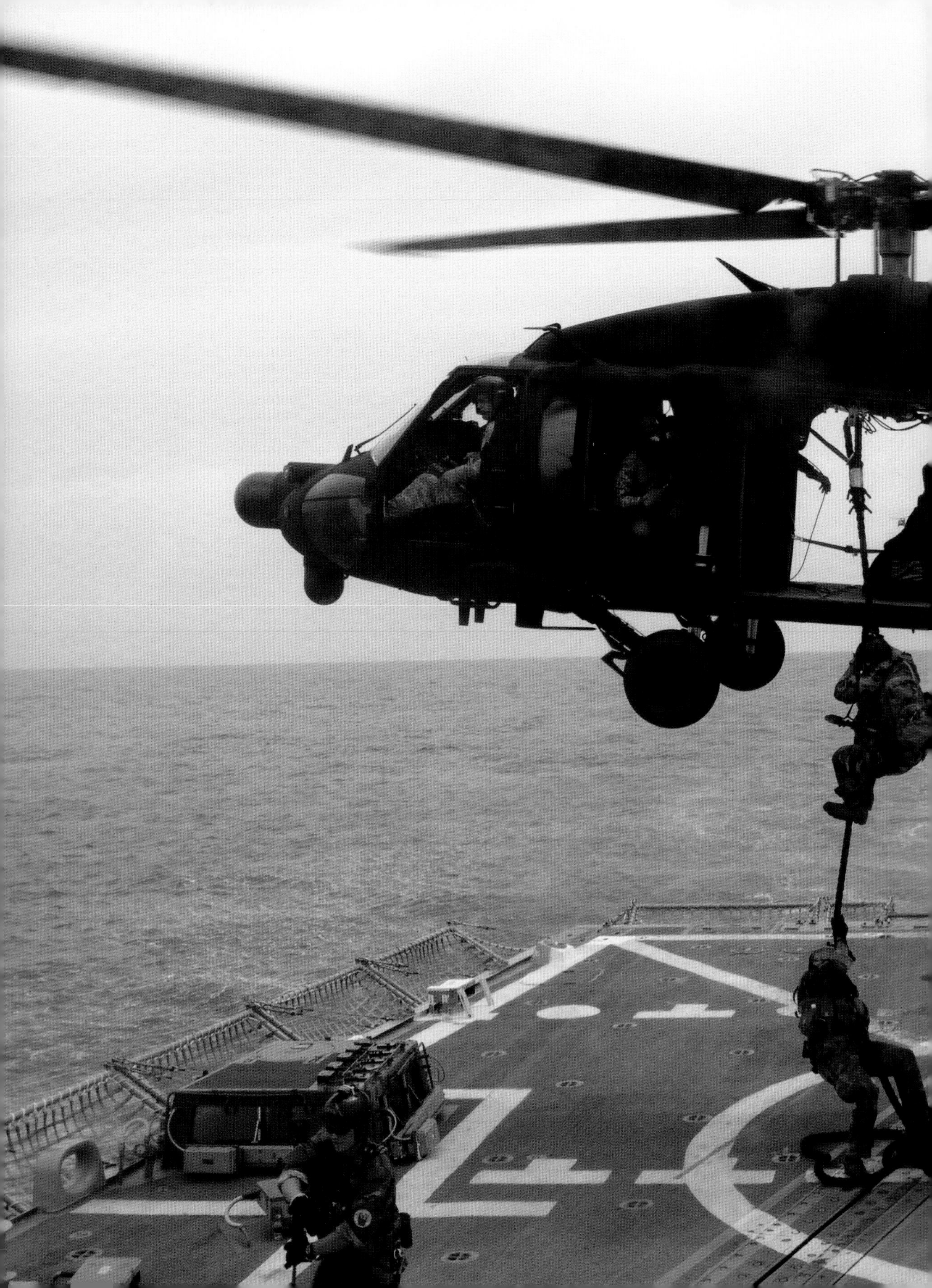

US Navy SEALs from SEAL Team Four fast roping from an MH-60L Blackhawk from the US Army's 160th Special Operations Aviation Regiment. Exercises such as these hone the SEALs' VBSS skills for operations against Somali pirates. (Mass Communication Specialist Seaman Shanika L. Futrell; US Navy)

An armed MQ-9 Reaper waits out a desert sandstorm in a hanger in Balad, Iraq, 2009. One Hellfire anti-tank guided missile is visible. The Reapers can carry a mix of JDAM bombs and Hellfires. (Senior Airman Jason Epley; US Air Force)

In less than a minute, and without a shot being fired, the operation was completed and the van sped toward an undisclosed Libyan military facility. Then the target was placed on board a waiting helicopter and flown to a US Navy warship in the Mediterranean. On board, he was interrogated by the High-value Detainee Interrogation Group (HIG) before being formally taken into custody by the FBI for criminal trial in the United States.

The next year Delta again hit the headlines with a further raid in Libya, which netted another high-value target. This time he was a senior figure in the al-Qaeda-linked militia that had attacked the US Consulate in Benghazi. An undercover

Delta team, accompanied by FBI HRT agents, managed to trick their way into the target's compound and subdue the individual, again without a shot being fired. The target was transferred to a US Navy ship and eventually into FBI custody.

Southern Libya remains a chaotic melting pot of armed militias and jihadists. To counter the influence of al-Qaeda in the Islamic Maghreb, JSOC teams and US Army Special Forces, French COS, and Algerian Special Forces have deployed to the region to hunt down AQIM (al-Qaeda in the Islamic Magreb) elements. The SEALs continued to conduct operations in the region too. In March 2014, a stolen oil tanker, the *Morning Glory*, was intercepted by SEALs off the coast of Cyprus who conducted a VBSS (Visit, Board, Search, and Seizure) operation to recapture the tanker and its stolen barrels of Libyan crude.

YEMEN

The first offensive UAV strike outside Afghanistan occurred in November 2002 in Yemen, a new battlefield in the war on terror. The target was Qaed Salim Sinaw al Harethi, the planner of the USS *Cole* bombing. A joint CIA and JSOC team, including a signals intelligence element from ISA, had been allowed to operate in Yemen as the country battled both Shia separatists and an influx of foreign fighters from al-Qaeda. The ISA team intercepted the target's cell phone as he was on the move, the NSA matched his voiceprint and a CIA Predator, flying out of Djibouti, launched two Hellfire anti-tank guided missiles at al Harethi's Land Cruiser. The target and five other al-Qaeda fighters were confirmed killed in the strike.

The Predator had been flying over Afghanistan since September 2000, watching for bin Laden. Before its armed capability was developed in early 2001, Tomahawk cruise missiles were the preferred stand-off attack option for the Pentagon. The Predator and its sister the Reaper now offered both surveillance and strike options in the one, unmanned, aircraft. The UAV could go to places into which the White House was reluctant to authorize manned flights, Iran for instance, where an advanced RQ-170 Sentinel (the same type of UAV that monitored the Abbottabad operation in Pakistani airspace) crashed in 2011 while apparently conducting a reconnaissance mission over Iranian nuclear facilities.

Years later, another airstrike would herald a renewed focus on Yemen. Admiral McRaven at JSOC argued for an "Iraq-style Task Force" to be deployed to hunt al-Qaeda cells in the country, but his requests were denied by both the Pentagon and the Yemenis. Instead, air strikes were the preferred option. However, JSOC and the CIA were permitted to establish a small command centre in the capital. December 2009 saw the first operation in almost ten years, with a Tomahawk cruise missile strike against a jihadist training camp in Abyan. A second strike in May 2010 ended in disaster when a Yemeni government go-between was killed as he met al-Qaeda representatives. The parallels with misplaced strikes years earlier in Afghanistan were uncanny but the strike largely stalled American counterterrorism operations for the next year.

With a secret CIA Predator base built in Saudi Arabia which was operational by September 2011, and with heavy losses to Yemeni forces fighting AQAP (al-Qaeda in the Arabian Peninsula), the CIA and JSOC negotiated their way back into Yemen. Covert UAV and conventional air strikes (by the F-15Es based at Camp Lemonnier) would be permitted under the guise of them being conducted by the Yemenis in an exercise of plausible deniability for the Yemeni people. A priority target had been tracked to Yemen: the American-born al-Qaeda cleric Anwar al Awlaki. A JSOC strike involving both Predators and F-15s had narrowly missed him. A second operation by a pair of CIA Predators finally killed him in September 2011. His son, also American born, was mistakenly killed by a JSOC Predator strike just weeks later as they targeted other AQAP leaders.

Yemen, like Somalia before it, was now subject to the attentions of two UAV fleets and two sets of sometimes misaligned targets. Occasionally these strikes go wrong, such as the one that targeted al Awlaki's son, or the December 2013 strike that killed not only a number of AQAP fighters in the midst of a convoy of vehicles heading to a wedding, but also a dozen or more civilian non-combatants; however, the vast majority are correctly targeted with no collateral damage. Each strike, such as those in Pakistan, must be examined for potential collateral damage, and in terms of human life and civilian infrastructure, before it is authorized.

In April 2014, a JSOC Lieutenant Colonel and a senior CIA SAD officer were off-duty and having a haircut in the expatriate area of the Yemeni capital, Sanaa, when a group of gunmen attempted to kidnap them. The JSOC and SAD officers responded with their sidearms, shooting dead two of their attackers and sending the others fleeing. The kidnapping attempt appeared more criminally inspired than jihadist, but it illustrates the dangers of operating in such locations. In the same month, SAD Air Branch pilots and crew flew Yemeni Special Forces into the rugged southern mountains of the country in a major combat offensive against al-Qaeda in the Arabian Peninsula (AQAP) which saw more than 60 terrorists killed. The Air Branch crews operated leased Russian Mi-17 helicopters and flew with night-vision goggles to give the Yemeni SF the element of surprise.

A late November 2014 hostage rescue attempt in Yemen was only partially successful. A reinforced troop from DEVGRU supported by US-trained Yemeni SOF launched a nightime raid on a number of caves in the Hadhramaut Province of eastern Yemen. They landed at an off-set helicopter landing zone several kilometres from the target and patrolled in on foot to maintain the element of surprise. Seven AQAP terrorists were shot and killed in the assault with one Yemeni SOF operator sustaining a light wound. Eight hostages including Yemeni,

OPERATION *SERVAL*, MALI, 2013

Key:
1) Combined conventional and SOF attack to recapture Gao
2) Combined conventional and SOF attack to recapture Timbuktu
3) SOF (supported by American ISR and AC-130s) operations targeting jihadist cells in the north
4) SOF and Paratroop drop to recapture Timbuktu

Saudi and Nigerian nationals were rescued, but five other hostages – including an American, a Briton and a South African – had evidently been moved immediately prior to the raid. The SEALs conducted an SSE and the Nightstalker MH-60s were brought forward to extract both the assault teams and the hostages.

DEVGRU conducted a second raid on December 5, 2014, after time sensitive intelligence indicated that an American hostage would be executed by AQAP imminently. A half squadron force infiltrated into Yemen by V-22 Osprey tiltrotors, which landed at an off-set HLZ some 10km from the target compound in the Abadan Valley to maintain the element of surprise, and patrolled into the location on foot using night vision goggles.

The element of surprise was lost when an AQAP sentry spotted the DEVGRU operators less than 100 yards from the objective. Both the American and a South African hostage were immediately shot by AQAP terrorists as the assaulters breached into the compound. The operators shot and killed all six terrorists at the location before discovering both hostages bleeding from gunshot wounds but still alive. A JSOC medical unit that had inserted with the assault force went to work to stabilize the wounded hostages while the operators secured the site to allow the tiltrotors to fly in and extract them.

The medical team worked on the wounded men at the objective for some 20 minutes until they felt that they were stable enough to be transported out of Yemen to a waiting US Navy ship in the Gulf of Aden. Tragically, despite the best efforts of the medical team, one hostage died on the extraction flight and the other passed away on the operating table on the US Navy ship as doctors struggled to save him. There were no reported injuries or wounds to the assaulters.

In other countries, Western SOF teams battle terrorists and hostage takers, including Nigeria where Boko Haram, an Islamic insurgency movement whose unlikely name means "Western education is forbidden," is aiming to establish its own caliphate. Boko Haram's recent kidnapping of 200 school girls has brought it to the attention of the world's media, however, it has been active for a number of years.

In 2012 the SBS attempted to rescue a British and an Italian oil worker held by Boko Haram in the Nigerian city of Sokoto. Signals intelligence indicated the hostages were to be moved, forcing the SBS assaulters to conduct a daylight rapid entry on the target building. As the assaulters breached into the location after a Nigerian Army APC rammed the gates of the target compound, the two hostages were

French special reconnaissance operators from 13e RDP train in Djibouti in preparation for operations in Mali. The weapon mounted on the swing arm is the 5.56mm FN Minimi. (CCH J. Bardenet; SIRPA Terre)

French operators from the Army's 1er RPIMa conduct a mounted patrol in Mali from their Panhard VPS Desert Patrol Vehicle. The passenger side swing mount weapon is the unique French 7.62mm AA-52 medium machine gun, which has been largely replaced in French SOF with the FN MAG and Minimi. (CCH J. Bardenet; SIRPA Terre)

murdered in a back room by Boko Haram members. The SBS team killed at least two jihadists and captured several more.

MALI

In the troubled northwest African state of Mali, Islamists came dangerously close to capturing the country and declaring an Islamic republic and the start of a global caliphate, an eerie premonition of things to come in a fractured Iraq later the following year. In January 2013, al-Qaeda in the Islamic Maghreb (AQIM) and affiliated jihadist groups including Algerian terrorists, along with Tuareg separatists of the Ansar Dine movement began a concerted push toward Bamako, the Malian capital. They had already captured large swathes of the north of the country, which borders Algeria, and were imposing their own harsh version of Sharia law, murdering civilians and burning down villages. Two long convoys of jihadists in technicals headed for the capital, Bamako.

Under a UN Security Council mandate, and in conjunction with the Malian government, the French military launched an operation to halt the advances of the jihadists under Operation *Serval*. Some of the first French forces into action were from the Mission Sabre Special Forces contingent based in Burkina Faso (along with US covert ISR aircraft that supported the *Serval* mission). Small teams of SOF on the ground guided in airstrikes from Rafale and Mirage fighters along with Special Forces Gazelle helicopters, which attacked the jihadist convoys, stopping them in their tracks.

The SOF contingent numbered some 150 operators largely drawn from the 1st Marine Infantry Parachute Regiment (1er RPIMa, which traces its ancestry to the wartime French SAS). They brought with them a number of COS Tiger and Gazelle attack and Puma transport helicopters. As well as conducting deep reconnaissance for the conventional force of mechanized infantry, light armor and

Marines, the 1er RPIMa launched joint operations with Malian Defense Force units deep into the north of the country. They also carried out advance reconnaissance and shaped operations in preparation for the January 27 parachute drop and air assault on the historic city of Timbuktu.

It is believed that both 1er RPIMa and the Special Action operators of the DGSE worked with teams from the SAS and JSOC elements to hunt actively terrorist leaders under Operation *Panther* (in 2012, two US Civil Affairs soldiers and a member of the ISA were killed in a road accident in Bamako, prompting speculation of earlier US counterterrorist missions, although Army Green Berets had long been deployed on a FID mission in the region). Across the border in Algeria the al-Qaeda-linked Those Who Sign in Blood Battalion seized an Algerian gas facility, killing over 30 foreign workers in the wake of an Algerian SOF action to free the hostages. American and British offers of assistance were refused.

Operations continue in Mali with French SOF supported by US Predators hunting jihadist remnants in the north. The leader of AQIM in Mali, Omar Ould Hamaha, known as Red Beard, was killed by undisclosed French SOF in a raid in March 2014. Another French SOF operation in the following month rescued five Red Cross workers, who had been held hostage by jihadists, ten of whom were killed in the operation.

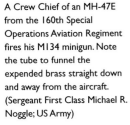

A Crew Chief of an MH-47E from the 160th Special Operations Aviation Regiment fires his M134 minigun. Note the tube to funnel the expended brass straight down and away from the aircraft. (Sergeant First Class Michael R. Noggle; US Army)

SYRIA

Mali is not the only recent trouble spot. In Syria the rise of Islamic State (previously the Islamic State of Iraq and Syria, and before that the Islamic State of Iraq and the Levant; it is still known as ISIL in Coalition militaries), spurred on by the civil war, has seen jihadists in pitched battles against both Syrian government forces and other insurgent groups. After the terrorists entered Iraq and linked up with remnants of AQI, they managed to seize several major cities, including Fallujah. At the time of writing they controlled up to a quarter of the country. With Baghdad and the Kurdish homelands threatened, US airstrikes commenced, supported by Green Beret adviser teams under Operation *Inherant Resolve*. United States SOF are also operating in Syria.

In northern Syria, on July 4, 2014, a classified "complex" hostage rescue mission was launched in an attempt to rescue several American hostages held by IS at a remote location, allegedly a former oil pumping station that was used by the terrorists as a prison camp. The night-time operation was based around a JSOC force of "several dozen" SOF operators, several four-man teams of Delta assaulters, and possibly supported by a Ranger security element, and according to some media reports, at least one Jordanian SOF operator acting as an interpreter.

The operation included 160th SOAR helicopters (apparently the so-called Silent Hawk variant used in Abbottabad and several MH-60L Direct Action Penetrators), fixed-wing aircraft and surveillance aircraft. The mission was probably launched from Jordan with AC-130 Spectre fixed-wing gunships and armed Predators overhead, and both manned and unmanned ISR aircraft for real-time surveillance. Syrian air defense radars would also have needed to be spoofed or jammed in a similar fashion to Operation *Neptune Spear*. Reports suggest local air defense positions were destroyed in a US airstrike moments before the helicopter assault force arrived.

The assaulters were contacted as they landed and a significant firefight developed, with a substantial number of terrorists killed. One member of the aircrew from the 160th SOAR was believed wounded when a helicopter was engaged by enemy ground fire "on their egress." A Delta operator was slightly wounded during the gunfight. There were no further casualties among the assault force. The AC-130 reportedly engaged and destroyed an IS reaction force heading toward the site.

Sadly, there was no sign of the hostages and the site was declared a "dry hole" (an SOF term for a target location where the objective is no longer located). The assault teams managed to conduct an SSE at the target site and unspecified materials were recovered. American journalist James Foley, reportedly one of the hostages JSOC hoped to rescue, was infamously executed in August 2014, his murder videotaped in a grim ode to Zarqawi.

CHAPTER 8
THE LONG WAR

At the time of writing, US air strikes continue in northern Iraq in an effort to support the Kurdish Peshmerga in its battle against the jihadist thugs of Islamic State, the latest incarnation of Zarqawi's al-Qaeda in Iraq. Some of these strikes, against artillery batteries, Grad multiple rocket launchers and similar targets, appear to have been guided in by UAVs. Others, including tactical strikes to support specific Kurdish and Iraqi Army offensives, must have been guided in by ground-based Forward Air Controllers (FAC).

Whether that FAC is an Air Force Special Tactics Combat Controller attached to a Special Forces ODA, a MARSOC Raider Team, a JSOC advisory team, or the CIA's SAD Ground Branch remains to be seen. What is certain is that, at a minimum, Special Forces ODAs have been deployed in the volatile region as advisers, apparently to conduct FID mentoring for Kurdish and Iraqi forces. It is unlikely that any of these teams have been directly involved in combat, yet. They have been joined by Canadian and Australian special operators to train and advise Iraqi and Kurdish forces. UK Special Forces have also been covertly deployed in the north of the country, working alongside the Kurds. It is also apparent that JSOC units are engaged in Direct Action operations after CENTCOM mistakenly posted an internet video of a flight of four MH-60Ms of the 160th SOAR conducting a mid-air refuelling over Iraq in October 2014. The video was hastily taken down once someone realized what it showed.

In related parts of the Muslim world, other groups are vying for attention. Boko Haram continues its reign of terror in Nigeria abducting schoolchildren and massacring whole villages. Mali remains an operational hot spot for the French (and, unofficially, US and UK SOF). Somalia continues to cement its reputation as one of the most dangerous regions on the planet, with no operating central government and al-Shebaab controlling much of the capital. Yemen too remains a constant source of concern where United States SOF have been operating relatively openly on partnered offensive operations.

In Yemen too, and in Pakistan, the drone war continues, with JSOC and CIA Reapers and Predators prosecuting targets from the Joint Prioritized Effects List (JPEL) – the much mythologized kill list of thriller writers. In many cases, UAVs have taken over the role of SOF in tracking and killing terrorists in inhospitable lands. The current US administration, with honorable exceptions such as the raid into Syria in 2014 or the Abbottabad operation to kill bin Laden, prefers the safety and deniability of the Predator and its ilk. There are no pilots to rescue if one crashes and there needs to be no formal acknowledgment of their use – targets in Waziristan die from an unspecified explosion, perhaps from a Hellfire missile, perhaps not. They are the near perfect tool for the War on Terror.

The special operators have no doubt evolved and many lessons have been learnt. Western Special Operations Forces are currently at their operational and professional pinnacle. The wars in Afghanistan and Iraq sharpened them to a knife's edge and gave them something that all of the expensive and grueling training in the world cannot – combat experience. They have seen what it takes to succeed in the field and have developed capabilities to match those needs.

A US Army Special Forces reconnaissance patrol is extracted by an Army UH-60 Blackhawk, Zabul Province, Afghanistan. (Staff Sergeant Aubree Clute; US Army)

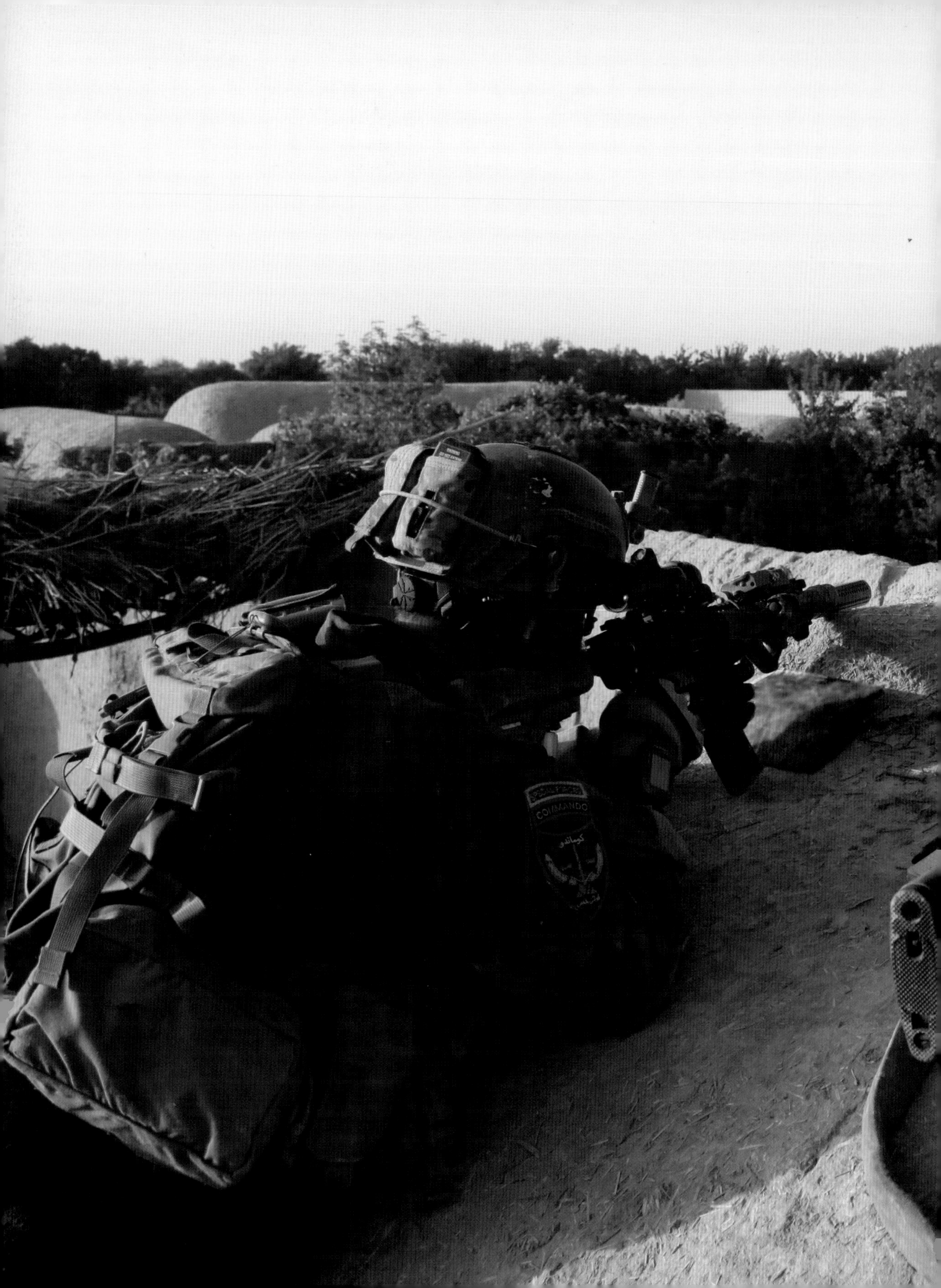
COMMANDO
کوماندو

"Watch and shoot." A MARSOC Marine provides overwatch from a compound roof through the Spectre sight mounted on his suppressed M4A1 carbine during an operation in Helmand Province, in 2012, as part of Special Operations Task Force-West. Next to him rests a suppressed M110 semi-automatic sniper rifle. Just visible to the left of the M110 is the sniper's DOPE book that will list range and bullet data for his weapon. See also the Afghan Commando flash worn by the Marine. (Corporal Kyle McNally; US Marine Corps)

US Army Rangers prepare for extraction by a MH-47E from the 160th Special Operations Aviation Regiment. Note how the Rangers are positioned to provide security overwatch in every direction as the helicopter lands. (Specialist Steven Hitchcock; US Army)

Most SOF have recognized the need for their own covert intelligence and reconnaissance gatherers in a similar form to Advanced Force Operations (AFO) at the beginning of the Afghan war. For example, SASR has added 4 Squadron, its principal tasks being covert reconnaissance, surveillance, and intelligence gathering, and it also provides a paramilitary capability to the Australian Secret Intelligence Service. The United Kingdom formed the Special Reconnaissance Regiment in 2005 to formalise these capabilities within UK Special Forces. In the US military, the Ranger Reconnaissance Detachment was placed under JSOC command to conduct Special Reconnaissance for all JSOC units. Other SOF expanded their size in direct relation to the increased tempo of operations since 9/11 – Delta added a fourth squadron, as did DEVGRU, while a fourth battalion was added to each Special Forces Group. In the UK, E Squadron was formed as a covert paramilitary unit for the Secret Intelligence Service while the Navy's SBS added a squadron to cope with its increased roles.

ISR (or ISTAR in the UK) has become the latest SOF buzzword. The incredible advances in signals and electronic intelligence gathering have created capabilities that simply did not exist before the War on Terror. Terrorists can now be targeted with a Hellfire missile purely on a few seconds of ill-advised conversation on a cell phone. If an ISR asset happens to be loitering high overhead at the time, the terrorist doesn't even have to make that phone call – he can be betrayed by his voice itself. Aircraft can beam color, broadcast quality footage, with sound, in real-time to SOF units on the ground. Micro UAVs are giving access to target locations never thought possible before – these tiny devices can fly in through an open window and, at night, are virtually invisible.

The mission has also evolved. After a long time when it was considered subservient to Direct Action, Foreign Internal Defense (and Civil Affairs) returned to prominence as perhaps the only way to ensure a future for a failed state such as Afghanistan. In the end, the kill or capture dynamic will not provide a guard for

US Army Rangers prepare to board a Nightstalker MH-47E on a kill or capture mission from Bagram Air Base, Afghanistan. Note the American flag used to mark friendly positions; judging by the radios also carried by that man, he is probably an attached Combat Controller. (US SOCOM)

the village when the Taliban creep in to deliver their night letters. Nor will it protect the villagers from insurgent retribution when a new school or clinic is built with government money and the Taliban, or an opposing tribe, want to burn it down. It won't train a local police force that the villagers can trust, at least to some degree in what is still one of the world's most corrupt nations. The US military understands this. The US Army Special Forces have recently raised a new command – the 1st Special Force Command – that will oversee all Special Forces Groups with a new emphasis on Unconventional Warfare and Foreign Internal Defense to counter so-called "hybrid warfare" such as that seen in the Ukraine or indeed Iraq. Additionally, every fourth battalion in the Special Forces Groups has been designated as UW specialists.

MARSOC Marines engaged in a firefight using HESCO barriers as cover at a remote patrol base, Badghis Province, 2009. (Sergeant Edmund L. Hatch; USMC)

Kill or capture is a necessary subset of counter-insurgency. The enemy who will not come to the table needs to be eliminated to allow more moderates a seat. Kill or capture also saved many, many lives – both military and civilian. In Iraq it had the added benefit of terrorizing the terrorists – sub-commanders were often unwilling to take over command from a leader killed by such a mission as they knew they could easily be next.

The other key development, and one which will always be difficult to balance, is the increased effort to arrest and prosecute terrorists as criminals. Delta's successful captures in Libya highlight two instances where, instead of the target dying in a hail of gunfire from an assault team, or from a Hellfire fired from high above, the target was arrested by US federal law enforcement and will go to trial

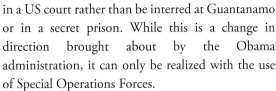

in a US court rather than be interred at Guantanamo or in a secret prison. While this is a change in direction brought about by the Obama administration, it can only be realized with the use of Special Operations Forces.

The War on Terror may have been renamed, but it continues, and regrettably it will continue into the future. Parts of Afghanistan will, in all likelihood, descend into something approaching another civil war following the eventual withdrawal of American combat troops. For as long as foreign forces remain, they will stem the tide with airstrikes and targeted SOF missions, while continuing to develop professional Afghan Security Forces. However, once the foreign forces leave, all bets are off. In Iraq too, only US intervention in the form of airstrikes and Green Beret advisers have stopped the murderous advances of Islamic State. In the near term, the battle against the radicals needs to be Iraqi led and that can only occur with some form of unity government supported by the Iraqi people.

Special Operations Forces will continue to be the tip of the spear in this global war against terrorism. They will continue to adapt to emerging threats and evolve to meet those threats through their unique skills and training. Technology will assist, but in the end it will be, as it always has been, the individual special operator on the ground who will make the difference.

GLOSSARY

AAR	After Action Report
AFO	Advanced Force Operations
AFO-North	Advanced Force Operations-North
AFO-South	Advanced Force Operations-South
AGMS	Armored Ground Mobility System
ALP/VSO	Afghan Local Police/Village Stability Operations
AMF	Afghan Militia Forces
ANA	Afghan National Army
ANCOP	Afghan National Civil Order Police
AO	Area of Operations
AQI	Al-Qaeda in Iraq
AQAP	Al-Qaeda in the Arabian Peninsula
AQIM	Al-Qaeda in the Islamic Magreb
ASG	Abu Sayyaf Group
ATV	All Terrain Vehicle
AVP	AeroVironment Pointer (a type of Unmanned Aerial Vehicle)
AWACS	Airborne Warning and Control System
BDA	Bomb or Battle Damage Assessment
BIAP	Baghdad International Airport
CAG	Combat Applications Group (Delta Force)
CENTCOM	The US military's Central Command
CIA	Central Intelligence Agency
CJCMOTF	Coalition Joint Civil-Military Operations Task Force
CJSOTF-Afghanistan	Combined Joint Special Operations Task Force-Afghanistan
CJSOTF-AP	Combined Joint Special Operations Task Force-Arabian Peninsula
CJSOTF-HOA	Combined Joint Special Operations Task Force-Horn of Africa
CJTF-HOA	Combined Joint Task Force-Horn of Africa
CJTF-M	Combined Joint Task Force-Mountain
CPA	Coalition Provisional Authority
CPIS	Close Quarter Battle Group of Division Action of Frech DGSE
CQB	Close Quarters Battle training (also known as CQC, close quarters combat)
CSAR	Combat Search and Rescue
CTPT	Counterterrorist Pursuit Team (CIA)
CTS	Counterterrorism Service (Iraqi)

DART	Downed Aircraft Recovery Team
DEVGRU	Naval Special Warfare Development Group (SEAL Team Six)
DIA	Defense Intelligence Agency
DOPE	Data-On-Previous-Engagements
DM	Designated Marksman
DPV	Desert Patrol Vehicle
EFP	Explosively Formed Projectile
EOD	Explosive Ordnance Disposal (US Navy)
ETAC	Enlisted Terminal Attack Controller (now JTAC)
FAC	Forward Air Controllers
FARP	Forward Armament and Refuelling Point
FBI	Federal Bureau of Investigation
FID	Foreign Internal Defense
FLET	Forward Line of Enemy Troops
FLIR	Forward-Looking Infrared Radar
FOB	Forward Operating Base
FORCE RECON	US Marine Force Reconnaissance
FRE	Former Regime Elements (Iraqi)
FSK	*Forsvarets Spesialkommando* (Norway)
GIRoA	Government of the Islamic Republic of Afghanistan
GMV	Ground Mobility Vehicle
GROM	*Grupa Reagowania Operacyjno Mobilneho* or Operational Reserve Group/Operational Mobile Reaction Group (Poland)
GPMG	General Purpose Machine Gun
GSG 9	*Grenzschutztruppe* 9 (Germany)
HAHO	High-Altitude High-Opening parachute jump
HALO	High-Altitude Low-Opening parachute jump
HESCO	the company that manufactures collapsible security barriers used at FOBs
HJK	*Haerens Jegerkommando* (Norway)
HLZ	Helicopter Landing Zone
HMG	Heavy Machine Gun
HMMWV	High Mobility Multipurpose Wheeled Vehicle (or Humvee)
HRT	Hostage Rescue Team (FBI)
HVT	High-Value Target
ICTF	Iraqi Counter Terrorism Force
IED	Improvised Explosive Device

IFV	Infantry Fighting Vehicle
IMV	Infantry Mobility Vehicle
IP	Iraqi Police
IRF	Immediate Reaction Force
ISA	Intelligence Support Activity (US)
ISAF	International Security Assistance Force
ISF	Iraqi Security Forces
ISI	Pakistani Inter Service Intelligence
ISIL	Islamic State in Iraq and the Levant
IS/ISIS	Islamic State/Islamic State of Iraq and Syria
ISOF	Iraqi Special Operations Forces
ISR	Intelligence Surveillance and Reconnaissance
ISTAR	Intelligence Surveillance, Target Acquisition, and Reconnaissance
JDAM	Joint Direct Attack Munition
JI	*Jemaah Islamiyah*
JIATF-CT	Joint Interagency Task Force-Counterterrorism
JIATF-E	Joint Interagency Task Force-East
JIATF-W	Joint Interagency Task Force-West
JPEL	Joint Prioritized Effects List
JSG	Joint Support Group (UK)
JSOTF-North	Joint Special Operations Task Force-North
JSOTF-South	Joint Special Operations Task Force-South
JSOTF-TS	Joint Special Operations Task Force-Trans Sahara
JSOC	Joint Special Operations Command (US)
JTAC	Joint Tactical Air Controller
JTF2	Joint Task Force 2 (Canada)
KCT	*Korps Commandotroepen* (Netherlands)
KSK	*Kommando Spezialkräfte* (Germany)
LITHSOF	Lithuania Special Operations Forces
LMTV	Light Medium Tactical Vehicle
LRPV	Long Range Patrol Vehicle
LRRV	Long Range Reconnaisance Vechicle
MI6	popular term (Military Intelllience, Section 6) for the British Secret Intelligence Service
MARSOC	Marine Special Operations Command
MBITR	Multi-Band Inter-Team Radio
MNF-I	Multi National Forces-Iraq
MSS	Mission Support Site
NATO	North Atlantic Treaty Organisation

NBC	Nuclear, Biological, and Chemical
NGA	National Geospatial Intelligence Agency (US)
NGO	Non-Governmental Organisation (e.g. charity)
NGSFG	National Guard Special Forces Groups
NSA	National Security Agency (US)
NZ SAS	New Zealand SAS Group
ODA	Operational Detachment Alpha (US)
OEF-A	Operation *Enduring Freedom-Afghanistan*
OEF-P	Operation *Enduring Freedom-Philippines*
OGA	Other Government Agency (CIA)
O-GPK	Objective Gunner Protection Kit
PJ	Para Rescue Jumpers (US Air Force)
PKM/PK	(*Pulemyot Kalashnikova* (Kalashnikov)) medium machine gun
POW	Prisoner of War
PUCs	Persons Under Control
PUK	Patriotic Union of Kurdistan
QRF	Quick Reaction Force
RAF	Royal Air Force
RIB	Rigid Inflatable Boat
ROE	Rules of Engagement
RPG	Rocket-Propelled Grenade
RPIMA	*Régiment de Parachutistes d'Infanterie de Marine* or Marine Parachute Infantry Regiment (France)
RRD	Ranger Reconaisance Detachment (US)
RSTB	Regimental Special Troops Battalion (US)
SAD	Special Activities Division (CIA)
SAM	Surface-to-Air Missile
SAS	Special Air Service (UK)
SASR	Special Air Service Regiment (Australia)
SAW	Squad Automatic Weapon (light machine gun)
SBS	Special Boat Service (UK)
SEALs	Sea, Air, Land Teams (US Navy)
SF	Special Forces
SFSG	Special Forces Support Group (UK)
SIS	Secret Intelligence Service (UK)
SMG	submachine gun
SMP	Special Missions Platoon (Iraqi)
SOAR	Special Operations Aviation Regiment (160th)

SOCCE-HOA	Special Operations Command and Control Element-Horn of Africa
SOCCENT	Special Operations Command Central
SOCOM	Special Operations Command
SOF	Special Operations Forces
SOG	Special Operations Group (Czech)
SOP	Standard Operating Procedure
SOT-A	Support Operations Team-Alpha (US)
SOTF	Special Operations Task Force
SRR	Special Reconnaissance Regiment (UK)
SRV	Surveillance Reconnaissance Vehicles
SSE	Sensitive Site Exploitation
TOC	Tactical Operations Centre
UAV	Unmanned Aerial Vehicle (drone)
USAF	United States Air Force
USMC	United States Marine Corps
USN	United States Navy
UW	Unconventional Warfare
VBIED	Vehicle-Borne Improvised Explosive Device (car bomb)
VBSS	Visit, Board, Search, and Seizure

SELECT
BIBLIOGRAPHY

The author can unreservedly recommend the following works that were essential for the development of this book.

Antenori, Sergeant First Class, Frank, and Halberstadt, Hans, *Roughneck Nine-One: The Extraordinary Story of a Special Forces A-Team at War* (New York, St Martin's Press, 2006)

Auerswald, David, and Saideman, Stephen, *NATO in Afghanistan: Fighting Together, Fighting Alone* (New Jersey, Princeton University Press, 2014)

Bergen, Peter, *The Longest War: The Enduring Conflict between America and Al-Qaeda* (New York, Free Press, 2011)

Bergen, Peter, *Manhunt: From 9/11 to Abbottabad: The Ten-Year Search for Osama bin Laden* (London, Bodley Head, 2012)

Bernsten, Gary, and Pezzullo, Ralph, *Jawbreaker: The Attack on Bin Laden and Al-Qaeda: A Personal Account by the CIA's Key Field Commander* (New York, Crown, 2005)

Blaber, Colonel Pete, *The Mission, the Men, and Me: Lessons from a Former Delta Force Commander* (New York, Berkley, 2008)

Blehm; Eric, *The Only Thing Worth Dying For: How Eleven Green Berets Fought for a New Afghanistan* (New York, HarperCollins, 2009)

Boot, Max, *War Made New: Technology, Warfare, and the Course of History: 1500 to Today* (New York, Gotham, 2006)

Bradley, Rusty, and Maurer, Kevin, *Lions of Kandahar: The Story of a Fight Against All Odds* (New York, Bantam, 2011)

Briscoe, Charles H.; Kiper, Richard L.; Schroeder, James A.; and Sepp, Kalev I., *Weapon of Choice US Army Special Operation Forces in Afghanistan* (Fort Leavenworth, Combat Studies Press, 2003)

Cantwell, Major General John, *Exit Wounds: One Australian's War on Terror* (Melbourne, Melbourne University Press, 2012)

Couch, Dick, *Down Range: Navy SEALs in the War on Terrorism* (New York, Three Rivers Press, 2006)

Couch, Dick, *The Sheriff of Ramadi: Navy SEALs and the Winning of Western Anbar Province* (Annapolis, Naval Institute Press, 2008)

Couch, Dick, *Sua Sponte: The Forging of a Modern American Ranger* (New York, Berkley Caliber, 2012)

Donaldson, Mark, VC, *The Crossroads: A Story of Life, Death and the SAS* (Sydney, Pan Macmillan, 2013)

Durant, Michael J.; Hartov, Steven; Johnson, Lieutenant Colonel Robert L., *The Night Stalkers: Top Secret Missions of the US Army's Special Operations Aviation Regiment* (New York, Putnam, 2006)

Fury, Dalton, *Kill Bin Laden: A Delta Force Commander's Account of the Hunt for the World's Most Wanted Man* (New York, St Martin's Press, 2008)

Gordon, Michael R., and Trainor, Bernard E., *Cobra II: The Inside Story of the Invasion and Occupation of Iraq* (New York, Pantheon, 2006)

Grau, Lester W., and Billingsley, Dodge, *Operation Anaconda: America's First Major Battle in Afghanistan* (Kansas, University Press of Kansas, 2011)

Lewis, Damien, *Bloody Heroes* (London, Century, 2006)

Lewis, Damien, *Zero Six Bravo: 60 Special Forces. 100,000 Enemy. The Explosive True Story* (London, Quercus, 2013)

Lowry, Richard, *New Dawn: The Battles for Fallujah* (Los Angeles, Savas Beatie, 2009)

Maloney, Sean, *Enduring the Freedom: A Rogue Historian in Afghanistan* (Virginia, Potomac Books, 2006)

Masters, Chris, *Uncommon Soldier: Brave, Compassionate and Tough, the Making of Australia's Modern Diggers* (Sydney, Allen and Unwin, 2012)

Maurer, Kevin, *Gentlemen Bastards: On the Ground in Afghanistan with America's Elite Special Forces* (New York, Berkley Caliber, 2012)

Mazzetti, Mark, *The Way of the Knife: The CIA, A Secret Army, and a War at the Ends of the Earth* (New York, Penguin, 2013)

McChrystal, General Stanley, *My Share of the Task* (New York, Portfolio Penguin, 2013)

Naylor, Sean, *Not a Good Day to Die: The Untold Story of Operation Anaconda* (New York, Berkley, 2005)

North, Colonel Oliver, and Holton, Chuck, *American Heroes in Special Operations* (Tennessee, Broadman and Holman, 2010)

Owen, Mark, *No Easy Day: The Autobiography of a Navy SEAL* (New York, Dutton, 2012)

Robinson, Linda, *Masters of Chaos: The Secret History of the Special Forces* (New York, Public Affairs, 2004)

Robinson, Linda, *One Hundred Victories: Special Ops and the Future of American Warfare* (New York, Public Affairs, 2013)

Schroen, Gary, *First In: An Insider's Account of How the CIA Spearheaded the War on Terror in Afghanistan* (New York, Presidio, 2005)

Stanton, Doug, *Horse Soldiers: A True Story of Modern War* (New York, Scribner, 2009)

Urban, Mark, *Task Force Black: The Explosive True Story of the SAS and the Secret War in Iraq* (London, Little Brown, 2010)

West, Bing, *No True Glory: A Frontline Account of the Battle for Fallujah* (New York, Bantam, 2005)

Weiss, Mitch, and Maurer, Kevin, *No Way Out: A Story of Valor in the Mountains of Afghanistan* (New York, Berkley Caliber, 2012)

INDEX

References in **bold** are to photos and illustrations

Abbas, Mohammed 190
Abbottabad 269–272
Advanced Force Operations (AFO) 31, 50–57
Afghan Arabs
  in Afghanistan 18, 19, 21, 69
  and Philippines 183
Afghan Militia Forces (AMF) 46–47, 50, 52, 148, 149–152
Afghan National Army 139, **148**, 157, 166–167, **258**, **272**, 273
Afghan Partner Unit (Kteh Kas) 162–163
Afghan Police 250
Afghanistan
  in the future 317
  history 18–22
  hostage rescue missions 236, 242–243, 263–266
  hunt for high-profile targets 232–239, 269–272
  kill-or-capture missions (2006–14) 228–277
  maps **33**, **39**, **79**, **143**
  see also Operation Enduring Freedom
AFO see Advanced Force Operations
Africa 11, 251, 280–301, **283**, 304–306, 310
aircraft
  A-10As 66, 90, 97, 120, 126, 130, 133–134, 152, 253
  AC-130s 25, 34, 36, 55, 57, 58–59, 75, 101, 126, 131, 190, 213, 225, 237, 263–264, 273, 285, 290, 294, 295, 303, 307
  Air Force One **169**
  AV-8 Harriers 117, 131, 284
  EA-6 Prowlers 131
  F-14 Tomcats 104–105, 121
  F-15Es 282, 302
  F-16 Fighting Falcons 61, 65, 90, 109, 110, 113, 216–217, 223–224
  F-117A Night Hawks 88
  F/A-18s 100, 101, 103, 105, 115, 117, 121, 250
  Iraq use overview 90
  ISR propeller planes 220

MC-130s 34, 42, 97–98, 116, 232, 233
  U-28As 282
  see also drones; helicopters
al Asad airbase **119**, 120–121, **120**
al Qadisiyah Research Center 133–134
al-Qaeda
  in Africa 282–285, 297, 300–301, 305–306
  Brigade 055 21, 48
  early days 18–19, 20–21
  and Enduring Freedom 24, 50–69, 70–82, 230, 232–236
  in Iraq 100, 170, 172, 179–180, 180–182, 197–227, 307
  and Philippines 183
  predicting behavior of 218
  in Yemen 301–305
Al Qaim 207, 225
Al Quds 224
al-Shabaab 282, 284, 285, 292–294, 310
Al Sukariya 225, **227**
al-Tikriti, General Abid al-Hamid Mahmud 191
Algeria 306
Algerian Special Forces 301
Ali, Commander Hazrat 46
Allex, Denis (pseud.) 292–295
AMF see Afghan Militia Forces
Ana Kalay Valley 250–251
Angoor Adda 236
Ansar al-Islam 98–101, 129, 170, 197
Ansar al-Sunnah 202
Apiata, Sergeant Bill "Willie" 80
Apostles 189
Ar Rutba 108–111, 113–114
Asad, Imam 233
assault tactics 221
Atta, General Mohammed 40, 41
Auerswald, David 141
Australian Special Forces
  in Afghanistan (2001–02) 30, 50, 54, 75–77, **76–77**
  in Afghanistan (2002–14) **8**, **145**, 162, **163**, **239**, 243–263, **246**, **247**, **248**, **249**, **254**, **259**, **262**, **263**
  before 2001 11

"Bubblies" 127
intelligence and reconnaissance 314
in Iraq **86–87**, 90, **90**, 97, 111, **112**, 118–121, **119**, **120**, 127, 130
and Philippines 185
SASR overview 246
Awlaki, Anwar al 302
Ayn Sifni 102
Aziz, Tariq 190

Ba'ath Party members
  and Basra 116
  and Fallujah 172
  and Haditha Dam 129
  and Highway 1 130
  hunting high-value 168
  and Najaf 117
  and Nasiriyah 118
  and Saddam's capture 195
  safe houses 190–191
  SOF treatment of former 113–114
  see also Fedayeen Saddam
badges and insignia **140**, **161**, **169**, **176**, **181**, **190**, **215**, **312–313**
Baghdad 178–179, 189, **199**, 200, **202**, 207, **214**, **215**, **225**
Baghdad Belts 213–215
Baghdadi, Abu Omar al 226
Bagram 38–40, **139**
Baird, Corporal Cameron 262–263
Balkans 11
Baqubah **203**, 213
Barawe 295
Basra 116, 211–212, **211**
Bastogne 42
Beckwith, Colonel Charlie 20
Beirut 280
Benghazi 297
Berg, Nick 172
Bergdahl, Sergeant Bowe 277
Berntsen, Gary 48
Bigley, Kenneth 172
bin Laden, Khalid 270
bin Laden, Usama
  2007 hunt for 233–236
  and Afghanistan 18, 20–21, 45–46, 48, 49

background 18
death 269–272
and 9/11 22
and Zarqawi 198
Blaber, Lieutenant Colonel Pete 51, 93, 96
black and white SOF 20
Blackwater contractors 172–174
Blair, Tony 70
boats **184**, **284**
Boivin, Sergeant Major Larry 174–175, **175**
Boko Haram 304–305, 310
bombs 38–40
Borneo 246
Briggs, SSgt Dan 174, 175
British Special Forces
  E Squadron 296–297, 314
  organization 14–15
  rules of engagement 202
  SAS
    in Afghanistan 30, 49, 69, 70–72, **71**, 75, 266
    in Africa 306
    in Balkans 11
    in Iraq (2003) 90, 97, 111, 116, 118–119, 123, 130
    in Iraq (2003–12) 188–189, **190**, 191, 195, 200–202, 207, 211–212, **211**, 213–214, **215**, 221, 224–225, 226–227
    overview 68
  SBS
    in Afghanistan 29, 49, 69, **70**, 72–75, **73**, 146, 162, 239–243, **242**
    in Africa 304–305
    expansion 314
    in Iraq 90, 97, 121–123, **122**, 195, 207–210
    overview 121
  Special Forces Support Group **188**, 189, 214, **240**, **242**, 243, **244–245**
  SRR 188, 239–241, 314
Buchanan, Jessica 285–290
Bulo Marer 293–295
Burillah Khan 40
Burkina Faso **283**
Butler, Major Dave 171

Caldwell, Major General Bill 216
Cameroon **283**
camouflage *see* uniforms and camouflage
Camp Lemonnier 280–282, 294, 302
Canadian Special Forces
  in Afghanistan 27–29, 30, 54, 77–78, 248–249

in Iraq 212
Carlson, William "Chief" 149–152
Central African Republic **283**
CFSOCC *see* Combined Forces Special Operations Component Command
Chechens
  in Afghanistan **54**, 232–233
  in Iraq 177
Chenartu 253, 259
CIA
  in Africa 281–282, 284–285, 296, 297
  Counterterrorist Center 22–24, 282
  Counterterrorist Pursuit Teams 149, 232, 236
  and intelligence in Iraq 218
  Special Activities Division
    in Afghanistan 22–24, **23**, **31**, 40–41, **41**, 46, 72–75, 138, 148, 149–153
    in Africa 282, 284–285, 296, 297
    in Iraq 92, 96, **133**
    and Philippines 185
    in Yemen 301, 302
  see also Jawbreaker team
Coalition Joint Civil-Military Operations Task Force (CJCMOTF) 25, 31
Cole, USS 301
Colombia 11
Combined Forces Special Operations Component Command (CFSOCC) 89
Combined Joint Special Operations Task Force (CJSOTF) 25–30, 83, 138
Combined Joint Special Operations Task Force-Afghanistan (CJSOTF-Afghanistan) 157, 161
Combined Joint Special Operations Task Force-Arabian Peninsula (CJSOTF-AP) 167, 168
Combined Joint Special Operations Task Force-North *see* Task Force Viking
Combined Joint Special Operations Task Force-West *see* Task Force Dagger (Iraq)
Combined Joint Task Force-180 (CJTF-180) 83, 86
Combined Joint Task Force-Horn of Africa (CJTF-HOA) 280, 284
Combined Joint Task Force-Mountain (CJTF-Mountain) 25, 30
Congo, Democratic Republic of the **283**
Cooper, CWO5 David 223
"Cosmo" (Special Forces sergeant) 100
Couch, Dick 160, 180
Croatian Special Forces **296**
Czechoslovakian Special Forces **141**

Dadullah, Mullah 241–242
Dailey, Major General Dell 93, 96
Dale, Senior Chief Matt 182
Danish Special Forces 54, 78
Daoud Khan, General 41, 42, 43
Dari-a-Balkh Valley 40–41
Dari-a-Souf Valley 38, 39, 40
"Dave" (CIA operative) 72–73, 74
Debecka Crossroads, Battle of the (2003) 102–105
Decker, SSgt Bart **25**
Delta Force
  in Afghanistan 15, 29, 31, 36, 44, **46**, 48–49, 52–54, 148, 274–277
  in Africa 297, 300–301
  as black SOF unit 20
  and *Desert Storm* **10**, **11**, 14, 35, **35**
  expansion 314
  in Iraq (2003) 93–96, 127–131, **128**
  in Iraq (2003–12) 172, 174–175, **175**, 178, 188, 189, 190, **190**, 191, 194–197, **197**, 199, 202–203, 207, 211–218, 220–227
  in other theaters 11
  overview 35
  in Syria 307
  term for members 20
  Wolverines 127–131
detainees, treatment of 200, 300, 317
DEVGRU *see* Naval Special Warfare Development Group
Diwaniyah 117–118, **177**
Djibouti 280–282, **283**
dogs
  in Afghanistan **230**, **231**, 251, **251**, **254**, **256–257**, **262**, 269
  in Iraq **71**, 127, **202**, 224
Donald, Lieutenant Mark 152–153
Donaldson, Trooper Mark 249–251, **250**
Dora Farms complex 88
Dostum, General Abdur Rashid 33, 37–38, 40, 41
drones (UAVs)
  in Africa 281–282, **283**, 293, 294, **300**
  in Afghanistan 65, 243, 263, 265–266, 273, 275
  in Iraq, 200, 206, 210, 219, 220
  in Pakistan 310
  in Yemen 301–302, 310
Dutch Special Forces 54, 143–144, 251

East Shah Wali Kot Offensive (2010) 252–259, **256–257**
East Timor 11

environmental reconnaissance 51
equipment
 Abseil gloves **226**
 assault ladders **216**
 assault packs **8**, **206**
 battering rams **216**
 cameras 285
 dump pouches **142**
 flashbang distraction devices 238
 GPSs **161**
 holsters **190**, **197**, **215**
 Hurst Rabbit Tools **238**
 Jawbreaker team **24**
 laser markers **22**, **30**
 night vision devices **163**, **216**, **222**, **230**,
  264
 radios 203, **234–235**
 wrist-strapped aides-mémoires **220**
Ethiopia **283**, 285
Explosive Ordnance Disposal teams **49**, 54
Extortion 17 **272–273**

facial recognition 220
Fahim Khan, General 32, 43
Fallujah 171–178, **175**, 182, 199–200,
 213, 307
Farrell, Stephen 243
FBI 220, 297, 300, 301
Fedayeen Saddam
 and Ar Rutba 109–111, 113
 and Basra 116
 and Karbala 115
 in Kirkuk 105
 and Nasiriyah 118, 132
 SBS encounters 121–123
 and Scud units 119–120
 and Tikrit 130
 uniforms and equipment 105
 and WMD facility 134
Fernandez, MSgt George "Andy" 130, 189
Foley, James 307
Force Recon *see* Marine Force
 Reconnaissance
Fox, Tom 212
Franks, General Tommy
 and Afghanistan 25, **34**, 48, 52
 and Iraq 86, 96
French Special Forces 78–80, 141,
 288–289, 292–295, 301, **304**, 305–306,
 305

Gaddafi, Muammar 297
Gayan Valley **152**
Geo Cell 219

German Special Forces 27–29, 49–50, 54,
 78, 80, 142
Ghadiya, Abu 225
Ghawchak 262
Gifford, Gunnery Sergeant Jonathan
 166–167
Grenada 11, **15**
Guantanamo Bay 77
Gulf War (1991) *see* Operation *Desert Storm*
Gurkhas 241

H-2 airbase 118
H-3 airbase 111–112, 118, 127
Haditha **174**, 260
Haditha Dam 128–129, **129**, **130**
Hallums, Roy 202–203
HALO parachute jumps 71
Hamaha, Omar Ould (Red Beard) 306
Haqqani (insurgent chief) 239
Haqqani Network 274–277
Harethi, Qaed Salim Sinaw al 301
Harrell, Brigadier General Gary 30, 86, 89
Harriman, CWO Stanley 55
Harward, Captain Robert 27, 126
Hathor Detachment 211, **211**
helicopters
 AH-1W Cobras 131
 AH-6 attack 275
 AH-6 Little Birds **10**, 94, 97, **98**, **128**,
  131, 223–224
 AH-6M attack 131, 133, 215, 225
 AH-6M Little Birds 284
 Apaches 52, 56–57, 66, 113, 115, 152,
  241, 242, 251, 253, 255, 258,
  272–273
 CH-46s 131
 CH-47D Chinooks **149**, **167**, 272–273,
  273, **274**
 CH-53s 131, **244–245**
 EC-725 Caracals 294–295
 HH-60G Pedros **82**
 Hughes 500 **133**
 Iraq use overview 91
 Jordanian Blackhawks **292–293**
 MH-6 Little Birds **275**
 MH-6Ms 133–134
 MH-47Es **32**, **64**, 94, **94–95**, 97,
  133–134, 156, 236–237, 263–264,
  269, **296**, **306**, **314–315**
 MH-53Js 127
 MH-60 Blackhawks **10**, **12–13**, **76–77**,
  94, **101**, 130, 131, 225, **236**,
  255–258, **256–257**
 MH-60Ks 133–134

MH-60L Blackhawks 284, **298–299**
MH-60L DAPs 94, 97, 130, 131,
 133–134, **168**, 199, 275, 307
MH-60M Blackhawks 277, 290
MH-D Little Birds 194, **198**, 199, **199**
Mi-8s **31**
Mi-17s **23**, 302
MV-22 Osprey VTOLs **281**
OH-47Ds **258**
OH-58s 194–195
Pumas 224
Seahawks **292–293**
"Silent Hawks" 269–270, 307
Tiger attack **294–295**
UH-60 Blackhawks **2–3**, 226, **246**, **311**
Hezbollah 224
High-value Detainee Interrogation Group
 (HIG) 300
Hollenbaugh, MSgt Don 174–175, **175**
horse riding **21**, **25**, 37
hostage rescue missions 198–199, 202–203,
 211–213, 236, 242–243, 263–266,
 302–304, 307
hunting permits, spoof **44**
Husaybah 207
Hussein, Mustapha 195
Hussein, Qusay 88, 191–195, **194**
Hussein, Uday 88, 191–195

ICTF *see* Iraqi Counterterrorism Force
Improvised Explosive Devices (IEDs) **145**,
 147, 177
intelligence 218–220, 260–261, 314–315
Intelligence Support Activity (ISA) 20, 29,
 31, 96, 195, 196, 241–242, 301
Intelligence Surveillance and Reconnaissance
 (ISR) 199, 200, 252, 253, 315
International Security Assistance Force
 (ISAF) 92, 230, 243, 247
Iran 35, 182–183, 301
 Iranians in Iraq 224
Iraq
 from 2003 onwards 167–183
 foreign fighter infiltration routes **173**
 Foreign Internal Defense 168–169, **179**,
  180
 in the future 317
 Islamic State in 307, 310
 kill-or-capture missions 317
 map **91**
 Unconventional Warfare 168–170
 see also Operation *Desert Storm*;
  Operation *Iraqi Freedom*
Iraqi Counterterrorism Force (ICTF) 168

Iraqi forces and police 168–171, **169**, **170**, **171**, **179**, 180, 182, 183, 211, 217, 226–227
ISA *see* Intelligence Support Activity
ISAF *see* International Security Assistance Force
Islamic State of Iraq (ISIS) 226, 307, 310
ISR *see* Intelligence Surveillance and Reconnaissance
Italian Special Forces 142, 242–243

Jaamat-e-Islami militia 40
Jaji Mountains **47**
Jawbreaker team 22–24, **23**, 32, 38, 46–48
    equipment and accommodation **24**
Johnston, Helen 265–266
Joint Hostage Working Group 198
Joint Interagency Task Force-Counterterrorism (JIATF-CT; Task Force Bowie) 25, 30–31, 50
Joint Interagency Task Force-East (JIATF-East) 218
Joint Interagency Task Force-West (JIATF-West) 218
Joint Special Operations Command (JSOC)
    in Afghanistan 233
    in Africa 281–282, 297, 306
    in Iraq 168, 196, 199, 200, 206
    overview 10
    in Syria 307
    in Yemen 301, 302, 310
Joint Special Operations Command Task Force 175, 177, 188–227
Joint Special Operations Task Force-Trans Sahara (JSOTF-TS) 281
Joint Support Group (JSG) 188–189
Jordanian forces **292–293**
Joseph, Dr Dilip 266
JSOC *see* Joint Special Operations Command

Kabul 43, **144**
Kahirkhawa, Mullah Khairullah 78
Kahlili, General Kareem 40
Kandahar 43, 44–45
Karbala 114–116, 224
Karshi-Khandabad (K2) airbase 22
Karzai, President Hamid **29**, 43, **43**, 44, 45, 58, 166, 231
Kember, Norman 212
Kenya **283**, 295, 297
Kirkuk 105
Kitty Hawk, USS 36
Konduz 43

Korengal Valley 263–265
Kteh Kas *see* Afghan Partner Unit
Kurds 92
    see also Peshmerga
Kush Khadir Valley 247–248
Kyle, Chris, 178

Latifiyah 213
Libya **283**, 295–301
Lithuanian Special Forces 143
Locke, Sergeant Matthew 247
Lodin, Commander Zia 52
Loney, James 212
Luttrell, Marcus **153**, 156
Lynch, Private First Class Jessica 131–132

Maersk Alabama (container ship) 290–292
Mali 281, **283**, **303**, 305–306, **305**, 310
Mansoor, Malawi Nasrullah 50–51
Mansoor, Mullah Shah 241, 242
Marcinko, Richard 58
Marine Force Reconnaissance (Force Recon) 14
Masoud, Ahmad Shah 21
Masri, Abu Ayyub al 226
Matin, Mullah Abdullah 241, 242
Mattis, General James 47
Maurer, Kevin 160
Mauritania **283**
Mazar-e-Sharif 33, 37, 41–42
McChrystal, General Stanley
    and Afghanistan 138, 156–157, 161, 230
    and Iraq 182–183, 197, 200, 207, 211, 213, 217–218, 219, 220, 224
McGough, Sergeant Paul "Scruff" 73–74
McRaven, Admiral William 163, 230, 301
Miceli, Ranger SPC Anthony **67**
Miller, Brigadier General Scott 161
Mirwais Hospital 78
missiles
    Hellfire **300**
    Javelin **86–87**, **103**, 104
    Scud 88, 108
    Tomahawk 301
    TOW 11 **191**, 194–195
Mogadishu 11, 251, 292–293
Mohammed, Khalid Sheikh 22, 197–198, 231–232
Monsoor, PO2 Michael A. 181–182, **181**
Morning Glory (oil tanker) 301
Mosul 102, 105, 194–195, 202, 226
MSS Fernandez 189, **199**, **215**
Mueller, Christopher 152
Mukarayin Dam 127

Mulholland, Colonel John 25, 88
Munadi, Sultan 243
Murphy, Lieutenant Michael 156

Najaf 116–117, **117**
Nasiriyah 118, 131–132
National Geospatial Intelligence Agency (NGA) 218
National Guard Special Forces Group (NGSFG) 138
National Security Agency (NSA) 218, 219
NATO 21, 82, 296, 297
Naval Special Operations Task Group 96, 123–127
Naval Special Warfare Development Group (DEVGRU; SEAL Team 6)
    in Afghanistan 31, **43**, 231, 232, 236–237, 263–274, **272**, **274**
    in Africa 284–292, **285**, 294, 295
    expansion 314
    in Iraq 96, 131–134, 188, 190, 207, 219–220
    overview 58
    and Philippines 185
    in Yemen 302–304
Naval Special Warfare Unit 10
New Zealand Special Forces 27–29, 54
NGA *see* National Geospatial Intelligence Agency
NGSFG *see* National Guard Special Forces Group
Nigeria 304–305, 310
9/11 22
Norgrove, Linda 263–265
Northern Alliance 21, **30**, 33–34, 37–50
Norwegian Special Forces 50, 54, 82, 144, **144**
NSA *see* National Security Agency

Obama, Barack 269, 282
Objective Medford 198–199
Objective Raptor 42
Objective Wolverine 42
Omar, Mullah Muhammad 20, 22, 36, 45, 75
Operation *Abalone* (2003) 195
Operation *Anaconda* (2002) 50–69, **53**, **56**, 77, 80, 82
Operation *Celestial Balance* (2009) 282–284, **291**
Operation *Cobalt Blue* (2003) 285
Operation *Crescent Wind* (2001) 22–24
Operation *Desert Storm* (1991) **10**, 11, **11**, 14, 35, **35**

Operation *Determine* (2001) 69
Operation *Enduring Freedom* (2001–2)
    16–83
    background 18–22
    command structure 25
    maps **33**, **39**, **79**
    opening 24–25
    special forces overview 15
    task forces 25–32
Operation *Enduring Freedom* (2002–14) **8**,
    82, 138–167
    ALP/VSO program 157, 161–167, 277
    Foreign Internal Defense 139, 157
    Green on Blue 162
    map **143**
    Night Raids 163–166
Operation *Falconer* (2003) 77
Operation *Gecko* (2001) 36
Operation *Ilios* (2006) 239–241
Operation *Iraqi Freedom* (2003) 84–134
    maps **99**
    organization 88
    planning 86–88
    task forces 88–96
Operation *Iraqi Freedom* (2003–12)
    186–227
    capture of high-value targets 190–198,
        215–217, 225, 226
    hostage rescue missions 198–199,
        202–203, 211–213
    intelligence 218–220
    Iranian activity 224
    maps **201**
    raids 202–206, **203**, **204–205**, **216**
    tactics 221–222
Operation *Jubilee* (2012) 265–266, **267**
Operation *Marlborough* (2005) 207–210
Operation *Mountain Lion* (2002) 77
Operation *Mystic Talon* 284–285
Operation *Neptune Spear* (2011) 269–272,
    271
Operation *Noble Venture* (2003), 231–232
Operation *Octave Fusion* (2012) 285, **291**
Operation *Prime Chance* (1987–89) **10**, 11,
    12–13, **14**
Operation *Provide Comfort* (1991–96) 92
Operation *Red Dawn* (2003) 195–197
Operation *Red Wings* (2005) 153–156
Operation *Relentless Strike* (2001) 42
Operation *Rhino* (2001) 34–36
Operation *Serval* (2013) **303**, 305–306
Operation *Slipper* (2001–2) 75–77
Operation *Snake Eyes* 207
Operation *Trent* (2001) 69–72

Operation *Urgent Fury* (1983) 11, **15**
Operation *Vigilant Harvest* (2006) 232–233
Operation *Viking Hammer* (2003) 98–101
Operational Detachments
    in Afghanistan (2001–2) **21**, 25, 27, 29,
        30, **31**, 32–33, **34**, 37–40, **38**, 40–43,
        44–45, 49, **81**
    in Afghanistan (2002–14) 138–140,
        138, **140**, **146**, 147–149, **147**,
        154–155, **160**, 161, **161**, 162,
        249–251
    FOB 102 105
    FOB 103 105
    in Iraq 88–92, 97–118, 168, **177**, 178,
        310
    ODA 043 102, 103
    ODA 044 102, 103
    ODA 051 102
    ODA 055 102
    ODA 056 102
    ODA 081 100
    ODA 391 102, 103–104, 105
    ODA 392 102, 103
    ODA 394 102, 103
    ODA 395 102, 103
    ODA 521 108, 110, 111, 114
    ODA 522 111
    ODA 523 108, 111
    ODA 524 44, 45, 108, 110–111
    ODA 525 **14**, **25**, 108–111, 114
    ODA 531 108
    ODA 534 40–41, 108
    ODA 551 114–116
    ODA 553 40
    ODA 554 116–117
    ODA 555 32, 38–40, 43
    ODA 561 49
    ODA 563 117–118
    ODA 570 44, 45
    ODA 572 46–49, 116–117
    ODA 574 29, 43, 44–45
    ODA 583 45
    ODA 585 40
    ODA 586 41, 42
    ODA 594 41
    ODA 595 32–33, 37–38
    ODA 911 89
    ODA 912 89
    ODA 913 89
    ODA 914 89
    ODA 915 89
    ODA 916 89
    overview and training 15, 26
    and Philippines 184–185

operator, origins of term 20
opium sites, attacks on 70–72
Owen, Mark (pseud.) 219

Pakistan 18, 20, 47, 48, 219, 231–233,
    252, 269–272, 310
pattern-of-life surveillance 51, 265–266
Persian Gulf *see* Operation *Prime Chance*
Peshmerga 86, 98, 100–101, 102–105, 310
Petraeus, General David 161, 227
Petry, Master Sergeant Larry 237
Philippines 183–185, **183**, **184**
Phillips, Captain Richard 14
Polish Special Forces 14, 96, 123–127,
    124–125, 144–146, **177**
Price, Gunnery Sergeant Daniel 166–167
Provincial Reconstruction Teams 31
psychological warfare ops 38, 42

Qala-i-Janghi 72–75
Qatari Special Forces 296, 297

RAF
    in Afghanistan 241, 242
    in Iraq 90, 122, 123, 189, 210, 224
    in Libya 296
    and SOCOM 15
Rahim, Mullah Abdul 242
Rahman, Abd al 215–216, 217
Ramadi 179–180, 180–182, **181**, 195, 199,
    214, 260
Red Beard *see* Hamaha, Omar Ould
rifles *see* carbines and rifles
Roberts, PO1 Neil Christopher "Fifi"
    59–66
Roberts-Smith, Corporal Ben **253**, 255,
    258–259
Robinson, Linda 138, 161–162
Romanian Special Forces 144, **296**
Royal Marines 96, 123–126
rules of engagement 202
Russell, Sergeant Andrew 77
Russia 8
    see also Soviet Union

Sabaya, Abu 185
Saddam Hussein 88, 171, 195–197, **196**
Sadr, Moqtada al 117
Sadr City 224
Saideman, Stephen 141
Sanaa 302
Sands, Phillip 213
Sangin 241
Sarbi (dog) 251, **251**

Sargat 100, 101
Saudi Special Forces 296
SEALs *see* US Navy SEALs; Naval Special
    Warfare Development Group
Self, Captain Nate 60, 64, 65
Sensitive Site Exploitation (SSE) teams **78**,
    101, 134, 203–206, 219–220, 270
Seychelles **283**
Shah Wali Kot Valley 162, 252–259,
    256–257, **264**
Shahikot Valley 50–67
Sherzai, Gul Agha 45
Show-of-Force missions 113
Sierra Leone 11
Simpson, John 105
snipers 253, 260–261
Somalia 11, 251, 281, 282, **283**, 284–295,
    291, 310
Sons of Iraq initiative 226–227
Sooden, Harmeet Singh 212
South Sudan 281, **283**
Soviet Union 18–19
    see also Russia
Spann, Captain Johnny "Mike" 72, 74, 75
Special Operations Command (SOCOM)
    10–11, 196, 220
Special Operations Command and Control
    Element-Horn of Africa (SOCCE-HOA)
    280–281
Special Operations Command Central
    (SOCCENT) 86
Special Tactics Combat Controllers **56**
Syria 225, 307

Taliban
    (2006–14) 230, 236–237, 239–243,
        247–269, 272–277
    and Afghan civil war 20–21
    and *Enduring Freedom* 24, 37–50,
        72–75, 78, 147–149
    and 9/11 22
    origins 19–20
Talil 223
Takur Ghar 50, 58–67, **60–61**, **66**, **67**
Taloquan 42
Tarin Kowt 247
Task Force *see* Joint Special Operations
    Command Task Force
Task Force 6-26 188
Task Force 7 90, 97, 111, 118–119
Task Force 11 (formerly Sword) 231
Task Force 17 182–183, 224, **225**
Task Force 20 93–96, 97, 127–131,
    131–134, 168, 188, 190–191, 194

Task Force 21 (later 121; 6-26) 188
Task Force 42 146
Task Force 58 30, 75
Task Force 64 (Afghanistan) 30, 50, 54,
    75–77, **76–77**
Task Force 64 (Iraq) 97, 111, **112**,
    118–121, **119**, **120**
Task Force 88 188
Task Force 121 (later 6-26) 188
Task Force 145 (later 88) 188
Task Force Black (later Knight) 188–189,
    190, 191, **202**, 211–212
Task Force Bowie *see* Joint Interagency Task
    Force-Counterterrorism
Task Force Central 188, 189, **198**, **199**
Task Force Commando 50
Task Force Dagger (Afghanistan) 25,
    31–32, 43, 50
Task Force Dagger (Iraq) 88–90, 97
Task Force East 188
Task Force Hammer 52, 55–57
Task Force Jacana 30
Task Force K-Bar 27–29, **49**, 50, 54
Task Force North 188
Task Force Rakkasan 30, 50, 52, 55–57, 66
Task Force Red 212–213, **212**, 214
Task Force Sword (later Task Force 11)
    29–30, 31, 36, 50, 52, 57, 67–69, 83
Task Force Viking 90–92, 97–105
Task Force West 188
Team India 54
Team Juliet 52–54, 58
Team Mako 21 58
Team Mako 30 58–67
Team Mako 31 54, 55
tier system 20
Tikrit 130–131, 191, 224–225
Tizak 255–259
Tora Bora caves 43, 45–49, **46**, 233–236
Tripoli 297–298
Turkey 92

UAVs *see* drones
Uganda **283**
"Ugly Baby" 97–98
Umm Qasr 96, 123–126, **124–125**, 127
uniforms and camouflage
    ACU pattern **174**, **206**
    AOR camouflage **166**, **233**, **259**,
        274
    "chocolate chip" desert pattern **11**
    combat swimmer **285**
    Desert Night Camouflage Pattern **81**
    Fedayeen Saddam 105

Gortex camouflage gear **67**
headgear **110**, **112**, **114**, **197**, **222**
MOPP suits 115
MultiCam pattern **8**, **76–77**, **188**, **197**,
    202, **240**, **259**
Paraclete vests **197**
plate carriers **2–3**, **233**, **240**
Protective Combat Uniforms **220**, **222**
three-color desert pattern **174**, **179**,
    197
Tiger Stripe camouflage 236
Woodland pattern BDUs **9**, **190**
Urban, Mark 200, 202
US Air Force
    Para Rescue Jumpers **139**
    and Philippines 184–185
    Special Tactics JTAC **276**
US Army 160th SOAR
    in Afghanistan 25, 29, 42, **43**, 58–67,
        148, 156, 231, 236–237, 266,
        272–273
    in Africa **298–299**
    before 2001 11, **12–13**
    in Iraq 90, 96, 97, **128**, 130, 188, 189,
        197, **198**, **212**, 215
    overview 94
    in Syria 307
US Marines
    in Afghanistan 30, 44, 157, 158–159,
        161, 162, **164–165**, 166–167
    in Iraq 131–132, 172, 174–175,
        177–178, 225
    overview 164–165
    in Philippines **183**
    training **286–287**
US Navy SEALs **9**
    in Afghanistan (2001–2) 15, 27–29, **43**,
        47, **49**, 55, 57–59
    in Afghanistan (2002–12) 153–156, 157,
        161, 162, 231–236, **231**, **233**,
        256–257, **258**
    in Iraq 123–127, **169**, 177–182,
        179
    organization 180
    in other theaters 14, **14**, 184–185
    overview 28
    Team 2 27, 54
    Team 3 27, 49–50, 54, 178
    Team 4 **169**, **298–299**
    Team 5 127, 178
    Team 6 11
    Team 8 27, 44, 54, 96, 123–126
    Team 10 96, 123–126, 153–156, **153**,
        178, **181**

training **281**, **290**
see also Naval Special Warfare
        Development Group (DEVGRU;
        SEAL Team 6)
US Rangers
    in Afghanistan (2001–2) 29, 34–36, **37**,
        41, 42, 46, **59**, 60–61, **62–63**, 64–67,
        67, **94–95**
    in Afghanistan (2002–14) **142**, 148,
        149, 162, **167**, **230**, 231, **234–235**,
        236–239, **237**, **238**, **255**, **261**,
        263–265, **264**, **268**, 269, 272, **272**,
        273, 277
    in Iraq (2003) 93, 128–130, **129**,
        131–134
    in Iraq (2003–12) 188, 190, **199**,
        204–205, **206**, 207, 210, **210**,
        212–213, **212**, **215**, 219, 220, **222**,
        226
    in other theaters 11, **15**
    overview 62–63
    Ranger Reconnaissance Detachment 239,
        314
US Special Forces Groups
    1st 161, 184
    3rd 27, 50, 54, 77, 81, 92, 102, **104**,
        105, **108**, **140**, 168
    5th 25, 26, 50, 73, **74**, 88–89, 92,
        108–118, **113**, **114**, **118**, 168, 177,
        178
    10th 90–93, 105, 168
    19th 89

VBSS operations and training 11, **286–287**,
    290, **292–293**, **296**, **298–299**, 301
vehicles
    ATVs 31, **146**, **162**, **240**
    Bushmasters **163**, 221, **247**, **249**, 252,
        254
    DPVs **43**, 126–127, **126**
    DUMVEEs **35**
    G Wagens 148
    GMVs **104**, **108**, **110**, **113**, **114**, **117**,
        158–159, **164**, **174**, **177**, **214**
    GMV-Navy variants **169**
    HMMWVs **31**, 148, **191**, **252**
    Kawasaki ATVs **158–159**
    Land Rover Pinkies 122–123, **122**
    M-ATVs **157**, **158–159**, **162**
    M1078 LMTV War Pigs **89**, **115**, **118**
    Menacity OAV/SRUs **240**
    NTVs 92–93
    Pandur AGMs 221, **221**
    Panhard VPS DPVs **305**

Perentie LRPVs **163**, 249
Perentie LRRVs **86–87**, **112**, **119**
pick-up trucks 127, 148, **162**,
    202
Pinzgauer SOVs 10, **35**, 80–81,
    127
Polaris ATVs 51, **160**
SRVs **86–87**
Stryker IFVs **142**
Vietnam 246

weapons
    ammunition **247**
    anti-aircraft guns **30**, 115
    carbines and rifles
        .50cal Barrett M107s **261**
        .338 Lapua Magnum Blaser R93
            Tactical 2s **259**
        AKM assault 24
        AMD 65s **239**
        Colts 11
        Diemaco CBs **70**, **73**, 176
        HK416s 176, **197**, **233**, **288–289**
        HK417s 188, **244–245**
        IR illuminators **264**
        Kalashnikov pattern **215**
        L85A2 assault **188**
        M3 Carl Gustavs **251**
        M4s **46**, 148, 176
        M4A1s **2–3**, **28**, **139**, **154–155**,
            164–165, 169, 176, **190**, **214**, **216**,
            226, **264**, **268**, **286–287**, **288–289**,
            312–313
        M4A5s **248**, **259**
        M16A2s **14**
        M40A1s **14**
        M82A1s **37**, 243
        M110s **312–313**
        McMillan .50s **14**
        Mk11/SR-25s **37**, **160**
        Mk12s **34**, 110
        Mk14s **250**, **253**
        Mk16 SCARs **268**
        Mk17 SCARs **237**, **268**, **285**
        Mk18 CQB-Rs **231**, **256–257**
        Mk21 Precisions **260**
        rails **264**, **268**
        snipers **261**
        weapon lights **264**
    fighting knives **274**
    grenade launchers **9**, **11**, **14**, 148, **152**,
        160, 176, **226**
        M79s 176
    grenades **2–3**, **139**

machine guns and SMGs
    .50cal **112**
    7.62mm **112**, **305**
    AA-52s **305**
    DShKs **26**, **54**
    FN MAG58s (M240s) **25**, **247**
    FN Maximis **259**
    FN Minimis **304**
    HK MP5A1s **73**
    M2s **89**, **104**, **157**, **164**
    M240s **89**, **104**, **110**, **117**, **184**
    M249s **164**
    Minimi Paras **70**, **188**
    Mk46s **62–63**, **146**, **222**
    Mk48s **56–57**, **274**, **285**
    MP5s 176, **288–289**, **290**
    MP7s 176
    MPSSD3s **14**
    PKMs **115**, **171**
    RPKs **215**
miniguns **184**, **306**
mortars **59**
pistols 24, 176
rails **264**
rocket launchers **175**
rockets **56–57**, **104**, **112**, 129, **144**,
    168
SAWs **67**
shotguns **226**
sights and pointers
    ACOGs **248**
    Aimpoints **11**, **67**, **110**, **226**, **239**,
        253
    EO Techs **46**, **169**, **238**, **253**,
        286–287
    laser **148**, **214**, **239**
    Spectres **2–3**, **139**, **237**, **264**,
        312–313
    thermal day/night **37**
SOF overview 176
weapons of mass destruction, hunting
    133–134, 190
Wells, CWO3 Kevin 168–169
Western Euphrates Ratline 207, 225
Whalen, Technical Sergeant Kevin **152**

Yemen 281, 282, **283**, 301–304, 310
Yusufiyah 213–215

Zaman, Commander Mohammed 46, 48
Zarqawi, Abu Musab al 100, 172, 175,
    197–198, 200, 206, 207, 215–217, 307
Zawahiri, al 233
Zawar Kili caves 49–50, **49**, 77